I'M HERE AND
I'M LISTENING

I am delighted to recommend *I'm Here and I'm Listening*, which is packed with helpful information for navigating through the early childhood years without the use of punishments or rewards. Parents who are not yet familiar with Aware Parenting will learn compassionate and effective skills for responding to children's uncooperative or aggressive behavior and for resolving everyday conflicts about bedtime, sibling relationships, eating, and screen use. For those who are already familiar with Aware Parenting, this book will deepen their understanding of the approach. Throughout the book, Marion Rose invites her readers to explore the root causes of children's behavior and to question common cultural assumptions. She also encourages parents to delve into their own childhood memories to better understand their reactions to their children's behavior. Perhaps most importantly, this book will help parents feel good about themselves while becoming the kind of parents they want to be.

– Aletha Solter, PhD, founder of Aware Parenting

Marion Rose has profound wisdom and expertise and offers such clarity and compassionate support to parents in this book. *I'm Here and I'm Listening* offers a clear description of how we can remember again who children are by nature, why they behave in ways that are not enjoyable for parents, and how we can support them with every challenge of parenthood, in the most effective and loving way. Marion gives us a map that we can use to navigate all that comes up for us parents in this journey, drawing on the latest evidence-based research on attachment, trauma and healing. I have been learning about Aware Parenting for 17 years, and yet reading this book was an exciting and remarkable experience. I felt new clarity, new understanding and profound optimism for the future of our world. She describes the innate wisdom of children and supports readers to cultivate deep trust in themselves and their children.

I felt so excited and passionate about Aware Parenting when I read *I'm Here and I'm Listening* for the first time. I experienced a renewed and enhanced love for this powerful approach and was touched to tears by the compassion and the information. I could not put the book down. This is a book that I will return to again and again, both in my own parenting and reparenting journey and for the parents that I support. Whether you are brand new to Aware Parenting or have been doing it for many years, this book will provide you with extraordinary support and guidance, inspiration, relief and compassion. I highly recommend it for all parents.

— Joss Goulden, Level 2 Aware Parenting instructor

Marion Rose, PhD has done it again with another outstanding book. The phrase, "I'm here, I'm listening" has become the way I speak to my children whenever they are upset and I know this creates the presence and connection they need to feel seen, heard and understood. Marion's work has profoundly changed my life as a parent and in my work as a therapist with families.

Marion has been in the field of developmental psychology for more than 30 years, studying the mother-infant relationship in her PhD, as well as exploring the experience of the child through various psychotherapy modalities. There is no-one I have come across who understands babies and children more deeply than Marion. She is a world leader in understanding what is driving our children's behaviour and this book will change your life.

*I'm Here and I'm Listening* will help you understand your child's needs and what is underneath the unenjoyable behaviours we often encounter as parents. If you want to understand the true nature of children and deepen the connection, love and understanding in your family then this is a must read. Marion's empathy oozes through the pages and it feels like a warm hug while you read. I highly recommend this book for all parents, grandparents, teachers, therapists or anyone who will be spending time with children. Marion has delivered another gift to the world.

— Shelley Clarke, Aware Parenting instructor, Marion Method Mentor, CranioSacral Therapist

The Aware Parenting model and Marion's work in particular, provides an evidence based approach to parenting and indeed all relationships, that promotes both long term psychological well-being and secure attachment. As a mother of three and a Clinical Psychologist, I have found this model and Marion's work to be profoundly impactful both personally and professionally, in fostering long term emotional health as well as more enjoyable, connected and deeply attuned parent-child relationships. Truly listening to and authentically accepting a child's feelings in their entirety, is one of the primary tenets of Aware Parenting.

*I'm Here and I'm Listening* has the potential to support an essential shift in intergenerational patterns of responding to feelings that will in turn cultivate healthy relationships and positive mental health outcomes for generations to come. My hope is that the words held within the pages of this book reach all parents, caregivers, teachers, allied health, medical professionals, and indeed all humans, for herein lies the potential to change the trajectory of human experience, relationships and psychological well-being across the life span.

– Dr Jessica Klug, Clinical Psychologist, Aware Parenting instructor

When you are ready, this book might just change your life. The wisdom in these pages might shift the way you understand and relate to children, yourself and all beings, and it might invite you into a profound journey of healing and reparenting. I can't think of a more apt title for a book by Marion, who has taught me what it truly means to be here and what it truly means to listen. The first time I met with her 1:1, I felt such an embodied sense of being truly seen, heard and accepted, that I cried for over twenty minutes before either of us had said a word!

Marion's compassionate presence accompanied by her depth of passion for, and knowledge and experience of Aware Parenting make her a real beacon of light for parents and caregivers of children everywhere. I don't quite know how to put into words the

metamorphosis that has unfolded in my life and in my family since first connecting with Marion through a podcast when my daughter was three months old. 15 months later, I am a mother who is deeply grounded in my knowledge and understanding of my daughter and her needs, as well as myself, and mine. I have unshakeable clarity about the reasons behind any of the things that can be challenging about parenting a toddler, from sleep, to food, to any unenjoyable behaviour. My daughter is a delight to be with and shines with awareness that is regularly observed by others.

I know that my my daughter knows that she is unconditionally loved. This is more than I ever could have imagined, and I believe it is what all babies, children and parents are really here to receive.

– Elllie Gut-Silverman, Aware Parenting instructor

I love how *I'm Here and I'm Listening* is structured. It invites readers to pause and digest the content through reflections and self compassion, which I think is really a beautiful way to help readers to connect to their inner knowing and inner loving presence. The simple *attachment play* ideas are very helpful for readers, especially those who believe that they aren't playful. I also find the practices for parents are very doable in everyday life. I think that overall this is a well written and easy to read book, both for readers who are new to Aware Parenting and those who have already applied it to their life. The compassionate approach both for parents and children makes this book different to other parenting books on the market. I'm so grateful for all the hard work that Marion put into this book. It will shine the light in so many homes.

– Amanda Trim, Aware Parenting instructor in training

*I'm Here and I'm Listening* is not an ordinary parenting book. I could describe it more as a guide for personal growth, which at the same time gives us the ultimate motivation for it: our children's well being, and a harmonious life. Even from the title I could feel its power, and wondered how the world will be when we start being present, and truly listening to the people we love, especially our children.

Marion Rose invites us to deeply trust our children's innate wisdom and ability to heal from stress and trauma, if we give them the chance to express themselves. She offers us an invaluable change of perspective on tantrums, rage and aggression. She gives us the tools we can use to connect with our children and give them the space to show us all their feelings. With so much compassion, she allows us to reflect on our conditioning from the society we live in, our experiences, thoughts, and beliefs, and to grow from our realisations. She reminds us of the significance of taking care of our needs, so we can be present and support our children in feeling their feelings. It's a book that I will definitely read again and again, and use as a resource for my practice. Thank you, Marion. Thank you for this book, and the motivation to be a part of this new generation of parents who will change the world!

– Eirini Anagnostopoulou – Parent Coach

This book is an absolutely fantastic deep dive into the practice of Aware Parenting. I would highly recommend it to anyone interested in learning more about themselves and any children in their lives. Marion has a lot of compassion and empathy which absolutely shines through in this book! I couldn't put it down!!! Thank you for putting such a beautiful offering out into the world Marion, we are all better off for it.

– Anna Haberfield

I came to Aware Parenting at a time in my life when things were very dark. The days were long and the nights were longer. I was exhausted and sad, struggling through from a very difficult pregnancy, to a birth that was completely different to what I wanted, simultaneously going through a challenging relationship and eventual separation and with a newborn baby on my own, who never slept. I was completely lost and overwhelmed with nowhere to turn.

Then when my daughter was almost four, a friend gifted me a beautiful course by Marion and my life was forever changed. Aware Parenting was the answer I had been looking for and more. Marion's voice in the course was like a warm hug that held me close in the night. The information deeply resonated and I dove further and further into Aware Parenting and subsequently her Marion Method work a couple of years after.

To say that Marion and her incredible work saved my life and my relationship with my daughter would be an understatement. Aware Parenting is the way forward to more connecting and loving relationships, not just with our children, but with ourselves and everyone we meet. Marion's decades of knowledge, experience and understanding of the parent/child connection, along with her clear communication style are invaluable in absolutely everything she creates.

If you want to truly revolutionise and transform your life with Aware Parenting, look no further than this amazing book by Marion Rose.

– Nic Wilson, Aware Parenting instructor and Marion Method Mentor

I love the structure of *I'm Here and I'm Listening*. The way that Marion Rose offers an overview and returns later for more details and depth makes it easy to read and to comprehend. I love the clarity of it all! And of course, the richness; there is so much without being overwhelming. I would just highlight the entire book, it is all so important. I just can't put it down! The way it is formulated means it's really such a pleasure to read!

– Linde Lambrechts, Psychotherapist and Aware Parenting instructor

Published in Australia by
Loving Being Publishing
PO Box 256, Doreen, VIC 3754
marion@marionrose.net
www.marionrose.net

First published in Australia 2024
Copyright © Marion Rose 2024

All rights reserved. No part of this publication may be reproduced, stored in a retrieval system, or transmitted, in any form or by any means without the prior written permission of the publisher, nor be otherwise circulated in any form of binding or cover other than that in which it is published and without a similar condition being imposed on the subsequent purchaser.

National Library of Australia Cataloguing–in–Publication entry

 A catalogue record for this book is available from the National Library of Australia

ISBN: 978-0-6455515-9-4 (paperback)
ISBN: 978-0-6459985-0-4 (hardback)
ISBN: 978-0-6459985-1-1 (epub)

Cover photography by Michael Rose
Cover layout and design by Jelena Mirkovic
Typesetting by Sophie White Design (sophiewhite.com.au)

Printed by Ingram Spark

Disclaimer: All care has been taken in the preparation of the information herein, but no responsibility can be accepted by the publisher or author for any damages resulting from the misinterpretation of this work. All contact details given in this book were current at the time of publication, but are subject to change.

The advice given in this book is based on the experience of the individuals. Professionals should be consulted for individual problems. The author and publisher shall not be responsible for any person with regard to any loss or damage caused directly or indirectly by the information in this book.

*Today, and every day, I acknowledge the Traditional Custodians of this land where I live and work, which include the Arakwal people, the Minjungbal people, the Widjabul people and the Bundjalung people. I pay my respects to elders past, present and emerging. I acknowledge and recognise them as the original storytellers and wisdom keepers.*

# I'M HERE AND
# *I'm Listening*

Empathic and empowering responses to needs,
feelings, and behaviours with Aware Parenting

MARION ROSE, PHD

*For Lana and Sunny,*
*my moon and sun.*

# ABOUT THE AUTHOR

You could say I'm obsessed with Aware Parenting and feelings! For 36 years, since I started my psychology degree in 1987, I've been passionately drawn to deeply understand why us human beings are the way we are, and how we can live more fulfilling, loving and connected lives. I have a background in academic developmental psychology (with a PhD from Cambridge University) and psychotherapy, but I most love working with parents.

When I was a psychotherapist in the nineties, I wanted to help my clients experience being deeply heard. I also wanted to support them to reconnect with who they really were, underneath all the ways they'd needed to shape themselves to get their needs met and stay safe as children. However, when I became an Aware Parenting instructor in 2005, I saw that it was even more effective for me to help parents to listen to their children's needs and feelings so that their children experienced both being deeply heard and connected with themselves in the first place. After a few years of supporting parents in this way, I realised that in order to do that for our children, we as parents need to experience a combination of transformative reparenting and what I call reculturing (getting freer from our cultural conditioning).

I don't know of anything as powerful as Aware Parenting to not only transform parent-child relationships but also to bring about profound change in the world. That's why, since the moment I learnt about it as a first time pregnant mother back in 2001, I haven't stopped talking about it to other people! I believe it understands babies and children in the most clear way we have on the planet right now, in particular, the genesis of dissociation, addiction and violence. Not only that, but it has tangible practices for helping children stay deeply connected with their unique self and their true nature, while knowing that they are unconditionally loved, exactly as they are.

My daughter and son are young adults now, and I see how deeply connected with themselves they are, even though there were many times I didn't parent in ways that I really I wanted to because of my own unhealed trauma at the time. This deep self-connection is a theme that I've heard from many other parents I've worked with who now have young adult 'children' parented in this way. Aware Parenting is powerful, even when we're practicing it while healing from our own childhood trauma and freeing ourselves from our cultural conditioning. In the process of parenting in this way, I've transformed, and my world view has changed beyond recognition. I love hearing, over and over again from the parents I've walked beside, how much Aware Parenting has also changed their family's lives. More connection, more love, more harmony, more sleep; you name it, and they've shared about it. Most of all, they've expressed how much more relaxed and present their children are, which affects every area of their children's lives.

In my books, mentoring, online courses, workshops, and *The Aware Parenting Podcast*, I'm here to help parents become the empathic, effective parents they want to be, while also embarking on their own reparenting journey, and in the process, gradually getting free from guilt and self-judgment, becoming more self-compassionate, healing from childhood trauma and deeply valuing their needs as parents. On that path, they become even more able to understand their children and respond to them in deeply effective, empathic and empowering ways. This profoundly affects how their children feel, think and behave, and has the kind of long-term effects I was looking for all those years ago. I'm honoured to do what I do, so deeply connected to my calling, and I'm delighted that you're here, reading this book.

## AUTHOR'S NOTE

This book is an educational resource focusing on the emotional needs of children; it is not intended to be a substitute for medical advice or treatment. Many of the behaviours and symptoms discussed can be an indication of serious emotional or physical problems. Readers are advised to consult with a competent health care provider whenever children display behavioural or emotional issues, a sudden change in sleep, eating or crying patterns, or when pain or illness are suspected. Furthermore, some of the suggested practices in this book may not be suitable under all conditions or with children suffering from certain physical or emotional challenges.

If you are ever concerned when your child is crying, or if your child's crying is suddenly high pitched, please seek advice from your health care provider. As outlined in this book, one of the reasons that children cry is when they are in physical pain, so please trust yourself if you're ever worried.

I ask that you don't do anything just because you read it in this book; rather, I invite you to always view yourself as your own authority in parenting – and to first listen in to whether what you read resonates with you, and if you do, experiment with it – and observe your child's behaviour afterwards. You are the researcher here. I will be talking about this process of you claiming your authority as a parent in more detail in the following pages.

Most of all, please listen to yourself. If you are concerned, please listen to that concern. You know your child the most. I invite you to deeply trust your perceptions and intuition.

# CONTENTS

| | |
|---|---|
| About the author | 12 |
| Author's note | 14 |
| Introduction | 23 |

### 1  The foundations of Aware Parenting — 35
| | |
|---|---|
| The three aspects of Aware Parenting | 37 |
| The three reasons for children's behaviour: thoughts, needs, feelings | 66 |
| The three options with feelings: expression, suppression and aggression | 79 |
| Understanding our place in healing our lineage as first generation Aware Parenting parents | 85 |
| Aware Parenting helps our child experience being unconditionally loved | 91 |
| Chapter summary | 93 |

### 2  Our own reparenting — 95
| | |
|---|---|
| Dropping the self-judgment | 98 |
| Tending to our own needs | 99 |
| Receiving support and empathy | 104 |
| Our relationship with our own feelings | 107 |
| Compassion for ourselves as we practice Aware Parenting | 109 |
| Chapter summary | 111 |

### 3  Understanding the effects of culture and creating new forms of community — 113
| | |
|---|---|
| Of course it's hard! Compassion for ourselves | 116 |
| Sharing with others and spreading the word in easy to hear ways | 118 |
| Creating new forms of community | 120 |
| Chapter summary | 123 |

### 4  Eliciting cooperation — 125
| | |
|---|---|
| Why don't children cooperate? | 126 |
| Eliciting cooperation | 128 |
| Using *attachment play* to elicit cooperation | 135 |
| An introduction to *Loving Limits* | 140 |
| Chapter summary | 142 |

## 5  Attachment play — 145

| | |
|---|---|
| Your childhood experiences of play | 147 |
| Non-directive child-centred play | 151 |
| Contingency play | 155 |
| Power-reversal games | 156 |
| Activities with body contact | 160 |
| Nonsense play | 162 |
| Separation games | 166 |
| Cooperative games and activities | 167 |
| Symbolic play with specific props or themes | 168 |
| Regression games | 171 |
| What happens if your child won't stop playing when you've had enough, or starts crying, or begins to get aggressive in their play? | 175 |
| The relationship between *attachment play* and crying and raging | 176 |
| Chapter summary | 178 |

## 6  Creating a welcoming space for feelings — 181

| | |
|---|---|
| Presence | 183 |
| Helping children be freer to express more of their feelings | 186 |
| Seeing feelings from a different perspective | 190 |
| How we can create a welcoming space for feelings | 193 |
| What we're thinking | 194 |
| Giving our child Aware Parenting information about feelings and behaviour | 198 |
| The extent to which our needs are met affects how we feel and how we behave | 203 |
| Reflecting on how your own feelings were responded to as a child | 205 |
| How our childhood affects our feelings now | 207 |
| How our suppression and dissociation affect our child's suppression and dissociation | 214 |
| Are you inadvertently suppressing your child's feelings? | 217 |
| Chapter summary | 220 |

## 7  Crying — 221
All children feel big feelings — 221
Hearing our child — 223
Your own experience of crying as a child — 224
When crying is most likely to happen — 229
Big crying after apparently small events – the *broken cookie phenomenon* — 232
Matching your child's crying times with when you are most able to listen — 234
Being present with your child *and* yourself when your child cries — 235
Chapter summary — 238

## 8  Healing from stress and trauma through raging and tantrums — 241
Why raging and tantrums are so healing — 243
Why it's so normal for us to find listening to raging and tantrums hard and how we can help it become easier — 247
Differentiating between aggression and expression — 249
Supportive responses to raging and tantrums: keeping them safe, supporting the healing and responding compassionately — 250
When our child is raging and tells us to *go away!* — 253
Chapter summary — 256

## 9  Being with our own frustration, anger and outrage — 259
How was your own frustration, anger and outrage responded to as a child? — 260
Befriending and welcoming frustration, anger and outrage in yourself — 262
The presence of another when we are feeling and expressing frustration, anger and outrage — 263
Expressing frustration, anger and outrage in safe and healing ways — 264
Modelling the safe and healing expression of frustration, anger and outrage to our child/ren — 266
Chapter summary — 269

## 10  Loving Limits and holding — 271

- The term *'Loving Limits'* — 274
- Differentiating *limits* from *Loving Limits* — 277
- What are *Loving Limits*? — 278
- When can we use *Loving Limits*? — 281
- Being the recipient of a *Loving Limit* as an adult when we're about to move into aggression — 286
- When are *Loving Limits* most likely to 'work'? — 300
- When do *Loving Limits* usually not 'work'? — 301
- If they aren't 'working', what can we do to build that foundation? — 302
- The *balance of attention* — 304
- Why *Loving Limits* can be so hard for us to offer — 305
- What shifts might we need to make in ourselves so that we can offer effective *Loving Limits*? — 306
- *Holding* — 308
- Chapter summary — 319

## 11  The *balance of attention* — 321

- The importance of the *balance of attention* in Aware Parenting — 321
- What is the *balance of attention*? — 322
- What do we need to provide the *balance of attention*? — 323
- The *balance of attention* with *attachment play* — 328
- The *balance of attention* with crying — 330
- The *balance of attention* with *Loving Limits* and *holding* — 334
- Chapter summary — 336

## 12  How we suppress and dissociate from our feelings with *control patterns* — 337

- Compassion for ourselves and our *control patterns* — 338
- The antidote to dissociation and suppression is compassionate presence — 340
- *Attachment play* with our *control patterns* — 344
- *Loving Limits* with our *control patterns* — 345
- Chapter summary — 348

| | |
|---|---|
| **13 Our child's *control patterns*** | **349** |
| Do all children have feelings to express? | 352 |
| Feelings accumulate | 355 |
| Understanding what's happening and having compassion (not judging ourselves or our child when they're using a *control pattern*) | 355 |
| Categories of *control patterns* | 358 |
| What we can do for ourselves when our child is engaging in a *control pattern* | 361 |
| What our child needs from us when they are engaged in a *control pattern* | 362 |
| When we don't recommend using *Loving Limits* with *control patterns* | 368 |
| Chapter summary | 375 |
| **14 Aggression – hitting, pushing and forcefully taking** | **377** |
| Compassion for us all | 380 |
| Exploring what shows up for us when our child shows aggression | 381 |
| Four things to reduce or prevent the likelihood of aggression in the first place | 386 |
| Immediate interventions – *attachment play* in response to aggression | 391 |
| Immediate interventions – *Loving Limits* and *holding* in response to aggression | 394 |
| Chapter summary | 398 |
| **15 Our own power-over and aggression and how we can repair** | **399** |
| Exploring when our own aggression shows up | 402 |
| The source of our aggression | 404 |
| Offering ourselves compassion and not punishing ourselves | 406 |
| Offering repair to our child | 408 |
| Chapter summary | 416 |
| **16 Eating, food and feelings** | **417** |
| Children's innate body wisdom | 417 |
| The self-connected approach to eating | 418 |
| Innate body wisdom and its interplay with culture and conditioning | 419 |
| What gets in the way of children being connected with their innate body wisdom in relation to food | 421 |

| | |
|---|---|
| General ways to help children be more connected with their innate body wisdom in relation to food | 433 |
| Helping children stay connected to their innate body wisdom (or reconnect with it) with the three aspects of Aware Parenting | 436 |
| What can make it hard for us to help our children eat in a self-connected way? | 439 |
| How might we experience these challenges? | 441 |
| Tangible actions we can take to help them stay connected with their innate body wisdom | 443 |
| Trusting them and supporting them to be connected with their bodily cues and sensations | 448 |
| Being relaxed and playful around food and aiming to make mealtimes enjoyable | 449 |
| Modelling a healthy relationship with food and connection with our cues and sensations | 451 |
| Having deep compassion for ourselves in relation to food, cooking and eating | 452 |
| My journey with eating, food and feelings | 453 |
| The process of practicing the self-connected approach to eating | 455 |
| Why hunger and feelings can often become intertwined | 455 |
| Differentiating hunger from a need to express feelings | 458 |
| Noticing eating *control patterns* in yourself and your child | 459 |
| Bringing in *attachment play* and *Loving Limits* with food and eating | 462 |
| *Loving Limits* | 468 |
| Chapter summary | 471 |

## 17  Screens — 473

| | |
|---|---|
| The interplay between self-connection and culture | 473 |
| How we can apply the Aware Parenting maps to screen use | 474 |
| Helping children be connected with what their bodies are telling them about screen use | 480 |
| Judgments and screens | 482 |
| Taking stock of your screen use and your child's screen use and being unwilling to judge yourself | 484 |
| Connection, needs, agreements and trust | 485 |

| | |
|---|---:|
| Differentiating between screens to meet needs and screens to suppress feelings | 488 |
| Staying connected before, during and after screen use | 493 |
| *Attachment play* and screens | 494 |
| *Loving Limits* with screens and listening to feelings | 499 |
| Why exploring our own powerlessness as parents is so important here | 503 |
| Chapter summary | 507 |

## 18  Sleep — 509

| | |
|---|---:|
| The innate wisdom of children's bodies to sleep peacefully | 509 |
| What gets in the way of children sleeping restfully | 510 |
| The three things needed for sound sleep | 511 |
| Creating connection before sleep | 521 |
| *Attachment play* before sleep | 524 |
| *Loving Limits* and listening to feelings before sleep | 529 |
| Chapter summary | 538 |

## 19  Supporting friendships and sibling relationships — 539

| | |
|---|---:|
| My children's relationship with each other, and my joy and grief | 539 |
| Preparing for harmony | 544 |
| How to support harmony | 547 |
| *Attachment play* in friendships and sibling relationships | 554 |
| *Loving Limits* in friendships and sibling relationships | 562 |
| Chapter summary | 567 |

## 20  Partners, exes and other family members — 569

| | |
|---|---:|
| Compassion for us all | 569 |
| Compassionate listening to your feelings and thoughts | 571 |
| Healing on the inside | 572 |
| Seeing what they are doing and understanding their feelings, needs and values | 575 |
| What conversations do you feel called to have? | 576 |
| Using *attachment play* to help our children heal from judgments from family members | 577 |
| Chapter summary | 579 |

| | |
|---|---:|
| **Conclusions** | **581** |
| Trusting our child | 581 |
| Trusting children is one of the core foundations of Aware Parenting | 581 |
| Exploring how we were trusted and not trusted | 583 |
| Trust in relation to attachment, food, sleep, healing, learning and play | 585 |
| Increasingly learning to trust your child | 586 |
| Chapter summary | 589 |
| | |
| Acknowledgements | 590 |
| Glossary | 592 |
| Recommended reading and resources | 596 |
| Your notes and observations of your child | 598 |
| Ways you can work with me | 602 |
| If you enjoyed this book | 603 |
| Author contact page | 605 |

# Introduction

Hello and a big warm welcome to you! I'm so glad that you're here, reading this book! I'm so excited to share about Aware Parenting with you, focusing on children aged one to eight years old[1].

I first learnt about Aware Parenting back in 2001, when I was pregnant with my daughter, my first child. However, my journey to Aware Parenting began way before that. In 1968, I was born at 30 weeks' gestation, and I was put in an incubator. Back in those days, they didn't think that babies could even feel physical pain, let alone painful feelings.

However, that five weeks alone was a profoundly painful experience for newborn baby me and it set up core beliefs and patterns which were woven through my childhood and teenage years – marked by feelings of fear, isolation and powerlessness, as well as beliefs that I couldn't be heard or understood, and that I couldn't really depend on people to be there for me.

As a teenager, I longed to feel less scared, to feel more confident, and to understand why I was the way I was. That longing took me to do a degree in psychology. From then onwards, I followed a parallel path of professional calling and personal healing which continues to this day.

I went to Cambridge University and did a PhD on the mother-infant relationship and postnatal depression. I didn't realise then that I

---

1   However, lots in this book is relevant to older children too.

was also wanting to heal from my own experience as a baby being separated from my mother. Looking back, I'm in awe of how each step I took was so apt for my own healing journey. For example, when doing my PhD, I made many visits to a maternity ward – the setting of my own early trauma – and saw mothers holding their newborn babies.

It was in Cambridge that I started going to weekly psychotherapy, wanting to understand more about how my experiences as a baby and child were affecting me. I continued this for 10 years, primarily because I wanted to experience lots of healing before becoming a mother myself.

It was in that same city that I walked along Mill Road one day, and was drawn to look in my favourite dusty old second hand bookshop, where I came across *The Continuum Concept*, about the Yequana people, by Jean Liedloff. Learning about babies' innate needs and their expectations for holding and belonging had a huge influence on me – as I connected with deep grief for how much closeness I had lost out on when I was in the incubator.

***Equally, learning about the Yequana people opened my eyes and ignited my fascination for understanding the powerful effects of the culture we live in on our parenting beliefs and practices. I began to see that much of what happens to us as babies and children in industrialised cultures is a very long way away from what we evolved to expect and experience.***

My passion to understand the experiences of babies grew and flourished while I lived in Cambridge. I read all the books I could about pre and peri natal psychology, and while doing my PhD, I watched the videos of mothers and babies that I had recorded, going through them millisecond by millisecond. Little did I know that this training in observing babies would be a profound gift a decade later when I was a new mother, learning to discern my baby's needs and feelings as I was putting Aware Parenting into practice.

I wanted to understand more about the healing power of expressing feelings, and to contribute to people who wanted to heal from their own painful experiences in infancy and childhood, so alongside my academic career as a researcher and lecturer, I did a four-year training in psychotherapy, with two more postgraduate years.

*As a psychotherapist, day after day I listened to clients who were sharing about the profound effects that not having their feelings heard as children were still having on them as adults. This sparked a passion in me for understanding how important it is for us to express emotions and be deeply heard during our early years.*

My thirties then involved putting into practice all I had learnt in the previous decade, as I moved to Australia (the land of my mother's birth), met the father of my children, and we conceived our first child.

It was while I was pregnant that I came across Aware Parenting. I had been looking for a parenting paradigm that would fit with all that I had learnt in academic psychology, combined with all that I'd experienced training and working as a psychotherapist, while also congruent with all that I'd discovered in all the therapy, workshops and healing modalities I'd experienced.

*And here it was – Aware Parenting. Developed by Aletha Solter, PhD, it included everything I'd been searching for, and more. It had attachment theory and attachment-style parenting at its core. It understood the impact of birth and early childhood, and any trauma experienced during that time, on babies and children, and it deeply valued the expression of feelings.*

*Yet, it had one extra aspect that was a revelation to me.*

# Babies and children are born with innate processes to heal from daily stresses as well as mini-traumas and larger traumas, right from birth.

They don't need to wait until early adulthood to start the healing process, and even more importantly, they can do that healing at home, with their own parents, either straight after the stresses or traumas happen, *or* at a later date.

And yes, it was so much about the healing power of expressing feelings! This was the missing link, which matched those stories I'd heard from clients as a psychotherapist about the huge effect of not having their feelings heard as children.

That was it for me. I had the biggest 'YES!' – I bought one of Aletha Solter's books, *Tears and Tantrums* – followed by *The Aware Baby*, and read them while I was pregnant.

I continue to be as passionate about Aware Parenting now as I was then, a little more than 22 years ago. As of January 2024, my daughter is 22 and my son is 17. I've been an Aware Parenting instructor since 2005 and in that time, have met many parents all around the world who are parenting in this way.

In the same way that I saw the profound effect practicing Aware Parenting had on my children and on our relationships, I saw similar experiences being replicated in the parents I worked with.

In the early years of parenting, my children's dad and I focused on meeting our children's needs and listening to their feelings as much as we could, and lo and behold, we found a wondrous thing.

**Pretty much all the things that parents find challenging, we saw very little of in our children. Through experience, I discovered that unexpressed pent-up feelings are the cause of most parenting challenges.**

Our children were generally relaxed, slept easily and peacefully, were gentle with each other and their friends and our dogs, concentrated for long periods, were very aware and present, and melted into cuddles.

Until, that is, their dad and I separated when they were five and nine, and as a result my son's behaviour changed suddenly and dramatically. I learnt first-hand about the effects of stress and trauma and how hard it can be to help our children heal from these when we're *also* immersed in really big feelings ourselves. This gave me even more compassion for all parents in my work as an Aware Parenting instructor.

I've worked with thousands of parents since 2005, in 1:1 mentoring, workshops and online courses.

> In the past 22 years, I've seen a big shift in the parenting world, with so much more openness and readiness for Aware Parenting nowadays. This has been clear in how many plays of *The Aware Parenting Podcast* there have been, (co-hosted with Lael Stone until episode 124). As of January 2024, it has nearly 3 million downloads.

When I trained as a psychotherapist, the word 'trauma' wasn't known about in the general population and still wasn't when I became a parent in 2002. Nowadays, the term 'trauma-informed parenting' has become very popular. Two decades ago, my attempts to share Aware Parenting with other parents often fell on deaf ears. Now, many more people are open, ready and resonant.

***I have a sense that Aware Parenting is on the verge of becoming very well-known, and I am so delighted to be a part of this community movement sharing Aware Parenting.***

I love being a Level Two instructor, the regional coordinator for Australia and New Zealand, and mentor to many Aware Parenting instructors and instructors-to-be. I'm writing this book with deep gratitude to Aletha Solter, her amazing work, and all her books, and with the desire and willingness to share about the feelings aspect of Aware Parenting that I am so passionate about.

If you haven't already, I invite you to visit Aletha Solter's website: **www.awareparenting.com** and to read all of her books.

## About *I'm Here and I'm Listening*

This book is designed to complement Aletha Solter's books. It focuses on children's feelings and the practical actions we can take to support children to stay deeply connected with themselves and their feelings and needs so that they grow up relatively free from unhealed stress and trauma (and their effects – accumulated feelings). This helps children feel more relaxed in their bodies, more present, more connected, and more willing to cooperate and contribute.

*I'm Here and I'm Listening* covers only *part* of the Aware Parenting approach and doesn't include all the elements, for example, about the learning process. I recommend reading all of Dr. Solter's books – particularly *Cooperative and Connected* and *Healing Your Traumatized Child* – to fully understand the whole spectrum of Aware Parenting.

This book follows my previous one, *The Emotional Life of Babies*, which focuses on babies' feelings and their effects on every aspect of a baby's life, and precedes my next book, which is about Aware Parenting and sleep.

In order to practice Aware Parenting with our children, having empathy for ourselves, our feelings and needs and reactions is vital, which is why I offer invitations for self-compassion throughout *I'm Here and I'm Listening*.

In what I call the *Disconnected Domination Culture*[2], we are taught to punish ourselves with guilt and other forms of emotional sticks[3] – harsh self-judgments that create painful feelings and sensations.

*In Aware Parenting, rather than punishing children to get them to do what we want them to do, we are aiming to search for the causes of their behaviour and compassionately attend to those reasons.*

With The Marion Method, which is the form of reparenting I created[4], we can also learn to stop punishing ourselves and be compassionate with ourselves for why we did what we did (or didn't do what we didn't do[5]).

Growing up in the *Disconnected Domination Culture*, most of us were shamed and judged when we didn't know things, or when we behaved in certain ways because we didn't yet have the relevant information. So, most of us internalised these shame and guilt sticks. As a result, we may feel guilt and/or shame when we discover new information that we didn't know before, or if we acted in certain ways because we didn't have the information we know now.

*You might be tempted to do this as you read this book.*

However, gaining new information and judging ourselves are not intrinsically intertwined. We *can* get increasingly free from our *Disconnected Domination Culture* conditioning. We *can* learn new information *without* hitting ourselves with guilt and shame sticks.

---

2   This is a Marion Method term, rather than an Aware Parenting term. It was inspired by the term 'domination culture' used by Marshall Rosenberg, the founder of Nonviolent Communication, who was influenced in the use of the term by Walter Wink.
3   A Marion Method term, not an Aware Parenting term.
4   Inspired by Aware Parenting and Nonviolent Communication.
5   Although this is inspired by Aware Parenting, this is specific to my work.

We can see the ways our behaviour in the past wasn't helpful for our children – because we didn't know what we know now – without picking up those guilt and shame sticks. Yes, we might mourn. We might feel sad, seeing the effects of what we did or didn't do. Feeling sadness in order to mourn these actions is very different from picking up guilt and shame sticks. Sadness flows and can leave our bodies. Repeatedly hitting ourselves with guilt and shame sticks means we can keep feeling those feelings forever.

***When we understand that we can be open to learning new information and to seeing things that we didn't see before, without judging ourselves for not knowing, the learning process radically changes.***

In my own life, I am unwilling to pick up guilt, shame or other self-judgment sticks. I'm also not willing to judge anyone else. We can replace guilt, shame and other self-judgment with self-compassion. It really is possible.

I used to feel shame and guilt more than anyone I knew. And now I never feel guilt and very rarely feel shame (and when I do, it's usually only for a few seconds, by which time I can replace the shame stick with deep self-compassion). There's no harsh judgment in my inner dialogue at all. I'm not willing to compare myself with others. Getting increasingly free from *Disconnected Domination Culture* conditioning is one of the most life-changing things I've experienced.

One of the reasons we do things that we later regret is simply because we didn't know then what we know now. So, any time you learn new information here that is different to what you have done with your child, I invite you to notice if you're picking up those sticks. You might even have a phrase for yourself, such as, "I'm not willing to judge myself for what I did and what I didn't know. I'm willing to be compassionate with myself now."[6]

---

[6] Another Marion Method phrase. If you want to remember which are Aware Parenting terms and which are Marion Method terms, you can find them in the Glossary.

I'm sending you so much love and compassion as you read this book and I'd love to share something else with you.

***With Aware Parenting, we can support our children to heal from any ways that we have hurt them or haven't met their needs. The more we understand their innate healing abilities, the more we can cooperate with those processes. As Aletha Solter says, it's never too late.***

## Invitation

As you read this book, I invite you to engage in a process of research, as follows:

1. Does this *information resonate* with you? Do you feel a 'yes' in your body when you read it? Would you like to continue learning about Aware Parenting, and would you like to experiment with the suggestions that you read about?

2. I invite you to *observe* your child, before, during and after what you do differently as a result of reading this information. In particular, I invite you to notice whether you see a difference in their eye contact, the relaxation or tension in their muscles, how much they smile, how much they melt into a hug, how much they cooperate, how much they are able to concentrate, how long they take to get to sleep, how long they sleep for, and how much they move around in their sleep.

3. If what you've done differently *has* clearly helped your child based on your observations (eg. they are more relaxed, they make more eye contact, they smile more, they concentrate for longer, or they sleep more peacefully), I invite you to keep on going, *listening to yourself* and observing them as you go. If it *doesn't* make a difference, do you need to return to the information, is there something you would like to tweak about what you're doing, do you feel called to reach out to an Aware Parenting instructor for help, or would you like to stop doing it altogether?

Taking into account the three pillars – information, inner listening and observation, you become your own parenting authority and expert, because you are the experimenter. Only *you* can connect in with what resonates with you. You are the one who is observing your child day after day.

In this way, you don't need to wait for 20 or 30 years to see the results of your parenting. You can clearly observe it from day to day when you know what to look for. You can keep tweaking and adjusting your responses as you go, based on what you see in your child and what you hear in yourself, while taking in new information about Aware Parenting when you need it.

***I'm here to emphasise how important this process is. If you ever feel unsure about what you are doing in practicing Aware Parenting, and you're concerned that what you are doing might not be helpful for your child, please stop!***

Then, I'd recommend returning to listening in to yourself. Does the theory resonate? Do you need to read more or understand more? You might want to get some support from an Aware Parenting instructor so you can gain clarity about what is going on. In this way, you'll be able to discern whether your concern is from your intuitive knowing or from your own conditioning and unexpressed feelings from your childhood.

# With this approach, parenting becomes a profound ongoing learning journey, since your child is always growing and changing and you will be invited to, too. Aware Parenting principles remain the same, but how they are put into practice morphs with a child's differing ages and with our own increasing comprehension and competence.

Thank you so much for reading this book, and for coming along on the ride. I'm so willing for it to be an enlightening, powerful and heartwarming experience for you.

CHAPTER ONE

# The foundations of Aware Parenting

What if we were under a great deception in this culture – a deception of who we really are as human beings?

And what if that deception began with our perception of children?

What if all the things our culture thinks are innate to being a child, the:

- agitation;
- sleeping challenges;
- conflict between siblings;
- pulling of the dog's tail;
- forcefully taking things from other children;
- biting and hitting;
- roughness in the playground;
- harsh words spoken;
- and so much more...

What if none of them were *intrinsic* to childhood?

What if these were symptoms of how a child *feels*?

What if the reason for us thinking that these behaviours are just a part of childhood was because we are believing inaccurate cultural beliefs about the true nature of human beings? For example, that these behaviours are innate developmental stages of childhood.

In Aware Parenting, we recognise them as indications of accumulated feelings from unmet needs and unhealed stress and trauma from growing up in this culture.

The cultural beliefs advocate punishments and rewards, or distraction and diagnosis, to get children to stop doing those things on the list. In Aware Parenting, we understand how to help children be cooperative, compassionate, calm and relaxed without ever resorting to punishments or rewards, blame or shame. This is because we recognise the true causes of these behaviours and how to create change at the causal level.

***This culture does not support parents to understand and welcome our children's feelings. I'm sending us all so much compassion for growing up in a culture which has so little understanding of the emotional worlds of children. I'm sending so much love to us for the myriad ways we weren't understood when we were growing up (as well as compassion for our parents, who also were not supported in these ways).***

In *I'm Here and I'm Listening*, you will see how Aware Parenting offers a deeply compassionate understanding of human beings. From this knowledge come ways of responding to children so that they feel much more deeply *relaxed* and *present*. As a result they *behave* very differently too.

I'm here to help you even more clearly understand your child's emotional world and all the ways it affects their behaviour. At the same time, I'm here to support you to also deepen your understanding of your own needs, feelings and thoughts, and how they influence your parenting. Building on that clarity, I'll offer you a set of practices to support both you and your child/ren to be more relaxed, present, calm, gentle and aware.

If you're not a parent, but you're interested in understanding children and yourself, I also really welcome you here.

Let's start by talking about the foundations of Aware Parenting.

## The three aspects of Aware Parenting

Aware Parenting is based on three core elements:

1. Attachment-style parenting;
2. Non-punitive discipline; and
3. Prevention of, and healing from, stress and trauma – including through empathic listening to children's emotions.

*We can go through this list of three whenever we're in a parenting situation and we're wanting clarity about the most optimal response.*

### 1. Attachment-style parenting

Attachment-style parenting is based on the understanding that babies and children have core attachment needs, and that meeting a child's attachment needs in a prompt and attuned way helps them feel far more safe, secure and confident than trying to promote early 'independence' ever can.

What I call the *Disconnected Domination Culture*, or *DDC*[7] has been trying to separate babies and children from their parents in so many

---

7   This is not an Aware Parenting term and is from The Marion Method.

ways and with so many contraptions for so long. We are all sold the deception that children and parents need to be separated early and often. This is just seen as the norm.

> *Self-Compassion Moment*
>
> I invite you to have deep compassion for yourself here, especially if you've believed that separation was necessary and were separated from your child in these ways. It's so understandable that we repeat what we've experienced and what we see being done around us.

Exactly because we live in the *DDC*, living in nuclear families away from extended families and our wider community, supporting secure attachment is much harder. In a healthy culture with a large interconnected clan of families, there would have always been plenty of adults, grandparents, aunties and uncles and even older children and siblings around to share the carrying of, and caring for, babies and children.

**Parenting was never meant to consist of one or two adults looking after one or multiple children.**

I am passionate about supporting parents to drop all of the guilt and self-judgment sticks (if they want to), because those sticks are all part of *DDC* conditioning too. In this book, I will be inviting you to do exactly that. But dropping the guilt is only half the journey. We can replace that harsh conditioning – that tells us that there's a 'right' or 'wrong' way to parent and that there are 'good' and 'bad' parents – with deep self-compassion.

When we understand *both* the core attachment needs of children *and* have compassion for ourselves as parents in this culture, we are more likely to be able to think clearly and find ways for both us and our child/ren to get our needs met, and we can then take steps to prioritise closeness and connection with our child, whatever age they are and whichever way we parented them when they were younger.

*Understanding the power of cultural conditioning can also help us tap into our own power to choose how we want to respond to our baby or child, freer from what other people tell us we 'should' do.*

Your parents might be telling you that your choice to still be co-sleeping with your two year old will be a 'rod for your own back,' and that your child will 'never want to sleep alone' but when you understand that they are speaking from their own cultural conditioning, you're more likely to feel free to continue doing what feels most resonant for you, and are less likely to feel hurt or upset when you hear their thoughts.

All your friends might tell their children that they have to stay in their own bed all night long, but as your child's parent, I invite you to choose what resonates with you, and if you want to support your child to come into your bed when they need closeness, that's your choice. I support you to deeply listen to yourself as well as your child.

Your five year old might have never co-slept as a baby, and might be crying whenever they're away from you. As you reflect on them being separated from you when they were a newborn, you might feel called to get a super big family bed and have them in close with you – to give them a reparative experience of the closeness that they didn't receive as a baby. You might choose not to tell your family if you know that they would judge you and shame your child for it.

Your eight year old might be asking for lots of cuddles after a series of stressful experiences. Friends might tell you that your child shouldn't need that many hugs at that age. Understanding the importance of attachment, you might ignore their suggestions and say yes to your child's requests for more closeness.

Ann shared her relief in finding out about Aware Parenting:

*"I discovered Aware Parenting last month and since then, I listen to* The Aware Parenting Podcast *episodes every day and I did your online free course, which made so much sense to me that I can't even put*

*into words. It just resonated so much with all the things that I learned throughout the years.*

*I'm a clinical psychologist and a psychodynamic psychotherapist and this approach pulls everything together and is really supporting me with the struggles that I was experiencing with my two year old!*

*It feels like, 'I can see him now, I can see what he needs and I feel more empowered and comfortable in being with him'. I wish I had discovered this much earlier.*

*I felt so uncomfortable listening to all the advice that I was getting from the health visitors, from relatives, from friends, and so fearful to be judged about my parenting style because I knew that that advice did not fit for me. I knew that they did not resonate with the way that I see life and relationships."*

Cultural conditioning is powerful, and when we do something different to *DDC* consciousness, we are likely to meet the cultural conditioning of others (and ourselves) at every turn.

So, what can we do when we are faced with new ideas that are different to the mainstream?

## We can listen in to ourselves and to what deeply resonates with us.

That process of trusting ourselves and our own inner barometer can be quite a journey, as we unlearn all the ways we were taught not to listen to ourselves in the *DDC*.

*If you've had your two year old in a cot and they stand in it, rattling the bars, are you willing to dismantle the cot and support them to sleep on a mattress on the floor instead, able to come to you whenever they need closeness?*

*If your four year old wants to come and sleep in your bed in the middle of the night, are you willing for them to?*

*If, after a work trip where you were away for a week, your eight year old wants to cuddle on a beanbag in their room every evening while you read to them, are you willing to set up your day so that can happen?*

As you read this, you might notice your own cultural conditioning emerging. The *DDC* is based on judgment, shaming and guilt – those *emotional sticks* I talked about. If you notice these arising in you, they come from the *DDC*. They are not innate to who you really are.

> *Self-Compassion Moment*
>
> *Whenever you notice yourself picking up guilt sticks, I invite you to put them down. You might simply notice the feeling of guilt, and then notice the thoughts causing it, which might be something like, "I shouldn't have done that." (Should is one of the key words that creates – and indicates – guilt.) I invite you to say to yourself something like, "I learnt to feel guilty in this culture. I'm not willing to feel guilty now. I am willing to be compassionate with myself instead." Dropping the 'should' stick can bring so much more ease in our parenting.*

I invite you to experiment with all of these attachment-style parenting practices. You have the opportunity to try things out and see what happens. You have choice here.

*That's what the father of my children and I did as parents of our newborn baby daughter, back in 2002. We tried out co-sleeping right from the start, open to see how it would go. We loved it so much that we kept on doing it. When our son came along four and a half years later, we moved a single bed into the bedroom and all slept in the huge combined bed together.*

However, there are so many ways for all members of a family to get their needs met. I've seen every different possible combination of co-sleeping over the last couple of decades. One couple I met in my *Aware Parenting with Marion Course* have a really ingenious arrangement. The working parent co-sleeps with the children on the days that they've been working, so they can make up for the lost connection in the day. The at home parent sleeps in another bed in another room and has more time to connect with themselves, and then they swap on the weekend. That way, the children have closeness with one parent every night, and the parents have more connection with their children at certain times and more connection with themselves at others. When you read the chapter on sleep (Chapter Eighteen), you will see that there are ways for *everyone* to get their needs met for both sleep *and* closeness with Aware Parenting's magical map of the three things needed for restful sleep!

I invite you to deeply listen in to yourself and your unique family. For example, there are important reasons for some families *not* to co-sleep.

***The more we put down the emotional sticks and our cultural conditioning, the more we can listen to ourselves, our partner if we have one, and our children, and find ways for us all to get our needs met – without telling ourselves that we 'should' do it any particular way, including the Aware Parenting way! One of my own favourite parenting mantras has been: "I'm willing for us all to get our needs met here.[8]" I wonder if that phrase resonates with you too?***

*I loved carrying my babies, and loved getting increasingly stronger as they got bigger. There is no need to do weight training at the gym when regularly carrying a young child! I loved that carrying them protected them somewhat from overstimulation when they were out. I loved being able to sense what was going on in their bodies and*

---

8 This is from The Marion Method.

*what that told me about how they felt, which was so helpful with the feelings and healing aspect of Aware Parenting. And yes, at times, I felt tired and overwhelmed and my body felt sore. We can make choices to promote secure attachment and be compassionate with ourselves when that is hard in the DDC! We can keep coming back to being willing to find ways for everyone to get their needs met.*

*Another powerful outcome from having lots of closeness with my children when they were babies and small children was that I experienced so much healing myself. My little inner baby, who had been so alone, experienced what it was like to be held, to be carried and to be kept close. I understood in my body the feelings that go with those experiences, albeit from the side of the mother rather than from the baby. This also supported me in my own reparenting journey, which I then developed into The Marion Method.*

I want to emphasise that understanding secure attachment isn't a reason for another 'have to' or another reason to pick up those guilt sticks. That would be part of the same old cultural conditioning. Rather, this information is an opportunity to see how vital attachment needs are, so we can do what we can to meet them while *also* honouring our own needs and challenges as parents living within the *DDC* – and to find ways that most meet everyone's needs in the family. Each of us will practice Aware Parenting in subtly different ways, depending on our own family circumstances, attachment and trauma history and so much more.

We can also hold in mind that we can give more closeness to a child later on if we didn't offer that so much when they were younger. In addition, with the healing from stress and trauma aspect of Aware Parenting, which we will be talking more about later, we can help them heal from any times when their needs for closeness weren't met.

> *Self-Compassion Moment*
>
> *I'm sending so much love to you and any feelings you might have when you read this. I want to remind you that it is so natural for all of us to have lots of grief and mourning in this culture that is set up against meeting attachment needs, particularly since most of us (growing up when attachment was even less understood than it is now) will often not have had our own attachment needs met as babies or children. Any feelings that come up for us when we see babies or children either getting their attachment needs met or not may stem from these early experiences of ours.*

## The foundation of Aware Parenting is connection.

Secure attachment is based on deep connection and attunement. Whenever you are in doubt about what to do as a parent, I invite you to always come back to connection! And of course, to be able to connect with our child, we need to be connected with ourselves, which is why our own inner work – including our relationship with our needs, our feelings and our past experiences – is so vital to our Aware Parenting journey, all of which we will be discussing in this book.

Attachment-style parenting involves understanding that connection is a core need for babies and children. They need a lot of it, including plenty of closeness, and prompt and attuned responses to their needs. That requires a lot from us living in the *Disconnected Domination Culture*, because not only do we lack large communities, but also the culture is set up so that financially, many parents need to work and be away from their children. This is why prioritising our own needs is so vital in Aware Parenting, and creating our own forms of support is essential too. As is self-compassion for how hard it can be to practice attachment-style parenting in this culture at this time.

However, Aware Parenting is about valuing *everyone's* needs in the family. Your needs matter too! So, although a child's attachment needs include lots of physical closeness, there may be reasons why you choose *not* to meet those needs at times. However, if you hold in mind their needs for closeness while *also* honouring your needs, I trust that you will find a way that meets everyone's needs in your family, such as aiming to give them lots of closeness whenever you *are* with them. Perhaps you have a back injury which makes carrying your toddler difficult. In this case, lots of cuddles on the couch may be a way for you both to get your needs met. Or maybe you work really long hours, or you are separated from their other parent and you don't see your children much. Prioritising lots of closeness and games with physical contact such as rough and tumble when you *are* together can support bonding and attachment for each of you.

*Amelie wanted to carry her son, Tobias, but once he was about 18 months old, her back got really sore. She came to me, full of guilt about not carrying him any more. I invited her to drop the guilt sticks and instead to be deeply compassionate with herself and to listen to her needs too. Then we talked about her willingness for both her and Tobias to get their needs met – hers to be comfortable and to contribute to him, his for closeness and support. She came up with an idea that whenever they were going places where she would need to put him in the stroller, that she would find ways to offer lots of closeness, such as ten minutes cuddling on the couch before they went out, and again when they came home again. Later, she bought a secondhand tricycle with a big handle which she could push him on. That met his need for fun and her need to care for her body.*

Please take into account that all the information I share here is *generalised*. Each child is unique, and each family situation is different. I invite you to tailor these practices to the particularities of yourself, your child and your situation.

**This is why listening to yourself and observing your child is so important. You are the only one who can know if what I am offering is relevant for your child, yourself and your family. Please trust yourself and keep on observing your child.**

There are going to be many different ways that we can all get our needs met in any family. I invite you to claim your own power here, and rather than doing things that others are doing or tell you to do, to connect in with what *you* want to do and how you can all get your needs met in *your* unique family. Some families might love daily cuddles on the couch, others might like to play pillow fights on the bed, others might love book reading marathons on cushions on the floor! I support you to do it your own way.

I will be inviting you to keep on reconnecting with your child/ren and yourself as much as you can, knowing that at any point, you can change things around. I invite you to experiment.

**There is no right or wrong here, there is only the invitation to understand the principles and practices and listen in to yourself about how you might implement them in your own unique family.**

*Self-Reflection Moment*

*Do you sense that your child is asking for more connection?*

*Would you like to meet their attachment needs even more than you do now?*

*If so, what do you sense might be helpful for them?*

*Do you notice any feelings or reactions in you when you read this part of the book?*

*If so, where might they be from?*

*Are you hitting yourself with emotional sticks? If so, are you willing to put them down?*

*Do you sense that your own experience of closeness as a baby or child is affecting your own willingness to be close to your child/ren?*

*What would you have loved as a child in terms of receiving connection and closeness from your parent/s?*

*Do your reflections invite you to do anything differently with your child/ren?*

## 2. Non-punitive discipline

The second aspect of Aware Parenting is non-punitive discipline. As the term indicates, this means not using punishments of any kind. Some parents are surprised to discover that this also includes not using rewards or bribes with children.

Punishments and rewards are designed to make children behave in the ways that we want them to and to stop them behaving in ways we don't want them to and are based on behaviour modification techniques – which means that they are about *just* attending to the behaviour and changing it on that surface level.

However, punishments and rewards don't actually address the cause of behaviour. They might appear to work, but they don't really – particularly in the long term – and they almost always have long term consequences that are unenjoyable for both the child's emotional wellbeing and the parent-child relationship.

> *Self-Compassion Moment*
>
> *If you do use punishments and rewards, or have in the past, I invite you to drop any emotional sticks of self-judgment or guilt if you are tempted to pick those sticks up. It's so understandable that you parented in that way, since this is what you are likely to have seen all around you, and probably also experienced as a child. And, it's never too late to change, if you feel called to, and it is never too late to help your child heal from those past experiences, using Aware Parenting practices.*

# If we're not using punishments and rewards, what can we do when children aren't doing what we do want them to do, or when they're doing things that we don't want them to do?

We can look for the underlying cause of the behaviour, and then work at that causal level, all the while focusing on the connection we have with our child (because attachment-style parenting is the foundation of this paradigm).

With Aware Parenting, we can understand *why* children do things that are challenging, and we can support them to feel more connected, calm, present and powerful, which means they will tend to behave in ways that lead to more harmony and peace. It also recognises *how* we can support children to be more willing to cooperate with our requests.

Instead of trying to coerce or bribe children to behave in ways we want them to, with Aware Parenting we can work with the true underlying causes, helping children be cooperative, gentle and relaxed without needing to resort to punishments and rewards.

We can also *respond* to behaviours – such as a lack of cooperation, hitting or not sleeping – in ways that actually help children naturally be able and willing to cooperate, be gentle and be able to sleep.

Sounds like magic, doesn't it?

> The Aware Parenting approach is based on a deep understanding of the true causes of behaviour, and so it doesn't need to use behaviour modification approaches of punishments and rewards. Rather, we know that needs, feelings and cognitive understanding profoundly affect behaviour, so we address those instead.

We are *also* invited to attend to the causes of our *own* reactivity, rather than punishing ourselves with guilt or self-judgment. This book isn't simply about how we respond to our child. Just as we are looking at the causes of a child's behaviour, and attending to their needs and feelings, so I will invite you to compassionately look at the causes of your *own* frustrations and outbursts – in your needs, feelings and thoughts.

> Understanding the true causes of behaviour and attending to those is so much more powerful and effective both in the short and long term, compared to using punishments and rewards – and has a profoundly beneficial effect on the parent-child relationship too.

Later in the book, we'll be looking at those causes of behaviour.

## The more we understand the causes, the more we can attend to them and make change there.

### 3. Healing from stress and trauma

The third aspect of Aware Parenting, in addition to attachment-style parenting and non-punitive discipline, is the recognition that children are deeply affected by their experiences. This invites parents to do what they can to prevent their child from experiencing stress and trauma wherever possible (while knowing that it's impossible to prevent this happening altogether).

*However, it also recognises that children have natural inbuilt processes to heal from stress and trauma.*

This is based upon core assumptions that:

1. Children are innately drawn towards emotional health;
2. Children inherently know how to heal from daily stresses and bigger traumas;
3. Children intuitively and spontaneously heal using innate biological healing processes when they feel a deep sense of connection, presence and emotional safety in the present while also reconnecting with unexpressed feelings from the past.

*Aware Parenting has a profound understanding not only of how children experience stress, mini-traumas and larger traumas, but also how they heal from them. This understanding differentiates Aware Parenting from many other parenting paradigms.*

> The major cause of most of the things that parents find challenging in their children is unhealed stress (including from unmet needs) and trauma. This is a completely different parenting perspective, which profoundly changes how parents choose to respond to their children.

*Given this, one of the core invitations to parents is to do what we can to prevent stress and trauma from happening in the first place. However, we also recognise that (in this culture in particular) it is impossible to protect a child from ever experiencing any stress and trauma.*

Even when we know how much children are affected on a day-to-day basis by what they experience in their lives, we can receive deep reassurance from knowing that Aware Parenting offers responses and practices that can help children heal from the effects of stress and trauma utilising their innate wisdom.

## These healing processes are primarily through play, laughter, crying and raging, within the context of a loving and connected parent-child relationship.

This is where we come back to connection as the foundation for this kind of parenting.

***Core to this healing process then, is trusting that children know how to heal from stress and trauma and will constantly be trying to heal, through play and laughter, as well as crying and raging. Since they need the loving support of an adult for this healing to happen, we need to know both how to recognise these calls for healing and how we can respond, so that healing happens.***

However, because most of us weren't brought up within a family or culture that held these beliefs – nor were our own innate biological healing processes known about, cooperated with, or trusted – as parents, we often need to learn about them anew. Otherwise, we often won't recognise these signs.

> Furthermore, our own conditioning and emotional hurts can lead to us inadvertently hindering these natural processes.

This means that our children may repeatedly attempt to participate in these processes, seeking our support.

Below, I offer some common cultural beliefs about children, contrasted with the understanding of children that Aware Parenting offers.

*Cultural belief:* Aggression in children indicates immaturity, 'misbehaviour', a trait, or a 'disorder.'

*Aware Parenting:* Aggression in children is caused by them being in a dangerous situation where fight/flight is actually required, or where they are reminded of an unhealed trauma, or by accumulated pent-up unexpressed feelings from past stress or trauma.

*Cultural belief:* Tantrums are a sign of immaturity or 'misbehaviour'.

*Aware Parenting:* Tantrums help children complete a recovery process after the fight or flight response, releasing the energy mobilised to fight or flee – with our loving presence and support. Their legs and feet release the physical energy to flee and fight. Their arms and hands release the energy from their readiness to fight. Their loud sounds release their readiness to shout out for help.

*Cultural belief:* Children fight sleep.

*Aware Parenting:* Children try to feel relaxed enough to sleep using their innate biological wisdom of crying, raging, laughter and play before sleep with our loving presence and support. However, we have been conditioned to work against those natural relaxation processes.

**Children are not inferior or flawed. They are actually more connected with their innate healing and relaxation response than us adults who have grown up in the Disconnected Domination Culture and who have been conditioned away from trusting our innate body wisdom and intrinsic drive towards healing and wholeness.**

I'm here to offer you loving support, compassion and clear information in that journey of *reclaiming deep trust* in the innate wisdom of children and how to cooperate with that intrinsic drive for healing and wholeness.

So, what might we need as parents to relearn how to deeply trust this innate and intuitive wisdom of children? What will help us, so that we can support them – through creating an environment of emotional safety, compassionate presence and apt and prompt responding to their calls for healing?

***First***, we need to understand that *all* children will experience daily stresses and at least small or mild traumas, *however* much we aim to meet their needs and refrain from punishments and rewards.

*When we realise that despite all our efforts, our children will experience emotional hurts, it is common for us to feel painful feelings. Of course we don't want our children to experience emotional pain. This may also help us connect with hurts from our own childhood, when we realise that many of our own feelings were not heard by our parents, even though they loved us deeply.*

We also need to hold in mind that *some* children will experience bigger traumas, including a stressful time in utero, birth trauma, being separated when they are not ready, witnessing parents arguing or separating, harshness at school, and so on.

Recent world events also mean that most children have experienced even more stress and trauma than they might have otherwise. And of course, in many areas of the world, children are experiencing severe stress and trauma, such as in war-torn countries.

> *Self-Compassion Moment*
>
> *How do you feel, having just read this? I'm sending love to any and all feelings you might be feeling. Really letting it sink in that our children regularly feel uncomfortable feelings and emotional pain can be so hard to be with. I'm here with you as you take in this information.*

***Second***, we need to understand that *many* of the things that we can find challenging in parenting are caused by a child's unhealed stress and trauma (as well as our own.) Taking a long time to go to sleep and not being able to stay asleep, agitation, not being able to sit still or concentrate, biting, hitting, throwing and forcefully taking; a large proportion of all of these kinds of behaviours is caused by accumulated painful feelings.

> *Self-Reflection Moment*
>
> *Does this resonate with you? Does it make sense to you that accumulated feelings lead to agitation, which affects a child's behaviour, for example, making it harder for them to be able to go to sleep and stay asleep?*

***Third***, we need to do our own inner work, including valuing our needs and listening to our own unhealed childhood hurts, trauma and unexpressed feelings. Through this work, we can create more of an environment of emotional safety, presence and connection, so our children are free to heal in the way that they innately know how to.

***Fourth***, we need to be able to recognise *when* our child is engaged in one of the natural biological healing processes (which consist of therapeutic play and laughter or crying or raging with physical movement) so that we can cooperate with that process.

***Fifth***, we need to know *how* to most helpfully respond to these healing processes so that they actually work. Children need adults to support them for the healing to happen. They need our loving presence and they need particular responses – which we may not know about or understand until we've learnt them from Aware Parenting.

## Children will repeatedly invite us to support them in their healing.

That is why the information presented here is so important, so that:

- we can *recognise* when a child is trying to heal;
- we know *what to do* to support that healing;
- we *see when our own* childhood feelings and conditioned thoughts are getting in the way of our ability to do that, so we can tend to them.

The welcoming of children's feelings as a natural and vitally important way for healing to happen – as long as we listen with respect, empathy and compassion – is again a significant move away from previous parenting paradigms, even those which aim to accept feelings but don't recognise or understand their incredible healing power.

## How do children heal from stress and trauma, anyway?

Aware Parenting recognises that children need three things to be able to heal from stress and trauma:

1. To feel a sense of security, love and emotional presence (often termed '*emotional safety*');
2. To *recall* the stressful or traumatic event and to *re-visit* it in some way *while* feeling safe in the here and now;
3. To talk, laugh, engage in therapeutic play, cry, rage, sweat or tremble when there is a '*balance of attention*' between feeling the emotional support and safety in the present combined with experiencing the emotional pain from the past. These processes are most effective when they are welcomed by a present and attentive adult.

In this way, they emerge from the fight, flight or freeze response, they feel and release the associated painful feelings, and they make movements which tell their brain that the trauma has now been overcome.

Children want to experience emotional health and are constantly striving for that – and are inviting us to cooperate with these inbuilt healing processes. They know how to heal from stress and trauma, and they will do so *spontaneously* when they feel deeply connected and emotionally safe.

***Aware Parenting has a deep trust in this innate and intuitive knowing of babies and children, which we are invited to match by creating an environment of emotional safety and offering them our compassionate presence.***

Children will invite us to support them in their healing over and over again! They will:

- *play* particular games – and invite us to join in with them;
- *cry* even when all their needs are met – and invite us to lovingly listen to them;
- *rage* and tantrum – and invite us to listen while keeping them and others safe.

However, this innate healing ability is not enough in itself.

## They need our understanding, loving presence and particular responses to enable the healing to happen. This is vital.

*Attachment play*[9]: If your child keeps asking to play hide and seek, they may be trying to heal from experiences of separation, either physical or emotional. If they keep wanting to create a tunnel and climb though it and be greeted by you at the other end, they might be intuitively trying to heal from their birth experience.

---

9   This is a type of play specific to Aware Parenting which we will talk about in more detail later in the book.

*Crying with loving support:* If your child starts crying over something apparently insignificant, they are probably releasing pent-up painful feelings from daily stresses or bigger traumas that have accumulated. If they tend to find a pretext to cry over something small in the evenings, they are probably using their innate healing and relaxation process so that they can feel relaxed enough to go fall asleep and sleep peacefully and restfully.

*Raging/tantrums with loving support:* If your child starts having a tantrum when you gently say no, the kicking and vigorous movement is probably releasing pent up tension that was mobilised in the fight or flight response. If they rage in your loving arms at the end of a busy day, they are likely to be letting out all the stress, muscular tension and feelings that have accumulated during the day.

If we are able to support our children in these natural healing processes:

- joining in with their *attachment play* and following their lead;
- listening lovingly to their tears and tantrums while keeping them and others safe,

they will generally come out the other side of these amazing natural homeostatic processes feeling *calmer* and *more relaxed*.

And that makes so much sense, doesn't it? They have:

- *engaged* in their natural and innate healing processes;
- *released* physical tension and stress from the fight or flight response, while feeling safe;
- *expressed* their feelings and had them lovingly heard,

all within a supportive, loving, safe and empathic parent-child relationship. They can then return to a state of calm, embodied presence.

**Aware Parenting offers a deep trust in humans and our innate striving for emotional wellbeing, in a culture that has demonised these beautiful, powerful and natural processes.**

If you find yourself feeling:

- *frustrated* when your child wants you to play families with their soft toys again;
- *angry* when your child starts to cry over apparently nothing;
- *powerless* when your child has a tantrum;

these are all normal and *natural* responses for you to have when your own innate, intuitive, natural healing processes were probably stifled or judged when you were a child.

> In order for us to be able to deeply trust these amazing healing processes in our child/ren, we often need to get freer from our own cultural conditioning about parenting, have our feelings heard, and reclaim trust in our own innate capacity to heal.

Then we are more likely to be able to:

- *recognise when* our child is inviting healing in these ways;
- *know how* to respond most helpfully to support that healing; and
- *be able* to offer safety, compassion and presence for the healing to happen successfully.

This is an incredibly powerful process that supports children to feel deeply calm and present in their bodies.

*I remember when my children were three and seven years old, and their dad and I used to go to cafés and restaurants. They would be sitting calmly and relaxedly throughout the meal, and the waitperson would often say, "Aren't they well-behaved?" or, "Aren't they good!?" And their dad and I would afterwards chuckle, imagining that the waitperson had thought that we'd told them to, "Be good," or to, "Sit still," when in reality, we'd listened to some big crying that day before going out for a meal. Sometimes we'd even say that to the waitperson, "Oh yes, they let out lots of feelings today so they feel really relaxed now!" They probably wondered what on earth we were talking about!*

*And then there were the days we used to go to a gift shop in Byron Bay, a nearby beachside town. It had lots of breakable items in there. We'd go in the shop and I'd see the shop person's eyes widen, seeing two young children. But because they'd had lots of their feelings heard, my children were calm and relaxed and picked up breakable things very gently. We loved having order in our house (which came from my passion for Montessori), so they would even put shop items in order that had been moved out of place. We could almost feel the sigh of relief from the shopkeeper at the counter!*

*Of course, my children weren't always like this – there were times when we'd had lots of busy days, or as parents we had less capacity to listen, and they had feelings bubbling and they were agitated and antsy. On those days, I would avoid taking them to a cafe, or a shop with delicate things. We'd do what we could to help them feel relaxed through crying and raging with our loving support before taking them to places where calmness and relaxation would make a big difference.*

I don't think any of us can listen to 100% of our child's feelings in this culture and at this point in time. However, understanding how they are feeling, and communicating that to them can make a huge difference, even if we are not able to listen to the feelings at times. Understanding that behind nearly all challenging behaviours are a child's painful feelings will mean that, even if we aren't able to listen to those feelings at the time, we are more likely to be able to respond compassionately to them and our child will be more likely to experience being loved and understood.

Mirroring their feelings to them makes a big difference to their experience of being unconditionally loved and understood. We can offer comments such as:

- "Did you feel scared?"
- "Do you feel overwhelmed?"
- "Are you feeling upset?"
- "I imagine you might be feeling sad?"

If we can *also* listen to crying and raging, that's *even more* helpful for them, because that's how the deep healing happens. Phrases such as, "I'm here with you. I'm listening. I welcome all of your feelings. I love you," while they cry or rage with our loving presence is a powerful way to communicate our willingness to be with them through their big feelings, leading to more emotional safety. I'll be talking about this in much more detail later in the book.

> *Self-Reflection Moment*
> *Does any of this resonate with you?*
> *Does any of it not resonate with you?*

In my own early years in parenting, I was amazed to discover that through simply understanding this and supporting my children in this way wherever I was able to, they generally:

- wanted to *cooperate*;
- were *calm and relaxed* in their bodies;
- were able to *concentrate* and be deeply *present*;
- were *gentle* with each other and other children, pets and objects;
- *slept restfully* and for long periods.

I was also surprised to learn that most of the things that parents find challenging were actually caused by pent-up painful feelings caused by unhealed stress and trauma.

I am so incredibly grateful for Aware Parenting and Aletha Solter, who helped me know how to recognise and support emotional healing and health in my children, and also made parenting so much more enjoyable, because children who don't have a lot of painful pent-up feelings are relaxed and present and a delight to be with.

> I love how Aware Parenting has this deep trust in the innate and intuitive knowing of babies and children, and our intrinsic capacity to support that healing through creating an environment of emotional safety and offering our compassionate presence.

> *Self-Compassion Moment*
> 
> *I'm sending you so much love if you feel painful feelings when you're reading this part about children being a delight when they don't have a lot of pent-up feelings.*
> 
> *I remember when my son and daughter did have a lot of pent-up feelings, after their dad and I separated, and how painful I found it, seeing my friends and colleagues enjoying their family life, when in my family, we were all reacting from the hurt we were feeling. So if you're feeling painful feelings right now, I do understand what you're going through, and I want to let you know that it really can be different. With enough emotional support and healing for ourselves, things really can change.*

## With this book, there are three key ways I would love to contribute to you

*Cognitive understanding:* I wrote this book to help parents understand that children innately know how to heal from stress and trauma, and when we support them in that, they feel so much more deeply relaxed, which affects almost all of their behaviour. I'm here to help you recognise when your child has an unmet need or when they are using their innate healing process, and I will be offering thoughts that might be helpful for you to think at those times.

*Emotional state:* I'm willing for this book to provide information and practices that help you feel calm and present in your body more of the time so that you can create the most conducive healing environment and more often have the ability to respond in loving and compassionate ways to your child's unmet needs and healing processes.

*Practical actions*: I'll offer specific examples of things you can say and do that will maximise the effectiveness of these opportunities for healing that your child presents to you.

**In addition, I will be repeatedly inviting you to stop judging yourself if you find yourself picking up those emotional sticks.**

> Just as punishment doesn't help children be more loving, neither does punishing ourselves help us be more loving. I invite you to be compassionate with yourself and to hold in mind that you were always responding in the ways that you thought were most helpful and in the ways that you were able to at the time, given all your previous hurts and traumas, and all the stresses and challenges you were faced with. In the parenting journey, we will constantly evolve, which means being deeply compassionate with ourselves for those times in the past when we didn't know what we know now and we couldn't do what we can do now.

Linde, a Psychotherapist and Aware Parenting instructor shares about the transformation that happened for her and her family when she first learnt about Aware Parenting:

*"When I was first pregnant, I thought that as a child psychologist I would have it in the bag. I thought; women have been doing this for ages, it's nature, I do not have to prepare anything. Looking back I did not take into account all of my own conditioning that was covering my*

*intuition and my need for information. So after giving birth I panicked when my son started to cry a lot after a few weeks – and when all of the contradictory advice came, I became so insecure. I started making lists on my phone of why my baby could be crying so I could go and check them when he was crying. I needed this list to check off what I could do because I could not think clearly when he was crying. I could not hear anyone else speak, his crying was all I could hear or think about and I felt this urge to fix it.*

*With my first son we did not know of Aware Parenting, so we had a more mainstream approach. We did everything during the day so he would not cry but left him alone to cry when it was time for bed. And it seemed to work. He cried every time I dropped him off at daycare, and they had to pull him off of me. It devastated me, but I thought this was normal.*

*By the age of two he had become very hyperactive and had a lot of tantrums. Six months later I gave birth to his brother. The combination of taking care of a newborn and a 2.5 year old with a lot of tantrums and all that excess energy had exhausted me. I remember my youngest waking up almost every hour his first night when I was alone at hospital while my partner was at home with my eldest. I was miserable. My youngest cried a lot from birth onwards and this was what made me reach out to other friends with kids for support and tips.*

*A friend then recommended Aletha Solter's book* Tears and Tantrums. *I remember thinking, 'This makes so much sense,' and struggling with it because at that time I had not cried in a long time. I started listening to my son's tears, however I don't think I had the capacity to really hold space for them. I did not read any other Aware Parenting books until a year later when we went into lockdown. By this time I did not enjoy spending time with my kids, I dreaded it. How will I survive these hours? I wondered to myself. I felt a huge weight on my chest all of the time and often had headaches. I remember one time my eldest had done something 'wrong' and I put him in time out. As a child* psychologist I was taught that you can modify your child's behaviour with punishments and rewards. That this is the way they learn, that they needed to be taught how to be 'good'.

We taped a square on the floor in the corner so he knew where time out was and that he had to stay within these lines until the timer went off. It worked a couple of times, he was affected the first times and a bit shaken, but then we always needed to get a bit harsher to get the same effect. As you can imagine, this was an invitation for a game for a 3.5 year old. First it was a toe over the line, then a foot, and then he escaped and ran as quickly as he could. I got so immensely triggered, I ran after him, put him back in the corner kicking and screaming and yelled at him.

By then we had already discovered that when we got him to his breaking point, and crying followed afterwards, he would cooperate more. Sometimes we got so triggered that we yelled, other times we did this on purpose just to get him to those feelings. But this time was different. I saw the fear in his eyes, the terror on his face, I saw him break down and forsake himself just to not lose our love. He asked me:'Mommy can I get a hug?' he clung to my leg and I could see the question on his mind: 'Do you still love me? Am I still loveable?' I got catapulted back to my own childhood and remembered how insecure I felt and how hard I worked to be seen and be loved, and I did not want that for my children. I decided; never again, this has to change. But I did not know how.

It was then that I started reading Aletha's books back-to-back, started experimenting and seeing the change in my children. I also started listening to The Aware Parenting Podcast which helped me with listening to my own needs. Listening to the podcast episode on motherhood and guilt was like an epiphany for me. I needed more space for me, I needed to allow myself to sit still and recharge, so I had capacity to hold space for them! I remember thinking: this all is so great, it makes perfect sense, but what is the catch? If this works, why don't more people know about this? I could not believe or trust it.

*But the evidence in my kids now is crystal clear, it works! My partner tries to take into account everything I tell him about Aware Parenting but he is not 100% on board. This means that I listen to tears most of the time, he connects mostly over games and screens with the kids, this is what he knows. So with my youngest I started listening to his crying soon after birth and with my eldest when he was 2.5. When I look at both my kids, I see the effects of that. My eldest is really sensitive and insecure, gets frustrated really easily and needs a lot of time to adjust, worries a lot and gravitates towards screens more. My youngest seems to have no fear and is a really happy kid and can play alone for a long time and has no difficulty with trial and error. I truly believe that this has something to do with my eldest being left alone to cry and my youngest always having cried in my arms.*

*When I started making space for their tears, I started with* attachment play *to get our connection back and to create safety. My eldest got really angry at first when tears came. 'I don't want to cry, stupid tears,' he said. The real turning point came when I started with* attachment play *and started prioritising my needs. We got big tantrums, big emotions, and also so much love and cooperation afterwards. My kids started saying, 'I love you Mommy,' started coming up to me and hugging me out of nowhere, asking me if they could help.*

*It has been quite the rollercoaster of being able to see their needs behind their behaviour and feeling in my body, checking in with myself before responding or offering a* Loving Limit. *I started enjoying spending time with them again and connecting with my inner child again. I find it difficult discovering what I like, what nurtures me and what I need. I'm not completely where I want to be yet, but I'm loving the journey and I'm trying to trust the process!*

*I even noticed that I was reacting differently with my clients. That I was looking through a different lens and all of a sudden, things made so much more sense. Gradually I started seeing the unhealed trauma from their childhood and their conditioning coming up in what they were sharing with me. I could see the trans-generational trauma and how things were passed on to yet another generation. Where will it end? The mental health waiting lists just get longer and longer, and I felt like the only way to really change this is by supporting parents in Aware Parenting their children so that the next generation is more resilient and compassionate.*

*I have seen such beautiful changes in my kids and clients, seen them connecting with themselves again and developing an inner compass. This all made me so excited that I want to help more people and want to share Aware Parenting with the world. I truly believe it can change the world and I want to be part of it. So I decided I want to become an Aware Parenting instructor myself. I believe this vision is more helpful than my previous psychology-psychotherapy training/background."*

## The three reasons for children's behaviour: thoughts, needs, feelings

We talked above about non-punitive discipline, and how this requires an understanding of what is actually *causing* a child's behaviour in the first place, so that we can attend to the origins. In this section, we are addressing *how* to attend to the reasons for a child's behaviour, which can be categorised into three causes.

This map of the three reasons for children's behaviour was created by Aletha Solter. It gives a profound understanding of what is *really* going on underneath the behaviour we observe. We talked a bit about it earlier on, but let's dive in deeper now.

The three things are:

- **a need for information;**
- **unmet needs in the here and now;**
- **painful feelings in the present or from the past.**

As shorthand, I call this what children:
- think/know/understand;
- need; and
- feel.

***In our parenting, we can repeatedly go back to this powerful map to discover what is really going on for our child, so I invite you to have this list of three causes clearly in your mind.***

What is equally powerful is knowing that as parents, our parenting responses are also caused by these three things:

**What we are thinking**

including:

- the *information* we have about children;
- our *understanding* of child development;
- our own *conditioning* about the true nature of children and human beings; and
- the *thoughts* we have about our child and ourselves based on our own childhood experiences.

**What we are needing**

I will be talking more about addressing your needs later in this book.

**What we feel in the present and from the past**

I will be inviting you to compassionately attend to your own feelings, particularly those that stem from your own childhood experiences!

However, because most of us were also brought up with punishments and rewards rather than non-punitive discipline, most of us *don't* attend to these three reasons when we act in ways we don't want to, including towards our children. Instead, most of us do the equivalent of what was done to us as children. We punish ourselves.

> *Self-Compassion Moment*
>
> *Do you punish yourself when you've done something to your child you wish you hadn't?*
>
> *Do you punish yourself if you don't do something that you wish you had?*
>
> *Do you judge yourself? Shame yourself? Pick up the guilt sticks?*
>
> *If so, how do you feel when you imagine not punishing yourself in these ways?*

Punishing ourselves in these ways is the result of us being punished and rewarded as children. Behaviour modification techniques of punishments and rewards don't change behaviour at the causal level. They also *don't* help us grow up into adults who know how to address the causes of our behaviour and make changes from there.

Instead, they lead to adults who are very competent at self-judgment and picking up the guilt and shame sticks. As a result, we often become adults who keep repeating behaviour that we don't want to repeat, because we don't know how to change our behaviour at the level of cause.

**Imagine responding to your child in a way that not only attends to the source of their behaviour and creates change there, but also helps them become adults who know how powerful they are because they understand the causes of their behaviours and actions and they know how to change those at the causal level!**

The other core element of this way of responding to children is that it is based on a fundamentally different belief about human beings. The behaviour modification model of behaviour change (and the religious beliefs that preceded it), is based on the belief that human beings are basically 'bad' (or 'sinful') and need to be 'taught' to be 'good' – hence the punishments and rewards. In other words, they need to experience painful things when they're doing unwanted things, so they stop because they want to stop experiencing pain. And following this is the idea that they need to experience enjoyable things when they are doing wanted things, so that they want to keep doing that to keep having more of the reward.

However, all that really happens with the behaviour modification model is a child experiences more painful things during threats and punishments that leave more traces of stress or trauma. With rewards, they are likely to disconnect from themselves and their innate desires such as to contribute and cooperate. For example, they experience wanting the sticker or the chocolate but still not intrinsically liking doing homework or eating vegetables.

> *Self-Compassion Moment*
>
> *I'm sending you so much love if you're tempted to pick up any guilt sticks right now. I want to remind you that changing our cultural conditioning is hard. When we're feeling stretched and stressed, it's so natural for us to return to the ways we were parented, and the conditioning we experienced growing up, which for many of us was threats and punishments, bribes and rewards. I also want to remind you that whenever we do that, we can repair afterwards, in ways that I talk about later in the book.*

## Aware Parenting is based on a totally different belief about human beings compared to behaviour modification.

I call it the three C's. That, whether we are an adult or child, we innately want to:

- Connect;
- Cooperate; and
- Contribute.

And if we are not doing those three C's, it's because of one of those three reasons.

We're **thinking** things that are causing our hurtful or difficult behaviour.

We have **unmet needs** that are so uncomfortable that they lead us to act in unenjoyable ways.

We have **painful accumulated feelings** from past painful, stressful or traumatic events that are causing the behaviour.

This is why Aware Parenting is so powerful, because it:

- is based on a deeply *compassionate* belief about human beings;
- understands the actual *causes* of behaviour; and
- has really *practical* ways to attend to those three causes.

By attending to the three causes, we can help children:

- have the *information* they need to understand what's going on and what's required;
- have their *needs* met so that they feel calm in their bodies; and
- express enough accumulated *feelings* so they feel deeply relaxed,

so that they:

- *want* to brush their teeth;
- *enjoy* clearing up their toys with us;
- are *naturally gentle* with other beings; and
- are *relaxed* enough to sleep when they're tired.

We help them do those things not though arbitrary punishments or rewards, but because they feel relaxed enough, connected enough, powerful enough, and have the information they need to simply be willing and able to do those things.

This attends to their mind, their body and their feelings by not adding unnecessary disconnection and emotional pain (like punishments and rewards do), but instead helping them have:

- clear *information* and understanding;
- enough of their *needs* met; and
- enough of their *feelings* heard,

so that they enjoy behaving in helpful, connected and calm ways.

How powerful is that! It not only helps them return to the connected, loving, cooperative, calm, concentrating person they are, it is also more likely to help them be an adult who, instead of punishing themselves when they act in ways they don't want to, knows how to attend to the causes, so they can ask themselves:

- is there something they're *thinking* or *believing*?
- is there something they're *needing*?
- do they have painful *feelings* that need to be expressed or heard?

It helps them know as children and adults that when they are behaving in ways they don't want to, they are not bad, that there is nothing wrong with them, and there is nothing to be ashamed of. They have simply disconnected from their connected, cooperative, contributing self because of harsh or inaccurate thoughts, unmet needs or painful feelings. What a huge change that will create in the world!

**Then rewards and punishments clearly become what they always were – outdated and inefficient carrots and sticks that miss the wonder and complexity of human beings.**

I would love to support you in this element of Aware Parenting (if you're not already doing so) – to help you parent without punishments and rewards and instead know how to parent through attending to the causes of your child/ren's behaviour.

In that process, I would also love to support you to attend to that list in yourself too, so that *you* have:

- more compassionate ways of *thinking* about your child and yourself;
- your *needs* met more, which also makes it easier to meet your child/ren's needs; and
- your own *feelings* lovingly heard, which will also give you more emotional spaciousness in yourself to listen to your child/ren's feelings.

As parents, we can go through this list of three things – thoughts, needs and feelings – whenever our child is doing something that we don't want them to be doing, or when they aren't doing what we do want them to be doing (and we can also go through it on similar occasions for ourselves!)

### A need for information

In our culture, there is often a focus on giving children information when they're not doing what we're asking them to do. I wonder if you've found that? If your child is pulling the dog's tail, do you find yourself saying over and over, "Be gentle! The dog doesn't like that!" Perhaps you might even find yourself speaking more and more loudly, thinking that somehow they aren't hearing you? Parents will often say, "My child doesn't listen," as part of this way of thinking.

> *Self-Compassion Moment*
> I'm sending you lots of love if you recall doing this with your child. It's really understandable if you have, because we live in a culture where the mind is seen as most powerful, and where many of us were taught to 'just do what we were told'.

I find it also helpful to reflect on this for ourselves too! Have you ever had information about something but kept on doing it? For example, perhaps you know that shouting at a child isn't helpful for them, but you find yourself doing exactly that when you're really stressed, overwhelmed or powerless? In this situation, it's not a lack of information causing your behaviour, just as it is often not a lack of information that is causing a child's behaviour. Having someone tell us, "You know that it's not helpful to shout at a child," is not likely to help us at all. In fact, we're likely to either pick up guilt sticks, or be reactive to the other person, as a result. This can also happen for children!

If we've repeatedly given a child information and they are still doing that thing that we don't want them to be doing, it's likely that their behaviour is *not* being caused by a lack of information.

> That's when we can move to
> the next cause, unmet needs,
> and address that possibility.

### Unmet needs

I imagine there have been times when you've been needing connection or empathy or support and haven't been getting those needs met and you've felt upset or agitated, and then have responded in ways to your child that you don't want to respond.

> **Self-Reflection Moment**
> Can you recall occasions where that happened? If so, I'm sending you lots of compassion. It can be really hard for us to get our needs met as parents in the DDC, so it can be common for us to have unmet needs.

Children are just like us, only they are affected by unmet needs even more, particularly because they are often dependent on us to meet those needs.

If they have unmet needs, that creates painful feelings for them. The sensations and feelings in their bodies are literally communicating important information to them – that they have immediate needs. When they're feeling those painful feelings, it's really hard for them to be able to hear what we are saying, or cooperate, or be calm. This isn't because they don't understand what we want and don't want. It's because their needs are calling more strongly in the moment to be heard.

So, if your child is not doing something you want them to do, or is doing something that you don't want them to do, the next step is to address their needs.

**Remember their core need for connection! Moving in with connection can often make a huge difference to a child's behaviour. If they feel connected with us, they are more likely to be able to take in what we are saying and to want to contribute and cooperate.**

Other core needs for children are autonomy and choice. When we offer our child choices rather than tell them what they have to do or should do, they are much more likely to be *willing* to cooperate with us.

We can do this preventatively and we can do it in the moment. To *prevent* challenging behaviour, the more we offer our child choices and honour their needs for autonomy, the fewer feelings of powerlessness they will feel, and also our respect for those needs will mean that they simply want to cooperate more.

Also, in the *moment*, offering choices about how something is done often leads to more willingness to cooperate.

> I recommend avoiding phrases such as "you have to," "you've got to," "you should" and "you must" and instead to make true requests. I love the phrase, "are you willing?" (as you will discover)![10]

We will talk more more about cooperation later in the book.

> In response to certain behaviours, we may go through this list of three things. We might give our child information, and perhaps they're not cooperating. Then we might address their needs – such as for connection and choice – and if they're still not cooperating, that's when we can turn to the last reason.

*However, there are particular situations where we don't need to go through the whole list of three, because the third reason is clearly the cause from the outset. This is generally the case for behaviours such as hitting – or aggression in general. However, remember, because Aware Parenting has attachment-style parenting at the core, a child needs connection in order to be able to express the feelings causing that behaviour.*

> Children will not hit because of a lack of information. Even very young children understand that hitting hurts.

---

10  I'm grateful to Marshall Rosenberg, who created Nonviolent Communication, from whom I learnt this information. Please note that the phrase "are you willing" is a phrase I love but isn't an intrinsic element of Aware Parenting.

It's also unlikely that they are hitting because of unmet needs in the present, although it is possible, for example if there is a chronic unmet need for connection or choice, and they hit us as those feelings become really big, or if an adult is using power-over them in the present. Of course, hitting is an adaptive response in a dangerous situation as the fight part of our fight or flight response.

However, in most cases, hitting and other similar behaviours are caused by painful feelings, generally those that have accumulated from the past.

### Painful feelings

*The understanding that painful feelings cause behaviour is a core difference between Aware Parenting and many other parenting paradigms. So many of the things that parents find challenging are created by an accumulation of painful feelings.*

When children have unexpressed feelings sitting in their bodies, they often feel agitated. When they are agitated, it's harder for them to be able to think clearly, hear what others are saying, concentrate, sit still, go to sleep and stay asleep.

## Agitation is uncomfortable for them and leads them to do things that they don't actually want to be doing.

Painful feelings consist of the feelings and sensations themselves, the stress hormones related to the feelings, and the physical tension from the fight or flight response, held in their muscles. In combination, these lead to behaviours like being silly and goofy, moving around a lot, hyperactivity, throwing, forcefully taking, pushing, biting, swearing and hitting.

This is such a different lens to look through, isn't it, compared to the behaviour modification model? In a behaviour modification approach, these children might be viewed as 'naughty' and 'misbehaving' and would either be punished for acting in these ways or rewarded to behave in other ways. But punishments and rewards would not address the painful feelings causing the behaviour. They probably wouldn't address *any* of the three causes of behaviour. They wouldn't help with the feelings, they wouldn't meet the needs, and they wouldn't give a child the information they were needing. All punishments do is create even *more* pain which then sits on top of the feelings already there.

But what can we do as parents, if our child has painful feelings that are leading to them not cooperating, not sleeping, or hitting? We will go into all of this in more detail in the book. However, for now, I will summarise the key information for us to hold in mind.

There are *two* key ways that children release painful feelings from their bodies:

1. With *attachment play*, which releases lighter feelings of fear, frustration and powerlessness. Play also helps children heal from past hurts and resolve frightening past experiences, helping them feel more relaxed and powerful. *Attachment play* is a special kind of play that happens when adults trust that children know how to heal and release painful feelings, and join in with their play in particular ways or offer specific kinds of play. We'll be talking in more detail about *attachment play* later in the book.

2. Through crying and raging (tantrums). When children cry and rage with our loving support, they express and release deeper feelings such as overwhelm, sadness and loss, fear and terror, frustration, anger and outrage. Those are the feelings sitting in their bodies making it hard for them to relax enough to concentrate, sleep, or be gentle. I'll also be explaining more about these processes in upcoming chapters.

The more we support our children through doing *attachment play* with them and listening lovingly to their tears and tantrums, the more relaxed they will feel in their bodies and the more they will naturally be able and willing to cooperate, concentrate, be gentle and be able to go to sleep and stay asleep.

When children's feelings bubble up into not cooperating, not concentrating, not sleeping, or hitting, we can respond in particular ways that help them express the feelings so that they can cooperate, concentrate, sleep or be gentle. Again, I will be talking about all of these in more detail later in the book.

> *Self-Reflection Moment*
>
> *Is there anything that your child has been doing that you are seeing in a different light?*
>
> *How are you feeling as you take in this information?*
>
> *This information can help us connect with our own feelings. As always, I invite you to be compassionate with yourself and refrain from judging yourself.*

Stephanie Heartfield, an Aware Parenting instructor in Australia, shares about her experience of not wanting to use behaviour modification and then coming across Aware Parenting:

*"When I was studying my psychology degree, I had a strong passion for developmental psychology, and it set the tone for how I desired to parent my own children when the time came. Behaviour modification did not resonate with me, so I knew I had no willingness to use punishments of any sort on my children. I valued unconditional love, compassion, empathy and acceptance. So that is what I decided to pursue when I was pregnant with my first child, 10 years ago.*

*I came across a beautiful essay about Aware Parenting written by*

*Marion which was at the back of a* CalmBirth *workbook. Before I had even finished reading the first paragraph, I had one of those deeply profound moments (kind of like when Harry Potter holds his wand for the very first time). Aware Parenting was the missing piece of the puzzle that I had been willing to see during my psychology degree. My husband also immediately resonated with Marion's words and all the principles and practices of Aware Parenting.*

*There is something truly magical about Aware Parenting, something that just cannot be put into words. It's an aliveness we feel, live and breathe. It is a paradigm that ripples through into every aspect of our lives, like a beautiful watercolour painting. I am so passionate about Aware Parenting, that my husband and I created our own special haven for children aged 1-8 years old in 2015, so that other children and their families could experience Aware Parenting, and see the beneficial impact in all aspects of their lives."*

## The three options with feelings: expression, suppression and aggression

Several years ago, in my *Aware Parenting Instructor Mentoring Course*, inspired by an idea from Maira Jorba (and with her permission), I created a map to help summarise the feelings element of Aware Parenting, which I will share below.

As we discussed above, *all children will frequently experience uncomfortable feelings*, however much we aim to meet their needs. Expressing feelings through laughter, tears and raging are the main ways that children heal from stress and trauma as long as we are lovingly present with them.

> Sometimes it can appear that children don't have feelings to express, because they hardly ever cry. However, perhaps they suck their thumb a lot, or hit other children. These indicate that there are accumulated feelings that haven't been expressed.

The thumb sucking is a form of suppression, and hitting is a sign of aggression (even if a child is laughing, because the laughter is the release of fear).

***This is why it can be really helpful to understand these three options with feelings, because then we can really understand what is going on with our child and how we can most help them.***

The three options with feelings are:

- expression;
- suppression; and
- aggression.

This list is a simplification of reality, because it's designed to be easy to remember. For example, the suppression category also includes dissociation, and the aggression category also includes agitation. It's a shorthand map designed for simplicity and clarity, so it doesn't include the full complexity of what is going on for children.

## Expression

Children heal from stress and trauma through expressing feelings during play and laughter, crying and raging. When children are expressing feelings, they can experience having their *feelings heard*, they are *releasing stress* and they are *letting go* of pent-up physical *tension*. All three of these have a huge effect on how they feel, the sensations they experience in their bodies, and how relaxed they are. As we talked about earlier on, this relaxation has a huge impact on many, if not all, of their behaviours.

## Suppression (and dissociation)

However, because most of us were brought up in a culture or family where our feelings were not seen and welcomed as the powerful healing processes that they are, we will often not realise that our child has feelings to express and we may instead try to distract them from those feelings.

When they have healing-feelings (ie. caused by stress or trauma), we might not always realise that they need to express those feelings and have them heard. We might think they have unmet needs which are creating needs-feelings and so of course, it's natural that we will do things to try to meet those apparent needs. At other times, we might understand that they have feelings to tell us, but we might not be able to be present with them while they are feeling their big emotions. At those times they will need to find ways to suppress their feelings.

We might try to distract them from their feelings, often in the same ways we were distracted from our emotions when we were children. For example, if we were fed when we were upset, we might tend to think our child is hungry when they actually have some feelings to tell us. Over time, they might learn to interpret the sensations of emotional hurt as hunger, and so then eat when they're upset.

At other times, we might just not be very emotionally available, so they might find their own ways to suppress their feelings. This is often the cause of behaviours such as thumb sucking, nose picking or hair twirling.

> *Self-Compassion Moment*
>
> *I'm sending you loving compassion if you're tempted to pick up the guilt sticks after reading this. I also want to remind you that it is so understandable that as parents in this culture, where we don't receive anywhere near enough support and acknowledgment for parenting, there will be many times when we are stressed, dissociated, or just really busy.*

***It's not your fault if your child dissociates from their feelings. You haven't done anything wrong. You simply grew up and live in a culture where needs and feelings aren't honoured and valued and where parents aren't given enough support.***

In Aware Parenting, the term to describe these ways of suppressing feelings is *control patterns*. These are habitual ways that children disconnect from their feelings, often through a form of mild dissociation.

## Being able to differentiate between calm relaxation and mild dissociation is vital in Aware Parenting.

I'd love to emphasise that it's very common that we do something to fix things when a child is upset, thinking that we have calmed them down and all their needs are now met, when actually, we have distracted them from their feelings and they are now dissociated.

### Self-Compassion Moment
*It's so natural that most of us do this, with the most loving of intentions.*
*I'm sending love to any feelings you might be feeling right now.*

There are a few major ways that children can suppress their feelings or dissociate:

*Movement* – such as repeated movements or running around whenever they are upset. This can be caused by rocking them or pushing them in a stroller when they needed to cry in our arms.

*Sucking* – eg. dummy, pacifier, thumb or finger sucking or bottlefeeding or breastfeeding. This might be from us giving them a bottle, dummy/pacifier or the breast when they had feelings to express, or they might start finger or thumb sucking when we were unable to be with their feelings or when we didn't understand that they had feelings to express.

*Eating when not hungry* – this often comes from us interpreting their upset feelings as hunger and feeding them when they were upset, so they learn to associate those sensations as hunger.

*Screens to suppress feelings* – screens are powerful ways that children (and adults) can distract themselves from feeling their feelings.

*Repetitive actions* – nose picking, hair twirling, nail biting, picking their skin, etc.

Almost anything can become a *control pattern*, a habitual way to mildly dissociate. A certain action may be taken to meet needs one day, and the same activity may be used to dissociate the next day.

Understanding suppression isn't another reason to judge ourselves or our child when they are dissociating. No! This clarity is so we can help them, whenever we are willing and able, to move from suppressing those feelings to expressing them.

> *Self-Compassion Moment*
> If you're tempted to pick up that emotional stick right now, I invite you to put it back down again! It is completely common in this culture for children to suppress their feelings. In the chapter on control patterns you will see how and why it is important to have a deeply compassionate perspective about them, and to refrain from judging ourselves.

**The antidote to suppression and dissociation is warm connection.**

One way we can remember this is to think of freezing, which is another way of describing dissociation. When we meet the freeze with emotional warmth, it can melt into water, which we can liken to emotions, feelings-in-motion, which often include tears and crying, but can also show up as raging and tantrums. With Aware Parenting, we can stay close with our child and keep offering them warm connection while they cry or rage.

*Attachment play* can also be part of helping those feelings bubble to the surface, so that they are expressed rather than being suppressed.

We will be talking more about *control patterns* later on – both your child/ren's and yours.

For now, I'd love to offer you a few invitations:

1. Would you like to observe your child/ren and notice when they might be suppressing their feelings with a *control pattern*?

   Clues that this is happening are that they:

   - *urgently* or *desperately* want to do that particular thing when they are clearly *upset*;
   - do it when they are *tired* (which is when healing-feelings naturally bubble up);
   - seem *disconnected* or *dissociated* when they are doing it, eg. their eyes are glazed or staring; or
   - have *tension* in their muscles when they're doing it.

2. Would you like to notice what your key *control patterns* are and when you use them?
3. I invite you to refrain from judging yourself or your child when there are *control patterns* around. They are simply one of the flags for feelings.

> The flags for feelings frame means that we can choose to understand that whenever our child is engaged in a *control pattern*, they have some uncomfortable feelings bubbling to the surface. I invite you to see that as an *invitation* for *connection*, rather than a judgment.

### Aggression (and agitation)[11]

Aggression is generally caused by painful accumulated feelings, that often (but not always) bubble up in response to something happening externally.

---

[11] This can also be the fight part of the fight/flight response in action.

This is a big shift in perception, isn't it?

*I wonder what you tell yourself when you see a child throwing or pushing or forcefully taking or hitting?*

In these moments, we might find it hard to see that they are actually feeling scared, powerless, frustrated or overwhelmed and instead of expressing those feelings, their emotions are showing up as aggression.

With Aware Parenting, we can do things both preventatively and in the moment to help with aggression in ways that actually attend to the root cause – feelings – and make it less and less likely for children to get to the point of aggression.

Again, we will talk about this in much more depth later in the book.

## Understanding our place in healing our lineage as first generation Aware Parenting parents

I believe that understanding our place in our lineage of healing is so important, particularly because it helps us be much more *compassionate* with ourselves. In talking to thousands of parents practicing Aware Parenting over many years, I have seen again and again parents judging themselves, thinking that they should be 'perfect' and generally giving themselves a hard time when they don't parent in ways that they think they 'should' be doing. I like to invite parents to remember where they have come from, and the amount of change that they have brought about in just one generation.

*I invite you to do that now.*

Your child/ren come after you and will bring about more change. Each generation has the opportunity to evolve beyond the one before. You are making a huge jump, but I invite you to drop the expectation that you 'should' get to some kind of parenting nirvana. What you are doing is making a huge difference. If you offer lots of closeness to your child/ren, they are already receiving more than many, many children. If you refrain from using punishments and rewards, they are experiencing something that very few children experience. If you listen lovingly to their tears and raging, even once, they are experiencing what 99% of the population have never experienced.

Instead of judging yourself, or comparing yourself harshly to others, I invite you to focus on what you *have* done. On all the changes that you have brought into your family and all the ways you have met their needs.

## Judging yourself, or expecting yourself to be some kind of 'perfect', is all part of *Disconnected Domination Culture* consciousness.

Just as Aware Parenting invites you to refrain from punishing your child, so I invite you to increasingly stop punishing yourself with self-judgment. Just as Aware Parenting invites you to trust your child's learning journey, so I invite you to *trust* your own learning journey with Aware Parenting. I also invite you to see the hugeness of what you are doing.

You may not have been responded to from an attachment style of parenting.

You were probably punished and rewarded.

You might have rarely or never been played with in an *attachment play* way.

You might never or rarely have had your feelings lovingly heard by an adult who understood that you were expressing feelings caused by stressful or traumatic events.

So, responding to your child in an attuned, connected and responsive way is big!

Avoiding punishing or rewarding your child is massive!

Doing *attachment play* with your child is a lot!

Listening to your child's crying and raging is huge!

***It is inevitably going to be hard at times to do this. Of course it is going to be a learning process, one where you'll understand more about Aware Parenting the more you learn about it and experiment with it, and you'll become more competent at it the more you practice it.***

It is also inevitably going to help you connect with your own feelings, including those from when you:

- didn't receive an attuned, empathic and connected response;
- were punished, rewarded, shamed and blamed;
- weren't played with in nourishing and fun ways; or
- were distracted, shamed or punished when you felt painful feelings.

## Practicing Aware Parenting, and making that shift in just one generation is a really huge ask.

I invite you to respond to yourself as much as you can in the way you would respond to a best friend, or to your child if they were the parent and you were the grandparent. Aware Parenting is hard enough as it is, without adding self-judgment, guilt and expectations of some kind of perfection onto the top!

## Increasing our capacity for self-compassion makes a huge difference not only in how we feel, but also in how we are able to respond to our child.

In addition, holding the lineage perspective can help us understand our parents more. I often think that if I had been born at the time and in the family system that my parents had, I would have probably parented in the ways that they did. For many of us, our parent/s responded to us with more connection, compassion and care and less harshness than they experienced from their own parent/s. This evolutionary journey is longer than just our parenting in the first decade of our children's lives. It began before us, and continues into the teenage years. It's also possible for healing to happen when our children become adults, as long as we are open and willing to hear their experiences and refrain from judging ourselves when we hear them share things that we did that were painful for them!

> *Self-Reflection Moment*
>
> *I wonder how you feel and what you think when you read this?*
>
> *Do you notice that you judge yourself, compare yourself, or think you should be some-kind-of-perfect in your parenting?*
>
> *If so, would you like to respond to yourself in different ways to this?*
>
> *How would you respond to a best friend if they had this inner dialogue?*
>
> *Are you willing to respond to yourself in these more friendly ways?*

Listening lovingly to a child's feelings and tears can ask so much more of us than distracting them with food or a screen, a dummy or a book.

Helping them be willing to cooperate can require so much more of us than offering rewards, threats or coercion.

Offering closeness and empathy to them when they need our loving presence requires more of us than leaving them when they are quiet but dissociated, sucking their thumb or gazing into space.

Offering *Loving Limits* when they are agitated or aggressive asks more of us than 'leaving them to it' or responding harshly.

Aware Parenting is certainly not an easy path. But in these early years, we are supporting the foundation of our child's psyche.

Leaving them alone physically or emotionally before bed when all their feelings are bubbling up may seem easier for us, but they are forming their core beliefs about whether there is support available for them when they need it and whether their feelings are welcome.

Distracting them from their feelings may seem easier too, and when they're twirling their hair, sucking their thumb or gazing off into space, all may seem fine, but those feelings are still there, and they will stay there until felt, expressed and lovingly heard.

***Our responses to our children make a huge difference to their future emotional wellbeing, their core beliefs and their relationships with their own needs and feelings.***

This isn't another reason to pick up sticks of guilt and self-judgment. This is an acknowledgment of how hard this is to parent in ways that we weren't parented and which still aren't mainstream (yet!) within the *Disconnected Domination Culture*. And it is never too late.

## It is never too late.

***Whatever age your child is, how you respond to their needs and feelings today makes a difference to them. However you've responded to their needs and feelings in the past, your response today is important. Every day is a new day and offers us new opportunities to start again, and to repair from the past.***

Oh, and another thing about ease! Yes, it requires SO much more from us to respond promptly, to understand when a child is dissociating, to listen to many, many hours of tears and raging, or to stay with them when they're going to sleep until they can do that alone without needing to dissociate.

However, the difference our responses make to how they feel in their bodies means that actually, parenting becomes easier.

The more we meet a child's needs, the more we respond non-punitively, and the larger percentage of their feelings and tears we listen to, the more connected and relaxed they feel. This affects all their behaviour.

They will:

- be more willing to *cooperate*;
- be more able to *concentrate* and be present in their bodies and sit still;
- naturally be more *gentle* with us, other children and animals;
- feel more *relaxed* which will help them go to sleep more easily and sleep peacefully; and
- feel *happier* and more joyful.

Being present, being compassionate and listening to feelings can all be really hard when we didn't receive them and live in a culture that works against these practices for families. However, doing whatever we can do to increase these makes a profound difference in our child's life, in our life, and in our family lineage.

## Aware Parenting helps our child experience being unconditionally loved

*Did you experience being unconditionally loved as a child?*

Most of us had parents or carers who loved us, but that love doesn't always translate into us experiencing being loved. *Why* didn't their love translate into us experiencing being loved? And even more importantly, as parents, *how* can we make it more likely that the love we feel for our children *does* translate into them experiencing being loved?

We can increase the following:

1. Being *attuned* to them – literally, understanding what is really going on for them underneath their behaviour – and responding promptly and accurately.
2. *Not* using punishments or rewards, shame or blame, but instead, knowing what is really causing the behaviour and attending to it at that causal level.
3. Listening lovingly to their *feelings*, including their tears and rage. This also means seeing when they are feeling painful feelings but suppressing them. It also means we can help them heal from the times we weren't attuned to them or did respond harshly to them.
4. *Repairing* when there are inevitable ruptures. This includes taking responsibility for our feelings, needs and behaviours without judging ourselves and feeling guilty.

> *Self-Compassion Moment*
> *If you're tempted to pick them up, I invite you to drop the self-judgment sticks. This is about increasing our capacity to do these things, not thinking it's possible to do this 100% and judging ourselves for the times we don't do them!*

You'll recognise the aspects of Aware Parenting in that list: attachment-style parenting; non-punitive discipline; preventing stress and trauma wherever possible – and helping them heal when they do inevitably experience painful experiences.

***From a child:*** *Mummy, I really do want to do what you want me to do. You are my world and I want to be like you. I know you were annoyed today when I left my drawings and pens all over the kitchen table and you really wanted me to tidy it all up before dinner, but I just felt so antsy and wriggly. I just couldn't tidy them up. I felt all strange being away from you all day today and it was like you were a long way away and I couldn't reach you, even when we were in the kitchen together. I needed to run around and be all silly. I wanted to feel all nice and melty calm in my body so that I could do what you wanted me to do. I felt even further away from you when you were angry. Please love me. I do really want to do what you want, but I just couldn't today. Please see me and what I need. I need you. I need you to understand me and love me and help me. I get scared when your mouth does that funny thing and then I can't even move and do what you want. It's like I'm floating away on a boat, a long, long way away from you. We're getting further away and my tummy feels more and more funny. I feel smaller and smaller. I don't like this. Oh Mummy, you're coming towards me. Our boats are getting closer. Oh, you offer me a big hug! I melt into your arms. You DO love me! I start to feel bigger again, and closer. We hug for ages and then you tell me that you missed me too! I missed you SO much, Mummy! Now I can tell you all about it! You look at me, and you listen, and I let it all out. I love it when your eyes are so soft. I'm big again, and our boats are close again. You say we can tidy the table together. Oh YES, Mummy! I would love to do that with you! I have a big smile as I get all the pens into my pencil case and you get all the paper together. I love that you noticed what I drew. This one is of you and me, Mummy. I love you.*

## Chapter summary

### There are three aspects of Aware Parenting

*Attachment-style parenting, non-punitive discipline* and *healing from stress and trauma*. Each of these brings a deep understanding of children and their behaviour and offers ways to support children to be securely attached, to experience non-punitive discipline and to heal from stress and trauma.

### There are three reasons for children's behaviour

*What they're thinking, needing,* and *feeling*. In any parenting situation, we can go through this list of three things, starting with giving them information. However, some behaviours will almost always be caused by feelings, eg. aggression.

### There are three options with feelings

*Expression, suppression* and *aggression*. Expression includes the healthy expression of feelings through laughter, crying or raging with loving support. Suppression involves distraction or mild dissociation from feelings, often through the use of repetitive actions called *control patterns*. Whatever feelings are suppressed end up accumulating and can show up in the form of aggression.

**The more we understand our place in healing our lineage as first generation Aware Parenting parents**, the more likely we are to be compassionate with ourselves, which also means we're more likely to respond empathically and effectively towards our child/ren.

> I'm so willing for you to clearly understand
> the foundations of Aware Parenting.

CHAPTER TWO

# Our own reparenting

*If you've had a hard day, it's not your fault.*

*You're not doing anything wrong.*

*You live in a culture which can be really challenging for parents and children.*

*If you're feeling stretched, overwhelmed, or full of feelings, there's nothing wrong with you and you're not alone.*

*I'm here with you.*

*I'm sending you so much love.*

*If you'd like to (and you're willing), I invite you to put one hand on your forehead and your other hand around your belly, and feel the presence of your hands there.*

*I'm sending tender compassion to all of your feelings.*

*Being stretched and overwhelmed is so understandable in this culture.*

*It's not your fault if things are hard at times.*

*You haven't done anything wrong.*

*I'm here with you.*

*I'm here to help.*

*I'm listening.*

## The reason Aware Parenting can be SO HARD at times is not because of anything you're doing wrong.

First, telling yourself that you've done something 'wrong' would be you punishing yourself!

Second, we live in a culture that is set up to be really hard for parents and children. In addition, if you're wanting to practice Aware Parenting, most of us were conditioned to respond in very different ways to what I am sharing about in this book.

**Attachment-style parenting:** This can be so challenging when we're bombarded with messages about how important it is for young children to be 'independent', and doubly hard when there are only one or two pairs of arms doing the work of dozens.

*We are not meant to be living in small families with only one or two parents or parent figures.*

**Non-punitive discipline:** Of course that's going to be hard at times when it's likely that we received punishments and rewards thousands of times, and probably still punish ourselves with guilt and self-judgment – unless we've consciously got free from that (I'm here to help you do just that!). Conditioning is meant to be passed down.

*Cultures are continued through conditioning. That's why it can be so hard to not do what was done to us, especially when we're stressed. At these times, we generally revert to what we've known the longest and took in the earliest.*

**Healing from stress and trauma through supporting natural expression via** *attachment play***, healing tears and rage:** Of course this is going to be hard! How many of us ever had an adult listen lovingly to us from a deep sense of presence when we were crying or raging to heal as children?

***How can we expect that to be easy when many of us don't yet have an embodied experience of feeling deep and intense feelings while at the same time having the sense that we are completely safe, held and loved?***

So, those are just a few reasons why our own inner reparenting journey is so vital if we are practicing Aware Parenting.

You will notice the same model of thoughts, needs and feelings affecting behaviour as we talked about in Chapter One.

## Our thoughts

The more we have a compassionate inner dialogue (ie. thoughts), the more likely we will also be able to think compassionate thoughts about our child when they are, for example, pulling all the books off the bookshelf. New information can support us in putting down any judgment sticks. This understanding can normalise how *hard* practicing Aware Parenting can be when we live in – and have grown up in – a culture that promotes the *opposite* practices to Aware Parenting.

## Our needs

The more our needs are met, the more we will feel ease in our bodies and the more emotional spaciousness we will have to be able to meet our child's needs and listen to their feelings. It really is possible to increasingly reclaim our here-and-now needs, change our beliefs about them, and be more and more willing for them to be met.

## Our feelings

Being increasingly able to feel our own feelings and express them in safe and healing ways through embodied talking, crying and raging to a loving external or internal presence can make a *huge* difference to our parenting. This is because it increases our ability to stay lovingly present in our body when our child is releasing stress or trauma through crying or raging with our support.

I will invite you again and again throughout this book to be more compassionate with yourself and your feelings. That also includes being deeply loving towards yourself on those days when you absolutely *do not have* any extra bandwidth to go exploring your internal world, and when chocolate-eating and Instagram-scrolling – without self-judgment – are the most self-loving things you can do.

That's why I invite you over and over again to *drop the self-judgment sticks*.

## Dropping the self-judgment

I have met so many parents over the years who are doing everything in their power to meet their child's attachment needs, parent without punishments and rewards, and listen to their child's tears and tantrums, yet are frequently judging themselves and their parenting.

I remember doing the same in my early years of being a mother, until I began to realise that when I was judging myself, I was actually *less* present with my daughter. If I was filled with *emotional bruises* from those *emotional sticks*, I had far less to offer her in terms of connection, presence and listening.

> ### Self-Reflection Moment
> *I wonder if you notice that too, or whether you would like to observe over the next few days whether that is the case for you?*

We judge ourselves because we were judged as children and so we internalised those judgments. We learnt to judge, and we live in a culture that judges, but it doesn't mean we need to keep on doing that. One of the wonderful things about our own reparenting alongside Aware Parenting is that we can gradually do the things that we are doing for our children for *ourselves* as well. As we parent them without punishments and rewards, trusting them and their journey and learning to respond by giving information, meeting their needs and listening to their feelings, so we can increasingly do these things for ourselves too, because we know exactly how to do that, and reparenting our inner children[12] is very similar to parenting our children!

*Self-Reflection Moment*

*When you are tempted to judge yourself or your parenting, how would you like to respond to yourself instead?*

*If your best friend was judging themselves about their parenting, what would you say to them?*

*If you were a grandparent and your child was now a parent judging themselves about their parenting, what would you say to them?*

*Would you like to write those phrases down somewhere?*

*Are you willing to say those things to yourself in those moments where you notice that you're starting to judge yourself?*

## Tending to our own needs

Core to the attachment-style parenting aspect of Aware Parenting is attending promptly and responsively to our child's needs. However, honouring our *own* needs as parents can sometimes be really hard. One of the core reasons is because of the practical set-up of parenting in this culture and how far it is from how we are innately meant to be living. Another cause can be because of the cultural conditioning we received related to parenting. Thirdly, our own relationship to our needs can often be impacted by how our own needs were attended to as children.

### 1. The practical set-up of parenting in this culture

Nuclear families with one or two parents and no grandparents, extended family or wider community is not how family life is designed to be for

---

12  Inner children is a Marion Method concept, not an Aware Parenting one.

humans. We are meant to live embedded in community, with support simply being a part of the fabric of life. Add in the complexities of making a living in this family system, with one or both parents often needing to work to be able to survive, and things become much harder. In many Indigenous communities, as well as in our own hunter-gatherer past, large clans lived together, created together, foraged, farmed and made food together.

**So much of what is hard about parenting is because of the very unnatural set up we live in today. I invite you to remember this as often as you can!**

> *Self-Reflection Moment*
> *I wonder how you feel when you read this?*
> *Does it help you to put down the guilt or other self-judgment sticks?*

In addition, when we have our first baby, many of us have not had much experience with babies, so the early months can be a huge learning curve that can often be full of confusion, fear or overwhelm. In a healthy community, we would have been around babies since we were ourselves a newborn. We would have seen how babies were cared for and would have probably done lots of caring for them right from when we were young children. We would also have internalised ways of being with babies and children and would have simply continued those ways when we ourselves became a parent.

> This is very different to what most of us are doing as first generation Aware Parenting folk. We are not only doing something without cultural support, we are also parenting differently from what we experienced and internalised growing up (and what we generally see around us still).

## This means not only are we learning as we go, but we are also called to do our own reparenting and changing our cultural conditioning at the same time. This is a HUGE, complex and challenging process.

Our beliefs about babies, children and humans will be changing as we practice Aware Parenting. Our own:

- experiences of *attachment* (or lack of it) will show up while we are aiming to meet our child's attachment needs;
- experiences of being *punished*, rewarded and coerced will probably show up at times when our children are doing things that we would have been punished, rewarded or coerced for;
- unexpressed *tears* may well show up when we are listening to our child's tears;
- unexpressed *rage* is likely to bubble up when we are aiming to listen to our child's rage;
- unexpressed *powerlessness* can come up when our child is unwilling to cooperate.

***All of these things make parenting so much harder and make meeting our own needs extra challenging. Practically and tangibly, meeting our own needs as parents is likely to be really difficult at times.***

### 2. The cultural conditioning we received

Growing up, it's likely that many of us saw our own parents not getting their needs met. We probably saw them feeling overwhelmed, frustrated and burnt out. We may have seen them leaving their needs until last, not even knowing what they needed, or not ever making specific requests about their needs. Others of us may have seen our parents valuing their needs and not our own, so we might have decided that we don't want to do that to our own children, and so we sacrifice our needs.

*Because this culture doesn't value parenting, it also doesn't value the needs of parents. These are all elements of conditioning that we may have internalised, making it difficult for many of us to know what we need, to value our needs, and be willing for our needs to be met.*

> Self-Reflection Moment
>
> Did you see your parent/s or carers valuing their needs and having their needs met?
>
> What did you learn about valuing needs as a parent from observing your own parent/s?

So, if you find that your needs for support, community, empathy, autonomy, rest, or other needs are not met, there is nothing wrong with you. You have been affected by this culture. *And* we can gradually change our relationship with our needs. You can change this. Your needs matter.

### 3. How our own needs were attended to as children

How our needs were responded to as children has a profound effect on how we go on to respond to our needs as adults. Sometimes this can show up even more strongly when we become parents, as we can often revisit experiences we had at a certain age when our child is at that same age. Even our position in the family can make a difference – for example, if we were a middle child and our needs often got overlooked, we may overlook our own needs in responding to the needs of our child.

> Self-Reflection Moment
>
> Do you notice a relationship between how your needs were responded to as a child and how you respond to your needs now?
>
> Do you generally know what you need?
>
> Do you find it easy to ask for what you need?

> Just like our children, if our needs don't get met, we will feel painful sensations and feelings – which will make it less likely that we can respond to our child in the ways that we want to.

The more our needs *are* met, the more calm and relaxed we will feel in our bodies, and the more we will be able to respond to our child in a compassionate and attuned way.

The more our needs are met, the more we will be able to move in with *attachment play* when they need it, and the more likely we will be able to listen to their tears and their rage.

> *Self-Reflection Moment*
> *Do you notice that when your needs aren't met, you find it harder to respond calmly and compassionately to your child/ren?*

Even though at times we may tell ourselves that our child doesn't want us to get our needs met, they really do. Your child/ren want/s you to get your needs met, because the extent to which you do affects your quality of presence with them.

> Tending to our needs as parents is vital to help us to be able to practice Aware Parenting. I so support you in taking whatever your next steps are in relation to knowing what you need, valuing what you need, being willing to get your needs met, and taking action (including making requests of others).

## Receiving support and empathy

Support and empathy are two needs that are particularly important to us if we are practicing Aware Parenting.

If we are to be able to offer our child support and empathy, we really do need to receive them ourselves.

I have witnessed so many parents really wanting to support their child yet finding it hard because they have so little support. I have seen so many parents being so stretched, and not being able to listen to their child in the ways they want to, because they have so many of their own feelings bubbling up.

As we talked about before, it is inevitable that our own unexpressed feelings from childhood will show up when we are parenting in this way. This is meant to happen. Just as our children will keep on trying to express their feelings to us through play, crying and raging, so our own unexpressed feelings will keep on bubbling up to be expressed and heard.

Our own support is so vital, not only to how we feel and what we are able to do as parents, but also so we are able to help our children to be free to express their feelings.

**Children will sense if we have lots of feelings bubbling up that we are holding in.**

We might need to be in states of mild dissociation to stop ourselves from feeling and expressing those feelings, which will make it hard for them to feel enough of our emotional presence to then express their feelings. At times, they may wait for us to feel and express our own feelings to another adult before sharing their feelings with us.

*If we want our children to be more free to express their feelings with us, we really need to receive empathy and support so that we get to feel and express our own feelings, facilitating more presence in our bodies.*

> Children live in the sea of emotions and they are picking up so much from us, including our unexpressed feelings and how we respond to our feelings. So often, parents can focus on aiming to listen to their child's feelings, without realising that their relationship with their own feelings has a huge impact on their children.

If we're wanting to support our child to feel comfortable to express their tears and rage with us, the most aligned thing we can do is to make sure that *we* are expressing our tears and rage to another person. This brings a congruence to what we are communicating to them and they will feel that. In our embodied presence, we will be communicating to them, "I'm willing to listen to your feelings, just as I'm also willing for my feelings to be heard," In addition, if we're dissociating from feelings, they will feel that and it will be hard for them to experience enough emotional presence to be able to cry and rage with us.

Often this will invite us to evolve in ways we might have never done. We might be willing to value our needs more when we see how much not valuing them is affecting our child. We might be willing to get more support so we can feel more comfortable with feeling and expressing our feelings, when we see that our own suppression and dissociation is preventing them from expressing their feelings.

> *Self-Reflection Moment*
> *Do you receive enough empathy and support?*
> *Are you willing to receive more?*

One of the ways that we can receive support and empathy is with a *Listening Partner*.[13]

---

[13] This is a term from Hand in Hand Parenting, used with permission. Hand in Hand Parenting use the term in a more specific way than is generally used in Aware Parenting.

Would you like a *Listening Partner*?

If you would, you can find one in the Aware Parenting community. The classical practice of a *Listening Partnership*, as practiced in Hand in Hand Parenting – which is an approach that is similar to Aware Parenting – is to connect regularly, for example once a week. When meeting, we can take turns, with each person having the same amount of time to share, and the other person listening empathically. This means not giving advice, interrupting, or making suggestions. It's simply listening with our full attention and compassion, trusting that through expressing their feelings, the other person will come to clarity about whatever it is they are sharing about.

In Aware Parenting, many parents also receive support in more informal ways than classical *Listening Partnerships*[14], such as using a voice note app and leaving voice notes whenever they have feelings that they want to express. This can make all the difference as a parent.

***Imagine feeling really frustrated, and rather than that frustration all coming out in harsh ways towards your child, you express that frustration to your* Listening Partner *in voice notes instead.***

I use a voice notes app to listen to my mentees, and I also use it to express my own feelings to my friends and colleagues (who are all Aware Parenting instructors).

> Just as listening to our children's feelings in the form of expression means that they have less and less need for suppression, dissociation or aggression; us getting to regularly express our own feelings means that we will be less and less likely to resort to suppressing them with chocolate or screens or dissociating at various times through the day. It will also mean that it is less likely that our feelings will spill out in the form of harshness towards our child (or others).

---

14  I sometimes call these empathy buddies.

Amazingly, even leaving a voice note when our *Listening Partner* isn't there in real time can make a big difference. Knowing that we *will* be listened to with absolute unconditional love, whatever we are feeling, thinking or doing – even if the other person is not listening at that exact moment, is so helpful. That knowing in itself is healing, even if there isn't someone else on the other end of the voice note app at the same time as us.

Ideally, we would have compassionate people around us all the time as part of our culture, as we talked about above. But since our culture and families aren't set up like that (for most of us), there are these other ways to get our needs for support and empathy met.

Each of us is so different and we all live in different circumstances, so the beautiful thing about *Listening Partnerships* is that they can be tailor-made for your own particular life situation.

> Self-Reflection Moment
>
> *I wonder what you feel called to do in terms of support and empathy?*
>
> *Would you like a Listening Partner (or three)?*
>
> *Would you like to reach out to an Aware Parenting instructor or Aletha Solter herself for support and listening? If so, you can find more details about instructors on Aletha Solter's website www.awareparenting.com and click on the page your country. You can find a list of instructors in Australia and New Zealand on my website (www.marionrose.net).*

## Our relationship with our own feelings

I remember when I first started practicing Aware Parenting with my daughter, and how focused I was on being with *her* feelings. I didn't realise back then that my own relationship with *my* feelings was a vital part of Aware Parenting too.

*I wonder if you have found that?*

If we feel uncomfortable feeling our feelings and crying and raging in safe and healing ways, we may feel uncomfortable to be with our child's tears and tantrums and may distract them, **even in subtle ways without realising**. The same goes with their joyful play, if it helps us connect with our own pain.

Our discomfort with our own feelings deeply affects the extent to which we are able to be lovingly present with our child while they are feeling and expressing those feelings.

This is why it is vital for us to receive loving listening, ideally from someone who feels comfortable being with and hearing those feelings. Because this is so core to the feelings part of Aware Parenting, we will be talking about it more in this book.

> *Self-Reflection Moment*
>
> *Are there particular feelings that you feel uncomfortable with in yourself, or that you find uncomfortable to witness when your child feels or expresses them?*
>
> *Do you recall experiencing not being understood when you were a child?*
>
> *Do you remember feeling really upset and dissociating through reading or biting your nails or watching tv and those around you didn't realise that you were dissociating?*
>
> *You weren't feeling contented at those times. You were dissociating from painful feelings.*
>
> *Do you remember feeling frustrated and outraged and being rough with another child or doing something your parents didn't want you to do, or slamming the door, or throwing something, and instead of grown ups understanding the cause of your behaviours, you were shamed or punished?*

> You weren't deliberately doing things they found annoying. You were agitated and had feelings bubbling.
>
> These experiences can be so painful, not only because of the lack of connection or the painfulness or being punished or shamed, but also because of not being understood.

Rebecca shares about how she healed from her experiences of not having her needs met as a child.

*"In a therapy session 12 years ago, I came to the inner picture of how my Mom left me crying alone: me, being small in a half-dark room, standing in a cot, being stiff from fear, holding on to the bar, looking to the door with the only hope: that my Mom would come and pick me up. When grown up Becci takes little Becci on her lap and listens to her feelings, little Becci would burst into tears: How??? How can my Mom leave me? My beloved, beloved Mommy? How can she forget me? How can she not know how much I need her? My lovely, lovely Mommy. I miss her so much. Where is my Mommy? And little Becci would cry and lean on to my chest. And I would caress her, kiss her head and say: 'I know. I'm sorry. I'm here for you. I'm here now. I'm here.'"*

## Compassion for ourselves as we practice Aware Parenting

### To your inner children

*I'm here with you.*

*I acknowledge all the times the adults around you didn't listen to your feelings.*

*I'm sending love to you every single time you were told that, "There's no need to be upset," or, "You're too sensitive," or, "Don't cry!"*

*I'm here now with all of your feelings.*

*I welcome all of your feelings.*

*None of your feelings are too much for me.*

*I am always here with you, whatever you feel.*

*I love you when you're suppressing your feelings or dissociating from your feelings.*

*I love you when you're crying or raging.*

*I love you when you're agitated and antsy from all the feelings you've been holding inside.*

*You've been holding them in for so long, sweetheart.*

*I invite you to take your own time in letting them out and finding people whom you feel safe expressing them to.*

*I trust your timing.*

*I trust your own healing journey.*

*I'm here with you.*

*I'm listening.*

*I love you.*

### To you now, as a parent

*I really appreciate all that you're doing.*

*Your needs are beautiful.*

*I welcome all of your feelings*

*I'm sending love to all of your feelings.*

*I welcome your sadness and disappointment.*

*I welcome your frustration and outrage.*

*I welcome your overwhelm and fear.*

*I welcome all of your feelings.*

*You are doing so much as a parent.*

*I see you.*

*I acknowledge you.*

*I appreciate you.*

*Thank you for all you are doing for your child/ren.*

*I understand how much it is.*

*It's so normal to find it hard at times in this culture.*

*You're not doing anything wrong.*

*There's nothing wrong with you.*

*I'm here with you.*

*I've got your back.*

*You're not alone with this.*

## Chapter summary

**Judging ourselves and our parenting comes from cultural conditioning.** We can learn to put down those harsh emotional sticks and respond with self-compassion instead.

**Tending to our own needs:** We can so easily overlook our own needs as parents when we aim to practice Aware Parenting, but the more our own needs are met, the easier it will be to practice Aware Parenting.

**Receiving support and empathy is vital** if we are to be able to consistently offer our child/ren support and empathy.

**Our relationship with our own feelings:** Our children invite us to be able to be with more and more of our own feelings, as we also listen to more of theirs.

**Compassion for ourselves as we practice Aware Parenting is so important.** It is inevitably going to be hard, and judging ourselves will only make it much harder!

> I invite you to drop the guilt sticks and to be deeply compassionate with yourself.

CHAPTER THREE

# Understanding the effects of culture and creating new forms of community

In *The Aware Baby* (p.2), Aletha Solter says, *"No culture is perfect. In most cases, the cultural values and economic constraints force parents to impose certain restrictions on their children and ignore legitimate needs, such as the need to express emotions, to be fully accepted, or to explore freely in a safe environment. The fact that infants survive and grow up able to carry on the culture and reproduce does not imply that their basic human needs have been met, or that they have attained their human potential for intellectual, emotional or spiritual development."*

The wider culture we live in is often invisible to us. Because it's the air that we breathe and the sea we swim in, we often don't see it as culturally imposed and generally experience it as 'the truth' or 'just how things are'. However, parenting is one of the key junctures in life where we have the opportunity to become aware of the core cultural beliefs we've grown up believing, the effects of those beliefs on how children and adults are treated, and how we can make powerful choices that are different from our original cultural conditioning.

In my own journey, my focus has widened, from my initial interest in the effect of the individual family we grew up in, to then include both our lineage and the wider culture.

For many years, my attention was on the direct effects of our family, and how unhealed trauma was passed down from generation to generation. This is what I used to focus on. In sessions and courses, I would invite people to reflect on their experiences in their family while growing up. While I still see this as important and still invite those reflections, in more recent years, what has become more and more apparent to me is the *wider cultural context* and the huge impact it has on us.

**Holding in mind this wider cultural context can have two particular effects. It can help us have deep compassion for ourselves and how hard it is to parent with awareness in this society. It can also invite us to have more understanding of our parents.**

As I shared earlier, I had a powerful 'aha' moment when I realised that had I been born into the family and time my parents were born into, I would have probably parented in very similar ways to them.

*Self-Reflection Moment*
*If you had been born at the time and place your parents were, might you have parented in quite different ways to how you do now?*

Now I see that many of the things that make parenting – and in particular Aware Parenting – so challenging at times are actually cultural and societal. If we had grown up in a family collective, embedded in a healthy culture based on connection, compassion, trust, empowerment and listening to feelings, I imagine most of us would experience parenting very differently. So many of the stresses in parenting are caused by the systemic set up we live in.

Many of us are part of nuclear families, or single parent families, often with little or no wider support. Many of us experience a disconnection from the land, from growing our own food, from the seasons, from rites of passage and from the honouring of elders. Day to day life is often dictated by work and school schedules which have never held emotional wellbeing at their core.

***So much of the stress, powerlessness and overwhelm experienced by parents are due to these elements.***

As a result, children often experience stress, powerlessness and overwhelm too, leading to lots of feelings that need to be expressed through play, crying and raging. If they aren't expressed, those feelings will lead to challenging behaviours.

It's no wonder that parenting can be so hard, given these symptoms of unhealed stress, as we either aim to listen to those feelings, or respond to the behaviours that come as a consequence of not listening to them.

There are more reasons why this cultural lens so important:

- As I mentioned above, it helps us be more *compassionate* with ourselves when we can see one of the key reasons why parenting can be so hard is this wider culture that we live in.
- It also invites us to find ways *of co-creating new structures and systems*, such as mothers' circles, hanging out with other families, cooking together, and sharing about Aware Parenting so that we find other families who resonate.

## Both in-person and online connection with other like-minded families is so vital to us experiencing support with Aware Parenting.

> *Self-Reflection Moment*
>
> *If you're already familiar with Aware Parenting, have you found ways to create new forms of community and support with it?*
>
> *Would you like to do more to find extra community support?*
>
> *If Aware Parenting is new to you, and you're resonating with what you're reading, would you like to meet other like-minded families?*

## Of course it's hard! Compassion for ourselves

I know I'm repeating myself here, but I don't think I can say this too many times!

I want to remind you that it is so natural for parenting to be hard, given all that we've discussed about cultural and community contexts that we parent in. You probably didn't grow up in an Aware Parenting community, and I imagine that you don't live in one (yet).

In parenting and consciousness work, it's very common to judge ourselves or think that we need to just do more inner work when things are difficult. I would like to emphasise again that one of the main reasons it's hard is because of the culture. If you had grown up with Aware Parenting, as part of an Aware Parenting community where everyone responded to children's needs promptly and in an attuned way, where punishments and rewards didn't exist, where children's agency, autonomy and choice was respected and children's tears and rage were welcomed by everyone, you would probably be having a really different experience right now!

### Self-Reflection Moment

*I wonder if you can imagine that?*

*Can you imagine if, right from when you were in your mother's womb, you were talked to with respect and consideration?*

*If, as a baby, you were held close, responded to promptly, and all your feelings were welcomed, including when you wanted to express your feelings from your birth experience?*

*Can you imagine never being told that you were naughty or bad, never being punished nor shamed and the adults around you always aiming to understand what the true causes of your behaviour were?*

*Can you imagine those around you doing what they could to be your advocate, preventing you from experiencing stressful or traumatic events as much as possible?*

*Can you imagine everyone around you understanding about feelings, stress and trauma, and at any time, there were many safe adults who you could go and express your feelings to?*

*Can you imagine your innate wisdom being deeply trusted, from what and when you wanted to eat, your capacity to heal, your journey of individuation, to your own unique learning experiences?*

*Can you imagine how you would feel now as a parent, if that had been your experience growing up?*

*In addition, imagine that you now lived in a supportive community of people who all understood children like this and who aimed to respond to them in these ways.*

*Imagine that there was always someone to sit with, cook with, eat with, and to listen to your feelings with deep love and compassion.*

*Imagine that any time you needed to work, or to go to the shops, or rest or sleep or exercise, there were other adults around who could care for your child/ren. Not only that, but your child/ren were securely attached with them and loved hanging out with them and you knew you could deeply trust them.*

*Parenting would be very different, wouldn't it?*

*Now I invite you to reflect on what you did experience as a child growing up, and what you are experiencing now in your family and wider culture, and the points of difference between what you just envisaged, and what you are experiencing now.*

*Does this help you be more compassionate with yourself when things are hard or when you do things as a parent that you regret?*

I invite you not to blame or judge yourself when things are hard, and instead to remind yourself about how much growing up and living in this culture affects our experiences as parents.

*And I would also love to say that even* **with** *these experiences in this culture, Aware Parenting offers ways of responding that mean that most of us can still have a much more enjoyable, connected and loving family life more of the time!*

*Self-Reflection Moment*

*How do you feel and what do you think when you read this?*

## Sharing with others and spreading the word in easy to hear ways

*Self-Reflection Moment*

*If you're already familiar with Aware Parenting, would you like to share about Aware Parenting with other parents and people who care for children?*

*If you're not familiar with it yet, I invite you to skip this section for now and come back to it at a later date!*

Over the years, I've so often heard from parents who would love to share Aware Parenting with others, but who are scared to say something to their friend or relative, because they really don't want the other person to think that they are being judged.

> Self-Reflection Moment
> I wonder if you've experienced that?

I'd love to share a few things that I have found helpful over the years.

In the early days of my parenting (before social media existed), I used to have some Aware Parenting articles printed out to share with people. If I was with a friend or someone I had met who was sharing about parenting challenges, I used to first offer them some empathy, and then I would say things like, "I've found this way of parenting that I really enjoy that has really helped. I wonder if you would like to hear more about it? I have an article here that I'd be happy to give you."

What I loved about that approach was that first of all I listened to them with empathy. (I found this really hard in the early days because I just wanted to tell them about Aware Parenting straight away!)

*Then* I shared a bit about my experience.

And only *then* did I ask them whether they were interested in the information.

And what I love about that process is it modelled Aware Parenting. First, empathy for their feelings, then sharing some information, followed by offering them choice. (Feelings, thoughts and needs, mirroring that list of three.) I found that people generally responded with wanting to hear more, but if they didn't, of course I honoured their 'no'.

We can also do that in the digital age. First offering empathy, then saying something like, "I have some information that I think you might find helpful about that. If you'd ever like to hear it, please let me know." Again, what I love about that is they are getting to experience us inviting them to choose whether they want to ask us about that information later on.

This can often be a reparative experience for many, because we were often told what to do and what to think, growing up in the *DDC*. In comparison, we are offering them empathy and choice about whether they want any new information.

*I wonder what you would like to say and do if want to share about Aware Parenting with someone?*

## Creating new forms of community

Most of us don't already have Aware Parenting community around us, so one of the ways to get our needs met for community is to build it ourselves. Our longing for like-minded community can become a gift!

*I remember the process I went through as if it were yesterday. My daughter was six months old and I was at my mothers' group. No-one else was practicing Aware Parenting and I felt so lonely and sad. I can picture myself now, going outside and sitting on a low wall, my baby in my arms, and crying. I was so longing to meet other mothers who would also resonate with this way of being with babies and children. That's when I envisioned an Aware Parenting community. And from there, I took action. I decided I was going to set up a mothers' group for people wanting to parent like this. I made some flyers and put them everywhere I thought that people who might be interested in Aware Parenting might go. The health food shop, the local library, the book shop. I went to the mothers and babies' yoga group and the mothers and babies' singing group and handed out the flyers and talked to mothers who were interested in this approach.*

*About ten mothers joined, and about five of us met regularly. Those mothers became my close friends. Each week, we would read a chapter of* The Aware Baby *by Aletha Solter. We would share our thoughts and feelings with each other, and if our babies had healing-feelings to express, we would listen to them. I loved that group! Having that community and those friends made all the difference for me. I had people I could share my passion for Aware Parenting with. I could express my feelings with them. My daughter could express her feelings with them.*

*I also bought lots of copies of* The Aware Baby *– one box at a time, and I took them to local libraries, book shops, pregnancy groups and mother and baby groups. Then I set up an online community (in the olden days of Yahoo groups), and I am still in contact with most of those parents now, many years later. That was the start of my ongoing passion to create Aware Parenting communities. Nowadays there are many in person and online Aware Parenting communities – you might want to join an existing one, or create your own.*

As this book is for parents of 1-8 year olds, you are probably at a different point in your journey than I was as a mother of a baby. However, if you are willing for more in-person community, I trust that you will find ways to find and create that!

> Self-Reflection Moment
> 
> I wonder if you are longing for in-person or online Aware Parenting community?
> 
> Have you connected in with any of the online communities that already exist?
> 
> Do you feel called to make your own in-person or online Aware Parenting community?

I trust that you will find a way to meet your needs for community and support.

I'm so willing for you to experience *more* community and support.

I'd love to add one more thing which also relates back to what I was saying earlier about community.

*I noticed that any time I was hanging out with another Aware Parenting family or families, my cup was so much more full. I could sense that in very tangible ways, because at those times, I found that practicing* attachment play *was much easier. I was able to keep calm and loving during challenging moments for way longer. I felt more relaxed and relieved in my body. I so often felt a sense of joy and connection.*

**That makes so much sense, doesn't it? We really are meant to live in healthy communities, and co-creating these for ourselves when they don't yet exist can make a profound difference not only to how we feel, but also to how we parent.**

Imagine being able to share your questions and ponderings about Aware Parenting principles. Envision being able to express your overwhelm, sadness or frustration to someone who totally gets what you're talking about and who won't judge you or your child! Imagine being able to share celebratory moments, like the time when you helped your child stop hitting or sleep soundly through *attachment play* and listening to their feelings. Envisage being able to work together with compassion and understanding when there are disagreements between the children. Imagine being inspired by other parents. Envision not seeing children being judged, shamed, punished or distracted from their feelings.

If you want to imagine me by your side as you do this, I'm there with you, sending you lots of love. I am so willing for you to have the community that you are longing for!

---

*Self-Reflection Moment*

Would you like to take action?

I invite you to write down any ideas you have about this.

## Chapter summary

**Any time you are finding Aware Parenting hard,** I invite you to connect with, "Of course it's hard!" and then choose compassion for yourself, remembering the bigger cultural picture.

**The more you get to share with other like-minded families,** the less you are likely to find it hard. Regularly sharing with others can make a huge difference.

**I invite you to trust any and all of the ways that you feel called to create new forms of community!**

> Our culture has a big influence,
> but you are powerful
> and can bring about change.

CHAPTER FOUR

# Eliciting cooperation

I'm sending you loving compassion as we move into this chapter on cooperation.

Do you ever feel really frustrated when your child doesn't do things that you ask them to do? If so, I'm sending you so much love and I so welcome all your feelings of frustration and any of other feelings you feel. Powerlessness and rage are common for us to experience as parents at times like this, especially in the *Disconnected Domination Culture*.

Children come into the world with two core needs:

1. To be themselves, to trust their innate wisdom and to respond from this deep self-connection; and
2. To learn to fit into the family, culture and place they are born into.

> A healthy culture will support them to be themselves and to stay deeply connected with their innate wisdom, so they don't need to make choices between those two needs. The *DDC* doesn't do that, so children will often experience an internal conflict between being true to themselves and needing to fit into their family and culture.

Have you ever noticed that children in Indigenous cultures are so often learning to be like the older children and adults they see around them? The children are often:

- carrying babies;
- weaving fabric or baskets;
- preparing food alongside the adults; and
- practicing hunting and food gathering skills.

***When we live in a culture where children don't generally get to witness the community collaborating together, including the children, this makes their cooperation less likely.***

Having this bigger picture can help us have more compassion for ourselves.

However, with Aware Parenting, even in non-Indigenous cultures, we can put certain things in place so children are more likely to be *willing* to cooperate.

First of all, we need to know why they *don't* cooperate, so that we can help them naturally be more *willing* to cooperate.

## Why don't children cooperate?

Do you remember back in Chapter One we talked about the three reasons for children's behaviour? I will remind you of them now:

- what they're *thinking*;
- what they're *needing*; and
- what they're *feeling*.

These are the same three reasons for children not cooperating. And when I say not cooperating, that can be either when they are *not* doing something that we *want* them to be doing, or when they *are* doing something that we *don't* want them to be doing.

The more we can remember these three reasons, the more likely we are to be able to respond compassionately to our child when they're not cooperating – while also knowing how we can help elicit cooperation.

Why can this help us respond compassionately?

***Because what we're telling ourselves can have a powerful effect on how we feel and what actions we take.***

> Self-Reflection Moment
>
> I wonder what you have told yourself the reasons are for your child not cooperating? Do you notice any thoughts such as:
>
> "What is wrong with them?"
>
> "They're doing this deliberately!"
>
> "They are doing this to annoy me!"
>
> "Why do they never listen?"
>
> As always, I invite you to put down any emotional sticks. I'm asking you to reflect on this for more clarity for yourself, not so you have more opportunities to judge yourself.
>
> When you tell yourself those things, what feelings do you feel?
>
> When you tell yourself those things and feel those feelings, what actions do you feel tempted to take?

If we are telling ourselves that our child isn't cooperating because they are:

- "doing it deliberately";
- "trying to wind us up";
- "being naughty"; or
- "not listening to us";

we are likely to feel frustrated, powerless or annoyed.

*Do you resonate?*

If we are telling ourselves those things and as a result, feel frustrated, powerless, or annoyed, we are likely to respond with trying to get them to do what we want through bribes, threats, repeating our question, shouting, or trying to force them to do things. None of those things really work! Whereas, if we can remember the *real* reasons for that behaviour, we are more likely to feel compassion towards them and respond in helpful ways.

> I used to have a little mantra when my children were younger, for times when I started telling myself harsh things about them. I would say,
>
> *"They're not doing this deliberately. They're not enjoying this. They need my help."*

---

**Self-Reflection Moment**
*I wonder what you might like to tell yourself at times like this?*

---

## Eliciting cooperation

Remember the three causes of behaviour?

- what they're *thinking*;
- what they're *needing*; and
- what they're *feeling*.

We can expand this list, and see that children are much more likely to be willing to cooperate with us in doing something we want them to do if they:

1. Feel a sense of *connection* with us:

We can support that to be more likely by getting close, offering eye contact, and expressing our request in warm tones. Remember that connection is key to Aware Parenting, and generally comes first in any of our helpful responses.

2. *Understand* the reason for the request:

   We can give information about why we are asking them to do that thing in a way that is apt for their age.

3. Have a sense of *choice* and *autonomy*:

   In our language and energy we can communicate our respect for those needs: *"Are you willing?"* and avoiding, *"You have to,"* or, *"You should,"* or, *"You ought to,"* or, *"You must."*[15]

4. Are feeling *relaxed* and happy:

   If they're feeling tense and have painful feelings bubbling, it's hard for them to be willing to cooperate. *Attachment play* helps them release painful feelings, as does simply listening to those uncomfortable feelings, including when they're crying or raging. This helps them feel more relaxed and more connected with their natural willingness to cooperate.

5. Can have *fun* doing it:

   When we find ways of making the thing fun, they're much more likely to be willing to do it.

So, if we are wanting our child to be willing to cooperate more of the time, the more we can bring all of these elements into our parenting, the more likely they will cooperate.

However, since that is quite a long list to remember, I'd love to share with you this helpful list of three things to remember when you are aiming to elicit their cooperation.

---

[15] Please note that this language is not from Aware Parenting but was inspired by Nonviolent Communication.

1 – Give *information*;
2 – Offer *choices*;
3 – Make it *fun*!

**Give them information** – for example, the reason why we want them to come to the car with us. "I'd really like you to come and get in the car with me after we've finished breakfast, so we can go and buy some food."

**Offer them choices** – this is choice about how to do the thing we've just given them information about. For example, "Would you like to run with me to the car, or would you like me to carry you?"

**Make it fun** – for example, we can offer to run to the car together like their favourite character, and pretend that it is a spaceship/farm truck/ whatever vehicle would be fun for them to play with.

> *Self-Reflection Moment*
>
> What little mantra would help you remember this list in the heat of the moment?
>
> Can you imagine doing this with your child/ren?
>
> What kinds of things do you think might be fun for them?

What happens if you've done all of these things and they still aren't willing to cooperate?

> I recommend avoiding power-over at all costs. Power-over is when we use our larger physical, emotional, cognitive or economic power to make others do what we want.

However, if you do choose to use power-over them to make them do that thing, for example because you're in an important or dangerous situation where you don't see any other choice or when you're simply exhausted or fed up and don't know what else to do, I recommend being deeply empathic with them, and listening to their feelings. You might say something like, "I'm so sad that I am forcing you to do this. I don't see any other option here. I really understand that you don't want to do it. I see how frustrated you're feeling. Of course you are! I'm here to listen to all of your feelings."

**The more they get to release any feelings of powerlessness, frustration or outrage during and after this experience, the more likely it is that they will be willing to cooperate next time you want them to.**

If we have forced them to do something, it can also be very helpful to offer power-reversal games to repair afterwards. You'll learn more about power-reversal games in Chapter Five.

*Self-Compassion Moment*
*I'm sending you so much love, and am inviting you to drop any guilt sticks, if you have used power-over your child.*

I find it helpful to remember that so many of the things that we require our children to do are caused by our culture, such as getting children to daycare or school 'on time' so we can go to work. If we lived in a healthy large community, there would be many adults around to support children, so if we needed to do something, there would be lots of people around to care for them so we would rarely need to rush to get them to do certain things at particular times. In addition, children would be naturally more willing to cooperate because they would see all the cooperation happening around them, including from other children, so cooperating would meet their needs for belonging as well as learning and competence.

A lack of cooperation can be caused by powerlessness and accumulated feelings. These can be caused by unmet needs for choice and autonomy, so the more we can help them feel powerful by giving them choices and helping them release past experiences of powerlessness, the more likely they are to cooperate in the present.

One of my mentees left a me a voice note about a situation with her daughter where she was wanting cooperation, and I'm so grateful that she was willing for me to share her words and my response here. This is such a common situation for parents, so if you experience things like this, you're not alone!

*"My three year old daughter was touching a painting in our bedroom, and I said, 'Don't touch the painting.' She looked at me, and she had her back to it, and she said, 'Don't touch the painting?' and she was basically touching the painting with her head. I felt really angry. I said, 'No, don't touch the painting,' and she said, 'No?' but she was. I was annoyed about it. Developmentally, where is she at with that, when I ask her not to do something and she isn't stopping, and can't seem to stop? I know I should be compassionate to her but I feel challenged by it and the inner dialogue that's going on in my head is like, 'Why are you doing this to me? Why aren't you listening?' And the anger switches on. I'd love to know your feedback on that."*

Here's my response:

*"I'm sending so much love to the anger that you were feeling. And I hear that you'd like to understand more about what was going on. I would love to offer a few suggestions.*

*When we say, 'Don't do xyz', children often don't hear the word 'don't'. If we say 'don't,' it will often actually encourage them to do that thing. I wonder if that resonates with you?*

*There can be two other causes of this kind of behaviour. Sometimes children are wanting clear information, so if we haven't been congruent in the past, they might keep checking and asking because they are wanting congruence this time. So that can be another reason why they repeatedly do things that we ask them not to do.*

*The most common cause for children doing things that they know we don't want them to do is if they have painful feelings to express. They are doing that thing because their intrinsic body wisdom wants a* Loving Limit[16] *so they can have a pretext to cry.*

*I also want to remind you, when you are asking, 'Why is she doing that?' you might ask yourself in the moment, 'Have I given her information?' In this case, yes, you've given her information and she's not cooperating, so that means it's not about information. It's not that she doesn't know that you don't want her to do it.*

*After information, the second thing to consider is needs. And number three is to consider is feelings. The more we have those things in mind, the less likely it is that we will get frustrated or angry and the more likely we're going to be able to respond at that causal level. This is why what we are telling ourselves is important. Remembering those reasons means we are much less likely to feel angry, frustrated or resentful. I wonder if that resonates with you?*

---

16  I'll be talking a lot about *Loving Limits* later in the book.

*I'm sending love, hearing what you were telling yourself when she was doing that. It's so often our thoughts, needs and feelings that cause our feelings and behaviour. We could then enquire into your thoughts, 'Why are you doing this to me? Why aren't you listening?' Is that what was said to you as a child? Are there people now who are doing things that you don't want or who aren't listening to you? The next step is for us to listen lovingly to whatever the cause of those thoughts is.*

*So when you go to the source of your thoughts and your feelings, the more you are going to be able to respond compassionately, without ever needing to 'should' yourself. How do you feel when you hear that?"*

She then went on to share her realisation about where those phrases had come from in her own childhood, so I invited her to see if she wanted to express the feelings from her childhood and receive reparative responses. Then I suggested that she might like to create a new parenting mantra that she can use at times like this to replace the words that she heard and internalised and found herself saying.

Rachael, an Aware Parenting instructor in Aotearoa New Zealand, shares about her experience of finding ways for her and her daughter to both get their needs met with Aware Parenting:

*"I love how Aware Parenting has supported me when in relationship with others. It is through Aware Parenting that I am now more clearly able to come from a place of curiosity with what others are needing and then seeking out solutions where both parties' needs can be met. This is so powerful and brings so much joy to my heart. I grew up in a family where often either my parents' needs came before mine or they sacrificed their own needs and felt resentment. This felt so painful for me as a child. I am in awe of how my six year old daughter can express what her needs are in any situation and how we work together to create solutions that aim to have both of our needs met. This leads to incredible levels of cooperation while both of us maintain our own sense of agency, autonomy and power.*

*Here's an example. Our lounge room is basically one giant playroom and throughout the day, it can get pretty full with stuff. At times, I feel frustrated with how much stuff is everywhere and I get concerned about the possibility of tripping over things and getting hurt. I love that I can express this to my daughter by saying, "I can see how much you are enjoying the creation you are making and I am starting to feel concerned that I might trip over something because there is so much stuff in the doorways. My need is to be able to get through the room safely. I wonder what your need is here?" She replies, "Well, I need to have the (play) house facing this way, because they need to have paddocks over here and this is the driveway so it can't go this way and the letterbox is over there." And I reply, "Ahhh, I hear you. I wonder what we could do to have both of our needs met?" She always comes up with a solution that works for both of us, and often one that I had not thought of. It really is incredible!"*

## Using *attachment play* to elicit cooperation

*Attachment play* is a powerful way to help children *want* to cooperate with us. That makes so much sense, doesn't it? As adults, we can experience things similarly. If we feel warmly connected with someone and they ask us to do something that will be fun, we are much more likely to be willing to do it.

> So often, the things we ask children to do aren't meaningful or important to them. Many children probably don't care about brushing their teeth, putting on pyjamas or clean clothes, having a bath, getting in the car or going on the bus yet again, going to places that we want to go to, and so on. However, if we offer *attachment play*, they are more likely to feel connected with us, and want to have fun with us. Then they are more likely to be willing to do things that are fun as well as feeling their innate desire to contribute to us.

Tidying up together can be a clear example. If you want your child to clear up their toys, and you shout from the other room that you want them to do that now, that isn't very conducive to their willingness. However, if you connect in with yourself and choose to be playful, and then go over to them, get down to their level, and say, "Ahoy there! The pirates are picking up all the treasure on the sea floor today and are putting it in the treasure chest! I'm the first mate, and you're the Captain! Which things do you want to pick up, Captain?" And then you might hum a sea shanty while pretending to be surprised about each piece of treasure (toys) that is put back into place, all the while talking to them about what treasure they are putting back.

The wonderful thing about *attachment play* is that it's not only fun for children. It also makes getting things done so much more enjoyable for us as parents. Instead of trying to convince them to tidy up, or getting frustrated and trying to coerce them to do it, joining with them and playing at the same time is much more connecting and fun for us too!

Nic Wilson, an Aware Parenting instructor and Marion Method Mentor, shares some of the games she's played with her daughter to support the tidying up process.

*"I find with tidying up,* attachment play *is so useful! I used to sing a song called 'Everybody pack away' as I would sing loudly and in a funny voice then pick up things and make funny movements to get them in their boxes. Another game was 'Don't you dare put those pens in the box, don't you even think about it!!'*

*Or, 'I'm going to close my eyes and turn around, if those pens walk themselves into the box I will turn around ten times and jump up and down on one leg' (or insert action you are willing to do!). I may even put the pens in my mouth like teeth and ask her in a funny voice to 'help us go home to our box, we don't want to be eaten by Mummy!! Arghhh!'*

*I liked to jump like a kangaroo and folded up my shirt like a pouch and put things in it to put away and pretended it's a cute baby kangaroo, and then I asked my daughter what type of animal she wanted to be to put the stuff away. Or I put a timer on and made a race to get everything away, shouting, 'I'm soooo sure I can beat you putting these things away!' (And I let her win, of course!)"*

*Attachment play* can also be really helpful if we're wanting our child to get into a stroller or car-seat, as the following examples – from participants of my *Attachment Play Course* – show.

Emily shares about the 'Fire Truck Loves the Buggy Game' with her son:

*"I was trying to get him into the buggy to go home. His fire truck toy happened to be there in the seat, and after stating that we were going home, I took the fire truck and told it to get out and make a place for my son. The truck replied that no, it didn't want to leave the buggy. Then I continued mock angrily to say, please fire truck, get out of here! Within seconds my son sat in the buggy voluntarily. And he was happy to go home with me."*

Sian talks about the power of the 'He's Disappeared Game:'

*"I used to use milk or food to get him into the carseat, until I found out about* attachment play. *Now I take a deep breath and pretend that he's disappeared! Right in front of my eyes! I can't find him until he touches me and then we both laugh at my obliviousness. 'Do it again, Mama!' (I loooove hearing that). And it doesn't actually take longer than it used to, struggling to get him buckled in. In fact he does his own top buckle now. I pretend that my hands are glued to the sides of my face in mock horror. I can't be unglued until his buckle is done. That always gets a laugh!"*

Andi found an *attachment play* game to help her daughter cooperate with her:

*"She still needed to get her boots off from coming home from school, and she was stalling and not really wanting to take them off. So finally, after trying other silly things, I said to her younger sister, 'I bet she*

won't take her boots off while I'm looking away! She better not take her boots off! Do you think she'll take her boots off while I'm looking away? She better not!' She ran to the living room, laughed, and took them off, and when I looked, and acted all surprised and with mock anger, shouting, 'Nooo no she took her boots off!' she laughed even more."

Samia shared how sometimes using *attachment play* to elicit cooperation can be really simple:

*"Quite often my son doesn't want to walk to the car and/or gets distracted by other things once we're out of the door. Today we didn't walk, but stomped, tiptoed, danced etc. to my son's delight!"*

Here's another simple example from Dee:

*"When my son is 'ignoring' us, I ask the same question using a toy or Lego man."*

And this time from Anya:

*"My daughters were in the basement where Papa was working. Then I wanted them to come back up. The two year old didn't want to, so I went to get her. She got all upset and said, 'I not!' So I stood in the middle of the staircase with her in my arms and said, 'Ready, set..., not. Oh oh, we're not moving'. I did the same thing again. And the third time I did it, 'Ready, set...' the little one answered: 'Go!' and I rushed up the rest of the stairs and she laughed."*

Penny was also happy to see more ease came about with *attachment play*:

*"I'm celebrating that the other day when I wanted my daughter to put socks on (our floors are cold and she has a cold) and she was refusing, and I wanted to say, "Just DO it", I made a game of pretending her hands were her feet and put socks and slippers on her hands and mittens on her feet and we laughed and then she simply let me switch the socks and slippers to her feet. And I thought, 'How incredibly easy that was!'"*

Maya also found the big difference *attachment play* made to both cooperation and fun:

*"I also often say silly instructions when I want the kids to do a few steps in the bath/bed routine. eg. 'Go and put your clothes in the bath tub, do a wee in the dirty clothes basket and hop in the toilet for a bath.' Much laughter and them correcting me – 'No Mummy, we put our clothes in the basket.' Much better than the power struggle of 'do this and that.'"*

> Self-Reflection Moment
> Are there situations where you regularly want your child/ren to cooperate and they often don't?
> Can you think of any fun games that you could play at those times?

I invite you to reach out for some empathy and support if you regularly feel frustrated when your child doesn't cooperate, or find it hard to refrain from coercion – or to choose play – at these times.

You might even find that you just start making up games spontaneously, like 'the Stuck in the Mud Game' that Yana invented at the supermarket to help her son keep walking.

*"I have a four year old boy. After starting to listen to Marion yesterday in the* Attachment Play Course, *I had some success today when we went to the supermarket and he was dragging his feet along. Normally this would really get me irritated, but I was able to turn it into a game where I pretended to be stuck in mud and asked him to pull me out... it worked!! He giggled and pulled me out, and you know what? Today has been generally so much fun and I've felt very close to him."*

*Attachment play* can not only be helpful when our child is not doing what we want them to do. It can also be helpful when they are doing things that we *don't* want them to do. Remember that two of the three causes of children's behaviour are unmet needs and painful feelings? *Attachment play* helps meet their needs for connection and if there's laughter, can help them release some painful feelings, so it addresses two of those causes.

Esme made up the 'We've Been Playing for 25 Years Now' game, after her daughter kept on playing and playing at bedtime.

*"I said to her, 'We've been playing for 25 years now, and I have fallen asleep,' and put on a big mock show of hardly being able to walk because of all the playing I'd been doing, and then falling over and falling asleep. She laughed and cuddled up with me."*

I had fun with *attachment play* to help my son with hair brushing and tooth brushing when he was going out one day.

*He was already in the car ready to go without having done either of those, so I held out the toothbrush in one hand and the hairbrush in the other and ran along the driveway in a funny way, saying, "Did you know that there is a new magic pirate called Mighty Mummy? Her superpower is helping children brush their hair and teeth!" I then did some big karate kicks and offered him the toothbrush! I did some more karate kicks while he was brushing his teeth. I loved that we both had fun!*

However, when behaviour is extreme, such as with hitting, it can often be that laughter and play isn't enough to release the underlying feelings and a *Loving Limit* is required to help the bigger feelings such as frustration, powerlessness or outrage to be expressed and released.

## An introduction to *Loving Limits*

We have a whole chapter on *Loving Limits* coming up, so I will talk about them in depth there. For now, I'd love to give you an introduction to this vital part of Aware Parenting. When children are doing challenging things that we don't want them to be doing, and they are not cooperating by stopping when we are asking them to stop, that behaviour is often caused by accumulated painful feelings.

> In particular, if a child is doing something that they *know* we don't want them to do, that tells us that in that moment their inner wisdom is asking us to offer them a *Loving Limit*.

The term '*Loving Limit*' is one that I created to describe an element of Aware Parenting that already existed, and the term has been taken up by Aletha Solter as a phrase used in Aware Parenting.

# The way I love to describe *Loving Limits* is that we say no to the behaviour and yes to the feelings that are causing the behaviour.

We are understanding in that moment that our child is doing that thing that we don't want them to be doing because of painful accumulated feelings. With a *Loving Limit*, we are stopping the behaviour but we are also willing to listen to the feelings underlying the behaviour. If you'd like to dive deeper into *Loving Limits*, you can do that in Chapter Ten.

***From a child:*** *Daddy, I do really know that you want me to leave the park, but I just want to stay. School was so hard for me today. I hate sitting still for so long and Mrs. Preston is SO boring. My hand hurts from holding a pen and my eyes hurt from reading so much stuff, and my legs are all antsy from that stupid chair. I just want to run around and I feel so free when I swing really high on the swing and climb to the very highest part of all the climbing things, and when I run and* *run as fast as I can. I get less tense, like I'm a dolphin getting free from a net. I want to shout and jump and twirl around. I can tell you want to go. You always get your phone out and your eyes get all scrunched and your mouth changes shape, and I just know that you're going to tell me to leave. Arrrgh! But Dad, what's going on? You're looking up from your phone and putting it in your pocket. Your mouth is turning into a big smile, and you're running towards me with your arms open! "Let's fly around this park like flying manta rays!" you say to me! Have you replaced my Dad with a robot? What's going on? I join in, a bit unsure at first at how this is going to go, but you stay smiling, and you're pretending to be a manta ray and you don't even seem to care that the other parents are looking at you! My heart warms up. You must have been listening to me last night when I told you how much I like sea creatures and how trapped I feel at school. I join in, becoming the biggest and most free manta ray that ever existed! I swim faster than you, and you follow me all around the park! We swim and fly under the swing set, and over the play train, and I feel giddy with joy. I become a dolphin, and you do too, and we jump and dive and smile big smiles together. My heart is defrosting and my legs are like fins. You sweep me up, and tell me how much you love me, and I just can't stop smiling! It's as if we've been here together for hours! Eventually, you tell me that the dolphins are swimming home for dinner, and we swoosh to the car, making squeaky dolphin noises. I jump into my seat with a big dolphin move, and you do too. All the way home, we make up silly songs about sea creatures. I love you, Dad. I feel so happy and relaxed. Gosh, I'm hungry! What's for dinner? I'm glad we're going home!*

## Chapter summary

**We can use the list of three causes of behaviour to remember why children don't cooperate.** The more we can think clearly and compassionately, the more likely we will put in place the elements that make it easier for our child to cooperate.

You might want to tattoo in your consciousness **the Aware Parenting list of three things for eliciting cooperation:** give information, give choices, make it fun!

**Play is a really powerful and helpful way to elicit cooperation.** Children are almost always way more likely to do things we want them to do if we include play.

**We can also offer *Loving Limits* when they are doing things that we don't want them to do because of painful feelings.** Often, one of the main reasons children deliberately do things they know we don't want is because their inner wisdom is asking for a *Loving Limit* from us.

> Children really do want
> to be free to cooperate.

CHAPTER FIVE

# *Attachment play*

Have you ever thought about the power of humour, comedy and laughter and its role in healing? If we are talking about really painful subjects, being with our feelings of sadness, fear and outrage is very important. However, laughter is a powerful way to help us release lighter feelings such as mild discomfort and embarrassment.

## I think that laughter and play are some of the most overlooked methods for transforming, healing and releasing emotional pain.

It makes sense that they aren't valued in this *Disconnected Domination Culture*, which devalues children and anything 'childlike,' and sees play as unimportant and a 'waste of time,' or alternatively, as an opportunity to sell products to people – often, in the form of toys that are overstimulating or that can easily restrict children's innate creativity and curiosity.

Yet play is incredibly powerful for children and adults alike. Just like many other mammals, children use play to understand their world and their role in it. The child who sees their parent often having a 'serious work call' is likely to play the 'serious work call' game later that day.

## In addition, children innately know how to play to heal from stress and trauma.

Has your child ever laughed when you have been seriously telling them not to do something? Did you feel frustrated, even outraged? Perhaps you might have told yourself that they "weren't taking you seriously" or were "being disrespectful?"

Does it resonate with you that they were probably feeling scared or powerless and were laughing to release that fear? You might have noticed yourself doing something similar – at a party, or meeting new people, at times when you feel a bit unsure or nervous, do you notice yourself giggling or laughing?

When I trained as a psychotherapist many years ago, I was taught that laughter is an escape from feeling emotional pain. So, I loved learning from Aware Parenting that it is actually a method for releasing and healing from painful feelings. So, it's like crying and raging and other incredible physiological processes that bring calmness and relief, as long as a child who needs this release has the loving support of an adult.

## Yet again, we are deeply trusting the innate healing processes that we are all born with.

In Aware Parenting, this kind of play is called *attachment play*, because the power of it happens within a connected relationship with an adult. Your child playing doctors alone with their dolls may be healing for them. However, if they invite you to join in and you pretend to be the patient, making funny noises when the stethoscope is placed on your body, the healing can often be even more powerful.

One of the least understood ways that children innately and intuitively use play to release pent-up feelings, stress hormones and tension is when they get playful before bed. When parents don't understand this innate healing process, they often think thoughts like, "Why on earth are they ramping up now, when it's time to sleep?"

*Self-Reflection Moment*
*I wonder if you've ever thought that?*
*Have you also ever thought, "My child is fighting sleep?"*

What a different way of looking at it when we see that rather than them fighting sleep, it's more likely that it is we who have been fighting against their innate relaxation process!

If we:

- *understand* what they are doing;
- know *how* to join in with their play in the most helpful ways; and
- have the *energy* and willingness to join the play in those ways,

the evenings can be transformed.

We will be diving deeper into this in the chapter on sleep.

## Your childhood experiences of play

### *I wonder if you ever say, "I'm not playful!"?*

From an Aware Parenting perspective, we would have *all* been playful as children in our own unique ways, had we been brought up in an environment where our natural playfulness was welcomed and supported.

However, many of us disconnected with that playfulness, for lots of important reasons.

*I wonder if you resonate with any of them?*

- Our parents *didn't respond* to our invitations to play;
- we were often *left alone* to play;
- playing was *shamed* in our family;
- we were *hurt* during play, e.g. by siblings;
- we were *overpowered* by our parents or siblings or other children during play, including with tickling; or
- we were exposed to lots of *competitive* games as a child and have painful unexpressed feelings related to pressure or 'losing'.

> If we don't remember what happened when we tried to play as children, we can often discover what we experienced by noticing our responses when our child invites us to play, or when we are wanting to offer our child *attachment play* to help them with an issue that they are bringing to us.

Having thoughts like, "This is silly!" or feeling *embarrassed* to be seen playing can tell us that playing was shamed in our family or we were shamed for being playful. (And then of course we needed to internalise that shame stick).

Feeling *powerless* can indicate that we were overpowered when we played.

*Dissociating* may tell us that painful things happened when we played that we needed to dissociate from.

Feeling *lonely* or *sad* when we try to play can tell us that we were left alone to play.

This is why, yet again, it is so important for us to refrain from judging ourselves in relation to play, and to not coerce ourselves to use *attachment play* with our child/ren. It's also why self-compassion is vital. Because *attachment play* is so powerful to help bring a sense of connection and for painful feelings to bubble up to be expressed, this can also happen for us when we play with our child.

*I remember several times having so much fun playing with my children, and then something would happen at the end of the play – like accidentally bumping heads with each other – and then us both having a big cry together. Playing would definitely stir up feelings for me.* These emotions can be *any* that have been suppressed, or they can be particular feelings related to memories of playing as a child.

*Self-Reflection Moment*
*I wonder if you've ever experienced something like this?*

So if you do have reactions like this to play, I want to remind you that if you had grown up in a family and culture where your invitations for play were responded to with enthusiasm and joy, and where there were plenty of adults who had loads of energy to play and who felt excited and happy to play, you would have probably stayed deeply connected with your playfulness.

Alternatively, you might be reading this and not resonating, because you *have* stayed connected with your playfulness. If so, I am so glad that you *are* still connected with it!

If you do find play hard at times, I invite you to be compassionate with yourself, *not* to force yourself to do *attachment play*, and to remember that we *can* heal from these childhood experiences and we *can* increasingly reconnect with our innate playfulness.

> *Self-Compassion Moment*
> 
> *If you find playing challenging, if you tend to say no to your child's offers for play, if you get bored or find yourself dissociating or thinking about what's for dinner when playing with your child, I invite you to be deeply compassionate with yourself. It's so understandable if you do have any of these responses, given the culture you grew up in and live in now. If we had all been brought up with Aware Parenting in large communities, with attachment play happening all around us, we would have very different experiences as adults.*

Another thing to hold in mind is that the more we are willing to experience fun and joy and pleasure in our lives, the more likely it is that *attachment play* will come easily to us.

If we're feeling joyful, it can be so much easier to add in playfulness and *attachment play* throughout the day such as while getting up in the morning, at mealtimes, getting dressed, leaving the house, moving between activities, toothbrushing, and so on. This comes back again to what we talked about with the importance of meeting our needs and receiving empathy for our feelings as parents.

## The more our needs are met and the more our feelings are heard, the more likely we are to feel joyful and playful in our everyday life.

We can also do things as parents to help us feel more happy and more joyful. For some of us that might be going out in nature, for others that might be doing exercise, for others that might be watching a comedian in person or online. These might be things that we can do with our children or they might be things that we can only do when our children are not with us.

> **Self-Reflection Moment**
>
> *I invite you to reflect on what helps you feel connected with joy, happiness or playfulness.*
>
> *What helps you laugh?*
>
> *Are you willing to bring more of these into your life?*

There are nine forms of *attachment play*, and I'd love to go through them all with you, and also offer examples of each type and in what situations they can be most helpful. If you want to dive in deep to *attachment play*, I invite you to read Aletha Solter's book of the same name.

The games I played with my children when they were younger were inspired by Aletha Solter's *Attachment Play* book[17], from Hand in Hand Parenting, Lawrence Cohen's *Playful Parenting* book, and those I learnt from Chiara Rossetti, an Aware Parenting instructor in Australia. I'm so grateful to all of them (and send apologies if I haven't credited any of them accurately).

## Non-directive child-centred play

Sometimes I call this *Present Time* as shorthand, because non-directive child-centred play can be a long phrase to say! However, *Present Time* isn't an official Aware Parenting term.

**What it is:** A space where you offer your child your undivided attention and presence, in a setting where they have choice about what they play, where there are objects and items for them to play with, and where you follow their lead.

**What it's helpful for:** Just about *everything* in parenting! If you're feeling disconnected with your child, or they seem disconnected from you, if you're going to be going out or having a busy day, if

---

17  However, it wasn't published until March 2013, when my children were 11 and 6.

you're reconnecting after being separated, if you're wanting your child to cooperate, if you're wanting time and space to concentrate on something afterwards, or with pretty much any parenting challenge, non-directive child-centred play can help.

**An example:** Some people like to set a timer, to make it easier to be present and attentive during that length of time. If you do use a timer, the end of the time can be an opportunity to listen to any upset feelings, tears or rage that a child feels. Following their lead during that time means doing what they want to do in an engaged way.

*I used to find that looking at the details of my children helped me during Present Time, especially if I was starting to dissociate or thinking about other things, for example cooking dinner. I'd look at the details of their skin, eyes, or eyebrows.*

**What it can bring:** A deep sense of connection! So often I have talked to parents who said that they were doing non-directive child-centred play to help their child, but they found that it not only helped their child, but also *they* felt so much more connected with and loving towards their child. Non-directive child-centred play has a magic combination of connection and choice which are two core needs for children, so it can really help them feel that deep relaxation that comes from those needs being met.

> However, it can also help deeper feelings bubble up, just like for us as adults. Can you remember ever going out for a lovely meal with a partner and then ending up having an argument? After warm loving connection, our child might feel really happy and filled up, *or* the extra connection might help unexpressed feelings rise to the surface. This might happen at the end of non-directive child-centred play, and they might have a big cry. Or it might occur later on that day, when suddenly they're not happy with anything we offer, and a *Loving Limit* leads to tears.

At these times I invite you to notice what you're telling yourself. If you're thinking, "I gave them all that *Present Time*, and look how they're behaving!" you're likely to feel frustrated or resentful. However, if you think something like, "Wow, that non-directive child-centred play really worked – look how connected and safe they feel now to express these deeper feelings to me!" you're likely to feel compassionate and expansive, and ready to listen. Holding in mind before offering this type of play that it is possible that tears may follow can help us listen in to see if we're willing for that, and prepares us to be ready for these big feelings.

**What we might need as parents to offer non-directive child-centred play:** In order to offer non-directive child-centred play, I have found it can be helpful to offer ourselves this same quality of connection and choice beforehand, even if just for a few minutes. For example, while our child is listening to an audiobook, we might have five minutes lying on the sofa, feeling the support under us, and choosing to listen to our favourite song. Or doing five minutes of yoga, dancing around the kitchen, lying in a hammock looking at the trees, or doing some of our favourite exercise.

I have found that the combination of *connection* with ourselves and our *choice* to do something that we want to do can help us then offer deep *connection* to our child and the *choice* to do what they want.

Another thing that is important is that we do actually *choose* to give our child non-directive child-centred play. In other words, that we're doing it from a place of willingness. If we coerce ourselves with an, "I should do this with them," we're less likely to really be able to support *them* to choose during that time.

I invite you to have a play with this and see what you discover!

> **Self-Reflection Moment**
>
> What helps you be more willing and able to offer non-directive child-centred play?

**What can show up for us as parents when we do this?** We might find it hard to be present and attentive, particularly when we have lots of unmet needs or painful feelings bubbling. I remember sometimes getting very sleepy – which for me was a sign I was dissociating (and sometimes it was because I was tired, and stopping and being still helped me feel that!) We might feel bored, especially if our child wants to play the same kinds of games each time. The presence might help us connect in with our own unexpressed feelings. We might feel resentful, especially if we weren't given this kind of connection and attention as children. Or we might feel a strong urge to teach our child, or correct them, rather than simply giving them our warm attention. Sharing about all these things with our *Listening Partner* or an Aware Parenting instructor can really help.

Rafa Guadalupe, an Aware Parenting instructor in Australia, shared about how she helped her son prepare for the arrival of his baby sister using non-directive child-centred play:

*"My son was two years old when I became pregnant with my second child. My partner and I gave him lots of information from the very beginning, read many books with him about it, and offered lots of* attachment play *and listening to feelings.*

*One day, when I was already in the third trimester, my son initiated a series of* attachment play *games with me during our non-directive child-centred play time. He started by asking me to pretend that I was a dog and he would pull me by my necklace around the house, and tell me when to sit, lay down etc. There were lots of laughs. He then initiated a hide and seek game. He hid behind the curtains and giggled while I pretended not to find him. When I finally found him, I gave him a big hug. While hugging me, he started to talk in a baby voice and say, 'Mommy, I'm your baby.' I picked him up and held him like a baby in my arms, I told him how much I loved my baby and sang a lullaby. Right after that, the special time was over and, as expected, there were lots of tears. I kept him in my arms until he finished crying.*

*Because of Aware Parenting, I was able to quickly identify that my son needed to process some painful feelings of powerlessness as he could see his life was changing and he had no control over it. He had more separation from me, as at this stage of the pregnancy I was becoming less available for him. Of course he had feelings too around welcoming a new baby in our family. Without Aware Parenting, I could easily have misunderstood all of this powerful healing process – by thinking he wanted to be the boss in asking me to be a dog, or that it was too silly of him to hide under the curtains, or even that he wanted to manipulate me by pretending to be a baby and that I had to make sure he knew he was a big boy and was soon going to become a big brother."*

## Contingency play

**What it is:** Play where we do something that is contingent on, i.e. caused by, our child's behaviour.

**What it's helpful for:** Helping a child feel powerful, in control and having a sense of agency that their actions affect their world. This means it's particularly helpful for children who have fears, don't speak up, or who feel powerless.

*You might find it helpful to remember that hitting and other forms of aggression are often caused by powerlessness, although power-reversal games are generally more helpful than contingency play for in-the-moment responses to aggression.*

Imitation or mirroring games, where we 'mirror' what our child is doing, can also help them experience being seen and heard.

**An example:** If a child has fears, for example of monsters at night, playing the magic wand game can help. In this game, they have the magic wand and they get to choose what we do. Each time they wave the wand and say a word, we as the adult do what they say. Another version of this is the remote control game, where they have a remote control, and they point it at us and tell us what to do, and we do it.

**What it can bring:** A sense of power and agency, and thus a reduction in fear and powerlessness. It can help heal fears of monsters or non-specific fears. It can also reduce aggression caused by powerlessness.

**What we might need as parents to play this:** We might need to also have a sense of our agency and power. That could be through doing a yoga power pose, or some jumping around the kitchen beforehand with our child. We might need to make clear choices beforehand, which can be about simple things, such as choosing what to eat or drink, or choosing to go to the toilet when our body first tells us we need to.

**What can show up for us as parents when we do this?** We might feel powerless when we are told what to do, especially if we're not getting many of our needs for choice met as a parent. We might feel frustrated or angry, or we might dissociate if this reminds us of childhood experiences of being told what to do. And again, you know what I'm going to suggest, don't you? Journaling or sharing with your *Listening Partner* or with an Aware Parenting instructor can help those feelings be lovingly heard so that they're less likely to show up when you're playing with your child.

## Power-reversal games

**What they are:** Where we play the less powerful one, often in a mock silly way. We also pretend that our child is bigger and more powerful than us and that we are scared or surprised at how big and full of power they are.

**What they are helpful for:** Feelings of powerlessness and behaviours that are caused by powerlessness, such as not cooperating, hitting, pushing, throwing and forceful taking. It can also be helpful to support healing if a child has been pushed, hit or overpowered by another child, or if we have used our bigger power over them and are wanting to repair.

**An example:** They chase us around the house and we keep on pretending to be surprised that they catch us, and perhaps we fall over in a big exaggerated way each time. Or they are on a swing and we pretend that they knock us over each time that they swing forwards towards us, and we exaggeratedly say, "You're not going to do that, again, are you?" Or we have a pillow fight where we pretend to fall over each time they hit us with a pillow, again, with lots of exaggeration.

**What they can can bring:** Children can feel a deep sense of connection and power from this kind of play that can reduce all the behaviours caused by powerlessness, such as hitting or a lack of cooperation. *And*, as with most *attachment play*, it can also help them connect with bigger feelings which can then come bubbling up into raging or crying. Powerlessness can be caused by developmental frustration or a lack of choice, as well as traumatic experiences, so power-reversal games can be incredibly helpful for children.

**What we might need as parents to play these games:** Again, we will generally n*eed to feel powerful to be able to play being powerless*! Doing things that help us feel powerful or that give us a sense of choice beforehand can make a big difference. Weight training, a bike ride, strong yoga poses, carrying our child and feeling our strength, reminding ourselves that we are the parent and we are so much bigger and have so much more power than our child – can all help with this.

**What can show up for us as parents when we do this?** Feelings of powerlessness from the present or the past can show up during this kind of play, particularly if our parents or siblings used physical power over us. If you find this happening, you might want to steer away from this kind of play for a while, and to attend to it with your *Listening Partner* or Aware Parenting instructor, or Aletha Solter herself.

Victoria shares about how she used power-reversal games to help her son heal from his fear of trains. She says,

*"We live next to a steam train line which runs a very noisy steam train a few times a week. Even though he grew up next to it, at about four years old, my son started to feel extremely scared of the steam train and would run and hide, or cling to me, covering his ears until the train had passed. I tried many things to help him through this fear and after reading Aletha Solter's* Attachment Play *book, I decided to try using play. So I told him that we were going to play a game where he was the big loud steam train. He enthusiastically started chugging like a train and trumpeting like the horn and I pretended to run away and be very scared. We played this game a few times over about two weeks and his fear of the train completely disappeared. It wasn't long before he was racing outside to wave to the passengers when he heard the train."*

Tanya shares about how power-reversal games help her daughter heal from past experiences of being talked at:

*"My three and a half year old daughter has created a game in the pool where she tells me to start to say something and she ducks under the water while I'm talking. I'm definitely prone to talking too much to her at times about things and I love that we have a big laugh about this now. I start with, 'I just need to tell you something really important and I need you to listen,' and under she goes. We do it again and again."*

Alia shares about how power-reversal games helped her son heal from experiences at school and how they met her needs too:

*"Power-reversal is really helping my youngest son, so we play the game 'Let's coach mama' – in the bath or outside, wherever really.*

*My son is the coach and gives me exercises or movements to do (so I can have my needs met for movement and he can role play at being the boss/teacher/trainer etc). So easy! 'Okay, Mama, 10 pushups!' and then he counts them out for me. And will tick off his list and I even get points for my hard work (acting out what happens at school obviously, and it is really helping him be with the frustrations of point systems, etc. at school too). Everything from pushups, giving him kisses on the forehead, squats into ninja kicks, running up and down the hallway, or, 'Mama, carry me on your back up and down the yard.' Whatever he says goes. Even the funny stuff like, 'Okay, do 20 hundred one thousand chin ups.' I just go for it and count in 20 hundred one thousand language and collapse on the floor, pretending to be exhausted. It's really giving me the energy I need to keep up with them and to also not resent waiting for my weekly moments to myself for yoga, etc because I am finding ways to play with them and also keep my body singing."*

Here's a suggestion I made to a parent who was wondering how to use *attachment play* to help her child have some medicine:

*"I'd suggest a power reversal game – for example, he gets to give you something to drink that looks yucky – maybe he could mix it up himself – and perhaps it could be eggs and fruit or something like that! And then you spend ages making all kinds of mock disgusted faces at it, and exaggeratedly falling over, and lots of 'it smells like poo' or snot or anything that will bring laughter, where he's being the powerful one where he gives you the 'medicine' and you're the less powerful one. The more you do that, the more he laughs, the more he is releasing feelings about taking the medicine. Another game you could play is the 'closer and closer' game – where you hold the medicine a long way from him, and tell him when to say 'Stop!' – and you slowly put it closer to his mouth, and each time he says stop, you also make a big exaggerated, 'Oh no! How will I ever help you take this medicine' kind of phrase, again to be the less powerful one, in ways that support*

him to laugh and feel powerful. And do it bit by bit until he is willing to take it."

And here's Amrita sharing about how she used power-reversal games to help her son heal from a medical procedure:

*"Since the CT scan (where my son was put under anaesthetic), I've played a little game with him before he falls asleep. I sit up next to him on the bed and encourage him to place my hand over my mouth, to symbolise a mask. Then I take a HUGE exaggerated breath in and flop down on the pillows snoring loudly. HE LOVES IT! Bursts out giggling and gets me to do it over and over, then he does it to himself but is too busy giggling to actually pretend he is asleep. I knew it must have made an impact when he woke in the middle of the night and got me to do it, then went back to sleep straight away."*

## Activities with body contact

**What they are:** Where we play while having physical contact.

**What they are helpful for:** Meeting needs for connection, helping children who have a lot of unexpressed feelings, particularly if that's showing up as lots of movement, and for children who feel scared or not confident in their physical abilities. It's also really helpful to support children to feel a deep sense of physical connection before going to sleep, given that feeling deeply connected is one of the three things children need for sound sleep (more on that in Chapter Eighteen).

**An example:** *There was a game that my son and I used to love when he was little. He would lie on top of me on the bed (a queen and single bed attached together) and we would roll over and over, all the way to the end of the bed, and back again, over and over again. Obviously, when I was rolling over the top of him, I would balance all of my weight on my arms so that I didn't squash him in any way!*

Belynda Smith, who is an Aware Parenting instructor as well as the Copy Editor of this book, says, *"We played this too and called it 'Roly Poly Guacamole!'"*

**What they can bring:** They can bring a deep sense of connection between parent and child, can help release some physical and emotional tension (although they don't replace crying and raging), can help children feel powerful, competent and strong, and can help children feel connected before going to sleep.

**What we might need as parents to play these activities:** We might need to feel energetic enough, rested enough or well enough to play these kinds of games. However, if we don't, there are often smaller versions we can play, such as clapping games or gentle massaging games.

**What can show up for us as parents when we do this?** Again, if we were physically overpowered by our parents, siblings or other children, those memories or feelings can emerge during this kind of play. As always, receiving listening from a *Listening Partner* or Aware Parenting instructor can really help us if we are experiencing this. Or, we might notice that particular kinds of play stimulate those feelings and might choose not to do those. We might also feel tired when playing in these ways, which might invite us to find creative ways to play restful games such as pretending to be a flying carpet, where we lie on the floor and our child lies on us and pretends to fly to faraway places. There are so many ways to be playful even when things are difficult or we are tired or not well (and it's so important that we also listen to ourselves if we simply are not willing to play)!

> Creativity makes a big difference, and inviting our children to come up with creative games can also help them experienced being valued, competent and powerful!

Adana shared about the power of 'The Love Gravity Game:'

*"My boy and I came up with a wonderful game! It just started out of the blue one day when I felt overwhelmingly in love and connected to him. I started kissing and hugging him like crazy, telling him that I couldn't help because my 'love gravity' for him was so strong! He really enjoyed that because he is really interested in space right now. As soon as he would say, 'Enough!', I would tell him, 'I'm sorry, but my love gravity can't stop!' and hugged and kissed more, and he would laugh! Eventually he started running away, but my love gravity could always seek him out and pull me to him, no matter what. It has been a lot of fun. (Of course, I would stop straight away if he clearly really did want me to stop!)"*

## Nonsense play

**What it is:** Playing being silly or goofy, nonsensical and strange, often in a slapstick comedy kind of manner, where we exaggerate our responses. It can also include games where we encourage a child to purposely do something in a different way to how it is usually done.

**What it's helpful for:** Feelings related to competence and not being able to do things or learning new skills and finding it difficult, and feelings related to rules and expectations.

**An example:** Pretending to be really serious but bumping into things and falling over things. Singing a song but singing the words differently to make up funny words. If a child is finding something difficult, we could play doing that thing and falling over or making unexpected actions.

**What it can bring:** Children can laugh a lot and then feel more comfortable to try new things. Seemingly paradoxically, if they are doing something like swearing, using nonsense play with them and pretending to not hear the words and to say other silly words, brings laughter and often stops the behaviour altogether! This is because we're attending to the source of the behaviour.

**What we might need as parents to play this:** If we're feeling really serious, this kind of play can be hard. So we might need to feel a bit light-hearted to start with. Watching some comedy online, and the contagious laughing this brings, might help us find a sense of playfulness. If we also have feelings related to not being able to do things ourselves, that can make it difficult, so as always, receiving loving listening beforehand can make a big difference so that we experience knowing what to do and being competent in our practice of *attachment play*; we can then often be really silly and goofy.

**What can show up for us as parents when we do this?** We might feel uncomfortable, or embarrassed, or we might tell ourselves that, "This is stupid," and feel shame, particularly if we were shamed as children for being silly or for not being able to do things. Receiving empathy while we share about these feelings can really help. However, you might also find that you laugh and actually release those feelings, because all of this play can help our healing too!

*A game that the father of my children and I used to love playing with our children was called 'The Laughter Police' game. They would run from one end of the house to the other, laughing, and we would run with them, repeatedly saying things like, "We're going to get the laughter police in here, you know there's no laughing in this house!" They would laugh and laugh more!*

*When my son was four, he started using some swear words. Every time he did, I would join in with nonsense play. I'd pretend to be like Mr. Saucepan man from* The Magic Faraway Tree *books, and I'd deliberately inaccurately hear the words he said and would replace them with other words. I'd pretend to love the words and to try to eat the words up. The swearing went away again within days and came back only once, and again I did more of the same play. He has never sworn again since (and he's 17 now).*

Rebecca shares a nonsense play game that she came up with when she was just about to use a threat:

*"When my kids were little I would sometimes catch myself resorting to threats like, 'If you don't do... you won't have ice cream'. One day we were out and we were in a bit of a rush to go somewhere and they started 'fighting' with each other, and I said, 'If you don't stop fighting...' and I somehow realised how stupid it was to try to persuade them with any kind of threat, so I said, 'If you don't stop fighting, a giant seagull will come and poo on your head!' We all started laughing and it lifted the spirits and since then I may use that not just with my sons but about myself. So I say a ridiculous consequence that will happen because of me not doing something."*

Emma shares about the power of nonsense play to bring about more warm connection:

*"The other day, when my seven year old was in bed in the morning she pushed away my kiss. I ducked down and popped back up and landed a few little ones on her, then I heard her shuffle away so I popped up and landed in the same place I had been doing, so ended up kissing the pillow (lots of laughter) and of course this developed into her hiding in different places and me missing her. In fact I did this with my eight year old too when she was under the covers so I felt on top of the duvet and pretended I'd found her head and gave it an over-the-top smooch, only for her to whip the covers back, so I pretended to be disgusted, scraping my tongue etc. etc., lots of laughter again."*

Stephanie Heartfield, an Aware Parenting instructor, shares about playing some nonsense play with her children:

*"Aware Parenting has made such a huge impact on my life. It has given me permission to feel my own feelings, express what is going on for me and recognise when I am dissociating. When I felt overwhelmed, exhausted and powerless, I often resorted to using a harsh tone with my children when I felt annoyed – basically, my parents were coming*

*out of my mouth, even though I knew better. It was self-compassion, self-awareness and play that really changed things for me, and as a result the connection with my children. We created a playful, nonsense game called Cranky Mama/Kind Mama. When I felt all the big feelings and I was really needing alone time and quiet, but my children had other ideas, out came Cranky Mama. I would say in mock anger, 'Oh no, Cranky Mama is here, she is feeling really mad and grumpy right now.' My children found this hilarious and would laugh and laugh; and I was able to express how I was feeling and growl out my rage in a playful way. We would then add a another aspect to the game. My son asked for Kind Mama while giggling, and I responded, 'Kind Mama is on holiday, you have Cranky Mama.' Then he would ask for Cranky Mama and out would come Kind Mama. He would say, 'No I want Cranky Mama, you poo bum. There I called you a name, so Cranky Mama needs to come out.' I responded in the kindest, sweetest voice, 'Oh that's the kindest thing anyone has ever called me, thank you so much, I love you.' This play elicited so much laughter, it lightened the mood considerably and released stress for both myself and my children."*

Rachael Butterworth, an Aware Parenting instructor in New Zealand whom you met earlier in the book, shares how nonsense play helped her daughter:

*"At the age of three and a half years old, my daughter was toileting comfortably on her own when needing to urinate. I could sense that she had some feelings coming up with pooing on the toilet which was why she would only poo in a nappy. I realised that using* attachment play *could work really well to support her feelings here.*

*We played lots of nonsense games about 'pooing' everywhere in the house. We would be on the bed playing and I would suddenly say in a playful tone, "Ahh! I need to poo!" I would then pretend to poo on the bed and say, "Oops! I pooed on the bed." She would then say to me, "Don't worry Mum, we can clean it up," and we would both pretend to clean up my poo. Just as we cleaned up, I would then do the same thing again, and again, and again, getting faster and faster each time, until there was so much pretend poo in every room throughout the house, that we would both be rolling on the floor laughing. Sometimes I would pretend that my poo was soap and wash it all over my body and face. This always got her laughing! We played these games many times a day over the course of about a week, and then my daughter started using the toilet independently to poo. And there have not been any difficulties with this since. It felt like magic!"*

## Separation games

**What they are:** These are games to support children to release feelings related to separation.

**What they are helpful for:** For helping children prepare for a separation, or to help with reconnection and healing after a separation.

**An example:** Hide and seek is a classic example of a separation game. In this game, it's really important that young children get to hide with someone else, preferably an adult. Reversing the power so that they come and find you can really help, too. If you are the one hiding, you might jump up in the air with a loud 'beep!' when you are found – you might find that it brings lots of laughter! With separation games, it's important that the separation isn't too much or for too long – because the separation is symbolic, to represent real and bigger separations.

**What they can can bring:** They can help children be more ready to separate from us, and it can help them heal from previous separations.

**What we might need as parents to play this:** If we have feelings related to separating from our child, or feelings from our own separation experiences as children at the surface, we might need to have those feelings heard before being able to play these games. We might also need to feel connected with our child before playing these games, such as through some non-directive child-centred play.

**What can show up for us as parents when we do this?** Feelings from being separated from our child or from separations when we were a child might bubble up for us. However, we might also find ourselves laughing a lot and healing from those experiences through the play!

*I sometimes played a game with my children where, when they were walking to another room, I'd lie on the floor and put my arms around their legs and say, "Please don't leave me," and they would kind of half drag me across the floor while I kept on repeating things like that. Another game was where they were sitting or standing with me and I'd put my arms around them lightly, saying, "You'll never get away from me!" and would keep talking about this, being goofy and whistling, and they would get away and I'd keep going, then suddenly pretend to be really surprised about how on earth they escaped!*

You can probably see that these some of the games have elements of other types of *attachment play* intertwined into them. I wonder if you can think of games with as many types of *attachment play* as possible, just for fun!

## Cooperative games and activities

**What they are:** Games where we cooperate to help each other rather than compete with each other. This can include cooperative board games or creating food or art or craft items together.

**What they are helpful for:** Children who always need to win, when there's a sense of disconnection between you and them, or if there's family conflict or sibling rivalry.

**An example:** Modified competitive games such as musical chairs where everyone needs to share the last chairs, or board games where you all help each other, or tennis or badminton where you aim to keep the ball or shuttlecock going back and forth as many times as you can together.

**What they can can bring:** A sense of family cohesion, warmth, connection and harmony, and a relief from competition.

**What we might need as parents to play these games:** We might need to have our own needs for support and cooperation met so that we are willing for the game to be cooperative.

**What can show up for us as parents when we do this?** We might feel jealous or resentful that our child gets to play games like this when we experienced a lot of competition. We might feel uncomfortable playing without the concept of 'winning' and 'losing' if we've been taught that games can only be fun if there is competition.

## Symbolic play with specific props or themes

**What it is:** Symbolic play is similar to non-directive child-centred play, except that the parent suggests toys or themes to play that symbolise a conflict or traumatic experience that the child has had, and then the parent follows the child's lead, which might include simply watching the child play with our full awareness.

**What it's helpful for:** Preparing for experiences – such as going to the doctor or dentist, and healing from experiences – such as being chased by a dog. It's also helpful for supporting them to make sense of – and heal from – new, stressful or traumatic experiences.

**An example:** If your child is going to the dentist, you could offer them a toy dentist kit and observe, stay present, and follow their lead. They might choose to play dentists with a doll, or they might want to pretend to be the dentist and ask you to pretend to be the patient. If they do invite you to play, you could add in contingency, power-reversal, or nonsense play to this, for example, you could make a beep sound each time they open your mouth, you could pretend to trip over the dentist chair, or you could pretend to fall backwards when they look in your mouth. Other examples include giving brown play dough, a doll, and a small potty to a child who is resisting pooing on the toilet; giving a doctor kit to a child who has experienced medical trauma; creating a tunnel to crawl through for a birth-traumatised child; and giving a teddy bear family to a child after the birth of a sibling.

**What it can bring:** Lots of laugher and a sense of power and willingness to try new things. It can help children heal from stressful or traumatic experiences so that those feelings don't show up next time.

**What we might need as parents to play this:** If we have unexpressed feelings related to the experience they want to play about, it's likely that we will need to have those feelings lovingly heard in order to be able to play these games, or we may need to go to our *Listening Partner* afterwards to share about feelings that bubbled up for us.

**What can show up for us as parents when we do this?** Our own painful feelings, either related to the experience in the present that they are playing about, or our own version of those experiences from our childhoods.

Stephanie Heartfield, a Aware Parenting instructor whom you met earlier, shares about the power of this kind of play to help children heal from medical procedures:

*"When my second and youngest child was 14 months old, he was diagnosed with a very rare and potentially life-threatening blood disorder. The next few years saw us going to Emergency every time he had a fever. Once there he would be subjected to poking, prodding, needles, cannulas and medication. He had to have routine blood tests every couple of months, for several years. Each medical and pathology visit involved my son being held down by medical staff, while they drew blood. He screamed and cried. He developed feelings of powerlessness, helplessness, fear and anxiousness. Once he could talk he would also start screaming, 'I don't want another blood test.'*

*Each time he was pinned down, I would gently stroke his face, meet his gaze and tell him, 'I am here, I am listening, it's okay to cry.' When he started saying, 'I'm scared,' 'It hurts,' and 'I don't want this,' I would reflect and empathise back all of these feelings and thoughts.*

*We loved using* attachment play *– specifically symbolic play and non-directive child-centred play, both before and after blood tests. Most of the time, we weren't able to prepare for the Emergency visits. We spent time playing nonsense games. This helped release the stress and trauma from our bodies through laughter. As my elder son was sometimes present (we are a Defence family and my husband was away a lot), the three of us invented a game called 'The Bumbling Doctor' (which is a form of power-reversal play because the parent is pretending to be silly and incompetent).*

*To start with, I would recommend that your child assigns the role of patient and doctor to each of you, and then you can swap roles. No matter what your role though, you will be acting like a bumbling, confused and silly patient/doctor. Remember, this won't mean that your child will act like this at their appointment/procedure, this is a means to get your child to release their scared feelings through laughter and connection with you, so that they feel more confident going into their appointment.*

**Bumbling patient:** *if you start as the patient, you can pretend you hurt a part of your body, you're unwell or just need fixing. Ask your doctor if you can lie down so they can see what's wrong with you. For example, maybe you pretend that you broke your arm. You can mock exaggerate the hurt: "Oh it hurts so much, it feels like it's fallen off!" and then indicate your arm or your foot. Your child will probably correct your complete incompetence at recognising your own anatomy. You can then say, "Thank goodness you know what's what, doctor." This will help your child feel powerful in their role as a doctor, which can counteract their feelings of powerlessness about their medical appointment/procedure.*

***Bumbling doctor:*** *you could have your child lie down and ask them how you can help them. They might say their tummy hurts. You can then go to their knee, "Oh here's your tummy, hmm it does look a bit odd." Your child will most likely giggle and re-direct you to their abdomen. You can overshoot their abdomen and look at their neck, "Oh here it is! I found your tummy." Once again there will be laughter and your child will show you where their tummy is. You can start to get mock confused, "What! that can't be right! Are you sure that's your tummy?" You can continue like this, as your child releases their fears through laughter, and finds your incompetence as a doctor hilarious."*

## Regression games

**What they are:** Regression games are when children spontaneously want to play games where they pretend to be younger than they really are.

**What they are helpful for:** Being ready to take a developmental leap, preparing for a new sibling, needing reassurance that they are still loved when they get bigger and older, needing more closeness and support after stressful or traumatic events.

> They can also offer reparative experiences by supporting children to experience what they missed as a baby (for example, in the case of adoption, early separation, or maternal illness).

Regression play can also be a way for a child to revisit early trauma in order to heal from it, including through reparative experiences.

**An example:** When a child has a new sibling on the way, they might pretend to be a baby, for example by talking in baby voices. They might want to be carried like a baby and be wrapped up in a blanket and make pretend baby noises. We can join in and make a big fuss over this little baby's tiny toes and fingers!

**What it can bring:** A sense of relief that they are still loved, a readiness to take the next developmental leap or become a big sibling.

**What we might need as parents to play these:** To understand why they are doing this and hold in mind that this is a natural and healthy behaviour which indicates that children are needing our support to connect, make sense of things, and heal. This will often mean refraining from judging ourselves or them, for example if we're tempted to tell ourselves that there's something wrong with them for doing this. We might also need to have our own feelings heard if we feel frustrated when they won't do what we know they can do, overwhelmed if this just adds more to our plate, or concerned that they will not return to their actual developmental stage and capacity.

**What can show up for us as parents when we do this?** We might feel uncomfortable, or old feelings of shame may come up if we were shamed for wanting to play regression play. We might want our child to stop. We might feel guilty for how they feel if there's a new sibling on the way. Again, refraining from judging or guilting ourselves, and receiving empathy, can really help.

Hannah shares how powerful *attachment play* can be in family life:

*"I could literally share a story every day about the difference Aware Parenting makes in our lives. I cannot imagine how we would be parenting without it – from the* attachment play, *to the awareness that when our kids' behaviour is off we know we need to find a way to help them express some feelings, to our own awareness of needing to listen to our own feelings when we are struggling.*

*An example the other night is that my seven year old daughter was very grumpy at supper, picking fights with her little sister. She lay on the sofa after supper and hid under a blanket. I went to sit at the other end of the sofa and just quietly sat with her for a bit. I started to squeeze her legs under the blanket and she shook them off with a 'go away' kind of feeling so I said, 'Aargh, there's something moving under the blanket, what is it?' so I started to investigate further, gently squeezing her legs through the blanket and pretending it must be a big scary animal under there. I worked my way up her body until I felt her hair sticking out under the blanket and then slowly peeled back the blanket and acted terrified as if her hair was a scary animal and then when she turned her face to me I pretended as if I suddenly saw it was her and acted all relieved that it was actually her. She looked grumpily at me but with a tiny hint of a smile and said 'again' and then hid under the blanket again. Through the next few repetitions of the game she gradually came out from under the blanket, laughing, making eye contact, connecting again, giving instructions and then we moved to the bigger sofa so her sister could join in and they both hid under the blanket together and had a wonderful time.*

*What could have been a moment of separation, anger, or punishment, which is maybe what the old paradigm would have expected of us after her behaviour at supper, was instead a recognition that she needed connection to come back to herself and then be able to be loving with everyone in her family. Afterwards my partner said thank you to me for remembering to do that – we make a great tag team between us, picking up when the other one might be getting too activated themselves! I am so, so grateful for Aware Parenting and all the amazing teachers I've learnt from. It makes a difference to our lives every day."*

---

### Self-Reflection Moment

Are you seeing any of your child/ren's invitations for play in a different light now?

Which forms of attachment play do you think will be helpful for your child/ren?

Which type do you think you would enjoy playing?

Which ones do you really not want to play?

Another wonderful thing is, if we have more than one child and we play *attachment play* games with them, they will often learn from us and play them with their siblings. For example, Anke shares about an experience with her two daughters:

*"Last week my four year old got out of school and immediately started kicking and hitting her eight year old sister, saying harsh things to her. Normally our eight year old would attempt to stay calm but would then lash out. This time, she looked at her sister and said: 'Okay, you can be the mum and you're really strict and mean. And I'll be the toddler and I don't want to hold your hand and I try to run off. And when we get home, you can be the teacher and you can be really strict and angry with me, because I forget everything.' They had a great time playing these games and I didn't even have to do anything!"*

You might love to know that *attachment play* can be really helpful if a child is pushing away one parent who goes out to work more of the time. In this game, the parent who is being pushed away can mock-plead, "Please let me take you to the shops? No? How about to the car? Oh pleeeeaaase? Can I look at you? Pick your nose?" and then get more and more silly about the suggestions, and more and more pretend-pleading. Or otherwise, they could come into the room wearing one funny item, like a cape, and then pretend to be looking for the other superhero to go out and rescue the moon. Responding like this can make all the difference for everyone: the child, who gets to experience how much they are loved; the parent who has been at home, because they get more support from the other parent with their child; and the parent who has been away, as they come to realise that, actually, their child really *does* want to connect with them!

Kat shared:

*"My husband had this issue. My two year old would be so excited to see him in the evening, saying 'Baba!!' all excited as we approach home, then as soon as we get in and he sees his dad who hugs him and*

*kisses him, he would push him away, say, 'No no no,' and get really upset and cling to me. Today my husband did something that worked really well: he saw him and said, 'Don't you give me any kisses, no, no, no, I don't want any yucky kisses!' in a playful voice. I couldn't believe it, but all evening long our son has been blowing kisses his way and even kissing his face, all the while my husband was fake protesting and wiping them away. It was so cute!"*

## What happens if your child won't stop playing when you've had enough, or starts crying, or begins to get aggressive in their play?

All three of these responses are very common, for all the reasons we talked about above.

**If they won't stop playing**, this could simply because the play is meeting their needs still, or it could be that they are tired and aren't quite getting to deeper feelings they're holding within so they can't yet fall asleep (if it's evening time). In either case, we can offer them a *Limit*, which would be to listen to our own needs for rest, or a *Loving Limit*, when it's clear that there are feelings bubbling underneath. In this case, the language might be the same for both, "I see that you want to play for longer, sweetheart, and I'm tired. I'm not willing to play any more," and then listen to the feelings that might show up. That might mean offering empathy, "I hear that you're disappointed. You really love playing. I so understand. I love playing with you too." Or it might mean that we're present with the tears or the rage, giving our loving presence, "I'm here with you. I'm listening. I understand."

**If they start crying**, we can listen lovingly to the feelings, knowing that the *attachment play* has helped bring the connection and has stirred up the lighter feelings so that they can show us the deeper feelings.

Elspeth shares her experience of how her daughter cried after *attachment play*:

*"We played the 'Mummy Penguin Game'. I was the mummy penguin and my daughter was the baby penguin. We picked a noise that the baby penguin makes to call for her Mummy. Ours was a high pitched 'beep beep'. Then Mummy had to keep her eyes closed and baby had to run across the room and then make her noise. Mummy then had to follow the noise to find her baby. After a while we swapped. My daughter LOVED being the baby, calling out for me to find her. She giggled and laughed so much and talked about it the rest of the day. I think she liked the separation, she could decide how far to go, and it was also a power-reversal game as I couldn't see and she was guiding me. She had a big cry before bed with lots of big tears rolling down her face which is unusual for her. I really think the play and connection helped with this."*

**If they start getting aggressive**, we can remember that the play has likely supported deeper feelings to bubble up that need to come out in raging and crying. In which case, we can offer a *Loving Limit* and listen to the underlying feelings that the play has helped come to the surface: "I'm not willing for you to hit me, sweetheart, because I'm here to keep everyone safe, and I'm right here and I'm listening."

We will be talking in more detail about how you can offer *Loving Limits* in Chapter Ten.

## The relationship between *attachment play* and crying and raging

As adults, we often see play and crying as very different things. However, for children, they are often very closely connected. Just as lots of laughter can lead to crying, so can crying be interspersed with laughter. I will be sharing in the chapter on *control patterns* how if a child is suppressing crying, we might move into *attachment play* with them, which might lead to laughter and then tears, once the connection and warmth have unfrozen the freeze (mild dissociation). Sometimes

I would find when my children were young that I would be listening lovingly to their tears, then we would move into *attachment play*, and then they would move seamlessly back into crying again.

This is very different from using play to distract a child away from their tears or rage, which we *wouldn't* recommend in Aware Parenting.

At other times, we might move in and invite *attachment play* when actually, our child really needs to cry or rage.[18] As with all of Aware Parenting, we can be in a continual nuanced experiment, inviting deep compassion for ourselves when we don't accurately understand what our child is needing in the moment. It's *through* experimentation that we get clear about what's really going on and what the most helpful response is. And indeed, the *attachment play* might help them move into the crying or raging. It's always an experiment!

Here's another invitation to put down any emotional sticks you might be tempted to pick up and hit yourself with, and instead to offer yourself and your child compassion. If they start crying or raging, we can listen lovingly and offer empathy, reflecting back any words that they might need to have heard, eg, "You really didn't like it when I tried to play? I hear you, I'm listening." This is also all related to the *balance of attention*, and there's a chapter all about that coming too.

> *Self-Reflection Moment*
>
> *How are you feeling and what are you thinking after reading this?*
>
> *Would you like to notice what thoughts and feelings show up for you if your child wants to keep on playing for a long time, or starts crying, or moves into aggression?*
>
> *What parenting mantra might help you to remember the real reasons for these behaviours so you're more likely to be able to respond compassionately?*

---

18  Thanks to Joss Goulden for reminding me to add this!

> *Would you like to express your feelings in relation to any of this with a loving listener?*
>
> *I'm sending love to any and all of your feelings!*

**From a child:** *Oh Daddy, I love it when we play games together! I know I want to play A LOT and I see that sometimes you look a bit grumpy when I ask you to play again. But playing with you brightens my whole world. Sometimes I feel tense and all squished up, and when we play that game where you carry me on your back and pretend to be a unicorn, and I get to choose where you go, all the tightness in my body just floats away like clouds through the sky. And when we play that toothbrush game, I feel so much happier. Those prickly things on the toothbrush tickle my tongue and the toothpaste tastes funny, and playing that game helps the tickle and the funny feeling feel fun, not scary. And when you let me push you over, and you fall right over with your arms and legs in the air, wiggling around, I feel a giggle of joy exploding from my tummy. I love it when we do that over and over again. Somehow I just feel more 'me' after we play those games. I know I ask to play A LOT but the games we play together help me so much. Can we play superheroes now? Pleeease?*

## Chapter summary

Many of us didn't experience our parents joyfully engaging in *attachment play* with us, so it can be really understandable for us to get bored, dissociate, or simply not want to play with our children. However, we can work towards having a different relationship with our own child/ren and with play, if we receive enough information, support and have our own feelings from the past and present lovingly heard.

**In this chapter, we talked about:**
- **non-directive child-centred play;**
- **contingency play;**
- **power-reversal games;**
- **activities with body contact;**
- **nonsense play;**
- **separation games;**
- **cooperative games,**
- **symbolic play with specific props or themes; and**
- **regression play.**

**If you want to dive deeper into *attachment play*, you can do that in the following ways:**

By reading Aletha Solter's book *Attachment Play*. I so highly recommend this – it's so detailed and clear, as are all of Aletha's books.

By reading Aletha Solter's book *Healing Your Traumatized Child*. This also includes more information about how *attachment play* can be used to help children heal from trauma.

By joining my *Attachment Play Course* – this includes lots of examples of *attachment play* in videos.

## CHAPTER SIX

# Creating a welcoming space for feelings

If we understand that *all* children have feelings to express to us, and that given our cultural conditioning, us parents may often unwittingly distract them from their feelings, how can we create a welcoming space for their feelings so that they can freely share with us what's really going on for them?

Let's recap on feelings first.

*Which children have painful feelings to share with us?*

All children!

Children who take *ages* to go to sleep.

Children who wake up *frequently* in the night.

Children who are *agitated* and antsy.

Children who aren't able to *concentrate*.

Children who have *big reactions* to small things.

Children who suck their *thumb* or a *dummy/pacifier*.

Children who *push* or *bite* or *hit*.

Children who *avoid* eye contact.

Children with lots of muscle *tension*.

Children who constantly *whine*.

Children who constantly *demand* attention.

I want to remind you that there may be other *physiological* reasons that are causing some of these things, or the feelings might be coming from unmet needs, such as for connection or choice, so please always check those first. However, in our culture, we overlook the centrality of feelings to the cause of children's (and adults' behaviour).

**All *children have painful feelings that they try to express through crying and raging with us.***

> *Self-Compassion Moment*
>
> *If you're tempted to pick up a guilt, shame or other self-judgment stick after seeing your child in this list above, I invite you to put that stick down now. You might even say to yourself, "I'm not willing to judge myself for what I've done or haven't done. I'm willing to be compassionate with myself instead." It's so common for children to have accumulated painful feelings. There's nothing wrong with you or your parenting if your child is doing anything on this list.*

This is an invitation to be deeply compassionate with ourselves and all parents, living in a culture that demonises feelings and the body.

I'm passionate about helping parents recognise their child's feelings. I am also *so* willing for parents to receive more support, community and compassionate listening for themselves, so that they can listen to a larger percentage of their child's painful feelings. If you'd like those things, I am so willing for them for you.

Earlier on in the book, I shared how expressing feelings through crying and raging are one of the key ways that children heal from stress and trauma. I want to remind you that when they have needs-feelings, our role is to meet the needs, and then the feelings dissipate. But when they have healing-feelings, our role is to listen lovingly to their crying or raging. This is what brings the healing.

Differentiating between needs-feelings and healing-feelings is vital in Aware Parenting. With needs-feelings, we can offer empathy for the feeling, "Oh sweetheart, I hear that you feel hungry and need some food. What would you like?" And then meet the need. With healing-feelings, we can simply be lovingly present with those feelings (although we might also need to take action, e.g. if they are kicking their legs vigorously – we will talk about this later on in the chapter).

To summarise, with needs-feelings our role is to help the uncomfortable feelings leave by meeting the needs, and with healing-feelings our role is to help the uncomfortable feelings leave through listening to them.

## Presence

*I think that presence underlies everything about Aware Parenting. We need to be present in order to be attuned to our child. If we're not present, we're likely to miss our child's needs and cues.*

And when we're not present, we're less likely to be able to offer the kind of environment that is conducive to them freely expressing their feelings, including their natural intrinsic process of crying and raging to heal from daily stresses and larger traumas.

It's easy as parents practicing Aware Parenting to overlook the importance of our own presence, because our presence is like the sea a fish lives in. We're often not aware of it.

> *Self-Compassion Moment*
>
> *Again, I invite you to drop any guilt sticks here and be deeply compassionate with yourself. Our culture does not support us to be deeply present and actually makes it really hard for us to be present. So it's so understandable that many of us will not be very present a lot of the time.*

So, what takes us away from presence? And what helps us to return to it?

Dissociation is one thing that takes us away from our natural presence. When we have uncomfortable feelings bubbling and we dissociate, or use *control patterns*[19], which are mild forms of dissociation, we literally either distract our presence from the feelings onto something else, we dissociate from the sensations themselves, or we tense up muscles, which prevents us from feeling the sensations.

Being busy and distracting ourselves takes us away from presence. If we're going really fast, it's very hard to be tuned in – to the sensations in our bodies; to the sights, the sounds, the features of our child's face; to our loving presence with them. The *Disconnected Domination Culture* trains us to be busy, and often sets up conditions which make it really hard for us to not be busy!

What can help us be more present?

**Experiencing loving presence helps us be present.**

---

[19] An Aware Parenting term to describe a habitual action used to mildly dissociate from feelings.

## I'M HERE AND I'M LISTENING

That is most often the loving presence of another human being – someone who is present in their body, with their sensations, feelings and experiences, being with us, and listening to us. At the most basic level, that might be us sinking in to a warm and loving hug with someone we feel safe with. That might be sitting next to a friend, knees touching, chatting. It might be feeling the warm presence of a hand on ours.

***But we are so wired for presence that this can even happen over the phone or on a video call.***

We can feel the presence of another non-locally. Us sharing our feelings or talking about our experiences over these platforms can help us feel more presence in our bodies.

When there's enough presence, we feel a sense of emotional safety to be able to feel the feelings we were trying to escape from.

> We can also feel presence with whatever else is present. Children are often way more present than us, partly because they have fewer accumulated feelings they need to suppress or dissociate from. So, connecting with them, pausing and noticing their eyelashes, the patterns of their irises, or the soft hair on their skin, can help us become present.

Animals are generally *really* present, so stroking a dog or cat or rabbit can help us return to being present in our bodies. And then there's that wondrous ever-present reminder, our breath. Being present with our breathing is powerful.

Nature is another focus point for us to experience presence – leaning up against a tree, feeling the breeze on your skin, watching a bird flying, or watching the tree move in the wind can all bring a sense of present awareness.

Finally, there's our internal presences – in my Marion Method work I call them our Inner Loving Presences. Connecting with them is a powerful way to return to presence. When we experience inner or outer loving presence while we're suppressing or dissociating from our feelings, we are more likely to be able to then express our feelings. The more we do, the less we need to dissociate, and the more present we become. This is also why children who get to express a large percentage of their feelings are generally very present.

> *Self-Reflection Moment*
>
> *Do you have a way that you love to return to presence?*
>
> *Do you notice that you don't really feel connected with your child when you're not really connected with yourself?*
>
> *Are you willing to be more present?*
>
> *What might help you to become more present?*
>
> *Are you willing to do more of that over the next few days?*

## Helping children be freer to express more of their feelings

Once parents understand how *healing* the expression of feelings is, most want to listen to more of their children's feelings.

However, if we have unwittingly suppressed our child's feelings, we often need to put in place particular conditions and practices to support them to be able to more freely express their feelings again.

> *Self-Reflection Moment*
>
> *Do you want to help your child to be free to express a higher percentage of their feelings?*

Before we go into this in more detail, I'd love to offer a few suggestions.

**Willingness:** You may *want* your child to feel free to express more of their feelings, but are you really *willing*?[20] If you imagine your child sharing their deepest and biggest feelings with you, loudly raging and crying for an hour in your loving arms, telling you about the hardest experiences in their life, how do you feel? When we enquire within in these ways, we may realise that we are not quite willing at the moment, which then invites us to have our own feelings heard – particularly those which are leading to us being unwilling to listen. Lovingness leads to willingness.[21]

**Our feelings:** Creating a welcoming space for our child's feelings requires us to have our feelings heard. One of the ways we can do that in Aware Parenting is to have a *Listening Partner*, someone with whom we share our feelings. We can also model this to our child, letting them know that we have our feelings heard by another adult, or when we're upset, telling them that we are going to share our feelings with our *Listening Partner*.

**How we talk about feelings with our child:** If we are wanting to create a welcoming space for feelings, how we talk about feelings matters. Giving accurate information to children about their feelings, the feelings of others, and our own feelings, is part of that process.

For example, if a child in the playground is sucking their thumb or hitting another child, we might say to our child, "It looks like they have some feelings that they're holding in."

**Noticing when we distract them:** We can begin noticing the ways we are distracting them from their feelings.

***They innately knew how to express their feelings and learnt from us and the culture around them how to suppress them or dissociate***

---

20  Willingness work is a central part of The Marion Method.
21  Again, in The Marion Method.

*from them. So, without judging ourselves, we can also reduce the amount of distracting that we do.*

We might use distraction with our words, for example, "There's no need to be upset," or it might be with our actions, for example singing songs when they need to cry, giving them food when they're not hungry, or trying to cheer them up through play and distraction. If we notice ourselves distracting our child in these ways, we can connect in to see if we're willing to stop distracting them, and aim to be as present as we can in our own bodies, and listen lovingly; "I'm here with you. I'm listening. I love you."

**Noticing when they distract themselves:** We can notice the ways they are distracting themselves from their feelings with *control patterns* or dissociation, which is anything they do repetitively when they clearly have feelings, for example, when they are tired.

*You can tell this is happening because they will have an urgency and an intensity to wanting to do this, may avoid eye contact (or have glazed eyes), won't be connected or present in their body (even if they are physically close or even cuddling with us), and are likely to have tense muscles.*

For example, thumb sucking, using a dummy, clutching on to something, wanting to eat when not hungry, or urgently moving from one thing to the next to distract themselves. When you observe these behaviours and see the quality of urgency or dissociation, you can connect with your willingness, and move in with compassion and warmth, bringing your presence to invite them to become present in their body. There are all kinds of specific *attachment play* games you can play to help loosen up the feelings that they are suppressing or dissociating from.

*In general, you can imagine that you are offering them the warmth of your love to melt away the freeze, which may turn it into tears, remembering that the antidote to suppression and dissociation is warm, loving connection.*

**Offering *Loving Limits*:** You might at times also offer a *Loving Limit*, for example if they're asking for you to read them the tenth book in a row when they clearly have feelings. In this instance, you might say, "I'm not willing to read you any more books after this one, sweetheart, because I don't think that's the most helpful thing for you, and I'm here and I'm listening," and then not distract them from their feelings.[22]

We can offer *Loving Limits* when our child is clearly telling us from their behaviour that they have feelings bubbling – if they are whining and nothing seems to be helping, or they are really upset in relation to something small, they are probably wanting to express feelings to you. You can move in with, "I hear that you're upset that I cut the sandwiches into squares not triangles, sweetheart, and I'm not willing to cut any more because there's not much bread left," and listen to the feelings.

If they're doing things that they know you don't want them to do, they may also be communicating that they need help to express their feelings. Again, you can offer a *Loving Limit*: "I'm not willing for you to climb on the table, sweetheart, because I want to protect the food from your feet, and I'm here and I'm listening."

If they're being aggressive, it's most likely that they have unexpressed feelings. Again, you can move in with a *Loving Limit*, doing the minimum necessary to stop the behaviour: "I'm not willing for you to hit Susan, because I'm here to keep everyone safe, and I'm here and I'm listening," and then welcome the tears and rage that follow.

**Loving Limits** *say no to the behaviour and yes to the feelings that are causing the behaviour.*

> It's natural for ALL children to have a lot of big feelings, and it's normal and understandable for our big unexpressed feelings to show up too. The more we are getting to feel and express our own feelings with loving presence, the more we will be able to be present in our body and able to listen to their big feelings.

---

22  I'll explain about the anatomy of a *Loving Limit* in the chapter on *Loving Limits*.

After that summary, let's dive into this in more depth.

## Seeing feelings from a different perspective

I think that the world would change overnight if everyone saw feelings in a completely new light instead of how the *Disconnected Domination Culture* perceives them. I am passionate about us bringing in that new world together. Instead of feelings and sensations being judged and shamed, to be avoided at any cost, seen as sinful or bad, or signs of immaturity or flaws, I am willing for feelings to be deeply *welcomed*.

> Feelings offer information and healing.
> I love seeing their beauty and am so willing
> for others to see them in similar ways.

Sadness honours what we have lost and where we have been separated or disconnected.

Frustration points us to what we want to do and haven't been able to do.

Anger and rage tell us that we had a no for something that happened, such as our needs not being met, or if we were coerced, overpowered or hurt in some way.

Overwhelm tells about what has been too much for us.

Fear tries to protect us from things that happened in the past happening again, and alerts us to possible threats or dangers.

Jealousy points us to what we really want.

*I think one day we will look back to this time and wonder, how on earth could a child having a tantrum be seen as 'misbehaving?' How did we get so far away from understanding our true nature and the innate wisdom of our bodies?*

> *Self-Compassion Moment*
> *I wonder if you find the following information helpful in supporting you to be more compassionate with yourself?*

In this culture, feelings, sensations and the body have been seen as inferior to the mind for thousands of years[23], so no wonder this is a huge journey. It's not surprising that creating a welcoming space for a child's feelings with Aware Parenting is so often such a mammoth endeavor. It's so understandable that trusting a child's innate capacity to heal from stress and trauma through laughter and play, crying and raging with our loving support is hard for so many of us as parents.

And yet it transforms everything.

This has been my experience. As I shared earlier in the book, when our children were little, their dad and I focused on two main things – meeting their needs, and creating a welcoming space for as many of their feelings as we could. We were surprised to discover that many of the things parents find challenging are actually caused by unexpressed, pent-up, painful feelings.

When we were listening to a high percentage of their feelings, in *general,* they:

- were happy and *connected*;
- made *eye contact*;
- were willing to *cooperate*;
- were deeply *calm* and *relaxed* in their bodies;
- were naturally *gentle* and loving with each other and with animals;

---

23  See Jeremy Lent's *The Patterning Instinct*.

- were able to go to sleep and had long *restful sleep*;
- were *present* in their bodies, and *aware* of their bodies in their environment;
- would *notice* all kinds of things, such as the distant sound of a bird singing; and
- were able to *concentrate* for long periods.

It really was like magic!

**I would love for every parent to enjoy the wonder of being with their children who are comfortable in their bodies, happy, relaxed, present and aware.**

> **Self-Compassion Moment**
>
> If you are experiencing emotions after having read this, I'm sending unconditional love to all of your feelings. If you're comparing your children, I invite you to drop that comparison stick. You might also find it easier to drop that stick when you read that after my children's father and I separated, I saw a lot of very different behaviours in my children, especially my son.
>
> I'm offering this list not to invite you to pick up guilt or comparison sticks, but to show what can be possible if we have the information and lots of support for ourselves to help our children feel relaxed and calm in their bodies through expressing lots of their feelings.

I feel so sad thinking about the cultural beliefs about children – that they are innately agitated and antsy, have to awaken frequently in the night for several years, go through developmental phases of hitting, and just can't sit still, when all of these behaviours are usually symptoms of accumulated feelings, generally from unhealed stress and trauma.

The *Disconnected Domination Culture* perception of children (and by definition the beliefs about our true nature as human beings, since all of us were children once), gets confirmed by parenting practices which don't understand the huge difference it makes when we really welcome all of a child's feelings (in reality as much as we are able to, given our own history and the economic and social situation we're in).

Children innately know how to release these feelings and to heal from stress and trauma. They want to sleep when they're tired as much as we want them to. They want to be gentle and calm, and to be able to sit still and concentrate on things they enjoy. They are so often trying to return to that relaxed presence, through *attachment play* and connected crying and raging.

**Our own conditioning and hurts mean that we are so often working against those natural processes.**

> *Self-Compassion Moment*
> *I invite you to be deeply compassionate with yourself for the time you didn't know about children's feelings. I invite you to offer yourself compassion for any time you found it hard to be with their feelings, or felt frustrated, powerless, angry or any other feeling when they had big emotions bubbling. OF COURSE you didn't know about this, growing up in the DDC. OF COURSE you might find that your own feelings bubble up at times. This is SO understandable, for ALL OF US!*

## How we can create a welcoming space for feelings

The first step is learning about the beauty of children's feelings and how laughter, crying and raging with loving support are all designed to help children heal from stress and trauma. However, our cognitive understanding is only one part of the picture.

The way we are thinking about our child's behaviour will definitely help us be more likely to feel calmer and more compassionate when our child is not cooperating or is crying. Yet, having information and changing our thoughts is not enough.

Let's return to the list of three causes of behaviour:

- what we're *thinking*;
- what we're *needing*; and
- what we're *feeling*.

## What we're thinking

What we think about *why* our child does something affects how we feel and how we behave. If they are agitated and antsy and we are thinking, "They're doing this on purpose to be annoying," we are likely to feel annoyed. We are unlikely to feel lovingly connected with them. If we feel annoyed and disconnected, they are going to sense that. And when they do, they are not going to experience a welcoming space for their feelings. They might also experience disconnection, and might be confused, overwhelmed or scared – on top of their feelings of agitation that were there in the first place.

Other thoughts that are common for parents in the *DDC* are:

"There must be something *wrong* with them for behaving like this."

"I'm a *terrible* parent for having a child who does this."

"They are *spoilt* and *manipulative*."

"I *never* get my own needs met. I give up. No-one cares about me."

"They're being like this because I haven't been *firm* enough."

> *Self-Compassion Moment*
>
> If you've had thoughts like this, I'm sending you so much love and compassion. It's so understandable that you would have thoughts such as these, given the culture you grew up in. You probably heard adults saying things like this to you or to children around you many times, and then internalised those thoughts. We are meant to internalise the core beliefs of the culture we grow up in so we can continue it. This is all normal.
>
> However, I want to remind you that it is possible to increasingly be unwilling to think these things, and to gradually replace them with compassionate thoughts about our child and ourselves.

What we think about ourselves affects how we feel and how we behave. If we are judging ourselves, we are going to feel emotional pain, and that is going to mean that we are less present with our child.

*I invite you to be as compassionate with yourself as you can possibly be at these times. Remember the suggestion to imagine what you would say to your best friend in this scenario? Are you willing to then say that to yourself?*

So, what we tell ourselves when they are clearly upset, or when they are doing things that are caused by upset feelings (many challenging behaviours are!) will have a big effect on the emotional field that we create. What you tell yourself about why they are doing this is powerful. You have so much power, and if you choose to think about them in a way that is most beneficial for both of you, you can affect your relationship and their experience in deeply nurturing and useful ways.

Joss Goulden, a Level 2 Aware Parenting instructor in Australia, shares about the process she used for herself in her parenting:

*'When big things were coming up for me about my children and what I was telling myself about them or about me, when I was comparing them to other children or comparing myself to other parents, that was*

*so deeply painful. I used to find it so helpful in those moments or on reflection later that day, to get out my journal and write all the things down in a long list e.g. they are x, y and z, they will never be able to....., I am such a bad mother, so and so's children are so much better, happier, more cooperative, have less accumulated feelings than mine, I am a bad Aware Parent, my family is so dysfunctional, etc etc in a long, long list. At the end of that process, I would then go back and re-read the list, offering myself deep compassion and ask myself for each one, "Is this true?" Doing this process again and again in parenting supported me so much to have a kinder internal dialogue about myself and my children and to free myself from the cultural conditioning that I had experienced. So often what I found to be really true when doing this exercise, was the exact opposite of what I had been telling myself. And this process supported deepening in the connection I felt with my children and with myself."*

> ### Self-Reflection Moment
> I invite you again to connect in with your parenting mantra. What do you want to be saying to yourself when your child is not cooperating, is crying, or is pulling the dog's tail?
>
> I invite you to make a note of it somewhere you can easily see it, such as on your phone.

**My favourite parenting mantra, as I shared earlier on was, "They're not doing this deliberately, they're not enjoying this, they need my help."**

What I love about that was that I was (without realising this when I created it), connecting with their choices, feelings and needs.

"They're *not* doing it *deliberately*" – they're not choosing to do it.

"They're *not enjoying* this" – they're feeling uncomfortable feelings.

"They need *my help*" – this reminded me to focus on their needs.

*Self-Reflection Moment*
*Would you like to add anything to your parenting mantra?*

**There's a wide variety of parenting mantras. The most important thing is that it addresses the habitual thoughts you might otherwise think, which may not include all of these elements.**

For example:

- "There is nothing wrong with my child. This is natural behaviour when children are upset."
- "I'm doing my utmost here. Parenting is hard, particularly in this culture."
- "They have real needs and feelings that are causing their behaviour."
- "I'm willing to get my needs met here as well as theirs."
- "Their behaviour doesn't mean I'm failing."
- "I'm not willing to judge them or myself."
- "I don't need to react immediately."
- "I can take time to breathe and think."

We would have probably heard the original judgments about children thousands of times when we were children. Replacing those thoughts with new ways of thinking about children requires repetition and practice too!

But it's not *just* about what *we* are thinking. Giving our child Aware Parenting information about feelings and behaviour is a core part of creating a welcoming space for their feelings too, as we touched on earlier.

## Giving our child Aware Parenting information about feelings and behaviour

If we see another baby or child crying, the information we give our child about that will have a profound impact on the way they perceive their own crying and the extent to which they experience their crying as welcome.

Imagine as a child, you heard (which you might have done!): "Look at that annoying/naughty/ spoilt child. Fancy crying over nothing!" What do you imagine you would have thought when *you* started to cry?

With Aware Parenting, we might choose to say things like:

- "Oh, it looks like they have some big feelings to let out."
- "I think they might need to have a big cry with their mummy or daddy."
- "They look upset, don't they? Let's imagine sending them a big hug."

Helen Attia, Founder of Feelings, Inc., shares an experience like this with her son:

*"Maxi, at three, is often telling us now that he's 'feeling frustrated' and so we ask him what he might need. There was a gorgeous moment recently when his friend was really upset about not being able to do something in the playground and Maxi went over to him and gently offered him the question, 'What do you need?'"*

> Self-Reflection Moment
>
> *Given what you've read so far, what would you like your child/ren to believe about crying?*
>
> *What would you like to say to your child/ren when they see another child crying?*
>
> *What about when they see another child being agitated, antsy, or hitting?*

The wonderful thing about giving this kind of information is that not only does it mean that your child is likely to think of their own behaviour in these terms, understand themselves more, and feel more a sense of being unconditionally loved, however they feel. It also means that they will understand other children much more too, and will be more likely to respond compassionately to them.

*I remember this with my children, even from a really young age. If they saw a child being really antsy and agitated, they would say things like, "I think they need to have a cry, Mummy!"*

**Can you imagine what kind of world we lived in if, instead of adults judging other adults, we all had a compassionate understanding of why people are acting in the ways that they are?**

Sarah Mason, an Aware Parenting instructor in Australia, shares her experience of Aware Parenting, and how she observes her daughter's compassionate understanding of feelings and behaviour. She wrote this a year ago:

*"Since Elsie was six months old, we have been listening to her feelings, one of the three aspects of Aware Parenting. I have made it a priority in our daily schedule to create space for connection and meeting her needs with joy. Through creating this space of emotional safety, Elsie is able to stay connected to her body and her tears flow easily. Elsie is two years old now will have at least one cry every day, varying in length and intensity. We speak regularly about our bodies and how we are feeling and I offer many words of loving compassion when feelings are being expressed.*

*Elsie and I have been spending time with a friend and her daughter, who also practice Aware Parenting. For the past six months, we have been meeting weekly. My friend and I are intentional in our time we spend together, ensuring we create a safe space for connection and emotions and allowing each person to show up exactly as they are. Our girls are similar in age, 26/27 months.*

*Through these regular meet ups, the girls have developed a beautiful friendship. We observe them play, laugh and interact with one another with love, compassion and empathy. Recently, we were all gathered together with many other babies and children and their parents. Both the other mother and I noticed the girls playing together. However, each time Elsie would come close to the other girl, her friend would connect with her feelings and want to move away from Elsie. This happened a few times. Elsie, unfazed, would try again moments later to be with her friend. Later in the day, the other girl was sitting on her Mum's knee while on the floor and she began to cry. Elsie, sitting with me, said, 'She's got some feelings.' and a moment later stood up and walked over to her friend. She stood in front of the two of them and gazing at her friend said, 'I am here and I am listening.' Elsie pulled her t-shirt up to her friend's face to dry her tears before walking back to sit with me.*

*One of the remarkable interactions I have noticed with Elsie and her friend is the deep respect the girls both have for the other's 'no'. The girls will continue to be with each other and this includes laughing, playing as well as conflict, though when one of the girls says 'no' the other will immediately respect and move away or stop as requested. I see this as a gorgeous embodiment of holding space for each other... When one of them is upset, the other doesn't shy away from the feelings, rather she stays with her friend.*

*The power of practicing Aware Parenting in our home continues to expand my reality of what can be. As I witness my two year old hold space for her friend, as she is internalising the words and experiences she has experienced, witnessing this moves me to tears of joy, gratitude and so much love."*

> *Self-Compassion Moment*
> *I'm sending you so much love here, especially if you're tempted to pick up a guilt or self-comparison stick. I want to remind you that these are both forms of cultural conditioning, and they won't help you, your parenting or your child/ren. Self-compassion will!*

Our thoughts really do have a powerful impact on our feelings and on our behaviour, which affects the emotional landscape we create for our child/ren. And the thoughts that we voice have a profound effect on the way our child/ren think about their own feelings and behaviour and the feelings and behaviour of other children and adults too.

I love speaking to parents who tell me that their child also understands when they, the parents, are upset or are behaving from upset feelings. Hundreds of times, I've heard parents share their child's words, such as:

"Mummy, I can see you're feeling upset. Why don't you go and message Marion and tell her about your feelings."

"Daddy, I don't like you talking to me like that. You have got some upset feelings."

Nic Wilson, an Aware Parenting instructor and Marion Method Mentor, shares about the powerful effects of responding to children in these ways, and giving them this information about feelings. She talks about a time where she dropped precious Christmas decorations down the stairs, and her 10 year old daughter came to her. Nic said:

*"I tripped on the stairs going up to our house. As I did, I accidentally threw the entire box of our very special Christmas ornaments down the stairs – into irreparable pieces. I was SO mad! Then sad – then mad again and sad. A myriad of feelings coming and going. The special ornaments that broke were ones we had bought together over*

*the 10 years of her life, one special ornament that we had chosen for each year of her life since her birth. Our Christmas tradition was in pieces all over the stairs. I burst into tears, yelling, "What have I done!" My daughter came running as she heard this HUGE smash. She didn't get upset at all. She stopped, and looked at me with the most compassionate face ever, came over to sit with me on the stairs and simply hugged me. Then she said, "I can see how sad you are, Mummy. They were our most precious ornaments and now they're broken. It's really sad, but I'm not willing for you to pick up any guilt sticks. It's no one's fault, it was just an accident. The most important thing is we have each other for Christmas, these are just things, they can be replaced."*

*In that moment she stayed calm, even when I was not. She sat next to me and hugged me to connect physically. She didn't try to distract me from my feelings. She deeply acknowledged my feelings of sadness with compassion and empathy. She reminded me not to pick up emotional sticks and hit myself. She supported me to feel seen and heard. She reminded me what was really important in this moment. She's 10 years old – and has been raised with Aware Parenting and the Marion Method for the last seven years of her life."*

Another beautiful effect of this is, when our children can understand that our behaviour is caused by our feelings and needs, they are far less likely to take responsibility for our behaviour, blame themselves, or think that it's their fault, especially if we avoid ever saying things like, "You made me feel …"

I invite you to clearly take responsibility for your own needs and feelings in the language you use with your child. This is a very important part of Aware Parenting.

> *Self-Compassion Moment*
>
> If you have said phrases like, "You made me feel," or if you have blamed your child for your needs, feelings or behaviours, I'm sending you so much love and compassion. It's so natural that we do that, given that is probably what we experienced, and when we're stressed, that's often what we return to.

*I remember so many times when I was connecting with some big feelings myself that I really wanted to blame my children for what I was experiencing. Whenever I could speak out loud something like, "I'm feeling some big feelings right now. You're not responsible for them," that would also help remind me that they really weren't causing my feelings nor were they responsible for them, even though my* DDC *conditioning really wanted to blame them!*

Thoughts and information form a powerful aspect of creating a welcoming space for feelings.

Second on the list is how our unmet needs affect our feelings and our behaviour.

## The extent to which our needs are met affects how we feel and how we behave

If our needs are chronically unmet, we are going to be feeling particular feelings and sensations in our body. Those feelings and sensations will be picked up by our child. I imagine you've experienced this!

> *Self-Reflection Moment*
>
> Have you had times when you're not experiencing enough support, understanding or sleep and you feel agitated and antsy?
>
> And have you noticed that your child also becomes agitated and antsy at those times too?

> When we have unmet needs, our body signals that to us through sensations and feelings.

If we're needing more connection, we might feel lonely. If we're needing more sleep, we might feel tired. If we're needing more support, we might feel sad or resentful.

*The more unmet needs we have, the more our body will be signalling those needs to us. The feelings that indicate needs (needs-feelings) are generally uncomfortable – that's the way our body is indicating to us to meet those needs – so that the discomfort will be relieved.*

*That discomfort will affect our child both directly and indirectly:*

- *Directly, we will probably be less present and attuned with them when we have a whole lot of needs-feelings in our bodies;*
- *Indirectly, they will also pick up on our emotional tone and feeling state. This will affect the extent to which our child feels comfortable expressing their feelings to us.*

---

*Self-Compassion Moment*

*Again, this isn't an invitation to pick up a stick when you remember all the times when your needs weren't met. Exactly the opposite! This is an invitation for deep compassion for yourself.*

---

It's also an opportunity to value your needs more. The *more* you value your needs and the *more* you are willing for your needs to be met, the more you will create an environment where not only are your child/ren's needs more likely to be met, but they are also more likely to experience a welcoming environment for their feelings.

---

*Self-Reflection Moment*

*Is there anything you feel inspired to do to meet your needs after reading this?*

We've talked about our thoughts and language, and we've talked about our needs, and how all of these affect the extent to which our child experiences their feelings being welcome.

Let's now turn to our own unexpressed feelings from the past.

## Reflecting on how your own feelings were responded to as a child

In this section, we're going to look at the third element – our own unexpressed feelings – and in particular, those from our childhood. This is particularly important when we are wanting to create a welcoming space for feelings.

# Children live in the sea of feelings. If we are feeling upset, and we are trying to hide it, we won't really be hiding it from our child.

We might be saying, "I'm here with you, and I'm listening," but if we're seething inside with frustration and resentment, or sadness and disappointment, or we're dissociated, that is what they will be picking up on, rather than our words.

*This is why it is so important to attend to our own feelings, not only those caused by our ways of thinking, not only those caused by our unmet needs, but also those feelings that were suppressed during our own childhood and that bubble up with our children – in The Marion Method, I call these thoughts-feelings, needs-feelings and healing-feelings.*

> I want to remind you that growing up in the *Disconnected Domination Culture*, where feelings are often judged, it is common for the majority of us to have a lot of suppressed feelings. It is also natural that those feelings bubble up when

we are with our children. This is how the natural process of healing is meant to happen. When we experience something in the present that reminds us of the past in some way, the feelings that we didn't get to express and have heard come up to be felt, expressed and heard this time.

***However, if we judge ourselves or judge our emotions – or if we didn't ever have anyone listen to our feelings so that we felt safe in our bodies while experiencing them – and if we needed to suppress our emotions a lot, all of those things can happen when the sensations come up – self-judgment, a sense of not being safe, and suppression of our feelings.***

> *Self-Reflection Moment*
>
> Do you tell yourself that you shouldn't feel those feelings, or that you're a bad parent for feeling those feelings?
>
> Do you feel scared when feelings start to arise?
>
> Do you notice yourself dissociating or freezing when feelings bubble up?
>
> Do you notice that you do things to suppress your feelings?
> (We'll be talking more about control patterns in Chapter Twelve).

> *Self-Compassion Moment*
>
> I invite you to be deeply compassionate with yourself. Remember about dropping the sticks and responding to yourself as you would a best friend.

I also want to say something very important:

***For some of us at certain times, we might already have a lot of feelings bubbling under the surface. Or we might be needing to dissociate, to protect ourselves from feeling overwhelmed by***

*feelings. Exploring our childhood at these times, especially if we don't have plenty of emotional support, can lead to us feeling flooded by feelings. Then we might need to dissociate even more. Clearly, that won't be helpful.*

*I am inviting you to really listen to yourself here.*

*If you feel hesitant when you imagine exploring more about your childhood feelings, if you already feel overwhelmed or flooded by feelings, if you know you're quite numb or frozen, or if you have a huge lot going on in your life already – if any of these scenarios apply to you, then I invite you to skip this next section.*

*You can always come back to it later. (If you want to and are willing to!)*

*I also invite you to reach out for support. Do you have a* Listening Partner?

*Do you need extra support from a counsellor, therapist or Aware Parenting instructor? If so, I invite you to do that if you feel called to.*

Given that, let's continue to explore how our own feelings from childhood might impact our parenting.

## How our childhood affects our feelings now

*Self-Reflection Moment*
*I'm going to invite you to reflect on your own childhood.*

I'm going to name some of the common ways that children's feelings are suppressed.

*As you read these, I invite you to imagine me, or someone you experience as supportive and compassionate, there with you. Perhaps you'd like to read it with someone there with you. Reading this list can help us feel painful feelings or connect with painful memories.*

*Distraction* – with food, movement, playing, screens, a dummy or pacifier (termed *control patterns*).

*Lessening* – with comments such as, "Oh, that didn't hurt, did it?" or, "There's nothing to cry about."

*Denying* – with phrases such as, "You don't feel upset," or, "No need to cry!"

*Shaming* – with comments such as, "Cry baby!" "Big boys don't cry!" "Sissy!" or, "What's WRONG with you?"

*Judgment* – with phrases such as, "Crying is so stupid."

*Threats* – with comments such as, "I will put you in time out if you don't stop crying," or, "If you don't stop crying, I'll give you something to cry about."

*Punishment* – such as putting a child in time out when they cry, or hitting a crying child.

*Abandonment* – such as putting them in a room or car and locking the door or refusing to talk to them.

*Scaring* – such as the parent screaming at the child who is crying.

*Physical power over* – such as the parent forcibly moving a child away when they are crying.

*Drugging* – such as giving the child drugs or alcohol if they are crying.

---

### Self-Compassion Moment

*I invite you to pause for a moment. Reading these things can help us connect with a lot of pain. You might want to put one hand on your forehead and one hand on your heart, and hear the words, "I'm here with you. I'm listening." I'm sending so much love and compassion to any feelings you might be feeling right now. And I invite you to listen in to yourself to check whether you want to continue reading this section. Please keep listening in to your yeses and your no's!*

***How we were responded to when we were upset can have a huge impact on both how we respond to ourselves now when we are upset, and on how we respond to our child when they are upset.***

We are meant to internalise what was done to us. We didn't have any choice as a child. We are designed to learn from the family and culture we were born into and to do to ourselves what was done to us.

Doing what was done to us would have at times protected us from more harm, more shaming, and more judgment. It might have met our needs for inclusion and perhaps safety. We needed to think that the adults around us knew what to do, and to believe that they knew more than us.

***I also want to remind you that we can change our relationship with our feelings over time.***

Let's look more at how we might *repeat* what was done to us. We might:

- *Distract* ourselves with eating or sweet things or alcohol, or with getting busy or tidying up or doing exercise, or with screens, or with biting our nails (*control patterns*).
- *Lessen* our feelings, for example thinking, "So many people have it worse than me."
- *Deny* our feelings, for example thinking, "I don't have any reason to feel upset," or, "I'm NOT upset!"
- *Shame* ourselves, for example thinking, "What is WRONG with me?"
- *Judge* ourselves or our feelings, for example thinking, "I shouldn't feel upset. I'm so weak/pathetic/stupid. I'm too sensitive."

- Feel *scared* or dissociated, and our body remembering being threatened, for example thinking, "I'll get hurt if I cry."
- *Punish* ourselves, for example thinking, "I'm pinching myself to stop crying. I'm digging my nails in my hand to stop feeling angry."
- *Abandon* ourselves, which might be through dissociating, which we can experience as leaving ourselves alone with the feelings.
- *Scare* ourselves, for example thinking, "Maybe I am going crazy! Maybe there really is something terribly wrong with me."
- Using *power-over* ourselves when we feel upset, for example thinking, "I have to stop crying NOW!"
- Give ourselves *alcohol* or drugs when we're upset.

Understanding the effect of how our feelings were responded to on how we respond to our feelings now can make a huge difference.

> For example, once you know this, you might become much more aware of when you are judging yourself, and you might start to realise that those judgments are not actually true. They are simply things that you were told and that you then internalised. The more we realise that these things are not true, and that we internalised them, the more likely it is that we will become unwilling to have those thoughts about ourselves any more and then to start to replace them with more helpful responses.

What next? What can we do with this information?

# The antidote to distraction and dissociation is the physical and emotional safety of warm connection and presence.

If we are wanting to be able to feel our feelings and express them in healing ways, we generally need to experience loving presence, empathy and connection from someone who is able to be present in their body while they listen to our feelings.

This is why I talk a lot about the importance of having a *Listening Partner* or Aware Parenting instructor to help us on our journey. The experience of someone listening to you, *whatever* you are feeling and whatever you are sharing, who does not distract you but instead is present with your feelings and invites you to be present with them, is profoundly healing. This deep listening might include:

- *loving you* unconditionally when you're using a *control pattern*;
- instead of lessening your feelings, *honouring* your feelings;
- not denying your feelings, but *validating* your feelings;
- rather than shaming you, offering you unconditional *love*;
- instead of judging you or your feelings, giving you *empathy* and *compassion*;
- rather than threatening you, offering you a sense of *safety* when you are feeling painful feelings;
- not abandoning you when you are upset, but *staying* with you;
- not scaring you, but being *relaxed* in their body and posture and gaze;
- not encouraging you to use drugs or alcohol, but supporting you in feeling *safe* and *welcomed* while you feel the feelings and sensations in your body.

## The more you receive this kind of compassionate support, the more you will internalise it and be able offer it to yourself and others.

> *Self-Reflection Moment*
> *I wonder how you would like to respond to yourself when you are upset?*
>
> *What things you would like to say to yourself when you are upset?*

The more that:

- you receive presence when you feel upset, the more you will be able to be *present* with your feelings;
- someone *honours* your feelings, the more you will be able to honour your feelings;
- your feelings are *validated*, the more you will be able to validate your own feelings;
- you receive unconditional love when you are upset, the more you will be able to offer yourself *unconditional love* when you're upset;
- you receive empathy and compassion in response to your feelings, the more you will be able to offer yourself *empathy* and *compassion* in response to your feelings;
- you experience a sense of emotional and physical safety with another while you're feeling feelings, the more you will internalise that sense of *safety* and will have that for yourself;
- you experience someone staying with you when you are upset, the more you will *stay* present with yourself when you're upset (i.e. not distract or dissociate);
- someone who is with you remains relaxed in their posture and gaze when you are upset, the more you will internalise that for yourself and be able to feel a *relaxed* sense of safety while also feeling uncomfortable feelings;
- you experience someone supporting you to stay present with the sensations in your body when you're upset, the more you will experience being able to stay *present* with the sensations in your

body when you're upset and won't feel the desire to numb those feelings with alcohol or drugs.

Being deeply listened to in these ways and becoming able to be with ourselves like this can literally be life changing, which has absolutely been my experience. I lovingly encourage you to reach out for a *Listening Partner* or to join a group, course or workshop, or reach out to an Aware Parenting instructor such as myself to experience this beautiful nurturing and support.

The more we receive these responses externally and internally, the more easily we will also be able to offer them to our child, which will also then be what they go on to internalise and express to others, as Nic's story earlier on so clearly illustrates.

I wonder if that inspires you to want to respond to your child/ren's feelings in those compassionate ways even more?

*Self-Reflection Moment*

*How are you feeling, having read this?*

*I'm sending you so much love and compassion. Understanding how we were affected by others' responses to our feelings growing up can be a huge process, let alone changing the internalised effects of that.*

> I imagine you have really taken in how important it is for us to be on our own ongoing journey to be able to be more present with our feelings and to express them in safe and healing ways, if we are wanting to support our child to fully feel and express their feelings.

If we want to communicate to our child that we welcome their feelings, but we are constantly suppressing our own and are not expressing them to a *Listening Partner*, partner or other compassionate listener, our child/ren will not get the full experience of our listening.

I imagine you really want them to receive the *full* effectiveness of your powerful listening!

## How our suppression and dissociation affect our child's suppression and dissociation

There are three key ways in which our protecting ourselves from our painful feelings (through distraction, suppression or dissociation) affects our child's relationship to their feelings.

1. *Directly*;
2. *Indirectly*, through them *copying* how we suppress our feelings;
3. *Indirectly*, when we don't understand that they have feelings to express or don't have the emotional capacity to listen to their feelings so they find ways to dissociate themselves.

### 1. Directly

This is where we suppress our baby or child's feelings in the ways that we suppress ours (often in the way that ours were suppressed as children).

*I wonder if you notice yourself suppressing your child's feelings in the same way that you suppress yours?*

> **Self-Compassion Moment**
> I invite you to refrain from picking up sticks. We are meant to pass down what was done to us. That's the whole reason cultural conditioning happens. It is meant to be hard to change our cultural conditioning. Judging yourself for doing what was done to you is just more punishing yourself. You wouldn't do these things if they hadn't been done to you.

However, suppressing our children's uncomfortable feelings is more than just repeating what was done to us. For many of us, hearing our child's crying and raging helps us connect with our own childhood pain and unshed tears and tantrums.

### Self-Reflection Moment

*Do you ever:*

- *distract your child/ren with food or drink?*
- *distract them with playing?*
- *distract them by moving on to the next thing?*
- *distract them with screens?*
- *distract them with a dummy or pacifier?*
- *lessen their feelings?*
- *deny their feelings?*
- *shame them when they are feeling feelings?*
- *judge their feelings?*
- *threaten them or punish them when they are upset?*
- *leave them alone emotionally or physically when they are upset?*
- *scare them when they're upset?*
- *drug them when they're upset?*

### Self-Compassion Moment

*This is a self-compassion moment x 10! I invite you to have so much compassion for yourself here.*

*If you have done any of these things to your child/ren, it is likely that you either experienced those being done to you, or saw a friend or sibling being responded to like that.*

What I want to remind you is that the *more* you have another person being lovingly present, relaxed and comfortable in their body, welcoming your feelings while you express them, and listening compassionately, the *more* you will be able to be lovingly present in your body with your feelings. And the *more* you are able to be lovingly present in your body with your feelings, the *more* you will be able to be lovingly present in your body with your child when they are feeling painful feelings.

> *Self-Reflection Moment*
> *How do you feel when you read this?*
> *What do you think when you read this?*
> *Is there anything you'd like to do differently after reading this?*

## 2. Indirectly

Children learn to be with their feelings in particular ways by observing us and how we respond to our own feelings. For example, if we always get busy when we're upset, to distract ourselves, or we dissociate from upset feelings with screens, or we talk fast, they may copy these ways and do them too.

## 3. Indirectly

When we:

- don't *understand* that children's feelings are natural and healthy;
- aren't able to *recognise* that our child is upset in this moment;
- don't have the emotional *spaciousness* to be present with them in that moment; or
- aren't *there* with them physically,

they will find other ways to suppress their feelings via mild dissociation.

This is commonly through things like:
- thumb or finger sucking;
- hair twirling or nose picking;
- clutching on to a blanket or soft toy;
- repetitive movements including head-butting;
- getting into a particular position;
- tensing up their muscles; or
- gazing off into space.

We will explore all of this more in the chapter on *control patterns*, where I will share about why and how almost anything can become a means to mildly dissociate.

### Are you inadvertently suppressing your child's feelings?

We can so easily suppress our child's feelings without realising it. We might think they are hungry and feed them, and if they aren't actually hungry, that is then suppressing their feelings.

How we respond to our child when they are feeling upset, or crying or raging has a huge effect on whether they stay present in their body, and feel and express those feelings, or whether they mildly dissociate from the feelings and thus do not express them. Our response to our child at these times – in our language, vocal tone, posture and actions – will also have a profound effect on how safe they feel to express their emotions and how much they experience that their feelings are welcome.

> *Self-Compassion Moment*
> 
> *It's so normal for all of us to have lots of ways that we suppress or dissociate from our feelings, given the culture we grew up in. So I invite you to drop the guilt sticks if you're telling yourself that you 'shouldn't' suppress your child's feelings, or to drop the self-judgment sticks if you're judging yourself when you see them using a control pattern. Perhaps you might like to replace those thoughts with, "I'm not willing to judge myself when I see them suppressing their feelings. I am willing to be compassionate with myself. There's nothing wrong with me or them that they suppress their feelings." You might also feel sadness when you have more understanding about all of this, and if so, I invite you to express your sadness to your Listening Partner or Aware Parenting instructor.*

Over the next few days, I invite you to notice how you respond to your child if they are crying, raging, 'whining', or are telling you that they are sad, disappointed, frustrated, scared or angry. What do you notice about your feelings, posture, tone and words?

> *Self-Reflection Moment*
> 
> *How would you like to respond with your posture, tone and words?*
> 
> *What might help you be more likely to be able and willing to respond in those ways?*
> 
> *Are you willing to do any of those things in the next few days or weeks?*

The more we feel comfortable in our bodies with our feelings, the more we will be able to respond calmly and compassionately to our child when they are feeling those feelings. However, we can also have choice about our responses. If possible, we can choose postures that are more welcoming, tones that are more warm and friendly, and words that are more empathic. This can also help us *feel* more compassionate too!

> **Self-Reflection Moment**
>
> What would you have liked to have heard when you were upset as a child?
>
> What kinds of things would you like to say to your child when they are upset?

I like to say things like:

- "I'm here with you."
- "I'm listening."
- "I hear that you're upset."
- "I see that you're upset."
- "I'm here."
- "You're letting it all out."
- "I welcome all your feelings."
- "I love you, whatever you feel."

> **Self-Reflection Moment**
>
> Do any of these resonate with you?
>
> Would you like to write down phrases that you enjoy?
>
> Would you like to put them on a Post-it or write a note on your phone to assist you in recalling these phrases when you are supporting your child?

**From a child:** *Hello, Daddy! I'm so glad you're picking me up from preschool. But I can't really show you that. I don't know why, but I just want to look out the window of the car. Everything goes past but I am still. My thumb is in my mouth. I'm here, but my thumb just wants to be in my mouth. I look over to you and I see you doing that too. Okay, it's not your thumb, cos you're biting your nails. We're both* *here but we're not here. Where are we? Kind of numb, with my thumb. I remember you said that once. It's like everything has stopped and nothing is happening. Kind of numb, with my thumb. I start singing it. Oh Daddy, you join in! We sing together! Kind of numb, with our thumbs! You start putting your thumb in your mouth too, and making big slurping noises! Then you make up new words, "Kind of numb, bum, bum, bum!" Daddy! Did you really say 'bum'? I'm starting to giggle! We get home and you help me out of the car, and we're still singing together, popping our thumbs in and out of our mouths, and laughing more and more. We get more and more silly, running around the kitchen together! I love this, Daddy! I don't feel numb any more! We sit down with a juice and I want to tell you about my day. Jenny said she didn't want to be my friend any more. I am so sad, Daddy. We talk and I want to tell you stuff, which often I don't. I love you, Daddy!*

## Chapter summary

Because in Aware Parenting we trust that our children are inherently striving for emotional health through expressing their feelings, we know that one of **our main roles is to create a welcoming space for their feelings**.

How our own feelings were responded to as a child has a profound effect on the emotional environment we create, and **reflecting lovingly on our past, along with receiving empathic listening, supports us** to create even more of a welcoming space for feelings.

**The ways we suppress our feelings affect our child's suppression.** Bringing more compassionate awareness to this helps us to be more present with our child's feelings as well as our own.

**We can so often inadvertently suppress our child's feelings.** The more awareness we have about this process, and the more empathic support we receive ourselves, the less likely it is that we will do this.

CHAPTER SEVEN

# Crying

*"The other day I asked my daughter if she felt loved and her response was, 'Yes, when I cry,' and I clarified, 'You feel loved when you're crying,' and she confirmed, 'Yes!'"* ~ Jaimee

## All children feel big feelings

All children long to have their feelings heard lovingly by their parents. They want to be deeply understood.

That is why I am *so* passionate about helping parents understand their children's feelings and the importance of children getting to express their feelings to us.

In working therapeutically with adults since 1993, I've heard over and over again the ongoing pain caused by not being heard or understood as a child. Being willing to understand, hear, and listen to our child and their feelings really *does* make a huge difference to them, not only in their childhood, but also for the rest of their lives.

This isn't just them *talking* about how they feel.

This is also about the deep sobs of sadness, the big loud crying, the huge rage, the LOUD expressions that are normal for *all* children to feel and express.

## I'm here to normalise that all children feel big feelings and need to express them in big ways.

And I'm here to support parents to really understand their children's feelings.

*Do you resonate with this collective movement of Aware Parenting to really understand children's feelings and behaviour?*

**There's nothing wrong with your child when they have big feelings!**

There's nothing wrong with your child if they have *really* big feelings. There's nothing flawed about them. They are not inferior in any way.

In our culture, they're called 'meltdowns' and 'outbursts'. In Aware Parenting, we see them as natural and healing feelings.

Parents so often say to me, "But my child has much bigger feelings than other children." But *all* children have really big feelings, *however* much we aim to meet their needs. We might not *see* those big feelings so much because we live in a culture that's built upon suppression and dissociation.

## The crying, the raging and the tears are either being expressed, or suppressed.

There's nothing wrong with your child if they have big feelings. In fact, from an Aware Parenting perspective, expressing those big feelings is very healthy. It's part of their intuitive and innate healing process in action. It's how they heal from painful and traumatic experiences. It's how they become calm and relaxed (as long as they have our loving presence while they're expressing those big feelings).

*And yes, certainly some children will have even more big healing-feelings, because they've experienced more stress or trauma, or because they are more deeply affected by what they experience, such as with Highly Sensitive Children or those with other sensitivities. But the big feelings in themselves are completely natural.*

## Hearing our child

All children feel what I call 'healing-feelings', not just feelings caused by unmet needs (which I call needs-feelings). They also try to cry and rage with our loving support to heal from stress and trauma.

The questions they are asking us are:

- *Will you listen? Or will you distract me?*
- *Will you stay here with me? Or will you leave me?*
- *Will you help me know I'm safe to feel?*
- *Do you love me, however I feel?*

Aware Parenting invites us to respond with our loving presence and our words: "I'm here with you. I'm listening. I see that you're upset. I love you."

---

*Self-Compassion Moments*

*Before you read these below, I invite you to put down any sticks. You may have responded to your child's feelings in the ways I will talk about.*

*I want to remind you that it is possible to learn new information without picking up the self-judgment sticks. It's so understandable that we will try to distract our children from their feelings if we think that their feelings are indicating unmet needs. Particularly if we don't know that crying and raging are the natural ways children heal from stress and trauma. Or in a particular situation where we think they*

> need something in the here and now, and only realise afterwards that they were trying to let out some feelings from the past. I'm sending love to any feelings you feel as you read what follows.

## Your own experience of crying as a child

Most of us probably received the message that our feelings weren't welcome – possibly even thousands of times as a baby and child. From the most well-meaning and loving of parents, we may have:

- Been given a dummy or pacifier, thinking it helped 'calm us down' or 'soothe us'. What we may have taken away from the experience was some version of, "I need to keep my mouth shut. My feelings aren't welcome."

> *Self-Reflection Moment*
> *Do you experience your feelings being welcomed by others now? Do you welcome your own feelings? Do you stifle your words or your tears?*

- Been distracted with food or books when we were upset, thinking that we were hungry or bored. What we possibly interpreted from it was, "These feelings are hunger or boredom," and then might find it hard to differentiate between hunger/boredom and painful feelings as adults.

> *Self-Reflection Moment*
> *Do you find it hard to differentiate between when you are hungry, bored or upset?*

- Been jiggled or moved, thinking we just needed movement. What we probably learnt from it was, "When I feel upset, I'd better move a lot," and then became children who got very busy or even hyperactive when feelings were bubbling.

> *Self-Reflection Moment*
> *Do you tend to get really busy when you're stressed or upset?*

Our parents did what they thought was the most helpful thing for us, but oftentimes unwittingly passed down to another generation that feelings aren't welcome.

**To your inner children:**

*I'm here with you.*

*I acknowledge all the times that the adults around you didn't listen to your feelings.*

*I'm sending love to you every single time you were told things like, "There's no need to be upset!" or, "There's something wrong with you for having such big feelings," or, "You're too sensitive!" or, "Don't cry!"*

*I'm here now with all of your feelings.*

*I welcome all of your feelings.*

*None of your feelings are too much for me.*

*I'm always here with you, whatever you feel.*

*I love you, whatever you feel.*

*I invite you to take your own time in feeling your feelings.*

*I invite you to choose how much you feel, and to go at your own pace.*

*I'm here with you.*

*I'm listening.*

One of my mentees, Kylie, shared her experience of increasing the amount of listening she was doing to her eighteen month old's feelings:

*"Last week, as you suggested, we made a huge effort for a couple of days to create space for Xav to have some really big releases. After a couple of days listening to these big cries, his energy has COMPLETELY shifted! He is calmer, so happy playing alone to the point that he will just wander off and play in his room by himself if I'm doing something! He has stopped biting, and has even stopped needing me all the time – he will happily interact with his dad and others around us!*

*Yesterday we had some friends here who have a three and an eight year old, and Xav just played with them the whole time! It's the first time ever that he has played with other kids like that – without me! I feel like I can breathe again!!!!! His sleep has improved too – he has even slept through a couple of nights! And this is all while transitioning from breastfeeding, too – which could have potentially been a huge thing for him! We definitely still have the daily build up but because the accumulation isn't there I can see his feelings much clearer now – and simply listening to them when they come up shifts his state with ease!"*

## All children have real feelings that need to be heard. The more we can hear them, the more they experience, "My feelings are welcome".

Those feelings are most likely to come out at particular times, as part of their body's natural relaxation and release process, such as:

- at the *end* of a *busy* day;
- *before sleep*;
- *after* an *overwhelming* or *frightening* experience;
- *after waking* up;

- *after* they have been *away* from us; and
- *after* lots of *closeness* and fun.

***Children who cry and rage in response to small things are not being 'manipulative' or 'spoilt' or 'crying over nothing,' they are not flawed or inferior, they are expressing healing-feelings that have accumulated, often because we have distracted them at other times.***

The wonderful thing is that it is never too late to start listening to our child's feelings, or increase the amount of listening we do. It's never too late to give them an even clearer message that we welcome their feelings. Just as we can change our own relationship with our feelings, we can welcome our child's feelings as the gifts that they truly are.

***I invite you to remember that crying is a beautiful natural process, designed to help children heal from stress and trauma – as long as they have loving support while they cry.***

Crying is stress-release in action, so if they are given support to cry with our loving presence as long as needed, they will complete the natural relaxation process.

## Healing from stress and trauma as a child is often very different from doing this as an adult.

This is because children have far fewer years of accumulated stress, unhealed trauma and emotional suppression, so they can heal more quickly and are much less likely to be overwhelmed by feelings than adults. Also, it's a very different experience to be healing from stress and trauma while a child – with one's parents, in the midst of everyday life, compared to going to someone who isn't a family member and having once a week sessions or being at a workshop for a day or weekend.

*Children know how to heal and are constantly inviting healing in particular situations that offer what they need for healing to happen. The more we understand these invitations, the more likely we will be able to respond in ways that support the healing to happen.*

Rafa Guadalupe, an Aware Parenting instructor whom you've already met, shares about helping her son heal from his early experiences of trauma through crying in her arms:

*"My son was born at 31 weeks of gestation and spent five weeks at the hospital. I knew there was lots of trauma related to that experience, mainly related to our separation and the medical procedures he went through, so I tried many times to talk to him about his birth story, show him the pictures of him at the hospital, but he would never show any interest.*

*When he was around three years old, he started to have some very unusual separation anxiety from me. In one night, while co-sleeping, I noticed he was having a nightmare and placed my hands on his chest. He started crying, said 'Mummy, I don't want to be by myself', and went back to sleep. On the next day, while preparing for bedtime, he noticed we had forgotten his train toy in the backyard since the day before and started sobbing deeply: 'Mummy, we forgot my train outside... He is by himself... He is feeling cold... He is scared.'*

*I immediately recognised he was talking about himself as a baby at the hospital. He didn't want to be alone, he felt cold and scared. I picked him up with his toy, held both in my arms while he was crying. He asked me to wrap the train in a blanket. We did it together. He came back to my arms and I started to tell him the story of his birth. For the first time he listened to it, asked some questions and cried in between. He then placed his train on his bed and we all slept together. On the next day, he shared about the train and some pieces about his birth story with his dad. His separation anxiety started to fade in the next days. I believe there is still much more in there to be healed, but I trust he is working on it in his own time, all I can do is to stay connected to him."*

There are two key ways that children move into crying/raging:

1. **Spontaneously** – including after *attachment play*;
2. **With *Loving Limits*.**

In this chapter, the focus is on feelings bubbling up *spontaneously* into crying. In Chapter Ten, I will discuss how *Loving Limits* help children move from suppression or aggression into the expression of feelings.

## When crying is most likely to happen

In this section, I'm going to offer ideas about when children are *most* likely to cry. However, please keep in mind that each child is uniquely different, and not all of these will be the case for all children.

Here are the occasions and times that the expression of painful feelings can be most likely to happen (both raging and crying):

1. **At the *time* of the event that is causing the feelings.**
   For example, if they're scared in response to a loud noise, or they have a physical injury and they start crying.
2. **Once the feelings have *accumulated* to a certain point.**
   For example, at the end of an overwhelming day (even if it's been a fun event like a birthday party), and the feelings have built to a level where they all spill out. It's as if the child can only hold in a certain amount of feelings, like a cup, and when that cup is full, it overflows. That's when the crying happens.
3. **When they are *tired*.** This is part of children's natural release and relaxation process, where feelings start to come out when they're tired. There's less capacity to hold in or suppress feelings, and a natural propensity to let them out so that their body is more relaxed and they are able to sleep more restfully and restoratively.

As I shared earlier in the book, so often parents say, "My child is fighting sleep," when we as the parents are inadvertently fighting our child's natural relaxation process. I will share more about this in the chapter on sleep (Chapter Eighteen).

4. **When they are *sick*.** It's often harder for children to suppress their feelings when they are sick. We might also experience this as adults. Making the choice of whether to listen to feelings when a child is sick, or suppress them and listen to the accumulated feelings once they are well again is a very personal decision. However, we can trust children to cry when they need to, whether they are sick or not. Very sick children (for example, with a high fever) don't cry much, but they spontaneously begin to cry when they start to feel more comfortable again and have more energy. We could also see this as the way that the body tries to release tension and stress hormones from the body, which might have even contributed to the sickness in the first place, so recovery might be quicker if we support the crying. On the other hand, for a breastfeeding toddler with a fever or diarrhoea, it's important to feed frequently, not with the goal of stopping the crying, but to prevent dehydration. My own personal decision was that if my children had mucous or coughs, and crying increased either or both of those, I would refrain from inviting crying. But as always, please listen to yourself and your own beliefs and observations about what's most helpful when healing from physical symptoms.

5. **Just after *waking*.** This can be where feelings have woken them up to be expressed. Or it can simply be that they're moving in between states of consciousness, where the feelings are more accessible and ready to be released.

6. **When something in the present is *similar* in some way to a past stressful experience.** For example, if a baby was separated from her parents after birth and didn't get to fully heal from this experience through crying in loving arms about it afterwards when all their immediate needs were met, then any time there is

separation later in her life, those feelings from the past are likely to bubble up to be expressed and heard this time around.

7. **When we say a loving *no* to something**, and they have past feelings of hurt, frustration or disappointment to express. Parents can often feel confused when they say "no" to their child and their child has a big cry. When they understand what is going on from an Aware Parenting perspective, many parents then experience clarity and relief.

8. **When they are feeling deeply *connected* with us and when we are feeling lovingly present and emotionally spacious enough to listen.** Children know how to heal from stress and trauma and can spontaneously do so when they are feeling deeply connected with us and we are offering the kind of loving presence that creates emotional safety which invites and welcomes those big feelings. So, during or after times of deep connection, children might simply express lots of big feelings, just as we might do when we're in the presence of people who offer us deep presence and compassion.

9. **After *attachment play***, because it helps them feel deeply connected and safe and helps the lighter feelings flow out, leaving the bigger ones at the surface. This is very common! Sometimes *attachment play* will simply help a child feel deeply relaxed, because of the combination of the connection and the release through laughter and the resolution through play. However, at other times, this connection and the bubbling up of lighter feelings will support deeper feelings to come up to the forefront and be expressed through crying. Understanding this can help us be more likely to welcome the crying after *attachment play* rather than respond with annoyance or frustration.

10. **When something small happens and it is a *pretext* for the feelings to come out.** This is called the *broken cookie phenomenon*, a term used in Aware Parenting which originated from Hand in Hand Parenting[24].

---

24  With permission.

## Big crying after apparently small events – the *broken cookie phenomenon*

I want to remind you that when children are crying even though their immediate needs are met, this is their amazing innate healing capacity in action, as long as we are lovingly present with them.

*Children know intuitively how to heal from stress and trauma, and they often will choose to revisit those stressful or traumatic experiences when they feel a sense of emotional connection and safety. They will do that through play, as we've already talked about, and they will also make use of minor pretexts to cry.*

When a child's feelings have built up and up and they are feeling uncomfortable, they try to heal through these small pretexts. The term '*broken cookie*' comes from one such example: when there is only one cookie left in the jar, and it is broken, and the child starts crying about the broken cookie.

This pretext is an opportunity for a child to let out a whole load of accumulated feelings from earlier experiences. We can also have this experience as adults – when we have a big response to an apparently small thing. Have you noticed that for yourself?

Understanding what is really going on here can make a huge difference to parents, who can otherwise feel confused, frustrated, overwhelmed or amused that their child is having a big cry in response to something like cutting their sandwich up into squares rather than triangles, or putting the cereal into the bowl in the 'wrong' way. Without this understanding, children might be judged in all kinds of harsh ways, which is why this information is so *important*.

## Children are so innately wise, and they intuitively know how to heal. They will use opportunities like this to release feelings caused by past stress and trauma.

> *Self-Reflection Moment*
> *How do you feel when you read this?*
> *Does this resonate with you?*
> *Does this make sense of what you've observed in your child/ren?*

It's also common for parents to keep think their child has an immediate need at times like this, and to keep trying to fix this apparent need. Perhaps your child asks for something, but when you get it for them, they are still agitated. Then they ask for something else, and you get that, and they're still not happy. This is another example of them trying to find a pretext to cry. When we realise that they are looking for a *broken cookie* moment, rather than doing thing after thing and feeling bemused or frustrated, we can move in with a *Loving Limit*. "I hear that you don't like the triangle sandwiches, sweetheart, and I'm not willing to make any more sandwiches for you because there isn't much bread left for everyone. And I'm here and I'm listening." And then listen lovingly to the feelings that have been waiting to come out.

*I recommend doing this as soon as you can after you realise that they are trying to express healing-feelings rather than needs-feelings. This is because the longer we try to keep fixing things, the more likely that we will feel frustrated and won't be in a place to offer a truly loving and effective* **Loving Limit** *which is required to help them express the pent-up feelings.*

## Matching your child's crying times with when you are most able to listen

If you are wanting to increase the percentage of your child's feelings that you listen to, one helpful way can be to match the times your child's feelings are most likely to be at the surface and ready to come out, with when you are most calmly and lovingly present to listen. In general, the more we remind ourselves with accurate information about Aware Parenting, the more we get our needs met, and the more we have our feelings from the past heard, the more of our child's feelings we will be able to hear.

However, there are also particular things we can do to create more of a match between our emotional spaciousness and our child's expression of feelings. For example, most people don't really want to listen to big feelings in the middle of the night. So, we can maximise opportunities when our child's feelings are most likely to be ready to come out with when we *are* most likely to be able to listen, and we can also do extra things to help ourselves so that we are even more able to listen at these times.

When we looked at the different times that children are most likely to cry, did any of those resonate with when your child/ren's feelings most often come up?

For many children, that is at *the end of the day*.

> *Self-Reflection Moment*
> Is that the case for your child/ren?
> If so, is this a time when you are able to listen?
> And if not, are there things that you can do to help yourself be more able and willing to listen then?

For example, if you have a partner, are you willing for them to be with your child/ren for 15 minutes in the evening so that you can do something that helps you feel re-energised, such as through doing some yoga, dancing, or talking to a friend?

> *Self-Reflection Moment*
>
> *Does this help you feel more present and loving and willing to listen to your child/ren's tears?*
>
> *If they tend to cry after attachment play, are you willing to offer attachment play at a time where you know that you will be able to listen to some feelings afterwards?*
>
> *If feelings tend to bubble up when they come home and you are reunited, is there something you're willing to do in those few moments before they get home that helps you feel more present and emotionally spacious?*

The more we can find a match between when their feelings are bubbling up and when we have most presence to listen, the easier the whole process is.

## Being present with your child *and* yourself when your child cries

What helps to maximise the healing power of a child's tears? What can we do? Of course, one of the main things is closeness and connection. So, the first thing we can do is move in close to them.

If they are already crying, we can simply offer our closeness, emotional warmth, eye contact, and loving phrases – "I'm here, I'm listening, I see that you're upset." If they are raging, we can take whatever actions are necessary to keep their body and the bodies of others safe. That might mean gathering cushions around them if they are lashing out or kicking their feet on the floor.

We can stay close, hugging them if they are willing to be held, and offering our warm loving presence until they finish crying and come out the other side of the feelings. Sometimes, they might need extra words to help the feelings come out.

Sometimes the crying will be really loud, and then there will be a pause but there are still feelings there. When we offer a few words, "I'm still here, sweetheart, I'm still listening," that can help them connect with the feelings again and cry more. This is related to the *balance of attention*, which we will talk about in Chapter Eleven.

So, throughout the crying, we can remain close, cuddling them if they are willing for that, listening, offering eye contact (although children generally do not make eye contact when they are in the middle of crying), and offering warmth in our voice and our words.

> Often, the bigger, louder and freer the crying is, the more stress and trauma is being released and healed from (and the more of a difference we will notice in their relaxation and presence afterwards).

However, especially when we are newer to Aware Parenting, we may feel concerned or worried when the crying gets big and loud. I want to remind you that any time you feel worried when you think that they have an unmet need rather than are healing, you can always offer your child what you think they might be needing, perhaps even telling them that you're unsure about what is going on for them. Then you can observe how they are.

If after meeting the apparent need, they appear dissociated – for example, their muscles are tense and they're avoiding eye contact or gazing into the distance – it's likely that they have suppressed their feelings and it wasn't an unmet need after all, and so you might return to inviting them to share more feelings with you. However, if they are relaxed in their muscles and making warm eye contact, that tells you that they did have an unmet need and now that need is met.

*Every time you listen to them expressing their big feelings, this makes a difference to them, and helps them feel more relaxed in their bodies, even if they don't get to finish expressing a whole chunk of those feelings. However, when they do complete the process of expressing all of those emotions, we are likely to see the most difference in how relaxed they feel, and thus to their behaviour.*

Because our own emotional state is also so important when they are crying, we can also keep connecting in with ourselves. We might want to bring our attention to our breathing, and to notice the points of contact we feel between our body and our child's. We could remind ourselves that this crying is helping them heal from stress and trauma.

*Self-Reflection Moment*
What will help you experience being supported while you're listening to your child's crying?

I want to remind you that it is also natural for our own unexpressed feelings to bubble up when we are listening to our child's feelings. Avoiding judging ourselves, being as present as we can with ourselves, and receiving empathy for our own emotions on an ongoing basis from a *Listening Partner* or Aware Parenting instructor can all help.

It's so natural for our own feelings to bubble up from times when we were left alone to cry, or when we cried and were punished, or were distracted from our feelings – in all the ways we reflected on earlier on in the book.

## I welcome all of your feelings.

I invite you to connect in with a *Listening Partner* or Aware Parenting instructor if you have emotions bubbling up after reading this.

***From a child:*** *Mummy, I don't know why, but I have a big rain cloud inside of me. It's getting bigger and bigger and it's blocking the sky. You went away today and the cloud blocked the sun. Everything was dark and grey, and I couldn't really think at all. My world got cold and icy. Oh, you're home! But I can't really feel you. The clouds are too thick. The ice is too cold. You sit next to me, and ask me about my day, but all I can feel is the clouds and the coldness. You get up, frustrated, and my world gets icy grey. I'm floating around, alone. But what's this! You come back, and you sit next to me again. You look really calm and warm. You smile at me and invite me to sit on your lap. I can feel something. Your hand is warm on my back, and something is happening. The ice is starting to melt. You tell me that you missed me and that you love me and that you're so glad that we're together again. I can feel your slow heart beat next to mine. The ice thaws and cracks and water begins to flow. I can feel more. You stroke my hair and the rain starts coming out of the clouds. I feel all these big feelings in my eyes and my heart. Tears start to flow as the ice melts and the rain comes down. I missed you Mummy, I missed you so much. The ice flows into water and the rain storm builds. I sob and wail. I MISSED YOU SO MUCH, MUMMY! I cry in your warm arms and you hold me, a warm ship of safety in a sea of tears. I cry and cry as we sail together in the stormy seas. Tears stream down my cheeks. The clouds were so full. The ice was so thick. The water is so clear. My sadness goes to the end of the world and returns. The ice is all gone now, and the clouds are moving away. I can start to see the blue sky and even the sunshine. I can feel my chest against yours and your arms around me. I sniff and sigh as the last drops of rain fall. I sit up, and I can see the sun. I gaze into your eyes, into the clear light. I'm a fresh new day after the storm. I can see for miles. The rain has washed the world clean. I love you, Mummy. I'm so glad that you're home.*

## Chapter summary

Crying is most likely to happen at **particular times**, such as when our child is tired, after a busy day, after deep connection with us or after *attachment play*.

Children sometimes cry after apparently small events. This is called the ***broken cookie phenomenon*** and is their natural healing process in action.

We discussed **matching** your child's crying times with when you are most able to listen, and the difference this makes to the ease and amount of crying that can happen.

I suggested **responses** you can offer to your child when they're crying, and things you can do to help yourself when you are with your child while they are crying.

> I so deeply acknowledge you
> every time you are present with
> your child/ren's crying.

CHAPTER EIGHT

# Healing from stress and trauma through raging and tantrums

I absolutely love how much Aware Parenting deeply *trusts* children. Rather than seeing tantrums as misbehaviour, signs of a child's immature nervous system, or as symptoms of something flawed about a child, it trusts that children's bodies are wise and know what they are doing.

> Children are constantly aiming towards emotional health. They intuitively and innately know how to heal from both daily stresses and larger traumas.

*They can spontaneously heal when they experience a deep sense of presence, connection and emotional safety, while also connecting with painful feelings from the past, and they rage while making movements that tell them the danger has been overcome and they are safe to relax.*

This is why children will so often have really *big* feelings in response to *small* events. They are not inferior beings to be pitied. They are using their innate healing processes to heal from past painful situations while they feel safe in the here and now. This is such a beautiful paradigm, don't you think? That children know how to heal, and do so through expressing their feelings.

> Raging and tantrums are completing the natural biological recovery processes after a previous fight, flight or freeze response. The loud vocalising and the movement of their arms and legs are all part of releasing the physical energy that was mobilised to fight or flee. When they get to do that and their expression is welcomed, they not only release their feelings and physical tension, they also experience power and completion.

I invite you to imagine a classic scenario of a toddler having a tantrum, with them stamping their feet and banging their fists.

When you think of the fight/flight response, doesn't it make perfect sense that the tantrum is them releasing the energy mobilised to fight or flee and is helping them negate past powerlessness?

- Their legs and feet felt all that physical energy to flee.
- Their arms, hands, legs and feet were ready to fight.
- Their voice was primed to shout out.

*Does this transform the way you see a tantrum?*

If you've ever simply lovingly been present with your child while they rage – staying close, offering love, and keeping them safe – I imagine you will have seen them come out the other side, having expressed that whole chunk of feelings, completing that biological healing process, feeling *calmer* and more *relaxed*.

You might:

- notice their eyes look *clearer* and they make more eye contact.
- see them *smiling* and asking if they can do anything to help you.
- observe how *relaxed* their muscles are and how easily they sleep that night.

*I remember so often my children completing that healing process, and then gazing into my eyes, their face looking luminescent, and they then wanted to contribute to what I was doing next, with such open hearts. It was as if they were feeling deeply connected with their true selves, their innate nature.*

> Human beings are amazing beings, ready-built to heal from stress and trauma, yet the culture we live in teaches us to mistrust, fear, judge and work against these natural healing and relaxation processes that return us to homeostasis.

When we trust children and work with these natural processes, we find that they are more:

- calm and present;
- able to sleep;
- gentle and cooperative; and
- able to concentrate.

Children want to sleep when they're tired. They want to be loving with their siblings and friends. They want to feel relaxed in their bodies. And they are constantly inviting us to support them in the natural processes that help them be all of those things.

## Why raging and tantrums are so healing

In our culture, raging and tantrums by children have often been judged as 'misbehaviour,' or as flaws or signs of inferiority or immaturity. However, raging and tantrums are a key way that children heal from stress and trauma, as long as they have an adult with them, listening to them, supporting them and keeping them safe.

Like crying, raging helps children heal through expressing feelings and releasing stress hormones and tension from their bodies. Raging and tantrums are often the expression of emotions such as powerlessness, fear, frustration and outrage – which are all common for children to feel. When children express these emotions, the accumulation lessens.

It's the unexpressed accumulation of feelings that leads them to:

- not cooperate;
- say no to everything;
- find it hard to go to sleep and stay asleep; or
- hit, bite, throw and forcefully take.

## We can also think of raging and tantrums as the resolution of the fight, flight or freeze response.

> Healing from stress and trauma is completing a natural biological recovery process. Children often need to make the movements that didn't work to prevent the stress or trauma from happening, so that they know that the trauma has been overcome. This means that we can support them by helping them feel protected and powerful while they revisit the traumatic memories and associated feelings, sensations and actions. Then they move out of the numbed state of hyperarousal or dissociation, they feel and express the unfelt feelings, and enter a state of calm presence.

The powerlessness and helplessness get released and revised when children complete the biological healing mechanisms while knowing they are safe. These big and active movements of their bodies during raging and tantrums release the energy that was mobilised for fight or flight. This is why lots of leg kicking and arm movements are often part of raging, as children express the fighting or the fleeing motions and transform powerlessness into power.

> So, although listening to raging and tantrums can be hard for us, children generally feel much more relaxed and calm afterwards, and are more cooperative, more able to go to sleep and stay asleep, and more naturally relaxed in general. Not only that, but they are literally healing from stress and trauma, and this has a profound effect on their long-term emotional wellbeing.

Pamela Quiery, a Hand in Hand Parenting Instructor (an approach similar to Aware Parenting) shared about an experience she had with her son which shows the power of supporting children to express their rage in healing ways when they need to:

*"Just before my son turned three, we moved house. I was aware of the impact this would have on my children, from the move itself and also from my distraction and stress. I did my best to stay connected to both of my children by doing a small amount of Special Time[25] each day but we were all affected by the upheaval of the move and I was less emotionally available than usual. All our normal routines and familiar ways of doing things were gone. All of our familiar belongings were packed up in boxes.*

*At first, my son appeared to cope quite well but a few days after the big move he developed a stutter. At first it only showed up when he was tired, but it progressed quite rapidly until he struggled to get any words out at all. He was really struggling to communicate which led to him feeling annoyed and frustrated.*

*Two weeks later we went on a much-needed holiday in a wooden cabin in a secluded end of a lovely quiet campsite. Four days relaxing*

---

25  This is the Hand in Hand term for non-directive child-centred play.

and connecting with each other and the beautiful countryside around us did us all a lot of good. I remember lying in the long grass and for the first time in several weeks allowed myself to have a big cry. My shoulders heaved and my whole body shook as I could feel the stress from those past few weeks release from my body. However, my son continued to stutter without any improvement. That evening the owner of the campsite was telling fairy stories to the children around the campfire. My son was agitated and restless and was unable to sit with the other kids. He kept wanting to go too close to the fire and was finding it difficult to listen to my requests to stay a safe distance away.

I was feeling calm and relaxed after my own cry so I decided to bring a limit (in Aware Parenting terminology, this would be a *Loving Limit)* and warmly told my son that it was time to go back to our cabin. He really didn't want to go so I lifted him and gently carried him back to the cabin. He was very unhappy about this. His body went rigid and he thrashed about in my arms. I sat down on the steps outside the cabin and he screamed and raged and cried in my arms for about 40 minutes.

Eventually, the crying subsided. My son's body relaxed as he curled into my lap. He had a big sigh and fell asleep in my arms. He slept deeply all night. The next day at breakfast we noticed his stutter was noticeably improved. He was relaxed and smiling and the words came easily. By the following day the stutter was completely gone, never to return."

### Self-Reflection Moment

How do you feel, having read this? I want to remind you that it's normal for our own feelings to bubble up when we envisage a scenario like this. I'm sending so much love and compassion to any and all feelings you might be feeling.

## Why it's so normal for us to find listening to raging and tantrums hard and how we can help it become easier

It is so normal and natural for us to have painful thoughts and feelings arising when our child is raging or having a tantrum.

There are many possible reasons for this:

### The effect of the culture we grew up in – and live in now

Given that the culture that most of us grew up in has so many judgments or fears about this expression, that means that as children, we would probably either have experienced a harsh or distracting response to our own attempts to rage or tantrum, or we would have seen those responses to other children around us.

### What we're telling ourselves about raging and tantrums

Because of the culture, most of us internalised harsh judgments about raging and tantrums. Those thoughts can naturally show up when our child is raging and tantrumming. Changing the way we think about raging and tantrums can have a huge impact on our capacity to respond helpfully to our child. This is why I believe it is so important for you to have lots of information about raging from an Aware Parenting perspective, so you can choose to replace your cultural conditioning with more compassionate thoughts about it.

### Our own childhood experiences

If we experienced a parent raging when we grew up, our child's tantrum might remind us of that. In which case it is so normal for the feelings that we felt as children to show up and the responses we had as children to arise. It's natural that we would have felt scared, especially if our parents became violent when they were angry. We might have moved into dissociation, or hid somewhere. We might have desperately tried to placate them or get them to calm down by pleading. We might have thought it was our fault, and desperately tried to act in ways that wouldn't 'make them angry' (in our perception). We might have moved into aggression ourselves.

If you experienced your parent expressing rage in unsafe ways, it's really natural that you might feel scared when your child expresses rage or tantrums. That's literally your body's attempt to heal from those earlier experiences. You might also feel scared or powerless if a sibling, teacher or peer was aggressive and used power-over you.

***If you feel extreme fear, powerlessness or outrage when your child expresses rage, it's likely that you are connecting with unexpressed feelings from your own childhood.***

If you are wanting to create an emotionally and physically safe space for your child's raging, it's really important for you to attend to your own childhood healing. I would invite you to receive regular empathic listening from a *Listening Partner*, counsellor, therapist or Aware Parenting instructor.

## There are so many reasons why it can be so hard for us to be with raging and tantrums.

I am going to invite you to explore the following questions. As always, please check in with yourself before starting and only take part in this enquiry if you have the sense of enough outer and/or inner emotional support to be able to be with the feelings that might show up for you.

If you have a *Listening Partner*, counsellor, therapist or Aware Parenting instructor, you might feel called to explore these questions with them!

> *Self-Reflection Moment*
>
> What thoughts do you have in relation to raging and tantrums?
>
> How do you feel when you see a child (or your child) raging?
>
> How do you imagine (or remember) you were responded to as a child when you raged or had a tantrum?
>
> How would you have liked to have been responded to?
>
> What thoughts would you like to think when your child is raging or tantrumming?
>
> I invite you to write them down in your journal or on your phone or on a Post-it or on your computer.
>
> How would you like to respond to your child when they are raging?
>
> What might you need to be able to respond like that?
>
> Are you willing to take action on that over the next few days or weeks?

## Differentiating between aggression and expression

Remember that list of three back in Chapter One – expression, suppression and aggression. Whatever feelings children aren't expressing through crying, raging and tantrums will need to be suppressed, and those emotions can bubble up in aggression. Aggression doesn't bring healing because it's a continuation of the fight or flight response rather than the resolution of it.

> A child hitting another child isn't releasing painful feelings. Quite the opposite. Being the one who hits is likely to lead to more painful feelings for them, especially if they have experienced receiving shame or guilt sticks and have internalised them, so increasing the amount of painful feelings that they are holding inside.

We can usually spot aggression because it doesn't include the vocalisations of crying and raging. It's still the fight or flight response, rather than release and resolution. If a child feels safe enough to heal, they won't need to defend themselves.

*In contrast, when a child is expressing rage in healing ways, there is often crying and raging with their voice involved, as well as vigorous movement, which releases the energy mobilised for the fight or flight response and helps them feel powerful again.*

If a child is in aggressive mode, our aim in Aware Parenting is to support the aggression to turn into expression by helping them know that they are safe now. There are two key ways we can do that – *attachment play* and *Loving Limits*. We will be talking more about all of this in the chapter on aggression (Chapter Fourteen).

When our child needs support from us to move from aggression to expression, it is normal for our own feelings to bubble up. It is so natural for our own fight, flight or freeze response to get activated when our child is hitting or pushing, especially if they lash out at us or their sibling. This is one of the many reasons why it can be so hard for us to stay calm when we are wanting to help our child shift from aggression to safe and healing expression!

## Supportive responses to raging and tantrums: keeping them safe, supporting the healing and responding compassionately

I want to remind you that when a child is raging or tantrumming, they are not only expressing feelings, they are literally releasing stress and tension from their bodies.
If we think of the fight or flight response, the energy that gets mobilised is either to fight with hitting and kicking, or fleeing through running fast. When a child is raging or tantrumming,

they are literally completing that process, through moving their arms and legs in ways that help their bodies release that fight or flight energy and tension.

In this way, they feel both more *relaxed* and more *powerful* afterwards. More relaxed, because they are no longer carrying all that held in tension and stress hormones. More powerful, because they have completed the resolution of the flight or fight response successfully and they know that they are again safe and that nothing frightening is going to happen to them.

So, because of this, we expect raging or tantrums to be full of lots of movement. Raging and tantrums by definition are not quiet and subdued! Children will often flail around, moving their arms and legs vigorously. As I shared above, our aim is to stop them from hitting, taking or throwing, while still supporting them in expressing all that powerful energy through their movement.

There are plenty of things we can do to keep them, us and others safe during the process. If they are raging or tantrumming on a hard floor, you might want to bring cushions or blankets to protect them from hurting themselves while they are flailing around. You could also pick them up and take them somewhere more cushioned, if that doesn't distract them from the process. You might want to be holding a pillow so you can put it in between yourself and them if they are kicking with their legs and there's a risk that they might kick you.

This part of the book is about being with the spontaneous expression of rage. We will be talking more about *Loving Limits* and *holding* in a later chapter.

**Children can often need something to push against when they are raging. Remember that beautiful resolution of the fight or flight**

*response? To feel powerful, they might need to push against your body with their hands or feet. In this way, they are getting to express their no, they are getting to feel powerful, and they are getting to express the energy that wasn't expressed at the time, while feeling a deep sense of safety and support (and without hurting anyone).*

There's quite an art to finding the most helpful response here. I see it as a bit like a partner dance, something like the tango. I call it the *crying dance*, in which we feel in to the amount of force they are exerting and meet that – not in a way where we get overpowered, nor in a way where we are pushing back too much. We are meeting their push with an *embodied presence* so that they feel the contact and support.

If a child is hitting and kicking and you sense that they are still in the fight or flight response rather than returning to homeostasis through the healing expression of rage, they will probably need your help to move into expression. We can usually tell if this is the case because their movements don't bring them relief and relaxation. We will often feel very different in our bodies too!

> I don't generally recommend inviting them to hit a pillow. Hitting a pillow is often a very different experience to healing raging and often doesn't bring much of a sense of relief, often because it doesn't include enough connection and emotional expression in the process to release the tension. However, some children might find it helpful, because each child is unique, and I invite you to trust them and yourself. Many children do enjoy games that include pushing, which helps with releasing energy mobilised to fight. That could be 'pushing hands' together with them, or both pushing a wall, or both pretending to be mechanical diggers or rhinos that love to push.

What kinds of words might we say when a child is raging or having a tantrum?

I'll offer a few suggestions. I wonder if any of them resonate with you?

- "I'm here with you."
- "I'm listening."
- "You're letting it all out."
- "I'm staying right here with you."
- "I welcome all of your feelings."
- "I'm here to keep you safe."
- "I love you."

> *Self-Reflection Moment*
>
> *What would you have liked to have heard when you were raging as a child?*
>
> *What would you like to say to your child when they are raging?*

## When our child is raging and tells us to *go away!*

When children are raging, they might tell us to *go away.*

> *Self-Reflection Moment*
>
> *I wonder if you ever remember doing that as a child or teenager?*
>
> *Did you really want your parent to go away, or did you want them to stay close and be able to be with you while you expressed those feelings?*

If you experienced that, I wonder if you would have liked to have heard something like:

*"I hear that you want me to go away, and I'm not going to leave you alone with these feelings, because I don't think that's the most helpful thing for you. I'm here with you."*

> Self-Reflection Moment
>
> Or would you have liked to have heard something different?
>
> What would you like to say to your child if they are raging and telling you to go away?

As always, I invite you to listen in to yourself, experiment, observe your child, and see what is most helpful for them to stay connected with you, themselves and their feelings. Each child is different and finding the exact *balance of attention* in terms of what brings healing will be subtly different for each child, also depending on their age.

Parents often think that their child really does want them to go away. However, I invite you to read the *balance of attention* chapter, and then to play with staying close with your child, while also offering empathy in response to what you hear them say.

**Often, young children need reassurance that we really can be with their big feelings, that they are safe while they're feeling those feelings, and that we're not going to leave them alone with those feelings. Our loving presence is often what is helping them feel the big emotions.**

We can also think of the *go away* as them expressing the *no* that they wanted to express in that fight or flight response. If we can offer emotional safety in the present and listen to that 'no' from the past, more healing can happen.

Again, I invite you to listen in to yourself and what resonates with you, experiment in terms of distance and closeness with your child, and observe them. If you stay relatively close while they are telling you to go away, what happens? If you move further away, what happens?

Understanding how to observe both dissociation and the *balance of attention* is vital here. If we move away from them, they might stop raging, but they might put their thumb in their mouth or start picking their nose – signs that they are dissociating. If we stay a few feet away when they are telling us to go away, their raging might intensify, and we might then observe them continuing to rage with us and then coming out the other side, relaxed and clear and wanting to cuddle with us. Again, I invite you to read the chapter on the *balance of attention* for more clarity about how to experiment with this to find out what's most helpful for your child.

> ### Self-Compassion Moment
> How are you feeling after this? I invite you to remember that this can stir up big feelings in us, so I invite you to be deeply compassionate with yourself and keep your Listening Partner close at these times! I'm sending you a big hug!

As the story below shows, it's very common that children will rage with us, and then their expression will become tears and crying. They might stop pushing and thrashing and melt into our arms, sobbing. This is a clear sign that the energy mobilised in their arms and legs to fight or flee has been released, along with the fear or terror and powerlessness or rage. Now they are expressing different feelings, which might include sadness, loss, disappointment, confusion or overwhelm. This change from raging to crying is often a distinct shift in the healing and releasing process.

**From a child:** *My feelings are like a volcano today. I want to roar like a lion and eat the whole world up in one big gulp. I tell you to GOOOOO AWAYYYYYYY and saying that is so satisfying in my tummy. I have so many feelings I want to express to you, Daddy. You* *do go away a lot with your work, and I feel feelings bigger than the moon when you go. I don't want you to go away. And I want to say GOOOOO AWAYYYY again! Oh, you start leaving the room. Please don't leave me alone! How can I tell you? I want to scream GO AWAY to you but I want you to stay with me and see me and keep me safe. These feelings are too big for me to feel when I'm on my own. You leave, and I feel kind of numb. I grab my teddy and hold him tight. I don't feel anything much. Oh, you are coming back in again! The volcano erupts again! I HATE YOU! I want to let it all out. But please stay, please love me, please be bigger than me. I want you to be bigger than this volcano. I want to be sure that my volcano won't hurt you, won't burn down your love for me, won't be too big for you. Oh, you stay! You're here with me. My volcano is throwing out big black and red fire. Oh Dad, you're still here. My volcano didn't destroy you. You look safe. Your face looks calm. You're my solid land while I'm a moving volcano. More lava erupts. I HATE YOU! GO AWAY! You stay! You stop me from hitting you but you stand there, with your hands out. I push with every bit of power I've got. I feel you there. You're with me. We're here together. I'm safe. My volcano is big but it doesn't destroy us. Oh Daddy, oh Daddy, I feel so sad. You go away so much. I miss you. Why do you go away? Don't you love me? I fall into your arms. You hold me and I cry and cry and cry. My volcano has become a waterfall. There's so much water. It's everywhere. It's flooding the world. But you are my safe anchor. You hold me like the rock under the waterfall. The tears flow and flow and flow. They start to dry. The rain stops, and the sun comes out. I sigh. I snuggle in to your melty hug. I love you, Daddy. I feel all soft and relaxed. I can see your face so clearly. I love you. I see you looking in my eyes. I think that you love me too. You can be with all of me. Let's stay snuggling like this some more, Daddy. I love you.*

## Chapter summary

**Raging and tantrums are deeply healthy and powerful healing processes** which help children heal from stress and trauma, as long as they are experiencing emotional and physical safety in the present.

It's so **natural for us to find listening to raging and tantrums hard**, given the culture we grew up in and live in now. However, we can help ourselves find them easier to be with!

**It's important to differentiate between aggression and expression**, and support a child to move from aggression to expression so they can move out of the fight or flight response into release and healing.

We talked about **keeping children safe while they are raging**, and how we can support the healing and respond compassionately.

## Supporting your child/ren's raging will help them feel more truly powerful and safe in the world.

CHAPTER NINE

# Being with our own frustration, anger and outrage

As a child, I was known for 'having a temper'.

*Nowadays, I know that I simply had a lot of unexpressed accumulated feelings. I experienced many painful and traumatic experiences – as well as being in an incubator as a newborn, I experienced further separations, such as sleeping alone in my room as a baby, followed by being separated from my parents for 18 months each some years later, and throwing in some traumatic dentist and school experiences! Added to these were the effects of the general parenting style that was prevalent in the 1970s.*

*Back in those days, very few people understood that babies and children have real feelings and are deeply affected by separation, medical procedures and punishments. Nor was there any understanding that children naturally try to heal from those experiences through play, crying and raging. Aletha Solter hadn't written any of her books back then!*

*Over years and years, those feelings accumulated, and I tensed up and dissociated to hold them in and not feel them. Occasionally they would burst out, such as when I felt frustrated, bashed my badminton racquet on the floor, and was told that I 'had a temper'. How misunderstood children are in the* Disconnected Domination Culture.

*Many years later, when I became a mother, those feelings of frustration or rage would suddenly bubble out when I felt overwhelmed or powerless. I began to realise that of course I had a whole load of unexpressed frustration, anger and outrage. As well as experiencing considerable stress and trauma, I'd also grown up in a culture where children's 'no's' are routinely overridden, and where most of us would have had our needs for agency, autonomy and choice not met thousands of times.*

*Learning to understand frustration, anger and outrage, to stop judging them and myself for feeling them, being able to be present with them in my body, and to express them in safe ways, have been vital steps in my Aware Parenting journey. I became unwilling to judge these feelings, became deeply comfortable with the sensations of them, and became able to release them. So much of this I learnt through being with my children's frustration, anger and outrage, which helped me understand my inner children[26] so much more deeply.*

## How was your own frustration, anger and outrage responded to as a child?

I invited you to dip your toe into this in the last chapter, and I'd love to invite you to dive in a bit deeper this time! As always, please listen to yourself and whether you have enough inner and outer emotional support, safety and loving presence to do this. If you don't, please skip the process and come back to it later if you want to.

I invite you to imagine me with you as you do this, or someone else you receive empathy and support from. Or you could literally go through this reflection process with your *Listening Partner*, counsellor, therapist or Aware Parenting instructor.

If you don't have any memories of your childhood, perhaps there are

---

26  This term isn't a part of Aware Parenting, but I use it a lot in the Marion Method.

family stories or photographs which can give you relevant information. In addition, you don't need to remember exactly what happened in order for healing to happen.

Belynda Smith, Aware Parenting instructor and the Copy Editor of this book, says,

*"I have very few memories of my childhood. One thing that has helped a lot is the phrase or idea, 'What's your best guess?' – when my* Listening Partner *says something like, 'You don't have to get it right, or remember exactly, but what is your best guess? How do you imagine it might have been?' This has opened the doors to feelings."*

So, if you don't exactly remember, how do you imagine things might have been for you?

*Self-Reflection Moment*

*Do you remember ever feeling frustrated, angry or outraged as a child?*

*Do you remember how you were responded to at those times, in both actions and words?*

*If your parent or parents are still around now, how have you seen them respond to your child/ren when they are frustrated, angry or outraged?*

*(Observing our parent/s as they respond to our children can be a powerful experience and can help us deeply understand the origins of our thoughts, feelings and actions.)*

*Do you see any links between how you were responded to then and how you respond to yourself now?*

## Befriending and welcoming frustration, anger and outrage in yourself

The more comfortable we feel with our own anger and outrage, the less we judge it. The more we can be with the sensations in our bodies without dissociating or moving into aggression, the more comfortable we will be with our child's similar feelings. We will be more able to create a supportive environment for the expression of those feelings so that they can feel safe, unconditionally loved and can heal from stress and trauma.

### Changing your thoughts about your own frustration, anger and outrage

*Self-Reflection Moment*

*Do you ever judge yourself if you are feeling angry or outraged?*

*If so, what kinds of thoughts do you have?*

I invite you to reflect on this book so far and what you already know about Aware Parenting. Remember that raging and tantrumming are the expression of pent-up feelings including from the fight or flight response; they help us heal from stress and trauma so that we can return to a state of calm and homeostasis.

*Self-Reflection Moment*

*What would you like your inner response to your frustration, anger and outrage to be, instead?*

As we've talked about for our children, it's not just our thoughts and understandings that have an impact on how we feel. Our capacity to be present in our body when we are feeling frustrated, angry or outraged is deeply affected by the presence we received as children when we were feeling those feelings.

## The presence of another when we are feeling and expressing frustration, anger and outrage

If we didn't ever have anyone else be lovingly present with us when we were feeling frustrated, angry or outraged, we would not have experienced being safe in our bodies to feel those feelings. Neither would we have had the embodied experience that we could feel those feelings and sensations, express them in safe ways, and come out the other side feeling relaxed, calm and present.

> This means that for many of us, we might feel scared when we feel these feelings. We might believe that we are out of control. We might think that we will never come out of the other side of these feelings.

This is why it is so important to have the experience of someone else who:

- has compassionate *thoughts* about the feelings and about us;
- can be *present* in their body with those sensations and feelings;
- knows that we are *safe* when we are feeling and expressing those feelings; and
- knows that *after* feeling and expressing those feelings, we will be relieved and relaxed.

Over time, through repeatedly experiencing this, you will then come to:

- have compassionate *thoughts* about yourself and these feelings when you're feeling them;
- be able to be *present* in your body when you are feeling the sensations and feelings;
- know that you are *safe* when you are feeling and expressing these feelings; and
- know that you will come out the other side feeling relieved and *relaxed*.

This is why I invite you so often to connect with your *Listening Partner*, counsellor or therapist, or Aware Parenting instructor!

## Expressing frustration, anger and outrage in safe and healing ways

How then can we express frustration, anger and outrage in safe and healing ways?

1. **Not being willing to judge ourselves when we are expressing it.** If we are thinking or saying, "I shouldn't be feeling this," or "I'm a terrible person for feeling this," it's unlikely that we will experience the healing effects of feeling and expressing these feelings.
2. **Not being willing to blame or judge another**, unless we are sharing these thoughts with someone who has agreed to listen to us, such as a *Listening Partner*, and we are expressing these blaming and judging thoughts as part of the process of releasing the fight energy of these feelings.
3. **Not being willing to physically damage items – and offering ourselves a *Loving Limit* (or asking another adult to offer us a *Loving Limit*) if we are tempted to do this**. That can literally be the inner version of what we might say to a child. "I see that you want to throw the phone, and because I'm here to keep everyone

safe and protect our belongings, I'm not willing for you to do that. And I'm here and listening." This helps us feel safe.

4. **Expressing the energy of the feeling in a way that brings relief and power through making noise**. That might be making a noise like, "Grrrrrr," or, "Raaaaaaa," or growling, while making sure our throat is open, our feet are firmly on the floor, and we're feeling connected with the sensations in our bodies.

5. **Moving our body in ways that support the release of feelings and energy and in ways that help us experience being powerful**, such as stamping our feet on the floor, or pushing the palms of our hands into a wall.

**Note:** Just as with children, simply hitting a pillow doesn't usually release the energy and feelings for many people. It can just continue the fight response, rather than moving into the release. It's also because the expression after the fight or flight response is emotional as well as physical, because we need to let out the feelings that we felt at the time, not just the physical tension that was mobilised to flight or flee.

6. **Naming the feeling we're feeling**, eg. "I am feeling SOOOOOOO frustrated and outraged right now."

7. **Expressing what it is that we are saying no to**, eg. "I do NOT want that! I have a NO for that! I am NOT WILLING for that."

---

*Self-Reflection Moment*

*How do you feel when you read this?*

*Have you experienced expressing frustration, anger or outrage in any of these ways?*

*If so, did you experience that as expressing and releasing the feelings? Did you feel relieved afterwards?*

*How would you like to express your frustration, anger or outrage in safe and healing ways?*

*What will help you be more likely to be able to do that?*

> *Are you willing to do any of those things that will help over the upcoming days?*
>
> *What support do you need to do that?*

## Modelling the safe and healing expression of frustration, anger and outrage to our child/ren

Older children or teenagers might feel quite comfortable seeing us express the feelings in the ways I outlined in the section above. However, younger children might feel scared seeing and hearing them, for example if we make loud noises or stamp our feet.

> A safe way to model this to younger children might be to say something like, "I'm feeling really angry right now. My feelings are not your fault and not your responsibility. I am going to go and share those feelings with my *Listening Partner* so that I feel calmer again and so I don't do anything I would regret."

***For children of all ages, hearing us express the name of how we are feeling is helpful. If we feel frustrated and aren't expressing it, our children will be able to sense that. Naming our feelings, eg."I'm feeling frustrated right now," can help them trust their internal barometer.***

Other actions that really help our children at these times:

- telling them that they are not *responsible* for our feelings, nor for looking after us, nor for listening to our feelings; and
- showing them that when we feel those feelings, *we reach out* for listening from another adult and express those feelings in safe and healing ways.

There are other ways we can express these feelings when we are with younger children so that they don't feel scared. One of those is through *attachment play*.

We could say, "I'm feeling frustrated, and I'm going to play being a frustrated lion. Would you like to be a frustrated lion too?" And then you could move around the room stamping your feet together and making lion roaring sounds.

Another way can be with nonsense play. If you're feeling frustrated, you could say, "Let's pretend I'm a grumpy mummy and I am stamping around the kitchen! I'm a grumpy mummy! I'm a grumpy mummy!"

In this way, *attachment play* can also help us release some frustration so it is less likely to boil over in ways we don't want.

Sian shared:

*"I've decided to start using blowing raspberries as my stress default. Every time I'm feeling angry, upset, hurt, overwhelmed, tense, and in particular when I feel the urge to yell or threaten or lecture... I am inserting raspberries! The more stress, the more raspberries! I'm finding this manages to diffuse almost any situation (both with my children and even just with myself!). No matter what is going on we all seem to end up rolling in laughter and giggles (and a good deal of spit when my four year old gets really excited). I've found this a really awesome way to insert more ease, joy and laughter in stressful moments and we're all more open to a more peaceful discussion afterwards."*

**In this way, we can release some of the frustration, but in a way that is playful and non-frightening for our child. If they laugh when we are doing that, they are releasing light feelings of fear.**

If we *do* express our frustration, anger or outrage either in front of our children or towards our children in ways that are frightening for them, or even if we blame them or make them responsible, we can still repair.[27]

---

27  I talk about repair in more detail later in the book.

We can:

- *Refrain* from judging ourselves;
- *Acknowledge* – "I really regret that I said that to you, because I value taking responsibility for my feelings so you feel safe with me";
- *Explain* – "I had some big feelings";
- Take *responsibility* – "You didn't cause them. My feelings are my responsibility";
- Offer *empathy* and listen –"Did you feel scared? I'm here and listening to how you feel"; and
- Offer *attachment play*. Often, power-reversal games are helpful. So, if we spoke loudly to them, we might want to offer a game where they shout loudly and we fall over each time they do, or they shout and chase us around the house and keep on catching us, or they shout and we jump in the air with mock-fright when they do!

> *Self-Reflection Moment*
> 
> *How would you like to model the safe and healing expression of frustration, anger and outrage to your child/ren?*
> 
> *What do you need in order to be able to do that?*
> 
> *Are you willing to bring more of whatever that is into your life in the next few weeks?*

### To your inner children

*Hello, little you!*

*I'm sending you love and compassion for every time that your frustration, anger or outrage was judged, shut down or shamed.*

*I acknowledge that the people around you didn't understand that there is nothing wrong with your anger.*

*I'm so sad that you didn't have people around you who felt really comfortable with your anger.*

*There is nothing wrong with your anger, sweetheart.*

*There is nothing wrong with you when you feel angry, either.*

*It's the role of the adults around you to keep you and others safe when you're angry, and to help you express those feelings in healing ways.*

*I will keep you safe and I will keep myself safe when you are expressing your anger.*

*I'm here to listen.*

*I love you when you're angry.*

*Your anger will not send me away.*

*I will always stay with you when you're angry.*

*Your anger is not too much for me.*

*You are not too much for me.*

*I welcome your anger.*

*I'm here with you.*

*I love you, whatever you feel.*

## Chapter summary

I invited you to connect with how your own frustration, anger and outrage were responded to as a child and to **offer those younger parts lots of compassion**.

We really can **befriend and welcome frustration, anger and outrage in ourselves**, however we were responded to as children.

We talked about the ways we can express frustration, anger and outrage in **safe and healing** ways and then **how we can model the safe and healing expression of frustration, anger and outrage to our child/ren**.

> Your rage
> is beautiful.

## CHAPTER TEN

# *Loving Limits* and holding

**From a child who is antsy, agitated, squirmy or aggressive**
*"I'm feeling uncomfortable in my body.*
*Please understand me.*
*I don't enjoy feeling this way.*
*I don't want to squirm in my chair.*
*I don't want to wriggle around in bed.*
*I don't want to move from one thing to the next.*
*I need your help.*
*I desperately want to feel calm and relaxed.*
*But I can't think myself into feeling calm and relaxed.*
*I need you to listen to the feelings that are making me agitated.*
*I have some really big feelings sitting inside me.*
*They are too big for me to be with on my own.*
*I need your help.*
*Please don't think this is my character or my personality.*
*I'm not 'strong-willed' or 'hyperactive'.*
*I've got lots of big feelings sitting in my body.*
*I'm not doing this on purpose.*
*I'm behaving this way because my body is full of stress.*

*When I keep on doing things that I know you don't want me to do,
I'm not 'pushing the edges' or 'needing boundaries'.
What I really want from you is one of those* Loving Limits, *where you gently stop me from doing that thing, and then listen to the big feelings that I'm holding inside.
Please don't shame me or judge me when I do these things.
When I laugh, I'm not laughing 'at you'. I'm releasing fear and powerlessness.
Please stop my behaviour and listen to my feelings.
I'm longing to feel calm again.
I really want to feel present in my body.
I'm longing to be able to cuddle up with you, and really feel your loving presence.
I really want to be able to feel deeply relaxed in my body and to sleep soundly.
I need your help.
Will you help me?"*

### To a child who is antsy and agitated and squirmy

*"Hello, lovely you!
I see how uncomfortable you're feeling, sweetheart.
I see you moving your body to try to feel more comfortable.
I know that you don't want to be moving from one thing to the next without stopping.
I understand that you don't want to be squirming away from a cuddle.
I get that you don't want to be wriggling around in bed.
I know that you really want to feel calm and relaxed in your body.
I recognise that you're longing to be able to be present.*

*I get that you're longing to gaze into my eyes.*

*I understand that you're longing to feel deeply relaxed so that you can fall into a peaceful sleep.*

*I hear what you're really feeling, sweetheart.*

*I am not willing to label you as a hyperactive child.*

*I know the squirming and agitation is caused by all those feelings you're holding inside.*

*You've been holding them in for so long, sweetheart.*

*I'm here to listen now.*

*I deeply regret all the times I distracted you from those feelings, so that you needed to learn to distract yourself.*

*I can be with your feelings now.*

*I will lovingly say no to you pulling all the books off the shelf, and I will listen to those feelings.*

*I will lovingly say no to you throwing your toys around the room, and I will listen to those feelings.*

*I'm here with you.*

*I'm listening.*

*I'm here to help you feel calm again, sweetheart.*

*I know your true nature.*

*I know who you really are.*

*I know your presence.*

*And I'm here to help you return to that presence.*

*I know how to help you feel connected with yourself again, sweetheart.*

*I'm here to help.*

*I love you."*

### The term *'Loving Limits'*

I created the term *'Loving Limits'* to describe the process already existing in Aware Parenting and I feel so honoured that Aletha Solter was then willing to include it as an official Aware Parenting term to indicate the process she had already described.

> I also love my definition of *Loving Limits*: It's where we say no to the behaviour, and yes to the feelings that are causing the behaviour.
>
> I don't talk about 'setting' *Loving Limits* (but of course, I so support you in using the language that you love). The way I see it, a *Loving Limit* is offered or given[28]. That's simply because, for me, the word 'set' helps me feel a different quality in my body from 'offer,' and the latter helps me feel the kind of open spaciousness and grounded power that I find so helpful when offering *Loving Limits*.

I find that choosing the language we use is one way to support ourselves to be more likely to feel compassionate towards our child and to stay connected with them, as well as staying connected with our true power as parents.

*We each have different interpretations, experiences and memories of words. I invite you to connect in with language that helps you find it easier to stay compassionately connected and emotionally spacious with your child/ren, while also feeling your power in your body (so you're less likely to move into powerlessness and then power-over or aggression and they feel loved and safe).*

---

[28] This is just my own personal take on *Loving Limits*. It's not an official Aware Parenting perspective or language. There is no official language for *Loving Limits* in Aware Parenting.

The practice of *Loving Limits* involves the connectedness that we have already created with the other aspects of Aware Parenting. It's built upon a relationship where connection, presence and emotional safety are prioritised, and where feelings are welcomed.

There are two key places where we might offer a *Loving Limit* to a child who has an accumulation of feelings:

- when they are in some form of *aggression* or *agitation* (eg. hitting, biting, throwing, forcefully taking, pushing, etc.); or
- where they are involved in *suppressing* or *dissociating* from their feelings through *control patterns* (for example, wanting us to read the 15th book in the evening, playing in a repetitive way for the second hour even though they're really tired, or sucking on a dummy/pacifier).

When we offer a Loving Limit, we're expressing in a calm, loving and powerful way that we are saying no the behaviour but we are saying a big wholehearted yes to the feelings that are causing that behaviour in the first place, whether that's an accumulation of feelings in the form of aggression/agitation or suppression/dissociation.

When we offer a *Loving Limit* in response to aggression, we also are doing the minimum necessary to stop that behaviour, so if a child is about to hit, we might put our hand out and stop their hand from hitting, along with, *"I'm not willing for you to hit Susan, because I'm here to keep everyone safe, and I'm right here and I'm listening."*

If they're asking for the 15th book to be read, because they're trying to suppress their uncomfortable feelings, we might say something like, *"I really hear that you want me to read you another book, sweetheart, and I'm not willing to read another one, because I don't think that's the most helpful thing for you right now."*

Whenever possible, it is important to give a child information about why we don't want them to do something. For example, to keep everyone safe in the case of aggression, and because it's not the most helpful thing when it's suppression and dissociation.[29] However, if we continue to repeat the *Loving Limit*, we might not keep repeating the information part.

**With a Loving Limit, *we are not expecting a child to say, "Okay!" and then stop the hitting or the book-asking (or whatever else they're doing in terms of aggression or suppression).***

What we *are* expecting is for all the feelings that have been sitting underneath that behaviour to come bubbling out instead. It's our role to stay with them, offering the *Loving Limit* again if required, and listening lovingly to those feelings that were causing the behaviour in the first place.

Aletha Solter describes two kinds of *Loving Limits*:

- *The first is useful when we need to stop a child from doing something dangerous, destructive or aggressive. We use language and sometimes firm, but gentle, physical restraint, and this* Loving Limit *often helps the child begin to cry.*
- *The other kind is when we choose to put a limit on what we are willing to do with (or for) a child. This second type of* Loving Limit *involves saying no to a child's requests, and this can also give them a pretext to cry.*

There is generally a correlation between these two kinds of *Loving Limits* that Aletha talks about and the key behaviours we might respond to with *Loving Limits*. With aggression or agitation (hyperarousal), we will generally be stopping them from doing something, and with suppression or dissociation, we are more likely to be refraining from doing something ourselves. However, this correlation does not always apply.

---

[29] I'm so grateful to my colleague Joss Goulden, who noted at this point: "So, coming back to the list of three, we are giving information in a *Loving Limit* too."

Offering *Loving Limits* sounds easy, the way I describe it here! So why can *Loving Limits* be so hard for us as parents?

There are many reasons, primarily because most of us didn't experience *Loving Limits* growing up. Instead, it's likely we experienced either a lack of limits or harsh limits.

Parents who hesitate to give *Loving Limits* to stop a child doing something might fear being harsh or controlling, while those who are reluctant to say no to a child's request might be concerned that they are not meeting their child's needs. Both of these experiences can have their origins in the parents' own childhood.

Learning to embody *Loving Limits*, where we feel both loving and powerful, can be quite a journey for most of us. However, when we do really get *Loving Limits*, they can transform our parenting! So, let's dive in deeper.

## Differentiating *limits* from *Loving Limits*

*Loving Limits* aren't simply saying 'no' in a loving way! In Aware Parenting, *Loving Limits* are different from *limits*.

### Limits

*Limits* are when we say that we're not willing to do something, or to continue doing something. Our child might ask us to go to the park, or play a game, or read another story, and we might say no. That's a *limit*. It's primarily about us and our willingness, rather than about them and their behaviour.

And yes, we would express it in a loving way, and they may feel feelings when we say 'no,' and we may offer them empathy when they feel those feelings, but the reason for the limit is *our* feelings, needs or preferences, not their feelings, needs or behaviour.

### Loving Limits

A *Loving Limit* is quite different. We are saying no, but it's not just no to anything. We are saying no to a behaviour that is being caused by accumulated painful feelings. When we say no, we're not just saying no to the behaviour. We're also saying yes to the feelings that are causing the behaviour and we're saying yes to their needs for support to express those feelings.

So the impetus for us to offer the *Loving Limit* is their behaviour – and their need for support to express the feelings that are causing the behaviour – and to have those emotions lovingly heard. The cause is not our feelings, needs or preferences.

So it is not just a no. In essence, it is a no and a yes.

The NO is always in service of the YES.

The YES is our willingness to:

- really *understand* what is going on for them;
- *create* a safe space for them to express their feelings in healing ways;
- *listen* to our child's feelings;
- offer them *unconditional love*, whatever they feel or do.

## What are *Loving Limits*?

When we offer a *Loving Limit*, we are saying a loving NO to the behaviour and a loving YES to the underlying feelings that are causing the behaviour in the first place.

In our nonverbal behaviour and our language, we communicate a deep sense of unconditional love to our child, while also offering a clear limit to their behaviour.

*Loving Limits* are given when we're saying no to a behaviour that is caused by painful accumulated feelings when our child has been in fight, flight or freeze (hyperarousal or dissociation) and hasn't yet completed the process of returning to homeostasis.

> The *Loving Limit* helps them feel and express those feelings and thus complete that process, so they can come out the other side, into a state of calm presence.

The loving 'no' of the *Loving Limit* is so powerful, because when we lovingly stop the behaviour from a place of willingness to listen to the feelings underlying it, they can then feel safe to express those feelings in healing ways.

The loving 'yes' of the *Loving Limit* is vital too, because it is through listening to the feelings and supporting the movements that go with them that we help our children to return to feeling much calmer again in their bodies, more connected with themselves, us and others.

This is literally a pairing of two things: *loving empathy ('I see that you're upset; I see that you really want that; I'm here, I love you, I'm listening; I regret that I wasn't here to help.")*.[30]

And *the limit ("I'm not willing for you to have any more, sweetheart; I'm not willing for you to do that, my lovely; I'm not willing to give you any more right now,")* all in a loving and connected tone of voice.

> *Loving Limits* are compassionate, calm and clear, without judgment, shaming or punishment.

---

[30] As stated before, there are many ways we can express *Loving Limits*. The language used here is simply my preference, and I invite you to find your own.

**What do *we* need so that we are able to offer *Loving Limits*?**
We need:

- to be able to clearly *embody* and *express* the no;
- to have the *emotional* spaciousness and compassion to be with the underlying feelings; and
- the ability to *continue* to offer the limit and listen to the feelings, even if they are *continuing* to do the thing that led us to offer the *Loving Limit* in the first place.

## *Loving Limits* can exist along a spectrum.

On one end we could express a simple and loving, *"No, sweetheart."*

Next on the spectrum might be a *Loving Limit* to stop a *control pattern* such as sucking on a dummy.

Then might come a *Loving Limit* in response to aggression.

And next may be a physical *Loving Limit* in response to aggression, including *holding*.

Loving Limits are the epitome of the practice of the *balance of attention*, with the love, presence and emotional safety on one side, and the limit on the other.

## With the *balance of attention*, our aim is to find that exact point where the most healing tears or raging happen, with the minimum amount of limit.

We will talk more about the *balance of attention* later in the book.

## When can we use *Loving Limits*?

We generally use *Loving Limits* when our children are doing things that are caused by painful accumulated feelings, ie. agitation or aggression (hyperarousal), or suppression or dissociation.

Up until now, we've categorised the behaviours we can respond to with *Loving Limits* into two categories (accumulation/aggression, and suppression/dissociation). Now, I'm going to dive in deeper, and widen that to three main forms (by dividing up accumulation and aggression).

1. in response to *accumulation/agitation*;
2. in response to *suppression/dissociation*;
3. in response to *aggression*.

Although the *Loving Limits* in the three of these have the same underlying principles, we will tend to offer them in different ways in each category.

### 1. Accumulation and agitation

When a child has accumulated feelings, they feel agitated. This agitation makes it hard for them to cooperate, concentrate, sit still, make eye contact, or feel relaxed enough to go to sleep and stay asleep.

> Agitation is really uncomfortable. They don't want to be feeling agitated, nor do they want to be moving from one thing to the next, not be able to sit still, and be unable to go to sleep.

When a child has accumulated feelings and they are agitated, we can literally see that in their body.

They might:

- be *running* around all over the place (this can also indicate part of the fight or flight response);
- *never* sit still;
- be *climbing* on the table when dinner is being served; or
- keep *jumping* up out of bed.

***They want to feel calm and relaxed as much as we want them to feel calm and relaxed! So, their innate wisdom will keep on trying to release those feelings.***

*They will do that through:*

- asking for *one thing after the next*, but still being antsy or whiny or agitated, because what they are really asking for is a *Loving Limit*;
- doing things that *they know we don't want them to do*, because they are wanting a *Loving Limit* so they can let the feelings out; and
- having *a big reaction over a small thing*; for example, if we cut the sandwiches into squares, they might say they want triangles and keep asking for them.

In each case, we can offer the *Loving Limit*, so that they can experience what they were actually needing, which is to express the feelings causing the agitation – which are getting in the way of them being able to concentrate, cooperate and sleep.

### The process of the *Loving Limit*

### Love

We can offer them connection, closeness and empathy: moving close, offering eye contact and warmth. If they are asking for one thing after the next, but still being antsy or whiny or agitated, we can say, *"I really hear that you want that, sweetheart."*

I recommend offering the *Loving Limit* as soon as you realise that is why they're asking for one thing after the next, before you end up feeling frustrated and are beyond the point of being able to offer a *Loving Limit* (because you're not feeling calm and compassionate enough any more)!

### Limit

If they are asking for one thing after the next, but still being antsy or whiny or agitated, we might then say, *"...and I'm not willing for you to have that,"* or *"I'm not willing to do that right now, sweetheart"*. It's generally helpful to give children information and include the reason why.

With suppression and agitation, that might be, *"...because I don't think that's the most helpful thing for you right now."*

### Listen

Because the behaviour was being caused by painful feelings, we are aiming for the feelings to come out, and they might do so along with words like, *"I really want it. That's not fair!"*

We can keep on listening, and offering empathy, *"I really hear that you want it, sweetheart, and that you think it's not fair. I'm here and I'm listening."*

### 2. Suppression/dissociation/control patterns

We can also offer *Loving Limits* when a child is trying to suppress feelings with a *control pattern* – when they want us to read them the tenth book despite being really tired, or they keep thinking of something else that they want just before bed.

*Control patterns* include things like: wanting screens when upset, a dummy or pacifier, clutching on to a soft toy, or anything that is being used to suppress the painful feelings that are sitting just below the surface. We will be diving in deeper to *control patterns* in Chapters 12 and 13.

> When a child is suppressing feelings, there isn't generally a huge urgency for us to stop the behaviour like there is with aggression (where we of course want safety), so I find that offering the connection and empathy before the limit is most helpful.[31] This is because the warmth that we bring helps create the emotional safety for the feelings to unfreeze, and for a child to be more likely to be able to move out of the mildly dissociated state and into the feelings.

So, we might say something like, *"I see that you want 'xyz', sweetheart, and I'm not willing for you to have that/do that, because I don't think that's the most helpful thing for you right now. And I'm here and I'm listening."*

The reason for the *Loving Limit* is to help the feelings that are sitting underneath that *control pattern* to be expressed, which will vary, depending on how often the suppression has been going on and how much it is used. In general, I recommend *Loving Limits* being the third thing that we do, after connection and *attachment play* (see below). Similarly with accumulated feelings and agitation, I would also generally recommend bringing in connection and *attachment play* first.

### First, connection

That might be coming close to them, getting down to their level, aiming to make eye contact, using gentle touch and a warm tone of voice. The more we can communicate our love for them, and our compassionate understanding of why they are suppressing their feelings, without any hint of judgment of them or of the ways they are doing that, the more

---

31  Please note that this is just my personal preference.

likely it is that they will feel the safety to express those feelings to us instead. If they are wanting their dummy/pacifier, we might say, *"I really hear that you want your dummy/pacifier, sweetheart."*

### Then *attachment play*

I'll be sharing more about what kinds of *attachment play* you can use with suppression in the chapter on *control patterns* (Chapter Thirteen). We can find specific ways to play with each form of suppression. With a pacifier/dummy, we might get another one and keep hiding it behind the sofa, making a big 'POP!" sound each time we find it.

### Then a *Loving Limit*

This is when you might say, *"I see you want to have your pacifier/dummy, sweetheart, and I'm not willing for you to have it right now, because I don't think it's the most helpful thing for you."*

### Then offer more empathy and listen to the feelings

*"...and I'm right here, and I'm listening."*

They might keep asking for the thing, and again, we can keep on repeating the *Loving Limit*, offering lots of empathy: *"I so hear how much you want your dummy/pacifier, lovely. And I'm not willing for you to have it for now. I'm here with you. I'm listening. I love you."* After we've given the information about why once, we will probably not need to give it again, but as always, please listen to yourself and your child here.

### 3. Aggression

Hitting, pushing, taking or throwing generally tell us that a child has painful accumulated feelings, often related to fear, powerlessness or frustration, or they're in fight or flight mode. They do not want to be acting in those ways, just like, if we get harsh with our child, we don't want to be acting in that way. They are communicating to us that they don't feel safe and they need our help.

The more we can get there *before* they hit, bite, push, throw or take, the more helpful it is for them, because if they do any of those things, it's likely that they will have additional extra painful feelings added to those already there. These will be as a result of seeing the pain and shock of the recipient, as well as any judgment or shaming from others which they may also internalise and do to themselves too.

## Being the recipient of a *Loving Limit* as an adult when we're about to move into aggression

Imagine if you had had a really hard day, and were feeling really stretched, and your child asked you to get them yet another snack when you were right in the middle of putting out the washing.

Imagine you were just about to say or do some things to them that you would later regret, and at that moment, an adult who you knew really well – and whom you felt a deep sense of emotional safety from – came close to you, put their hand on the small of your back with deep loving presence, and said, *"I'm not willing for you to speak to them like that, because I'm here to keep everyone safe. I'm right here and I'm listening. I welcome all your feelings."*

> *Self-Reflection Moment*
>
> *What do you imagine might happen?*
>
> *Would you breathe a sigh of relief?*
>
> *Might you burst into tears?*
>
> *Would you start telling them about how frustrated you feel, or how hard things have been for you?*
>
> *Perhaps you'd start raging at them?*
>
> *Does this change anything about your perception of Loving Limits?*

## Putting ourselves in our child's shoes

Imagine you're five years old, and you've had a really big day. You went to school, even though you would much prefer to stay at home. You wanted to cry when Dad dropped you off, but your friends laughed when you did that last time, so you hold the tears in and then get a bit of a headache. You are told to sit down to listen to the teacher and you get put beside that girl you don't really like. You know that your teacher won't let you change chairs, so you feel powerless. Ingrid takes your favourite pens, just as you're creating a new picture, and Sam spills her paints on your drawing. You're hungry but you don't get to eat until break time, and then you don't even like the food that you've been given, and it's gone a bit soggy in your sandwich box. Rob has some chocolate in his lunchbox that you would really like, but he laughs when you ask him if you can have some of his and then throws the empty packet at you. Back in class, you need to wee, but the teacher says you have to wait until afternoon break, so you need to tense up your muscles to hold it in, and that hurts. In afternoon lessons you have no idea what the teacher is talking about and you feel confused and overwhelmed. You get asked a question you don't know the answer to and wish you could hide when you see your teacher's face and the other children's laughter. Your feet hurt in your new shoes, your waistband is too tight, the temperature of the classroom is all wrong and there's a funny smell. When your dad comes to pick you up, your big brother is talking to him, and you don't get a word in edgeways. You get home, and start to do do a jigsaw puzzle and your little sister comes along and treads on the puzzle and it all breaks apart, and you move forwards, about to push her over.

I'm going to offer three different scenarios about what could happen next, and I invite you to connect in with how you might feel, and what conclusions you might make about yourself.

Dad: *"That's not okay! Be gentle, you know we don't hit in our family! It's not nice to push, you know that!!"*

> *Self-Reflection Moment*
> How would you feel?
> What conclusions would you make about yourself and your dad?

Dad: *"NO! Don't you dare do that to her! What is WRONG with you today?"*

> *Self-Reflection Moment*
> How would you feel?
> What conclusions would you make about yourself and your dad?

Dad: (moving in between you and your sister, gently but clearly holding your hand so you aren't able to push or hit) *"I'm not willing for you to hit your sister, because I'm here to keep everyone safe. I'm right here, sweetheart and I'm listening. I'm here with you both."*

> *Self-Reflection Moment*
> How would you feel?
> What conclusions would you make about yourself and your dad?

What would happen if you started crying or raging, perhaps while trying to hit him, and he stayed calm, repeating, *"I'm not willing for you to hurt me, and I'm here with you, sweetheart. I'm listening."*

> *Self-Reflection Moment*
> How would you feel?
> What conclusions would you make about yourself and your dad?

With a *Loving Limit*, we move in to stop hitting, biting, pushing, taking or throwing[32], and lovingly listen to the feelings that were causing the behaviour in the first place.

---

32 Please note that another option with throwing is to offer them soft things to throw safely.

> Children can then move back to natural gentleness without being shamed or punished, knowing that they are unconditionally loved and that their parent is there with them when they need help.

A child who is hitting isn't doing it deliberately.

They:

- are *not* enjoying it;
- *don't* need to learn to be gentle;
- *do* have painful feelings from unhealed stress or trauma.

We can help them stop the hitting, and help them heal from the stress or trauma, through supporting them to express the feelings that hadn't been expressed. The same is the case for pushing, forceful taking, throwing, biting, roughness and many other behaviours.

To repeat, if we are offering a *Loving Limit* in response to aggression, I like to offer the limit first and then give the empathy.

These are the steps I like to offer for aggression and *Loving Limits*, described in further detail below:

1. Move in close.
2. Offer the *Loving Limit* physically.
3. Express the *Loving Limit* verbally.
4. Give information about the reason you don't want the child to take that action.
5. Use supportive language.
6. Be with their feelings.
7. Continue to offer the *Loving Limit* and listen to the feelings.

### 1. Move in close

Closeness is required for the child to feel a sense of connection and physical and emotional safety, which are essential if they are to experience enough emotional presence to feel and express the feelings that are lying underneath the aggression.

### 2. Offer the *Loving Limit* physically. Do the minimum possible to stop the behaviour, ideally before it happens.

If they are about to hit, hold their hand to stop the hitting.

If they are about to throw something, hold the item while it's still in their hand to prevent it from being thrown.

If they are about to take something, hold their hand to prevent that, or hold the item while it's still being held by both of them.

If they are about to bite, putting your hand on their forehead can be a helpful way to prevent the biting.

**I *don't* recommend:**

- holding their hand *roughly*;
- *taking* an item out of their hand (unless absolutely necessary for safety reasons);
- *forcefully* removing an item from them and giving it back to the other child.

### 3. Express the *Loving Limit* verbally

For example, *"I'm not willing for you to hit Susan ..."*

**A note on language:** I'm not suggesting these language choices because there is a 'right' or a 'wrong' way to say things; I'm offering them to contribute you being most likely to be able to offer an embodied *Loving Limit* so your child can stop the behaviour and feel and express the feelings lying underneath!

***As I've shared earlier, I prefer the word 'willing'.***

The reason I enjoy the phrase "I'm not willing..." is because of how I feel in my body when I say it: I experience a grounded strength that is solid but not in a power-over way. The word 'willing' helps me embody the *Loving Limit* and create deep safety.

# I invite you to find a word or phrase that helps you embody the *Loving Limit* when you're expressing it to your child.

I have heard from parents over the years who speak European languages such as French and German that there is no direct translation for the word 'willing'.

Many people who practice Aware Parenting enjoy the phrase, "I don't want you to," especially when talking to young children, since children understand the word 'want' very early in life.

When I offer phrases, I invite you to play with them for yourself. One way of doing that is noticing how you feel in your body when you say that and whether it helps you embody the *Loving Limit*. Another way is to pretend you are a child and tune into how you might feel if you were at the receiving end of these phrases and what would help you feel safe and loved.

Here are suggestions for phrases that we can say when we want to stop a child from doing something, if you'd like some other word ideas in addition to "willing":

- *I'm not willing for you to [fill in verb], because...*
- *I don't want you to [fill in verb], because...*
- *I'm going to stop you from [fill in verb], because...*
- *I don't think it's safe for you to [fill in verb].*

- *I'm holding your hands (or holding you close) so nobody gets hurt.*
- *When you [fill in verb], I'm concerned that… (the window might break, etc…)*

### 4. Give information about the real reason you don't want the child to take that action

To help children understand why we are intervening, we might use phrases such as:

- *"I'm here to keep everyone safe."*
- *"I'm here to protect everyone."*
- *"I'm not willing for anyone to get hurt."*

These statements avoid blame and include the child who is being aggressive in a circle of safety and protection.

> *Self-Compassion Moment*
>
> *I invite you to refrain from judging or shaming yourself if you have spoken phrases that I don't recommend. Doing that is punishing yourself, which you've learnt to do in this culture, but won't help your child or you. You might want to say to yourself, "I'm not willing to judge myself or shame myself. I am willing to be compassionate with myself for all the reasons why I said what I did. And I choose to say the phrases that resonate most for me and that I find most helpful for my child."*

I invite you to see this as an offering for you to connect in with what language resonates with you, and to play with it, and then to make your own choices about the phrases you enjoy.

**More on language:** I prefer *"I'm not willing…"* rather than *"I can't let you…"*

That is because I don't feel a sense of the embodied power of a no if I say, "I can't let you…"

> **Self-Reflection Moment**
>
> *I invite you to do two things while experimenting with different phrases:*
>
> *Feel in to your body and how you feel as a parent saying this phrase. Does it help you embody a Loving Limit?*
>
> *If you imagine being a child and being at the receiving end of this phrase, how do you feel?*
>
> *As a result of this experiment, what phrase would you like to say?*

**What about the phrase:** *"I won't let you..."*

I used to say this to my children, until I realised that, for me, it still had a slight quality of power-over to it rather than the true power I was looking for, and I found that my children were less likely to express their emotions if I said this. They were more likely to move into feelings if I expressed the phrase "not willing" instead. For me, "I won't let you," doesn't have the precise quality of love and power that I am wanting with a *Loving Limit*.

> **Self-Reflection Moment**
>
> *What do you notice in your body as a parent saying this phrase? Does it help you embody a Loving Limit?*
>
> *If you imagine being a child and being at the receiving end of this phrase, how do you feel?*
>
> *As a result of this experiment, what phrase would you like to say?*

**I don't recommend:** *"It's not okay to hit."*

**Why not?**

***For them:*** I perceive this as a judgment and think that a child at the receiving end of this is likely to experience being judged, or feel shame, which again is not what we are wanting here – since we are wanting to offer an environment of unconditional love and emotional safety so that the child feels safe and loved.

***For us:*** If we keep on saying, *"It's not okay to hit,"*, we are likely to get frustrated or angry ourselves if they keep on trying to hit, because it's a judgment, and our feelings are affected by judgments. We're more likely to feel frustrated or angry when we use this phrase. These feelings will not help us offer a true *Loving Limit* that is both powerful and loving.

> *Self-Reflection Moment*
>
> *What do you notice in your body as a parent saying this phrase? Does it help you embody a Loving Limit?*
>
> *If you imagine being a child and being at the receiving end of this phrase, how do you feel?*
>
> *As a result of this experiment, what phrase would you like to say?*

**I also don't recommend:** *"Be gentle!"*

**Why not?**

***For them:*** This assumes that a child is being rough/hitting etc because they don't have the information that this action is not enjoyable – so it doesn't address the real cause of their behaviour and, even if they are able to choose to stop hitting and do so, those feelings will still be held inside, likely to come up again later.

***For us:*** For the same reasons – if we're saying this, at some level, we're thinking that, if we give them the information, they can choose to stop, and if they don't, that they are doing that deliberately, rather than that it is caused by painful feelings that they're not choosing. For this reason, we are also likely to get frustrated or angry if they keep on doing it, which again, isn't going to help the lovingness and emotional safety required for an effective *Loving Limit*.

> **Self-Reflection Moment**
>
> *What do you notice in your body as a parent saying this phrase? Does it help you embody a Loving Limit?*
>
> *If you imagine being a child and being at the receiving end of this phrase, how do you feel?*
>
> *As a result of this experiment, what phrase would you like to say?*

**I also don't recommend:** *"We don't hit in this family."*

**Why not?**

***For them:*** If they have the impulse to hit, or they have already hit, they can feel confused if they hear this phrase. Does it then mean that they are not a part of the family, or that they are not welcome in the family? It also doesn't have the quality of connection that is most helpful for a *Loving Limit*. It can also have a shaming quality to it, and if they feel shame, that may get in the way of them feeling our loving presence required for the healing experience of expressing the feelings that are causing the behaviour.

***For us:*** This is a thought and doesn't connect us with ourselves and our embodied no. Instead, it connects us with our mind. The generality of it and the fact that it is a thought means that if they continue hitting after we say this, we are likely to get frustrated or angry – because they are doing something that is different to what we are thinking about our family. It is less likely to bring healing tears and more likely to bring new hurt.

> **Self-Reflection Moment**
>
> *What do you notice in your body as a parent saying this phrase? Does it help you embody a Loving Limit?*
>
> *If you imagine being a child and being at the receiving end of this phrase, how do you feel?*
>
> *As a result of this experiment, what phrase would you like to say?*

***Another note about language:*** I find that 'I' statements are more likely to create the quality of connection that is most helpful for *Loving Limits*.

For example, "I'm *not willing for you to...*" rather than: "It's *not okay to hit*," or "We *don't hit in our family.*"

Again, I invite you to connect in with this for yourself and see if it resonates.

## 5. Use supportive language

I like to say things like: *"... and I'm here, and I'm listening..."*

I like to include endearments such as, *"lovely"* and *"sweetheart."*

The expression of the words can go together with our warm tone, eye contact, and gentle touch, so that they know that we are there to support them in what they are going through, and that we are willing to listen to their feelings.

> *Self-Reflection Moment*
>
> *What kind of language do you enjoy for Loving Limits?*
>
> *I invite you to write down some examples here that you could use in exact situations with your child.*
>
> *I also invite you to practice saying them out loud at other times, on your own, or with a Listening Partner, counsellor or therapist, or Aware Parenting instructor.*

The more we practice them, the more they can become second nature, and the more likely we will be able to access them – even in highly charged situations.

## 6. Be with their feelings

Once we have stopped the behaviour, and expressed our lovingness and willingness to listen to their underlying feelings, we are inviting them to express those feelings through crying or raging.

Our role is to keep staying calm and offering that warm connection to communicate that we are there with them, keeping everyone safe, and willing to listen to their feelings. So, you might want to remind yourself that one of the main points of the *Loving Limit* is for them to express the feelings underlying the behaviour.

It is normal and natural for them to keep trying to do the thing they were doing.

They might try to *keep on*:

- hitting;
- throwing things;
- taking things; or
- biting.

They might start:

- thrashing around:
- moving around a lot; or
- expressing their feelings in words or sounds.

## 7. Continue to offer the *Loving Limit* and listen to the feelings

Even if they are continuing to do the thing that led us to offer the *Loving Limit* in the first place.

Our role is to:

- stay as *calm* and relaxed as we can;
- keep offering the *Loving Limit*; and
- keep connecting with our *willingness* to listen to the feelings.

This means that we might keep on repeating the same phrase:

*"I'm not willing for you to hit, sweetheart, and I'm right here, and I'm listening."*

*"I'm not willing for you to hit, and I'm here with you. I'm here to keep everyone safe."*

## Remember, they are not continuing to do it because they're not listening to you.

They're doing it because you are saying no to the aggression, which is helping the feelings underlying the aggression to start to bubble out, and along with those feelings can come completion of the fight or flight response.

***I want to remind you that the reason for the* Loving Limit *isn't just to stop the behaviour in the short term.***

So we're not expecting them to say, "Okay," and then feel calm.

The *whole* reason they're doing the behaviour is because of painful feelings.

***So, when we stop the behaviour, in Aware Parenting, we want, and expect, the feelings to come out instead.***

Which means that they might keep on doing whatever they were trying to do. They may also start to tussle, or wriggle, or avoid connection. My invitation is to stay close and stay loving.

The feelings that bubbled up in the hitting are still there, and if they don't let them out, those feelings will still be there, ready to come out at another time. So, if you stop them from hitting, but there is no expression, it is possible that they will come out *again* in hitting, or in some other way. Staying close is a protective and supportive response for them and for whoever else is around.

There's no 'right' or 'wrong' here.

What *might* happen is that they then start tantrumming, raging or crying. *That* is the underlying feelings showing up. That's when we can listen. The more of these feelings they express, the less those feelings will show up in aggression or other behaviours that we don't enjoy.

Or we may not find the *balance of attention* and the crying and raging might not happen. I invite you to refrain from judging yourself or them! You might want to stay close, knowing that those feelings are close to the surface, and be ready to step in again, and ideally prevent anyone from getting hurt.

If there's lots of aggression and you don't seem to be helping your child release those feelings, there can be a couple of things you can do to help:

- move in with *attachment play* when you have a sense that they're about to hit; and
- keep practicing! I found that *Loving Limit*s took a lot of practice to really embody.

**What can we do if we get there after they have already hit, bitten, etc?**

I love a response inspired by Patty Wipfler of Hand in Hand Parenting and Marshall Rosenberg of NVC: "I regret that I didn't get here in time to stop that happening, because I really want you all to be safe."

This puts us in the role of advocate and supporter, taking responsibility as the parent for keeping the children safe, including the child that is doing the hitting. This can bring a great deal of emotional safety and can support the child who has acted aggressively to refrain from picking up shame or guilt sticks themselves.

If the child is trying to continue with the aggression, then we can offer the *Loving Limit* as above.

If the moment of aggression has passed, we can move in and offer empathy to each of the children involved, including the one who has hit. We can share our observations and offer both children support, for example, *"I see that you wanted to use the iPad, Seb, and Johnny, you weren't willing to give it to Seb, and Seb, you then hit Johnny. I'm here to help you both. Johnny, Seb, how are you feeling? I'm here to listen."* We can ask each of them to express their feelings, needs and thoughts, and listen to each other. Once everyone has had their feelings heard, we might ask the one who has done the hitting if they would like to do anything to repair – without inducing shame or guilt and without the expectation of an artificial, "I'm sorry".

## When are *Loving Limits* most likely to 'work'?

- When we already have a foundation of *connection* such as through lots of closeness (remember that attachment-style parenting is the core foundation of Aware Parenting) and regular *attachment play*, particularly *non-directive child-centred play*.
- When we are really able to *embody Loving Limits* – which means that we feel loving *and* powerful – not in a power-over way, but an embodied experience of true power that helps them feel safe.
- When we have available *presence* to listen to the feelings that arise from the *Loving Limit*.
- When we are able to hold in *mind* why our child is behaving as they are, and why we're offering the *Loving Limit*.
- When we're able to be *compassionate* with ourselves in the process if our own feelings bubble up.
- When we are really willing to *listen* to the feelings that arise after a *Loving Limit*.

## When do *Loving Limits* usually not 'work'?

- When we have *avoided* offering a *Loving Limit* for hours, and our child has been running round, throwing things, not cooperating, or doing everything that they know we don't like, and we've reached a peak of frustration. We are unlikely to be able to find that place of love and true power that *Loving Limits* require. That is why I recommend offering a *Loving Limit* as soon as you realise that this is what your child is really needing, so that you are most likely to be feeling compassionate towards them and connected with them.

- If aggression has been going on for weeks or months and we are both feeling *disconnected* from each other. Connection may be too buried for the feelings to flow out easily when the *Loving Limit* is offered.

- When we are *thinking harsh thoughts* about our child or ourselves that get in the way of how much we love them, for example, "He's so rude, he's a bully, he is annoying, he won't ever change, he'll end up a delinquent," or, "She's so manipulative, she's mean, she will never learn, I'm such a terrible parent, I did it all wrong." These painful thought patterns are likely to prevent connection with ourselves and our child.

- When we don't feel connected or *loving* towards our child for other reasons.

- When our child has been experiencing *harsh limits* such as punishment and isn't feeling enough emotional safety yet to express the underlying feelings.

- When we feel *powerless* or *frustrated* or full of *rage* ourselves.

> *Self-Reflection Moment*
> *If you have found that Loving Limits don't tend to lead to healing expression, do you sense that one or more of these is going on?*

> *What do you sense might help?*
>
> *Are you willing to bring more of whatever that is over the upcoming days and weeks?*

## If they aren't 'working', what can we do to build that foundation?

We can try some of the following suggestions.

- Make sure that we're *not* using punishments or other harsh responses to our child.
- Support increased *connection* with our child through more closeness and cuddles.
- Address any harsh judgments that we might be harbouring about our child and their behaviour and replace it with more *compassionate*, Aware Parenting-style thoughts about their behaviour and what they need from us.
- Offer more *choice*, *agency* and *autonomy* to our child.
- Start up a regular *non-directive child-centred play* practice.
- Focus on practicing more of all the forms of *attachment play*, and power-reversal games in particular.
- Share about our *own* feelings with our *Listening Partner*, counsellor or therapist, or Aware Parenting instructor, which might focus on our own aggression as a parent or child, or any aggression we experienced from parents, siblings or other children when we were a child.
- Notice whether we really are offering an *embodied Loving Limit*, or whether we are expressing the love but not the limit, or the limit but not the love.

*Loving Limits* help children release the feelings that sit underneath the agitation, aggression or suppression, that would no doubt be showing up in other areas too. Remember that when a child cries or rages with our loving support, they are healing from stress and trauma. *Loving Limits* are a key part of that process.

Chelsie Spence shares how she effectively used *Loving Limits* with her son in response to his aggression:

*"My three-year-old son, Maximus had progressively become aggressive since the birth of his baby brother Finn, now one. He was aggressive towards Finn and myself, and generally carried a lot of tension in his body, often roaring at us in a tense stance. We started working with Rafa Guadalupe, an Aware Parenting instructor, to address his aggressive behaviour. She broke down the main reason for his aggression being lack of expressing his uncomfortable feelings and stress towards the arrival of his brother.*

*So, we started unraveling Max's pent-up feelings by looking for places where we could place* Loving Limits. *It arrived one day when he asked for a book, the way he asked was tense and demanding so I practiced* Loving Limits *and told him I was not willing to read a book right then. He burst into raging tears and further demands (other books, television, wanting dad, etc). This lasted an hour and throughout I held him or had a hand placed gently on him while speaking loving words.*

*Throughout this time I could feel Max slowly softening into me. Once he had finished his rage he loving looked into my eyes, gently patted my face and asked for a drink.*

*We noticed an enormous impact immediately after this huge release. He spoke and moved more softly and looked brighter and happier. We felt we had been given our boy back, the boy we had always known, who is loving, gentle and kind. It was like our home gave a sigh of relief."*

> *Self-Compassion Moment*
> *How do you feel, having read this information, as well as Chelsie's story? If your child is showing aggressive behaviour, do you believe it's possible to help them stop using Loving Limits? I invite you to reach out for some empathy and listening for whatever feelings are showing up for you. I'm sending you so much love!*

## The *balance of attention*

The *balance of attention* is key to *Loving Limits*. The *balance of attention* is when, on the one side, we are creating and offering emotional safety from our presence, our willingness to listen, and our spaciousness to be with their feelings. On the other side is whatever is helping them revisit and feel the feelings from the past.

A *Loving Limit* that 'works' is the epitome of the *balance of attention*. This means that if the *Loving Limit* didn't lead to feelings being expressed, we can ask ourselves what might we need to do in terms of the *balance of attention*.

Do we need to do more to create *more emotional safety*? Could we try:

- Moving in *closer*?
- *Speaking* more?
- Offering more *endearments*?
- Going for more *eye contact*?
- Connecting in with our *own loving presence* in our body?

Or,

Do we need to do more to help them *revisit the past* and connect with the feelings? By;

- *Repeating* the limit?
- *Changing* the wording or the tone of the limit?
- Checking in if we're feeling an *embodied* 'no'?

I invite you to play with all of this as you develop your own practice of *Loving Limits*.

## Why *Loving Limits* can be so hard for us to offer

### The *Disconnected Domination Culture*

Most of us growing up in this culture haven't experienced being on the receiving end of *Loving Limits*. We've either experienced no limits or harsh limits. So learning to offer and embody *Loving Limits* can be new for most of us.

In our recent history, parenting paradigms have taught parents that if a child is agitated or aggressive, to either turn a blind eye, feel powerless and give up, to try to calm them down, or to get frustrated and use power over, punishment, shame or blame.

***It's quite a practice to be able to offer and keep holding a* Loving Limit *instead. I found that it took me quite a long time to be able to express a powerful and embodied* Loving Limit.**

Here are some more reasons why offering *Loving Limits* can be so challenging for us:

### Old beliefs and judgments

We probably also internalised old *DDC beliefs* about children and humans in general when we were children, and those can emerge when we are feeling frustrated – thoughts such as that children need to be punished in order to be caring and helpful members of society. Old ways of judging children can also arise that we heard as children, such as, "He's a bully!", or "She's manipulative". If we're thinking this, it's going to be hard for us to offer a true *Loving Limit*.

### Our own experiences from the past

We generally haven't experienced *Loving Limits* ourselves as children. For most of us, our parents were either permissive (lots of empathy, not many limits), or authoritarian (lots of limits, not much empathy). In times of stress, we tend to either veer towards what was done to us, or go to the other extreme.

### Our own feelings

When our children are agitated, are suppressing feelings or are aggressive, we can feel deeply frustrated. Our own feelings can get in the way of us feeling loving towards our children. *Loving Limits* require love to work, so if we aren't feeling loving, they generally don't work!

### Thoughts that we told ourselves as children

These can come up, such as, "I can't do this," or, "I have no power." When we're thinking these thoughts, it's going to be hard for us to be connected with our true adult loving *power*, which is necessary for *Loving Limits* to 'work'.

## What shifts might we need to make in ourselves so that we can offer effective *Loving Limits*?

- *Replace old beliefs* that 'limits are inherently punitive' with the knowing that *Loving Limits* are deeply loving and effective because they are responding to the root cause of a child's behaviour.
- *Replace old thoughts* that children need to be taught a lesson when they are aggressive, and instead, to choose thoughts that children really *need our help* when they are being aggressive.

- *Attend to our own healing* from childhood experiences when we were punished and when limits were harsh and painful for us.
- *Heal from our childhood* experiences when our parents were permissive and avoided hearing our painful feelings.
- *Practice Loving Limits* when our child is inviting them, so that we become more comfortable and skilled at offering them.

As always, receiving compassionate, loving support from others can be a vital part of this process.

Karin said this about *Loving Limits*,

*"The shift from, 'I'm saying no so she stops,' to, 'I'm offering a Loving Limit so she can let her feelings out,' has been transforming for my ability to stay calm and loving. And for our relationship. The whole family's relationships!"*

## I would love to invite you to reflect on *Loving Limits* for yourself.

As always, please only do this if you sense enough outer and/or inner availability to be lovingly present with your feelings, and if you're not already overwhelmed, flooded or dissociated from lots of feelings.

---

*Self-Reflection Moment*

*Is there something you're concerned might happen when you offer a Loving Limit?*

*Have you offered your child/ren a Loving Limit?*

*What did you experience in your posture, sensations and feelings when you did?*

*Did you find it hard to offer a Loving Limit?*

*Did you experience feeling both powerful and loving?*

*How would you like to feel when you offer Loving Limits?*

> *What is your next step with* Loving Limits?
>
> *What do you need to support you with that?*
>
> *Are you willing to do whatever that is in the next few weeks?*

## *Holding*

*Holding* is at the most physical end of the spectrum of *Loving Limits*.

*Holding* is a very contentious topic, and I invite you to always listen to yourself in relation to this practice. If you have a *no* to *holding*, I invite you to skip this section.

> I would like to state very clearly that *holding* is a very powerful practice and is only ever to be done with extreme sensitivity, presence and nuance. I recommend only using it as an advanced practice, by someone who is well-versed in all the elements of Aware Parenting and only if you are practicing all the aspects of Aware Parenting. I definitely recommend NOT using *holding* if you are new to Aware Parenting or if you are still using punishments, force or coercion.

*Holding* may be harmful if there is not a deep connection between parent and child and if the parent is using punishments or other forms of harshness towards their child.

As a philosophy based on attunement to a child and their needs, particularly for agency, autonomy and choice, Aware Parenting advocates being very cautious with *holding*.

In addition, I would recommend **not** to practice *holding* if you are feeling powerless, frustrated, angry or outraged. A child is likely to feel scared and to experience being powered-over if we hold them with these feelings. (Unless of course the child is in danger and *holding* would be the only option to keep them safe eg. running into a busy road.)

> *Self-Compassion Moment*
>
> *If you have used* holding *in ways I don't recommend above, I invite you to drop the guilt sticks and be deeply compassionate with yourself. You can help your child/ren heal from those experiences, particularly through power-reversal games, which I talk about more in the chapter on attachment play. You might feel sad and want to express that sadness to your* Listening Partner, *so that you can mourn what you did rather than hit yourself with sticks.*

If you are going to use *holding* at any time, I invite you to check in with yourself before and during the process, to see whether you are feeling calm and present and are doing this from a place of compassion for your child.

## Given all of these caveats, what IS *holding*?

*Holding* is when we hold our child as the limit part of a *Loving Limit*. In the *holding*, we might stop them from moving away from us if they are about to do something dangerous, such as running towards a cliff or a busy road, or we might hold part of their body, for example, if they are kicking us or another child, we might hold their feet or legs to stop the kicking.

*When might it be used?*

*Holding* is generally for situations where a verbal *Loving Limit* or one with minimal physical contact (eg. *holding* a child's hand to stop them from hitting) is not enough to prevent the behaviour. For example, if a child is continuing to hit, bite, push, throw or cause physical harm to other people, themselves or objects in other ways.

With *holding*, we are providing more containment than with a verbal *Loving Limit*. It not only stops the behaviour, but also can provide *more of a safe container* for the feelings to emerge. Sometimes children have a lot of big unexpressed feelings of *deep rage or terror* that require more containment for them to be expressed.

We can sometimes see a similar picture when a toddler is in a car seat and starts crying strongly. It can be that the car seat can help them connect with and express memories of their time in utero or during their birth. (Although, it's important to check that it isn't because of their unmet needs for agency, autonomy and connection.)

With *Loving Limits*, the aim is to use the *minimum* limit to support both safety and the expression of the feelings. The same is true of *holding*. If a child is running around, pulling things off shelves and throwing things, we might bring them into our loving arms and hold them to stop them doing those things.

Initially, they might start to move their arms and legs strongly, pushing against the support of our arms. Remember we talked about the fight or flight response, and how, in moments of stress or trauma, energy is mobilised to move to the arms and legs to either fight or flee? This is often the unexpressed energy that is trying to be released when a child is agitatedly pulling things off shelves or trying to hit their sibling.

> When we offer a loving space for them to push up against, they can truly release that fight or flight energy, so that the feelings, physical tension and stress hormones can literally be freed from their body. So, when we first contain our child, they might kick and push and vigorously move.

***Remember that we are always doing the minimum necessary to support the release. We might find that after a few moments, if we stop holding them, they still keep raging with us.***

However, as with all of Aware Parenting, we can keep connecting in with ourselves, and keep observing them, and take our next actions as a result.

You might feel concerned that you are not meeting your child's needs for agency, autonomy and choice. I want to tell you that, for every parent I have ever worked with about *holding*, that concern has come up.

**And I'm so glad that it does.**

**OF COURSE** we never want to inflict harm by using power-over our child. Meeting children's needs for agency, autonomy and choice and using non-punitive discipline are part of the core aspects of Aware Parenting.

SO, if you **EVER** feel concerned about what you are doing, **PLEASE STOP.**

**PLEASE DO NOT EVER** do *holding* because you think you should or because someone told you to, or because you are reading about it here.

More than almost any other element of Aware Parenting, I believe that it is **VITAL** that you listen to yourself in relation to *holding*.

## I would like to say it again.
## If you ever feel unsure, please STOP!

And if you do find yourself habitually using *holding* to help your child cry, or you feel frustrated or angry when you do, I invite you to reach out to an Aware Parenting instructor for help *as soon as possible*.

Remember, Aware Parenting is all about *observing your child* and staying *deeply connected with yourself*, and these are particularly important if you're considering *holding*.

I'll give you an example. Let's say Amber is clearly agitated. She's running around with other children, pushing and hitting them, taking things from them, pulling things off shelves and throwing things.

From an Aware Parenting perspective, this isn't a 'strong-willed' child. This is a child who has some big feelings bubbling, is in fight or flight (hyperarousal), and who needs the help of an adult to feel safe. We might move in close and offer a *Loving Limit* when she's about to hit another child. We might hold her hand and say, *"I'm not willing for you to hit Susan, because I'm here to keep everyone safe, and I love you and I'm here and I'm listening."*

However, if she starts kicking Susan, we might then move in with *holding*. We might say something like, *"I'm not willing for you to kick Susan. I'm going to hold you to stop you from kicking her. I'm here with you. I'm listening. I love you."*

And then we might hold her in a way that prevents her from hitting or kicking others. She might start raging, kicking her legs out, flailing her arms around and sweating. Remember the fight or flight response? This looks like the energy from that being released, doesn't it? Imagine that terror, that powerlessness, that rage, all coming out. That is what is going on here.

> I see this process as like a fine-tuned partner dance. So the *holding* isn't rigid and hard. It's *fluid* and *responsive*, *attuned* and deeply *connected*.

Imagine salsa dancing, and the amount of responsiveness required. This is what is required in *holding*, so we are not overpowering our child. We're deeply listening to what is going on for them in their body and we're responding to that.

So, we might *loosen* our hold and then *observe* her.

Amber might continue raging and crying, still pushing up against us, even though she can easily jump down and run off. She might move away, and then start throwing and hitting again. She might move away but then come back again. She might actually ask for us to hold her again, often in a non-verbal way, eg. she might get back into the same position and move our hand to the same position. In each case, I would invite you to respond in the most attuned way.

If she continues raging and crying without *holding*, simply stay present with her, offering loving words. Obviously, no *holding* is required, because she's expressing the feelings underlying the agitated and aggressive behaviour and is not using aggression any more.

If she moves away and starts throwing and hitting again, you might move back in with a *Loving Limit*, and then *holding* if the *Loving Limit* alone is not enough to stop the behaviour.

If she comes back and asks to be held, then you might return to *holding* again.

As always, I invite you to keep experimenting and observing.

As well as observing and connecting in with your own body, there are other things you can do to meet your need for reassurance that this is helpful rather than harmful.

Once she is raging, you could let go but just hold on to her clothing between your finger and thumb. Sometimes we can shift the focus so that the pretext for the release gets associated with something else. So, she might continue raging hard, but it's all focused towards you holding her t-shirt. Or perhaps she wants to leave the room that you're both in, so you could offer a *Loving Limit* about her leaving the room. Perhaps you might sit down on the floor at the door, with an, *"I hear that you want to go out, sweetheart, and I'm not willing for that right now because I don't think that's the most helpful thing for you. I'm here and I'm listening."* She might then continue raging in response to that *Loving Limit*, pushing against the door, *without* you needing to hold her for the feelings to be released.

## With holding, *it's important to always do the least necessary to hold the limit.*

During *holding*, children can have *really big* feelings emerge. If you're still feeling a yes to continue, you might see that. You might even find yourself thinking about your child's birth, or if they've had any medical procedures, you might find yourself remembering those. You can trust that you are picking up on what they are healing from. *Holding* can provide the closeness and safety for terror, powerlessness and rage from the past to be felt and expressed, such as from when a child was in a similar physical position.

That might be while they were in the *womb* and there were stressful or traumatic events going on. That might be during their *birth*, with the titanic forces they were moving through. That might be past experiences of being *constrained*, such as if they experienced medical or dental procedures or were held down and tickled.

It can also help them reconnect with experiences of *powerlessness*, such as being left alone to cry, being left at kindergarten when they didn't want to be, and so on.

**Remember that the key to healing from stress and trauma is for the experience to be similar in some way to the past so that the child can revisit it, but this time they are safe and powerful in the present and get to complete what they didn't complete. The vigorous movements**

**of their arms and legs and loud vocalisations are all part of that completion process. They are getting to do what they didn't do the first time around and be lovingly heard while they do that. Sweating can also be a part of that release process, as can tears.**

*Again, I want to say that it is totally normal and natural to feel scared if you ever do this, and if you do ever feel scared, please stop. Most of us have never experienced this type of* **holding.**

However, if you *have* done any kind of processes where you were held while you raged, you might have an embodied experience of the kind of safety that *holding* can offer when used in alignment with all the precautions we've named above.

If the *holding* is being done in the spirit and presence I am talking about, a child might express really big feelings and movements, and then, while still being held in exactly the same way, they might move into sadness and sobbing, and then they come out the other side of the expression, in a very different feeling state.

They might then feel deeply relaxed in their body,
in ways that we can clearly feel in feeling their muscles.
The tension has all gone.

They might snuggle in with you while you are *holding* them in *exactly the same position* as you were before. This can be particularly important evidence that the *holding* was acting as a safe container, and now the feelings have been released, the *holding* is a cuddle.

You might hear some big sighs from them and you might see that they feel a huge sense of relief. Their face might look clear, even luminous. They might gaze into your eyes and tell you how much they love you. They might get up and move around the space in a completely different way. With so much less tension, but not in numb or a dissociated way, but with an alive, embodied sense, and with much more presence.

This is the power of *holding*, when practiced with deep awareness, nuance and subtlety.

**This is how you can tell that it was helpful, not harmful – through observing them before, during and after.**

For some children, especially if they have experienced birth trauma or a long birth or medical interventions, *holding* can be transformative. Children can move from a general deep agitation, aggression and challenges going to sleep and staying asleep, as well as pushing away connection and closeness, to feeling deeply relaxed in their body, connected and calm.

> The purpose of *holding* is to create connection and emotional safety. Crying is not the aim. Crying is the natural, spontaneous by-product when the child feels safe. The message that we want to convey is that our connection with them is stronger than their anger, that there is room in our relationship for their deepest, most painful, emotions, and that nothing can destroy the bond. We want our child/ren to know that there is plenty of room in our relationship for their painful feelings.

Aletha Solter does not recommend *holding* on a regular basis, regardless of the child's behaviour. In her book, *Tears and Tantrums* (page 145), she recommends *holding* primarily for when children are behaving in harsh or aggressive ways *"and cannot seem to reach the point of crying without some assistance."*

If you've ever tried *holding* and have been concerned about how it was for your child, I would recommend offering them lots of agency and choice, and lots of power-reversal games. In that way, if they did ever feel powerless, you can help them heal from that experience. I would also highly recommend having a consultation with an Aware Parenting instructor to get clear about what happened and what might be most helpful moving forwards.

So, in summary, *holding* is an incredibly powerful practice that can be transformative to children who are extremely agitated or aggressive, to help them heal from past stress and trauma. However, it is to be used with **great caution** only when we are feeling calm, and only in conjunction with all the other elements of Aware Parenting. There are many children and families where we would recommend *never* using *holding*.

I also *highly recommend* receiving support from an Aware Parenting instructor if you are wanting to implement *holding*.

> *Self-Reflection Moment*
>
> *How do you feel, having read this?*
>
> *If you ever experienced physical power-over in the form of being tickled by a sibling, being punished physically, or your own birth experiences or medical interventions were traumatic, those can show up if we contemplate holding.*
>
> *Have you experienced any of these and do you have a sense that they are coming up when you think of this topic?*

If you do ever contemplate *holding*, I think it is vital to be receiving emotional support and empathic listening yourself, as always with a *Listening Partner*, counsellor or therapist, or Aware Parenting instructor.

**From a child:** *Please help me. I can't stop hitting. I feel a wild energy in me and I want to destroy everything I see. I'm a raging tornado, destroying everything in my path. You come close, Mum, and I really want you to help me, even though I'm still a tornado trying to destroy you too. I feel so wild. I want to destroy. I lash out and hit you. My body is the wild wind. I keep trying to hit you, and you hold my hand and do that* Loving Limit *thing. That's not enough, Mum, not enough. I'm too big and wild and strong for that to stop me. I want to wreck everything. I can't stop. Oh you come close and you hold me. I fight at first, because I start to feel more feelings in my body when you do that. I'm scared, Mum. These feelings are so big. Will I be okay? Am I safe? Will I destroy everything? I'm still fighting you, but I can feel you there, like a strong brick house, not moved by the tornado. It changes to a storm. The wind rages around, but there's ground now. I can feel you. I feel safe. But still SO ANGRY. Why do you spend so much time with Savannah? I know she's my sister and all that, but DON'T YOU LOVE ME ANY MORE? I'm soooo mad. I NEED YOU! Oh, the storm changes, the wind turns to rain. The tears fall. I feel so, so sad, Mum. I miss you. I'm getting bigger and the world is so confusing and I just want to cuddle up with you like how things used to be. I want you to love me like you love Savannah. I cry and I cry and you hold me. I can feel the warmth of your arms around my back. I can feel the warmth of you all around me as I sit on your lap. My tears and snot go all over your top. Ahhh, the storm is dying down now. Wow. I feel so different. I can look around me and see you clearly. The world looks all fresh and new after lots of rain. You hold me and I melt into your hug. I feel our hearts beating together. I love you, Mum. We stay like this for a really long time. I feel so relieved. I could drift off to sleep like this...*

## Chapter summary

***Loving Limits*** **are when we say no to the behaviour and yes to the feelings underlying the behaviour.** We can use them in response to accumulation, suppression and aggression.

*Loving Limits* can be so hard for us because most of us grew up without experiencing them. **However, we can learn to embody *Loving Limits* so that you feel both loving and powerful and so that your child feels loved and safe.**

I invite you to connect with the **language that most helps you to embody *Loving Limits***.

***Holding*** **is one form of *Loving Limits* that requires particular awareness, presence and nuance,** and is certainly **not** for everyone.

> I so celebrate any willingness you have
> to deepen your practice of *Loving Limits*.

CHAPTER ELEVEN

# The *balance of attention*

## The importance of the *balance of attention* in Aware Parenting

The more you understand the *balance of attention*, the more you will know what is going on for your child in any situation where they have painful feelings to express and will know what actions you can take to maximise the healing and relaxation process.

The *balance of attention* is key to understanding the process of healing from stress or trauma through *attachment play* and connected crying and raging.

The *balance of attention* is the exact balance that we create by on the one side, offering our loving presence and creating emotional safety – and on the other, helping our child stay connected with the feelings from the past when they were scared, sad or angry.

So much of what we are doing as parents is aiming either to increase the presence that we are offering so that our child feels safe enough to heal through play, laughter, crying or raging – or, helping them stay connected with the feelings from the past. When we find that exact *balance of attention*, the laughter and play pour out. The tears flow out. The rage rushes out. The feelings are big and loud. There's a quality of ease in the whole process and our child comes out the other side, calm, connected and clear.

If your child is constantly sucking their thumb or a dummy, or they keep on asking for the iPad whenever they're upset, it's the *balance of attention* that you may be looking for, so that they can express their feelings through crying with your loving support instead.

If your child keeps on hitting, throwing, taking or pushing, then you are being invited to play with the *balance of attention*, so that they can move into expressing healing tears and raging.

When parents really understand the *balance of attention*, that is often when they experience their own true power and authority as a parent, because they know exactly what they can do to support their child to heal. I would love for you to feel that sense of confidence in understanding the theory of Aware Parenting, being able to hold in mind the *balance of attention*, and always coming back to listening in to yourself and observing your child.

## What is the *balance of attention*?

The *balance of attention* is a cornerstone of the 'healing from stress and trauma' aspect of Aware Parenting. The *balance of attention* is when a child reconnects with the feelings from a past experience which was emotionally painful, stressful or traumatic for them while at the same time experiencing emotional safety in the present. The *balance of attention* is necessary for healing emotional release to occur, whether that is through laughter and play or crying or raging.

So many of the questions parents ask about Aware Parenting can be answered for themselves when they deeply understand the *balance of attention*.

If a parent is wanting to help their child to heal from stress or trauma through laughter, crying or raging, and they are doing all that they can to support that, either though offering *attachment play*, their loving presence, or a *Loving Limit*, and the healing laughter, crying or raging is not happening, this can often be because the *balance of attention* isn't there.

## What do we need to provide the *balance of attention*?

On the one hand, we need to communicate to our child a profound sense of emotional presence and safety. This is why our own inner work is so vital and is one of the reasons why I talk about it so much!

A child is *less* likely to experience that deep sense of emotional safety if we are:

- *judging them*, through thinking harsh thoughts about them and their behaviour;
- *judging ourselves*, and feeling either guilt (telling ourselves we've done something wrong), or shame (telling ourselves that there's something wrong with us);
- feeling painful feelings from our *unmet needs* (such as frustration, agitation, resentment, sadness, desperation or exhaustion);
- feeling *painful feelings* from our own *childhood* eg. scared, confused, overwhelmed, powerless, or outraged;
- *distracted* and thinking about all the other things we need to do;
- *dissociated* or disconnected from our body and feelings.

> *Self-Compassion Moment*
> *I invite you to be deeply compassionate with yourself here and to drop any sticks that you might be tempted to pick up! It's so normal for us to do all of these things a lot of the time, given that we grew up and live in the DDC!*

However, the *more* we receive support and are willing to keep growing in all of these areas, the more we are going to be able to offer that connected presence side of the *balance of attention*.

We will increasingly be able to offer the kind of loving presence that supports them to heal from stress and trauma if we gradually:

- *replace* our judgments of our child and their behaviour with compassionate thoughts about them and why they are doing what they are doing;
- *exchange* our judgments of ourselves and our behaviour with compassionate inner dialogue;
- *value* our needs more and are more willing to get them met;
- *receive* more loving listening externally and internally for our childhood hurts;
- are more able to *focus* on our child even when there are a million other things to do; and
- *receive* more loving support and presence so we can increasingly stay present in our body with our feelings.

> *Self-Compassion Moment*
> *If you feel overwhelmed reading this list, I'm sending loving compassion to the overwhelm. I want to remind you that this process takes time. Each step you take will make a difference.*

What about the other side of the *balance of attention*, where they are reminded of the original painful, stressful or traumatic experience?

Often life events *naturally* and *spontaneously* bring that about.

For example, a child who:

- was *separated* after birth might feel those original feelings when their mum wants to go out and leave them with their dad;
- experienced *medical interventions* after birth might feel powerless when they are in their car seat; or
- had a *frightening experience with a dog* might feel scared every time they see a dog on a cartoon or at the park.

When we understand what is happening at those moments when a child *spontaneously* starts crying big tears with dad, or in the car seat, or when they see a dog, we will be able to continue supporting that *balance of attention* rather than believing that those feelings they are feeling are all about the present.

The *balance of attention* invites us to be deeply *attuned* to our child. This is because it is like a dial on an old-fashioned radio. We can move the dial a very small amount and the music comes through loud and clear. But move it a little way in the other direction, and there's static and buzzing. The *balance of attention* is just like that.

**Our attunement is literally us turning the dial on the radio, fine tuning the connection between ourselves and our child and themselves and their feelings.**

Sometimes we might need to move the dial up towards more *closeness, presence and emotional safety*.

*How can we move the dial more that way?*

We might connect with our own *presence*, our *breathing*, our connection with ourselves, our *willingness* to be deeply connected with our child and to deeply listen. We might move *closer* towards them, we might make more eye *contact*, we might *touch* their hand or hug them, we might call them *endearments* such as, *"Sweetheart,"* and we might express our loving presence to them, for example, *"I love you. I'm here with you. I'm listening. I welcome all of your feelings. I hear how upset you are."*

All of these things can help our child feel *more deeply connected* with us, and that connection brings the emotional safety for them to connect with their body, their sensations, their feelings, and their innate healing processes rather than turning to suppression or aggression.

What if our child clearly has upset feelings but they are needing support to move a little further the other way along the dial?

*How can we move the dial more that in that direction?*

This is where we might *gently draw their attention* to the thing that is helping them feel the feelings from the past.

*Loving Limits* can often be an example of this. For example, say a child keeps asking for things but each time we give them that item, they are still agitated and whining. We might ascertain that rather than having an immediate need, they actually have some pent-up painful feelings. Once we realise this, we might offer a *Loving Limit* to the next request: *"I really hear that you'd like me to make new sandwiches and cut them in triangles rather than squares, but I'm not willing to make another lot, sweetheart, because there isn't much bread left for us all. And I'm here and I'm listening. I really hear how much you wanted them to be triangles. I'm here with you."* The limit part of the *Loving Limit* offers a reminder for the upset feelings that are sitting underneath the agitation.

**As mentioned, life events often bring that other side of the balance of attention, but sometimes we may do specific things that help that happen.**

This example above, with the *Loving Limit* of not making another lot of sandwiches to replace the first ones, might be seen that way. So, if your child clearly has unexpressed painful feelings from daily stresses or larger traumas, and you don't seem to be helping them to express those feelings through *attachment play*, crying or raging, one of the things you could attend to is the *balance of attention*. We will talk more about specific examples of this in the upcoming sections.

> Another way of looking at the *balance of attention* is the 'colder colder, warmer warmer' game. Did you ever play that as a child? In this metaphor, the *balance of attention* is the warmth. The closer a child is to the centre of the feelings, the warmer they are.

An example here is if a three year old has some feelings to express in the evening before going to sleep, but they are moving all around the room, avoiding being present in their body with their feelings. I have spoken to many parents over the years who have shared that it has taken a really long time to help their child to go to sleep in that scenario.

That's because the child keeps on going to the colder, colder point – they keep on moving away from the feelings that they actually need to feel and express so that they can feel relaxed enough to go to sleep. Here, they need us to move the dial of the *balance of attention* towards the warm spot. This might mean us staying close, crawling around next to them and playing some fun *attachment play* games.

## I also see us as being a bit like an emotional shepherd dog. We are keeping close to our child so that they actually feel our presence, which creates the emotional safety and connection to feel and express their feelings rather than suppress them.

## The *balance of attention* with *attachment play*

Have you ever played a particular kind of *attachment play* and one day your child laughs and laughs, and another day they show no interest in playing it, don't want to play it, or they get upset when you suggest it? Or perhaps you've read that a particular game is helpful for a certain issue, and you play that game, and nothing happens? Or maybe you have more than one child, and one of them loves a particular game and another doesn't at all?

This is all related to the *balance of attention*.

Remember the core understanding that children *naturally know how to heal*, and will *spontaneously* do so when there is the combination of revisiting an experience from the past while experiencing emotional support and safety in the present. This is very nuanced and means that in any moment, attending to the *balance of attention* is most likely to help the specific *attachment play* to bring about healing.

> This is why following our child's lead when they are inviting play can be most likely to create healing, because they innately know how to heal, but need our loving and present support to bring the emotional safety element to the equation.

I so understand that you might not want to play while doing the weekly food shop, or while cleaning the house, folding the washing, getting some uninterrupted work done on your laptop, or wanting them to just brush their teeth and go to sleep. But if we *do* have the emotional presence in ourselves to do so, that can be most effective for bringing the exact kind of play and laughter that elicits relief, release and repair.

Other times we will be offering *attachment play* because we're wanting to help prepare our child for an experience, or to help them heal from something that they don't seem to be bringing up themselves during play, or there is a particular issue showing up that we think *attachment play* will help with.

In this case, it can be really helpful to hold in mind the *balance of attention* while we are offering the play, because our child will show us what they need in terms of the position of that dial.

For example, say a child has had a scary experience with a dog and now they don't want to go anywhere where there is a dog. You could play with the *balance of attention* here. To give them that sense of emotional and physical safety in the present, we can offer games where they know that they are in *absolutely no danger*. That might be, for example, a power-reversal game, where they pretend to be a doggie and they chase you around the house and you pretend to be scared and keep jumping up in the air whenever they catch you.

They will let you know if you need to move up or down that *balance of attention* dial. If they are too scared to play, you might then make the situation even more *different* from the original traumatic one, by inviting them to be a lion rather than a dog.

However, if it is *not close enough* to the original experience to help healing happen, you might ask a friend with a friendly dog to help by meeting in the park with the dog on the lead, and you and your child hold hands and run towards the dog and away from it, again and again. If your child is laughing lots and clearly enjoying it while healing, you know you have the *balance of attention*.

I supported two siblings with fears related to dogs while holding in mind the *balance of attention*. First of all, we started with soft toy puppies. Then they moved to the approach-avoidance game I mentioned above. Then they went and touched the dog in the approach-avoidance game. Then they held the dog's lead. They got completely free from fear and now love playing with dogs!

It really is possible to help our children heal from fears, prepare for new situations, and release pent-up feelings from past stressful or traumatic events, all with *attachment play*. However, I want to remind you that *often, play is not enough for healing to happen*, and crying or raging is required.

Again, this might happen *naturally* and *spontaneously*. You might be doing *attachment play* and then during the play, your child suddenly bursts into tears. I invite you to trust that this is all part of the healing, and to listen lovingly.

Or it might be that half an hour after the play, your child suddenly has a *broken cookie* moment and starts crying, apparently in response to the way that you put the toothpaste on their toothbrush – but of course, actually because all that lovely play has created the safety and connection for those feelings to come up and out.

> Self-Reflection Moment
> Have you had any aha moments reading this?
> Is there anything you would like to do differently as a result?

## The *balance of attention* with crying

Again, we can see the *balance of attention* operating with crying for healing too. The most obvious example is if a young child is crying alone. Since by definition, children need the emotional safety of a listening adult for crying to be healing, we know that this is not healing. Babies need to be held for crying to be healing. However, as babies become mobile and particularly if we regularly listen to their feelings, as they and get older, they do not always need to be held for the crying to be healing. They can choose to come to us to receive the hug we're offering if they need more closeness. They might feel safe enough to cry without being held because they know that they can come to us for safety if they need to.

This is why I talk about the *crying dance*. This is us dancing with the *balance of attention*, finding that exact point where a child feels both completely connected with themselves, their body and their painful feelings, while feeling a deep connection and sense of presence and safety from us.

Sometimes that means us moving *closer* or *further* away. With a small child, that can literally mean walking along beside them to help them feel our closeness and connection while they are crying so that we maintain that *balance of attention*.

If breastfeeding has become a *control pattern*, which it does for many children, this can make the whole situation a bit more tricky, even once they are no longer breastfeeding, because when we are holding them, they might dissociate, if the *control pattern* has spread to us cuddling them. We can tell that they are dissociated rather than that their needs for closeness have been met by how relaxed they are in their body and how much eye contact they make.

> ### Self-Compassion Moment
> I invite you to put down any emotional sticks if your child has a breastfeeding control pattern and you're tempted to pick the sticks up here. It's so common for children to have acquired a breastfeeding control pattern and to find it harder to express their feelings with their mother as a result. You are not alone in this, and it's absolutely possible to support children to feel more comfortable to express their feelings again in these situations.

If they stop crying when we hold them, but they are tense, avoid eye contact and want to only stay in one position, or there's an absence of presence in their body, or they're twirling our hair or picking our skin, or sucking their thumb, it's likely that they are dissociating rather than feeling the natural calm from their needs being met.

In contrast, if they are relaxed and make eye contact, that tells us their immediate needs *are* being met.

If they are dissociating when we hold them, we might play with the *balance of attention* by still offering closeness, but in a position that is very different from breastfeeding. Or we might sit on the floor with our knees up and cuddle them, but so they are not able to get into the position where they dissociate. (I call this the 'knees-up' hug'.) Or if a child is crying but they dissociate when we pick them up, we might lean down, put our arms around them, and offer our loving words and warm presence but not pick them up. (I call this the 'bending-down hug'.) This may support the healing crying to continue.

I want to remind you that the whole basis of this is about:

- *listening* to yourself; and
- *observing* your child.

## If at any point, you feel uncomfortable, please stop whatever it is that you're doing.

I would also invite you to take that discomfort to be heard by a loving listener, or to journal about it, so that you can differentiate between discomfort from you tapping into the sense that this is not helpful, and discomfort because your own painful feelings from the past are bubbling up to be lovingly heard.

If you are ever unsure about whether the crying your child is doing is healing, or if you sense that your child needs to cry but isn't, I invite you to reflect on the *balance of attention* and ask yourself these two questions:

### 1. Is my child experiencing enough emotional presence and safety with me?

If not, do I need to get my needs met more or have my feelings heard?

Do I need to help myself become more present? Do I need to change what I'm telling myself about me, them or this situation? Do I need to move in closer, make more eye contact, offer more loving words, or verbally reassure my child that they are safe and protected?

## 2. Is my child feeling connected enough to the original stressful or traumatic experience?

If not, do I need to remind them about it so they can revisit it?

Here are some ways of helping children revisit trauma. (For more information, see Aletha Solter's book, *Healing Your Traumatized Child*.)

- *talking* about the experience;
- engaging them in *symbolic play* with the trauma theme;
- inviting them to *draw* a picture of what happened;
- gently *touching* the part of their body that was hurt (if relevant);
- returning to the *location* where it happened; or
- offering a *Loving Limit*.

As with all the elements of the 'healing from stress and trauma' aspect of Aware Parenting, this is something to tread very carefully with, receive lots of support with, and be very nuanced about in your practice. If in doubt, you can always stop.

Chiara Rossetti, an Aware Parenting instructor you've already met before, shares about the *balance of attention* in practice. She says:

*"A few months after a very close family member passed away, there were so many huge feelings needing to be heard, in all of us. One day, we all seemed to be fairly content and were all playing in the garden. I decided to saw a branch off a tree that was potentially an eye poker! I started sawing and Luca (age six) started screaming not to chop her head off (this was relevant to the health condition that the family*

member had). Her dramatic reaction seemed to have come out of the blue and took me by surprise. I then realised it wasn't about the branch (it wasn't a special or meaningful tree for her) and I'd told her a few times in days prior that I'd need to saw the branch.

Anyway, I slowly kept cutting the tree branch while connecting with her, and her screams escalated to the point that I was concerned neighbours would intervene. She was yelling, 'Don't cut me,' 'Stop hurting me,' 'That's my head you're chopping off,' 'You always hurt me,' etc. At one point I stopped sawing (when she was in full throttle) and she continued to cry and rage for quite a while. She had a look of terror in her eyes and her body was lashing out and she was stomping about like someone possessed.

At a certain point I would gently remind her that the branch needed to go but that I would listen to all her 'angries' about it. It felt so significant and huge! She was definitely processing and releasing so much pain from the year she had spent with her dying relation. It was incredibly heart warming to be able to hear all those massive emotions coming from her wee body. Phew.

After she had calmed down, this fresh version of her appeared – centred, loving, present and cooperative. The next day she helped me carry the branch out to the bin as if nothing had ever happened."

## The *balance of attention* with *Loving Limits* and *holding*

As we talked about in the previous chapter on *Loving Limits* and *holding*, the *balance of attention* is vital here. What *Loving Limits* and *holding* do is help create the emotional safety and the reminder from the past required for the child to experience the balance of attention to spontaneously express the feelings underlying the behaviour.

For both *Loving Limits* and *holding* this means that it is very important that we are:

- relatively *calm* rather than agitated, frustrated or angry;
- relatively *present* rather than dissociated; and
- thinking *compassionate* rather than harsh thoughts about our child and their behaviour.

If we're agitated, frustrated, angry, are dissociated, or are thinking harsh thoughts about them, it is possible or even likely that the *Loving Limit* or *holding* we offer will be more harmful than helpful.

> *Self-Compassion Moment*
> *I invite you to be compassionate with yourself here, as always, especially if you have offered* Loving Limits *or* holding *when you were doing or feeling one or more of those things. I want to remind you that we can repair if we have done this, through attachment play, particularly power-reversal games.*

These practices can be challenging for us. If you are a bit frustrated, and a bit dissociated, you are probably still going to be able to offer a *Loving Limit* and listen to your child's feelings in a way that is helpful. If we all needed to be completely calm, completely present and have completely compassionate thoughts for *Loving Limits* to be helpful, there would probably be very few helpful *Loving Limits* ever offered in the world!

**However, if we *are* feeling connected with our true power and with enough presence and compassion, a *Loving Limit* or *holding* can bring the most profound sense of safety and healing presence for our child's deep hurts and pain.**

> *Self-Reflection Moment*
> Are there any things that you want to do differently in relation to Loving Limits and holding?

***From a child:*** *Daddy, remember when I used to be so scared when a dog came near me and I just wanted to climb up your legs and be safe? I remember how much I didn't like being scared like that. I wanted to see my friend Bez's new puppies and I wasn't even going to his house 'cause I was so scared. You played that game of pretending that you were a dog but I still felt really scared. Then I played being the dog and chasing you and I laughed so much, it was like I couldn't stop laughing. Then I already felt much less scared. Remember then you took me to Bez's house and said I could see the puppies but that was too much for me. I loved it when you played that fun game with me where we held hands and ran towards Bez's front door and then ran back to the car again and we did it over and over again. We both laughed so much, didn't we, Daddy? I don't know how, but somehow it was just like magic, and when you asked me if I wanted to see the puppies, I said I did. You held my hand when I gave them a stroke and I giggled and giggled. Then after that I got to hold one and she was so soft. After that I didn't feel scared any more. That was so super cool! Can we look at the pictures of them again now, please?*

## Chapter summary

**The *balance of attention* is a key element of Aware Parenting**. When we really understand the *balance of attention* we can often know exactly how we might most helpfully respond in any situation related to our child's feelings.

The *balance of attention* is vital in all forms of healing, whether that's with *attachment play*, crying, *Loving Limits* or *holding*. **We need to create a *balance of attention* in order for healing to happen**.

CHAPTER TWELVE

# How we suppress and dissociate from our feelings with *control patterns*

> *Self-Reflection Moment*
> How do you suppress your feelings or dissociate from them?
> Are you suppressing them right now? Are you twirling your hair while you're reading, or eating chocolate or chips, or picking your nose!?

> *Self-Compassion Moment*
> If you are, I'm sending you lots of love. Remember to put down those guilt or shame sticks. Pretty much all of us have learnt to suppress our feelings or dissociate from them in the DDC. You are so not alone! We needed to do this to be safe, belong or be loved growing up.

The *antidote* to *suppression* and *dissociation* is the safety created by *loving, warm presence*[33]. If you'd like some loving and warm presence, *I'm here. I'm listening. I welcome all your feelings.*

In Aware Parenting, the repetitive ways we use to mildly dissociate from, or suppress our feelings with, are called *control patterns*, and they tend to get passed down in families. That might be through eating, busyness, or talking a lot, for example.

---
33 Remember the warmth melting the frozen water!

> **Self-Reflection Moment**
> Do you see that in your family?

The more we can get support to be present with our feelings, the more we will be able to be present with our child/ren's feelings, and the less they will learn to suppress their feelings. Being with people who welcome our feelings can make all the difference, so we're more able to welcome the full range of our child/ren's feelings.

## Compassion for ourselves and our *control patterns*

In the *Disconnected Domination Culture* it is very common for us to learn to judge ourselves or our *control patterns* when we are doing them!

> **Self-Reflection Moment**
> Do you find yourself doing that? Do you notice yourself scrolling Facebook and dissociating, or reaching for the chocolate when you're feeling overwhelmed, or going to the fridge when you're tired, or suddenly getting really busy when you're upset?
>
> And perhaps you judge yourself or tell yourself that you 'shouldn't' be doing that. Perhaps you stop yourself from doing that in a harsh way? I'm going to invite you to pause, and reflect back on why control patterns *are* there in the first place.

*Control patterns*, as *mild* forms of *dissociation*, are there because we grew up in a culture where people:

- did not *understand* the healing power of expressing feelings;
- had harsh *judgments* about tears or tantrums;
- thought there was something *wrong* with a child who cried or raged;
- had rarely or *never* experienced someone being lovingly present with them while they expressed feelings; and

- *couldn't* stay present in their bodies with their own feelings, and thus ours.

  So, every time we felt a feeling and were trying to use our innate wisdom to heal from the stress or the trauma, but didn't experience the emotional safety of a lovingly present adult welcoming those feelings, we would have needed to do something else with those feelings.

We would have either learnt to suppress our feelings in the same ways that our feelings were suppressed by the adults around us, eg. to eat when we are upset – or, we would have learnt to suppress our feelings in the same ways as we saw around us – or, we would have found our own ways to suppress our feelings, eg. to suck our thumb, tense our muscles, or hold on to a soft toy.

Many of these *control patterns* morph as we get older.

If we sucked our thumb, we might have been shamed at school and so started biting our nails instead. Then perhaps our parent painted horrible smelling concoctions on our nails, so we started biting the end of a pencil instead. When we left school, that might have morphed into biting our lip when we have feelings bubbling.

*Self-Reflection Moment*
*As you reflect on this, do you feel more compassion for yourself?*

Warm compassion is one of the *antidotes* to suppression and dissociation, which we will talk about in the next section.

*Self-Reflection Moment*
*I invite you to notice your control patterns.*
*Can you track whether they morphed in your life, or are they the same as they probably were when they first began?*

I invite you to be REALLY gentle with yourself here. Our *control patterns* can be holding a multitude of feelings at bay, so if we are to explore them, it's really important that we feel enough of a sense of emotional presence, either internally or externally. Otherwise, we can just end up flooded and dissociating even more.

> Your *control patterns* may have distracted you from thousands of hours of crying and raging. If you hadn't used them, you might have been shamed, punished, excluded, sent to your room, or hurt in even more ways than you already experienced being hurt growing up in this culture. In other words, *control patterns* not only protect us from feeling emotions that would be overwhelming to us as children with no adult to listen, but they also probably protected us from many other painful experiences.

> *Self-Reflection Moment*
> Do you feel more compassion towards yourself now?
> What thoughts would you like to have about yourself when you're engaged in your control patterns?
> How would you like to respond to yourself at those times?

## The antidote to dissociation and suppression is compassionate presence

In my own journey, I went from harsh and frequent judgment of my *control patterns* to a deep gratitude for them and compassion for myself whenever I was using them.

> *Self-Reflection Moment*
> I wonder if you would like to have deep gratitude for yours?
> I wonder if you would even like to express your gratitude to them?

Might you imagine all the ways:

- they helped you mildly *dissociate* from painful feelings when you didn't have an adult with you who could listen to them;
- they helped you *distract* yourself from your feelings when being with them would have been too much for you as a child on your own with those feelings; and
- they *protected* you from being shamed, judged, punished or excluded.

*Would you like to express your gratitude to them?*

*You might even want to write a letter to them in your journal.*

For example, "Dear eating chocolate *control pattern*. I so *appreciate* you. Thank you for all the times you helped me stop feeling feelings when I didn't have an adult with me to listen. Thank you for being there when I came home from school, feeling so upset but knowing that my feelings wouldn't be heard. Thank you for being there when I was a teenager and felt so alone and so uncomfortable. You helped me not feel those feelings and I'm so grateful to you. Thank you for being there when crying at school would have meant being outcast, when I could eat you at break times instead. Thank you so much for all the times I've needed to cry as an adult, but just didn't realise, didn't have the support, or didn't have the inner presence to be with those feelings myself. Thank you so much."

*Would you like to write something like that to each of your* control patterns?

**The antidote *to dissociation and suppression is warm*, compassionate presence. Having more compassion towards ourselves when we're suppressing our feelings or mildly dissociating is going to make it more likely that we can be present with our feelings at those times. We couldn't feel and express those feelings when we were younger because we didn't receive enough emotional presence from the adults around us.**

We haven't been able to feel and express those feelings as adults because we didn't internalise a loving presence from our parents (or we didn't internalise it for particular feelings). So, if we are wanting to use less suppression and less dissociation, that means feeling and expressing our feelings *with* emotional presence. Generally, we need that from outside of ourselves, especially if we didn't receive it from our parents and thus didn't internalise it.

The importance of emotional presence for us is why I keep inviting you to connect with your *Listening Partner*, counsellor, therapist or Aware Parenting instructor, so that you can experience the compassion, presence and emotional safety of someone who can be with you and your feelings as you feel and express them.

My Marion Method work includes developing our own *Inner Loving Presences*, which include our Inner Loving Mother and Inner Loving Father.[34]

Let's explore what's *actually* happening when there is suppression or dissociation, or a *control pattern* is in action. Our conscious awareness is either being moved away from the painful feelings to something else, such as the distraction of eating or reading something. Or, our consciousness is literally aware of less, when we dissociate or freeze.

Dissociation is akin to the freeze in the fight, flight or freeze response, and is adaptive because it numbs our sensations and feelings, to protect us in times of danger or threat.

There are different *levels* of not feeling the feelings.

The most *minimal* distraction might include biting our nails, twirling our hair, picking our nose, through to *more* dissociation such as when scrolling social media or eating a whole piece of cake without tasting it. *Further* along might be drinking alcohol, or getting drunk. Then

---

34  You can find out more on my website: www.marionrose.net

the most *extreme* end would be losing consciousness, either through alcohol or drugs, or fainting.

These are all ways our system is trying to protect us from feeling feelings when we don't feel the emotional or physical safety, compassion and presence to stay present in our body with our feelings.

We are each so *unique* and have had different life experiences.

Some of you might have experienced *chronic or complex trauma*. I would say that all of us growing up in this culture would have experienced many stressful and painful experiences and acute trauma. Some of you might have already been on a journey of healing from past painful events for many years.

Each of us will be in a *very different place*. Some of us might *often* be dissociated or in freeze mode. Others might only be *occasionally* mildly dissociating.

> This is why, throughout this book, I invite you to listen to yourself as much as you can, to be as gentle with yourself as possible, and to put down the book or skip the self-reflection parts at any time if you feel overwhelmed or you notice yourself dissociating.

## What can you do if you're about to pick up the chocolate or your phone or a glass of wine?

Here's one suggestion:

1. *Drop* the judgment *sticks* ("I'm not willing to judge myself.");
2. *Offer* yourself *presence* and *compassion* (You might put your hand on your heart and say something like, "I'm here with you. I hear that you want some chocolate/Instagram/wine. I'm listening.");

3. Know that you have *choice* ("I'm free to still do that thing if I don't feel present enough. Or I could listen to the feelings or reach out to my *Listening Partner* on voice note to tell them how I feel.").

> *Self-Reflection Moment*
> *What would you find helpful to think and do when you next notice yourself using a control pattern?*

## *Attachment play* with our *control patterns*

If we feel called to, doing *attachment play* with our *control patterns* can be a powerful way of helping increase our sense of emotional safety and presence, and releasing lighter feelings through laughter, just as we can help our child.

Just as *attachment play* for children requires the presence of an adult or older child, so *attachment play* for ourselves can be most effective if done with someone else. How might we do *attachment play* as an adult? Often, just bringing a quality of playfulness to us doing the *control pattern* can make a difference. Instead of being serious, judging yourself, or trying to work things out, being playful when we're about to suppress can make a big difference!

If you're:

- Wanting to eat cake, how about creating a cake party!
- Going to the fridge for the third time for chocolate, how about making a song of it, "I'm going to the fridge, I'm going to the fridge, yipppeee!"
- Getting busy tidying the house to distract yourself, how about singing and dancing while you do it?
- Wanting to scroll online, how about finding a music video and dancing around the kitchen?

- About to have your third glass of wine, how about having an out-loud conversation with it, where wine says, "Noooo, don't drink me!" and you say, "Yes! I'm going to drink you and *love* you!"

Bringing in silliness, lightness, goofiness and fun can all help at times.

And I want to remind you about the *balance of attention*. If you've got some really huge feelings bubbling up, it is likely that *attachment play* is not the most apt thing to do at that time. Only you can know whether playing might be helpful!

*Self-Reflection Moment*

*Have you ever been playful with your control patterns?*

*Would you like to play with being playful?*

*Is there a control pattern that you think you might be able to play this with?*

*What ideas do you have to play with it?*

## Loving Limits with our control patterns

If you've thought of offering a *Loving Limit* to yourself in relation to your *control patterns*, I want to remind you that as with children, if you say no to the suppression but you don't have the inner or outer support, safety and presence to listen to those feelings, you will need to find some other way to suppress or dissociate. I imagine you might have experienced that in the past, or seen someone else going through that. Perhaps you 'gave up' wine but ended up scrolling social media much more? Maybe you stopped drinking alcohol but started biting your nails?

If you do offer a *Loving Limit* to your *control patterns*, I invite you to have a few things in place:
- To do it because you really want to and are *willing* to, rather than because you think you 'should'. "I'm willing to stop drinking alcohol before bed," rather than, "I should stop drinking alcohol before bed."
- To do it from a place of being *compassionate* with yourself and the reasons why you use the *control pattern*, rather than from a place of self-judgment.
- To have extra *support*, empathy and listening time in place ready for more feelings.
- Doing things that support you, eg. dance classes or a massage.
- Not to do it if you are really *busy*, *stressed* or *overwhelmed*.
- To know that you are *welcome* to choose to pick up that *control pattern* again at any time if you're feeling overwhelmed by feelings, and that you will *celebrate* yourself *rather* than *judge* yourself for doing what you need to do.

I invite you to really listen in to yourself here.

> *Self-Reflection Moment*
> *Do you feel called to offer a Loving Limit to a control pattern?*
> *If yes, what extra support would you like to bring in beforehand?*

I want to remind you that this is a big experience, and even if you've only had this *control pattern* for a short time, it probably morphed from a previous one and there could be lots of feelings that it has been holding at bay. Please be *compassionate* with yourself and remember that you have the power to choose what you do (which will help you feel safe). I also recommend you reach out for *lots of extra emotional support while you go through this process*.

## To the younger parts of you

*I'm sending so much love to you at exactly the first time that you used that* control pattern *that you're still using now.*

*I deeply acknowledge that you really needed to mildly dissociate from those feelings at that time, because you didn't receive enough of the presence that would tell you that you were safe to feel and express the feeling you were feeling.*

*I celebrate how wise you were for developing that* control pattern.

*There's nothing wrong with you for using that* control pattern.

*You're not doing anything wrong when you use that* control pattern.

*I'm sending so much love and compassion and gentleness to you every single time you use that* control pattern.

*I welcome all the feelings that the* control pattern *is holding at bay.*

*You don't need to judge yourself any more, sweetheart.*

*I acknowledge that the adults around you weren't able to be with those feelings.*

*That wasn't your fault.*

*Your body is so wise.*

*I deeply trust that you will get more and more comfortable with feeling and expressing your feelings to someone who really knows how to be present with you and to listen to you with love.*

*It will happen.*

*I trust you.*

*I'm here with you.*

*I'm listening.*

## Chapter summary

I invite you again and again to **have compassion for your *control patterns***. They kept you safe and protected you when you were growing up.

Warm compassion is particularly important here, because it's the antidote to dissociation and suppression. If you're judging yourself for suppressing your feelings, you'll have even more feelings to suppress. **We need compassion when we have painful feelings**.

We can also add in ***attachment play*** **and** ***Loving Limits*** **with our *control patterns***, but I recommend always doing that from a foundation of compassion and plenty of emotional support for yourself.

I'm sending you so much tender compassion any time you're suppressing your feelings.

## CHAPTER THIRTEEN

# Our child's *control patterns*

***From a child who is sucking on a dummy or their thumb,
or who is constantly picking their nose or biting their nails:***

*I may look calm when I'm doing these things,
but I don't feel truly calm.*

*I feel kind of numb and not really here.*

*Doing those things is helping me stop feeling those feelings,
but they also stop me feeling connected with you.*

*I know it seems like I really, really want to do these things.*

*But what I'd much rather do is express the feelings that doing
those things is holding in.*

*I want to tell you how I really feel.*

*I want to let the feelings out rather than hold them in.*

*I want to feel present and connected rather than numb
and disconnected.*

*But I need your help.*

*Would you come and be close with me when I'm doing those things?*

*Please let me know you love me when I'm doing those things.*

*Please don't judge me or shame me, or judge yourself when I'm doing those things.*

*I just feel more disconnected from you when you do that.*

*Maybe we could play a bit? I loved it when you played that game where you pretended to have a dummy/suck your thumb/pick your nose and we laughed and laughed and laughed.*

*And then I didn't need to distract myself for a while after that.*

*I felt relieved and connected.*

*Remember when you offered me that* Loving Limit *thingy? When you stopped me from distracting myself from my feelings and listened to them instead?*

*Remember when I cried and raged and you listened to all of my feelings?*

*Oh Mummy and Daddy, I felt so relieved afterwards.*

*I didn't need to do things to stop myself from feeling.*

*I could feel the sensations in my body.*

*I could see the colours and the shapes and the patterns around me.*

*I felt so relaxed.*

*I loved how I could go off to sleep that night without doing anything to stop myself from feeling.*

*Please listen to my feelings more.*

*Please offer me more of those* Loving Limits.

*I want to feel connected and relaxed and present.*

*Please help me."*

**To a child who is sucking on a dummy or their thumb, or who is constantly picking their nose or biting their nails:**

*"Hello, lovely you!*

*I see you!*

*I understand what's really going on for you.*

*I know that you are doing those things to stop yourself from feeling your feelings.*

*I understand that you're not calm at those times. You're probably feeling numb.*

*I'm here with you.*

*Can you feel my hand as I gently touch the centre of your back?*

*I'm here with you.*

*I'm here to help you know that I welcome your feelings now.*

*I can be with you when you're feeling sad.*

*Your big feelings are not too much for me.*

*You are not too much for me.*

*I welcome all of your feelings.*

*I can be with you when you're feeling frustrated.*

*I am here to listen to your sadness, your overwhelm, and your rage.*

*I can be with all of your feelings.*

*I'm here, present in my body, ready to welcome your feelings.*

*I'm here to help you feel those feelings and let them out, so you can feel really relaxed in your body, so you don't need to do things to stop yourself from feeling.*

*I'm here to listen.*

*I love you."*

## Do all children have feelings to express?

Over the years, I've heard parents say, "My child isn't a crier," or, "My child doesn't seem to need to cry," or, "My child doesn't seem to ever have any upset feelings."

I so understand those ways of thinking. The 'feelings' aspect of Aware Parenting is such a huge learning curve for most of us. It certainly has been for me since becoming a mother back in 2002.

So, how might there be signs that a child actually *does* have feelings that haven't been expressed? How can we actually see what's going on in their inner world? The amazing thing is that, when we know what to look for, children show us clues that they are holding in feelings.

I call these *flags for feelings*.

And I find it really important that we refrain from judging ourselves if we see these flags. They are simply flags that tell us what's going on for our child. When we understand what is really going on for our child when they are doing these things, we already understand them more and they will already experience being understood more.

Some of the flags include:

- sucking their *thumb* or fingers with a glazed look;
- sucking on a *dummy* or pacifier;
- clutching on to a *blanket* or soft toy and needing to take it everywhere with them;
- repeatedly *twirling* their hair, picking their nose, biting their nails, or picking their skin; or
- desperately wanting *food*, chocolate or sweets/lollies/candy even though they've just eaten.

These are all things that they are doing to suppress their feelings or to mildly dissociate.

In Aware Parenting they are called *control patterns*.

Anything that seems to be needed with great urgency – often at bedtime and other times when feelings usually bubble up, such as when in a new or overwhelming situation – and that is accompanied by a glazed look and a sense of disconnection, might be a *control pattern*.

Other indications that control patterns are being used include behaviours that are caused by feelings being suppressed – which include most of the things we might find challenging – such as agitation, an inability to sit still, not being relaxed enough to sleep or stay asleep, not being able to concentrate or cooperate, a lack of awareness of others' bodies, roughness, and hitting.

## Almost anything can become a *control pattern*, if it is done to dissociate from sensations and feelings rather than be present with them.

> **Self-Compassion Moment**
> It's really important to drop any self-judgment sticks here! I invite you to do that now if you were tempted to. Remember what we've talked about already, about the family lineage and how it's so understandable that our children will have control patterns when we're first generation Aware Parenting families.

The wonderful thing is, just as it was often our absence of understanding or ability to be present with our child's feelings that caused the *control patterns* in the first place, so can our own understanding and ability to be present with our child's feelings transform their relationship with their feelings and *control patterns*, and thus radically change their behaviour.

This is such a gift for our children, so that they are able to be more present and aware, and to have fewer accumulated uncomfortable feelings sitting in their bodies.

## If you see your child suppressing their feelings with thumb sucking or clutching a soft toy, you haven't done anything wrong.

It can be so helpful for us to understand that when a child is biting their nails or sucking on a dummy (pacifier), or whatever it is they do when they have feelings bubbling, this is a message for us so that we can understand what is really going on for our child.

***This isn't an invitation to pick up the guilt or shame sticks. I don't believe that any of us will be able to listen to 100% of our child's feelings at this time, in this culture, as first-generation parents practicing Aware Parenting. This means that all children will show signs of suppressed feelings or dissociation at times.***

If we put down the guilt and shame sticks that we learnt growing up in this culture, we can see those flags for feelings as *invitations* for *even more compassion* for ourselves and our child.

Even if we're not able to listen to their feelings when they are sucking their thumb or clutching a blanket and carrying it around, *understanding* that they are feeling painful feelings changes everything. They can experience feeling deeply understood, because we understand exactly what is going on for them.

*Even* if we're not able to listen to those feelings right at that moment, or for some while.

So, I'm offering both an Aware Parenting understanding about the causes of children's *control patterns*, and as always, I'm *also* inviting you to put down any guilt and shame sticks.

## Feelings accumulate

We want our children to be happy, but if we repeatedly distract them from their feelings, it has the opposite effect. Those uncomfortable feelings have physiological correlates, such as sensations, physical tension and stress hormones. Each time we distract them from their feelings with play or food or a dummy/pacifier, those feelings are still there. We are taking their attention away from those feelings, but the feelings remain.

And in fact, the feelings accumulate. It's this accumulation of feelings that is one of the main causes of so many of the things that parents find challenging – the not being able to sit still or concentrate, the not being able to go to sleep or stay asleep, the agitation and the hitting and the throwing and the forcefully taking.

If we want our children to be able to feel and express their feelings, if we want them to not need to suppress their feelings with distraction, alcohol or busy-ness as adults, the way we respond to their feelings as babies, children and teenagers has a profound effect.

It is never too late!

## Understanding what's happening and having compassion (not judging ourselves or our child when they're using a *control pattern*)

I'm imagining that you really want your child to be happy and to have a joyful life. However, if we distract our child from their painful feelings that they are trying to express, it can actually have the opposite effect.

That's such a paradox, isn't it? Let's look at why that is in more detail.

When children are expressing feelings that indicate unmet needs (needs-feelings), when we meet those needs, the feelings are gone. The feelings were there to signal the need, so when the need is met, the feeling is no longer required.

If a child is hungry and we feed them, the hunger goes.

If they are upset because they need connection, the upset goes when we give them connection.

However, healing-feelings are caused by stress or trauma. Once the stressful or traumatic event has passed, those feelings don't just go away. As we've discussed before, the feelings have physical correlates in the form of stress hormones and physical tension from the fight, flight or freeze response.

## So, if our child is crying and all their needs are met, and we distract them from the crying, we are literally taking their awareness away from their connection with the sensations and feelings in their body. In addition, if they are raging and we distract them or stop them in other ways, we are literally stopping that physiological completion of the recovery from the fight or flight response.

Our child may no longer appear upset, but the feelings haven't gone away. Those feelings are still sitting in their bodies. The stress hormones are still in their system. Any physical tension from the mobilised fight or flight response is there too.

Distraction in whatever form might appear to work, but what happens over time?

> Over time, those feelings accumulate. Those stress hormones add up. That physical tension increases. Each time we distract them by giving them food, offering a toy, or singing them a song, those feelings accumulate in their bodies.

We are likely then to see – if we know what to look for – the following three things:

1. the *effects* of that *accumulation*;
2. the *increased need* to *dissociate*; and
3. *behaviours* that are caused by pent-up feelings, stress hormones and physical tension.

### 1. The effects of the accumulation might be things like:

- agitation, not being able to sit still, running around everywhere;
- moving from one thing to the next;
- hyperarousal or hyperactivity; and
- wriggling around when going to sleep and restlessness during sleep.

### 2. The increased need to dissociate might be things like:

- using suppression and *control patterns* more of the time – eg. thumb sucking, dummy or pacifier, screen use to suppress, eating to suppress, carrying around a soft toy, etc. – more and more and more!

It's also common that they will increasingly avoid connection – less eye contact, less willingness to cuddle and be held, pushing away offers of closeness and warmth. This is because the eye contact, closeness and warmth offer one side of what's needed for the *balance of attention* that is required for feelings to be expressed, which they are working against with the dissociation.

### 3. Behaviours caused by pent-up feelings, stress hormones and physical tension include things like:
- pushing, biting, forcefully taking, throwing, hitting;
- swearing, harshness to others;
- not being willing to cooperate; or
- challenges going to sleep and staying asleep.

If *all* children have accumulated feelings to a larger or lesser degree, why do these symptoms show up at *particular* times?

> Often this can be when the feelings are bubbling to the surface, either because there has been more connection and presence from us, which supports the feelings to come up, or because there has been more stress or overwhelm, which piles on more feelings and stress, so that the feelings spill over. Or something could happen that reminds them of the original feelings or experience.

## Categories of *control patterns*

There are three main categories of *control patterns*:

### 1. Those they acquired *directly* from us

Our children have acquired these, either from us, or from others. For example, we put a dummy in their mouth when they need to cry and they then start wanting a dummy when they need to cry. Or we give them food when they're upset, so they then ask for food when they need to cry. We might have rocked and jiggled them as babies when they had healing-feelings to express, and they then move a lot as a child when they're upset.

### 2. Those they acquired *indirectly* from us

This is when they have observed us suppressing our own feelings in certain ways, and they imitate us. Examples include doing the following when they have healing-feelings to express:

- eating;
- entertainment;
- screens;
- movement;
- being busy; and
- intellectualising.

### 3. Those that they created themselves

They started the *control pattern* themselves when people around them didn't have the understanding or the capacity to be present with their feelings, for example:

- thumb sucking;
- nail biting;
- hair twirling; or
- nose picking.

> *Self-Compassion Moment*
>
> *Remember to put down any emotional sticks if you're tempted to pick them up. It's so natural for all children to have control patterns in this culture. I'm sending you lots of love and compassion if you're seeing your child's suppression or dissociation even more clearly and if you're feeling painful feelings.*

**A note about 'unconscious' talking as a *control pattern*:** Does your child seem to talk constantly? Or perhaps you have a friend or colleague who doesn't stop talking and you notice yourself drifting away from listening to them? Did you know that talking can be a way of suppressing or dissociating from feelings? It's really common for both children and adults to do that.

Of course, if we're connected with ourselves and our feelings, talking can be a profound way for us to deeply *connect* with others and *express* feelings.

How is this possible? How can it be both a way to suppress or dissociate AND a way to connect, feel and express?

Well, us humans have so much innate body wisdom.

## Almost anything can be used to suppress or dissociate from feelings.

We are so wise, that when the conditions are available to connect, be present, feel our feelings and express them in healing ways, we will do that.

And when those conditions aren't there, we can do *the same things* to distract ourselves from our feelings. And those ways can become patterns we use repeatedly.

**How can you tell if your child is talking to distract or talking to connect?** If you are present with yourself and listening to them, you might notice that you don't actually feel *connected* with them. The talking might have a quality of agitation that is different from excitedly wanting to tell us things. They might avoid eye contact or closeness. You might start off the conversation feeling calm, and then pick up on their agitation once they start talking.

**While we're on this topic, how can we tell if *we* are talking to distract, suppress or dissociate?** You might talk and talk but not feel any sense of connection or relief. You might not have much connection to your feelings or body sensations.

With Aware Parenting, we can support our children when they have a talking *control pattern*, so that they can reconnect with their body and their feelings more.

Aren't we amazing humans, that we can do almost anything to feel more connected and present, and we can do that *exact* same thing to help us dissociate or disconnect from our bodies and sensations! Eating, exercise, talking, reading, all of these we can do *with* deep presence, or we can do them to take ourselves *away* from presence.

> *Self-Reflection Moment*
>
> I invite you to reflect on your child/ren's behaviour.
>
> As always, I invite you to refrain from picking up the self-judgment sticks, and to also avoid judging your child/ren too.
>
> Remember all the cultural, historical and familial reasons that your child needs to suppress their feelings at times.
>
> What kinds of behaviours indicate to you that they have accumulated feelings?
>
> What kinds of things do they do to suppress or dissociate from their feelings?
>
> What kinds of behaviours show up from pent up feelings, stress hormones and physical tension?

## What we can do for ourselves when our child is engaging in a *control pattern*

### Compassionate clarity

To *understand* the cause of *control patterns* and have compassion for ourselves and our children in that. This includes putting down the guilt and self-judgment sticks, and also being unwilling to judge our child.

### Expressing our feelings

To *express* our own feelings about their *control pattern* to another adult – eg. if we feel fear or rage, or we're judging ourselves or them, or we're scared about their future. Also, exploring our own feelings is useful, especially if we had a similar *control pattern* as a child. For example, if our child sucks their thumb and we did too as a child, we might express our own feelings and memories of doing that and how we felt when the adults around us responded as they did.

## What our child needs from us when they are engaged in a *control pattern*

In the moment:

### 1. Connection and presence

Moving in to connect with them with our loving presence. *Warm connection is the antidote to suppression and dissociation* (as I mentioned earlier on in the book, it's like the warmth melting the freeze).

The first step is connection. This is why I've already invited you to do so much work on dropping the judgment in relation to *control patterns* – because we won't really be able to connect as deeply if we're judging ourselves or judging them.

I'm going to be inviting you to deeply connect with your child next time you see them suppressing their feelings. How might you like to do that?

Would you like to:

- Remember when you suppressed your feelings as a child, and how you would have wanted to be unconditionally loved.
- Imagine exactly what you would have wanted your parents to say when you were: sucking your thumb; clutching on to a soft toy; glued to the TV; holding a bag of chocolates; picking your nose; or twirling your hair.

- Remember that your child is suppressing their feelings for important reasons – without judging yourself when you hold that in mind.
- Cuddle up with your child when they're sucking their thumb, and communicate unconditional love to them for what they are doing. Perhaps you might like to gently stroke their thumb.
- Snuggle up with them when they're sucking on a dummy, and tell them, "I'm here with you, sweetheart." Would you also like to reflect back on when you gave them the dummy, and be compassionate with yourself as you do that?
- Lie next to them on the bed when they are clutching their soft toy, and lovingly ask them about their toy, look at it tenderly, and gently touch it, while talking to it.
- Sit next to your child while they're looking at a screen, and simply feel your loving presence as you make body contact, communicating unconditional love that they are watching what they are watching, while asking questions and showing interest.
- Sit with your child as they are eating their sweeties/lollies/candy/chocolate, and ask them all about the flavours, and what they love about them.

## With each of these, offering a deep sense of compassion both gives them a sense of being unconditionally loved when they are suppressing feelings, and also paradoxically creates even more emotional connection, presence and safety for the underlying feelings to be expressed.

Depending on their age and your willingness, you might want to talk to them about the *control pattern*, particularly if you gave it to them in the first place. Or you might choose not to say anything, and simply work on supporting them to need it less.

> *Self-Reflection Moment*
>
> *What would you like to do?*
>
> *Would you like to say anything?*
>
> *What might you need to be able to do this?*
>
> *Are you willing to do what you need to be able to do this?*

## 2. Attachment play

*Attachment play* is often really helpful to loosen up feelings that are held in with suppression. eg. the thumb sucking game, or, the "Whatever you do, you're not going to …" game. Bringing in connection and play helps release lighter feelings and helps the child know that we love them even when they are suppressing, and that we are there to help them.

After creating lots of connection with your child when they're suppressing feelings, the next step I invite you to do is offer some *attachment play*.

**If they are sucking their thumb, would you like to:**

Suck yours too, but add in nonsense play, where you make big loud sucking noises and funny faces, or where you keep on taking it out and saying things like, "Mmmmm! Chocolate! Mmmmm! Vanilla!" And then ask to suck their thumb, ask what flavour it is, pretend to suck their thumb and then be surprised that it is snot flavour. "You said it would be chocolate flavour!!!! You won't do that again, will you?" And then repeat and repeat! I once played this game for about 45 minutes with two children during an in-person consultation, and one of them went on to have a huge cry with their mum.

Lily shares about how she helped her son with his thumb sucking *control pattern*:

*"He was lying on the couch sucking his thumb, I lay down next to*

*him and started sucking my thumb too, and said to him, 'Let's see if I can suck something out of this thumb!' And sucked a bit in a playful way, and then I pretended my thumb was a bird and I whistled and my thumb flew (and accidentally dropped a poopy on his head) and flew back in my mouth again, and I played the same.' See what I suck out of my thumb this time!' And then I was a grasshopper, jumping, jumping, underneath his shirt! Same thing again...and was another animal...he also made something out of his thumb twice and laughed and seemed to enjoy this game!"*

**If they are picking their nose, would you like to:**

Pretend to pick yours too, and pretend to eat the bogies and be surprised about how delicious they are! Say, "Whatever you do, you're not going to pick your nose, are you?" and turn around and mock whistle, and turn around again with mock shock when they are picking their nose. "YOU SAID you wouldn't pick your nose!!" You're not going to do that again, are you?" and so on!

Chiara Rossetti, an Aware Parenting instructor you've already met before, shares about the power of *attachment play* with nose picking *control patterns*. She says:

*"One of my kids started to pick their nose lots when they were four. It mostly didn't bother me but I could tell it was a control pattern and not a need to remove an obstruction! I started playing loads of games around nose picking – curiously trying to look up their nose to see what they were digging for and seeing if I could have a turn, running to get a plate, knife and fork to anticipate the lovely meal they were preparing and hoping they would share with me, singing nose picking songs like, 'I am the world's best nose picker and my snot won't make me sicker, if it does then I'll get you a sticker to wear on your knicker(s)', playing soft games with plenty of facial touching and focusing on the nose area. Loads of giggles and connection were had, and a few months later I noticed the nose picking had gone."*

**If they are eating to suppress, would you like to:**

Make the food into funny shapes or words on the table and be surprised with what you see. Or make up funny words for the food: "Is that a chocolate pea? Or a chocolate wee? Or a carrot from an elephant on Mars?"

Sandra shares about using *attachment play* with her daughter, who had a breastfeeding *control pattern*:

*"I played a lot of breastfeeding games with my daughter. She was two and a half. I would get a baby doll and pretend that the baby was having boobie but she would accidentally bite me or want to feed upside down or anything ridiculous. She would laugh a lot. And then I would pretend the baby wanted boobie off my daughter and my daughter would pretend to feed the baby and then the baby would make a loud burp noise or something ridiculous and my daughter would cackle and cackle. It was actually lots of fun. The sillier we were the more she laughed, and it really did create some spaciousness around the feeding."*

**If they are on screens to suppress, would you like to:**

Say, "Oh look, there is a new kind of phone stand, and it looks just like a child. It's really realistic! Look, you can move the arms and the legs and put it in different positions so you can watch more easily" (moving their arms and legs). Or draw a tablet on your tummy and lift up the bottom of your top and ask them, "I'm a lovely tablet, what would you like to play? Look, I can …" (and offer their usual games).

Watching with them, or joining them to watch the last part of them watching or playing can help bring connection. Showing interest in what they're watching or playing if that doesn't distract them can help. Then finding ways of playfully linking what they've been doing with an off-screen activity. For example, if they've been watching something about lions, perhaps you could pretend that you are lions going off to play together on the savannah.

> *Self-Reflection Moment*
> *Did any of these appeal to you?*
> *What games can you imagine playing with them?*

### 3. *Loving Limits* and listening

*Loving Limits* and listening to the feelings is a third way to work with *control patterns*. It might be that we tell them that we are going to help them go to sleep without the dummy/pacifier, or we're not going to give them screens right before bed[35]. Then we can listen to the feelings. *"I hear that you really want the dummy, sweetheart, and I'm not willing to give it to you, because I don't think it's the most helpful thing for you at the moment, and I'm here and I'm listening."*

It's important to note that if the *control pattern* has been around a long while, one cry isn't likely to release all the feelings that the *control pattern* has been holding in. So, when they have finished crying with us, or we have run out of emotional spaciousness to listen, they are free to use that *control pattern* again, if they still have feelings at the surface. For example, if it's a dummy and we aren't willing to give it back and they still have feelings at the surface, they might need to acquire a different *control pattern*, possibly a more internal one that might be harder for us to help them get free from.

I also want to remind you about the *balance of attention*. If you are feeling really stretched, or full of feelings yourself, you are probably not going to have the spaciousness to listen to the feelings underneath the *control pattern*. In that case, it may be preferable to wait until you do.

With a *Loving Limit* with a *control pattern*, you might want to give them advance notice. So, if they use a dummy before sleep, you might tell them that morning that you are going to help them go to sleep without the dummy in the evening.

---

35 Please note that there are particular things to hold in mind with *Loving Limits* with screens and food, which I talk about later in this chapter.

Remember with *Loving Limits*, we can offer the empathy:

*"I really hear that you want the..."*

and the limit:

*"...and I'm not willing for you to..."*

and the information:

*"because I don't think that's the most helpful thing for you right now."*

### 4. Ongoing listening

Understanding that this isn't something that will be shifted in one laughter or crying session. We will probably need to do this for some while, and receive our own ongoing listening too. Whenever a child experiences more stress in their lives, they will have more feelings to express. We'll be able to tell that's the case if they go back to using an old *control pattern*, if they start using an existing one more or they begin a new one. This is a flag for feelings, inviting us to increase our own listening time as well as listening to our child.

## When we don't recommend using *Loving Limits* with *control patterns*

**Thumb sucking:** If your child sucks their thumb, in Aware Parenting we *do not* recommend ever taking it out forcefully. This would be working against a child's own sense of the emotional safety available to express their feelings to us. Instead, I invite you to offer connection and *attachment play*, to build more on the emotional safety side of the *balance of attention* so that they can express their feelings.

**A *food* control pattern:** Similarly, in Aware Parenting, we don't recommend *Loving Limits* with eating food, again because we are aiming to support a child's connection and reconnection with their innate body wisdom. The two exceptions are if it's a breastfeeding *control pattern* (because it's the mother's body and she is saying no to what happens to her body), or if a child has health issues, particularly related to food, including with their weight. I go into this in more detail in the chapter on eating.

*A screen* **control pattern:** In Aware Parenting, we also wouldn't recommend simply offering a *Loving Limit* to get off a screen unless we had already had a discussion with the child and come to a mutual agreement about their use of the screen. The *Loving Limit* would then be an application of the agreement we've already made together. Here, the information part of the *Loving Limit* would be, 'Because I want us to stick to the agreement we made'. We are offering the *Loving Limit* in the context of all the aspects of Aware Parenting, particularly attuned connection, respectful conversation, conveying trust in their innate wisdom and meeting everyone's needs. I talk in more detail about this in the chapter on screens.

> *Self-Reflection Moment*
> Are you wanting to offer your child a Loving Limit with a control pattern?
> How do you feel when you imagine doing that?
> What will you need so that you are able to do that?
> Are you willing to tend to those needs?

Danni Willow, an Aware Parenting instructor, shares the beautiful story of how she helped her daughter gradually give up her dummy.

*"When my first daughter Marley was born, I practiced* Classical Attachment Parenting*: rocking, chatting, jiggling, breastfeeding, doing anything I could to stop her from crying. I believed that if she was crying, something was wrong and it was my job to fix it, to change it, to stop it because crying was bad or it meant something was wrong with the baby.*

*I had no idea about feelings at that stage in my mothering journey and I just thought I had to stop all the crying. And so I did that for two and a half years. But then breastfeeding and rocking and patting her throughout the night was no longer sustainable because I fell pregnant.*

*I moved on to a dummy. It was interesting because everyone around me had been saying she needed to have a dummy right from the start. And then she actually became this toddler who had this dummy in her mouth all the time. I then had everyone saying, you need to get rid of the dummy.*

*So for two and a half years I never listened to her feelings. She was a red haired little girl. And so I had this label on her that as a redhead, she's introverted. I believed that.*

*I found Aware Parenting when my second was born and she wouldn't take a dummy and she wouldn't settle with the rocking and the patting and any of those things. I think she came here to really show me I had to look for other ways. I had to become familiar and able to be with the crying, and that took a long, long time.*

*Fast forward to a time where I decided after many sessions and a lot of my own crying and tending to my own younger parts, particularly as a baby being left to cry it out and having a dummy myself and having it taken away from me often – I decided that I wanted to do the process of helping her get rid of the dummy really consciously, and there were multiple layers to this process. I needed to trust her and I needed to trust the process really deeply, and that meant it took about two years; that's how long it took for her to come to a place and say, I'm ready to give up the dummy every single day.*

*I would say to her, 'I deeply trust that when you are ready, you will give up. I deeply trust that you know that I can hold these feelings for you, and when you are ready to be in this space to let those feelings out, I'm here and I'm with you.' So over a period of time, I started to offer some* Loving Limits *with it, as well as started doing* attachment play.

*The* Loving Limits *were that I was only willing for her to have the dummy to the car and then we put it in the car door. I was only willing for her to have it in the house was the next* Loving Limit. *And then it was only for bedtime. And then the last part was releasing it in relation to sleep.*

*So there's a few things that I'd love to say about that. Firstly, I made sure that I offered lots of time wherever we went out to really listen to those feelings. So for example, when we were at the car door and she put it in and then we went out somewhere to meet friends. There were often big feelings then, so I'd make sure that I'd arrived places earlier so that she had time and space to release, and I would make sure that I built up my own capacity so that I could really listen and give her what she needed.*

*And I was really present during those times. What also made it easy was having my own feelings listened to throughout this, and I began to see this deep journey that we're on with our children that the more listening and crying and feeling we do, the more they can bring to us. And that just kept being reflected over two years.*

*She was just under four when she gave it up. I could just see that this was so much about me because I had suppressed those feelings for the first two and a half years of her life, and so I gave her so many opportunities to release.*

*The other thing was I did loads of play. I would play things like I would suck dummies and I would pretend to dip them in different things and that they would taste disgusting, or, 'This one tastes really nice!' and we were really, really silly around the dummies.*

*We continued to do lots and lots of power reversal games, where she felt really powerful, such as: knocking me down with pillows; doing piggyback rides; having a magic wand; lots of symbolic play with dollies who had dummies and lost them and then couldn't find them, and then found them again; and playing hide and seek with the dummies.*

*So it was this shift that I started to notice – the more I played around with it, the more I let her have her feelings, the less she started to need the dummy. There was this great shift because she started to need it less, but she also started to ask for it less, and I just really held those* Loving Limits *until she got to about three.*

*And at this point I started to see huge changes in her. So, she was really shy and didn't like participating in group activities and I really already labelled her as a redhead and an introvert. And, slowly she became this whole new person. She went to activities. She was confident. She started speaking and she was full of life. She was vivacious and it was amazing to see that actually none of those labels I had given her were true. Yes, she's a bit sensitive and she might be cautious and stay back before she joins in. But when she feels safe and confident in something, she's so willing to do it, which was the opposite of what happened when she had a dummy. So, it was amazing to witness it and see this transformation. This whole growth happened within her.*

*And so the last part of this journey was very much the night's sleep. I'd always held this story that they need something to suck or to have some sort of movement to have sleep during the night. And I remember I had suggested to her just over three and a half years of age that maybe she could stop the dummy when she felt ready. I deeply trusted when she felt ready to give it up in the night. I said to her, 'I'm trusting that when you feel ready and feel willing, you do the thing you need to do.'*

*And one day she came to me out of the blue, and she said, 'Mama, I'm ready. I don't want the dummy anymore.' And I had tears rolling down my face because she had this autonomy and this choice around when it was going to be no longer serving her. Lots of fear came up for me because I was thinking, "Is she going to sleep? And how's she going to sleep without it? And oh, I'm going to be up all night with her!" So that night, I sat with that, and spoke to those parts of myself. 'She's not you. She's done this safely, she's had choice, she's had independence. Let's just see what happens. Let's see how it plays out.'*

*And so that night, I went to sleep and she didn't wake through the night. She didn't cry. She didn't look for the dummy. We were co-sleeping at the time. So I was with her the whole night and the next morning she said to me, 'I don't need this dummy anymore.' And I said, 'What should we do with the dummies?' And she said, 'Let's give it to other children who need a dummy.' And what I was in awe around was that she got to choose the whole process when she was ready with the support of* Loving Limits *and playing.*

*If I reflect back on what were the most important things that contributed – one was having clear* Loving Limits. *When you have older children, you can often work these out together. Also having my own listening time so that I had space and capacity to listen to her. And doing loads of play. Lots and lots and lots of attachment play. And most importantly, the trust. 'I deeply trust you, sweetheart. I deeply trust that when you are ready, you'll feel willing to share your feelings with me and I'm here.'*

*And so over those two years, with all of the accumulated feelings, there was hours and hours of crying over periods of time. I think the longest I listened to was an hour and five minutes, but there were lots and lots of times of listening. But what a journey, and it just showed me how amazing Aware Parenting is when we're willing to put all the pieces of the journey together."*

> ### Self-Compassion Moment
> How do you feel after reading this, especially if your child uses a dummy or used to, or if you used one as a child?
>
> I invite you to be deeply compassionate with yourself if your child has (or used to have) a dummy and you have used different ways to help them stop. I want to remind you that if you have done things in the past that you would do differently now, it's never too late to repair! So much love to you.

***From a child:*** *I love my toy Bunny, Nanny. I always have to have him with me when I come and stay with you. I need him so much. I get scared when I think I've lost him, but he just falls down the side of my bed sometimes. I know I'm seven now, and Mummy tells me I'm too old now for Bunny and I shouldn't need him any more, but I just do. I feel lost without him. Daddy says I've had him since I was a baby. He showed me a picture of me in my cot, clinging on to him. No wonder he is falling apart a bit. Thank you for making him a new coat. I really like how red it is. Oh Nanny, look, I dropped him in the mud. Nanny, Nanny, he is so muddy! Help! Help! Oh, thank you for washing him and making him all clean again. Oh but do you really need to hang him in the sunshine to dry? I don't think I can do without him. I feel all wobbly inside. Let's sit next to the washing line, Nanny. Can I sit on your lap and watch him? Seeing him there, I feel so sad. Oh Nanny, I'm crying. I'm crying and crying. I feel so sad. I miss him so much. Tears are coming out of me like that time I left the tap on in the bath and it overflowed and Mummy and Daddy got angry. Hold me, Nanny, while I cry. I feel alone forever. I feel so sad. I want to cry until it's night time. I want to cry until I'm eight. Oh, you tell me that you're here with me and you're listening. Oh Nanny, I can keep on crying with you. I want to cry until it's Christmas. I feel all hot and sweaty, too. There are so many tears. Oh, the crying is coming to an end. Oh I'm not crying any more. The tears are all gone. Oh Nanny, I can see Bunny up there, but I feel all calm sitting here with you. I don't feel that scary feeling any more. I love him, but I'm not lonely without him. Wowsers, Nanny, that crying was like some kind of magic. Can we go and play puzzles inside while we wait for him to dry? He's safe here. I'm safe with you. I love you, Nanny.*

## Chapter summary

The more we understand *control patterns*, what's going on for our child, and having compassion for both them and ourselves, **the more likely we will be able to respond to *control patterns* in helpful ways**.

If we're wanting to help our child move from suppression to expression, the most helpful way is to **start with connection, then move to *attachment play*, and then to *Loving Limits*.**

I share about **certain cautions in responding to *control patterns*, such as not using them with thumb sucking, only in two situations with food, and only after conversations and agreements with screens.**

Your compassion for your child when they're suppressing their feelings is such a beautiful gift to them.

## CHAPTER FOURTEEN

# Aggression – hitting, pushing and forcefully taking

***From a child who is hitting:***

*"I'm feeling scared, overwhelmed, powerless and frustrated – all mixed together.*

*I don't want to hit, but I have some really big feelings bubbling.*

*Please stop me from hitting.*

*And please don't shame me, judge me or punish me (even with an, 'It's not okay to hit.')*

*I didn't choose to do it. I don't want to do it. I want you to get here and stop me before I do it.*

*Please help me.*

*I feel even more feelings when you don't stop me from hitting, and I see the shock and hurt on other people's faces.*

*You keep everyone safe when you stop me from hitting.*

*Please listen to my feelings that are causing me to hit.*

*They're really uncomfortable and I'm not able to feel them on my own. I can't even feel them when I'm hitting.*

*Please give me one of those* Loving Limit *things.*

*I may start raging, but that's because the* Loving Limits *help me feel safe enough to let those feelings out.*

*Please keep saying no to my behaviour and yes to my feelings so I can cry and rage with you.*

*If I keep trying to hit or throw, it's not that I'm not taking you seriously.*

*I just need more safety to let out these big feelings I'm holding inside.*

*I need your help.*

*Please help me."*


**To a child who is hitting (or biting, forcefully taking or throwing);**

*"Hello, lovely you.*

*I see you. I see your feelings underneath the hitting.*

*I know you are loving and caring, and that it's painful feelings that are causing you to lash out.*

*I wonder if you are feeling scared, confused, overwhelmed, or frustrated, sweetheart?*

*I'm here to help.*

*I know that you don't enjoy hitting and that you don't want to hit.*

*Whenever I can, I will get in there before you lash out, and I will stop you.*

*I'm here to listen to all the feelings that lie underneath the hitting.*

*I know that you're really wanting to feel the relief from raging and crying with my loving support.*

*I see the loving you that is always there, hiding underneath this behaviour.*

## I'M HERE AND I'M LISTENING

*And I'm here to help you return to that lovingness.*

*When I stop you from hitting, I'm here and listening.*

*I can be with all of your fear and confusion, your overwhelm and frustration, your anger and outrage.*

*I welcome all of your feelings.*

*Your feelings are not too much for me.*

*And if you laugh, I know that the laughter is releasing fear.*

*And if you keep on trying to hit after I come in and tell you that I'm not willing for you to hit, I know that you're feeling big feelings. I will keep saying no to the hitting and yes to those feelings.*

*I won't take what you're saying personally.*

*I will keep on listening to your feelings.*

*My love for you is big and wide.*

*Your feelings are not too much for my love for you.*

*I will keep on saying no to the hitting and yes to your feelings.*

*I see who you really are and what is really going on for you.*

*I am not willing to punish you, shame you or judge you when you hit.*

*And I'm not willing for anyone else to punish you, shame you or judge you when you hit.*

*And I will do all I can to help you feel safe enough to express the feelings that are causing the hitting, so that you don't need to hit any more.*

*I love you."*

## Compassion for us all

When my son was hitting and head butting after his dad and I separated, I found it so *incredibly* painful, so if you're experiencing anything like that, I am sending you so much love and compassion. I have an understanding of how you might be feeling.

Or perhaps your child is experiencing things like this at the hands of another child and if so, I also understand how painful that can be and I send you lots of love.

I remember when my son stopped hitting and head butting, after helping him heal from the powerlessness of experiencing his family change so much.

*It was as if I had my son back again.*

I love helping parents see that children who are hitting really need our help, and that we can support them, without ever turning to harshness, ignoring or other painful methods.

This culture often doesn't take aggression seriously, with comments such as, "Oh it's just a phase that all children go though," or, "Just leave them to it, they'll be fine." From an Aware Parenting perspective, no! and no!

> Hitting is not just a phase, and I would not ever recommend leaving children who are hitting or being hit. Hitting (and pushing and forcefully taking) are generally caused by painful accumulated feelings from past stress or trauma.

> When a child is hitting, they're not feeling powerful, and they're not enjoying it. They might appear to feel powerful and they might be laughing, but that doesn't indicate enjoyment. Laughter at times like this is often an indication of fear that is being released.

A child who is hitting doesn't feel powerful. They're in fight or flight mode (hence the fighting) and it's possible that they're feeling a combination of feelings such as fear, powerlessness and frustration. Or, they might be feeling numb, because hyperarousal can disconnect them from their sensations.

*Hitting is not a developmental phase, and children need adults to lovingly and powerfully intervene when there's any kind of aggression going on.*

*There are two key actions we can take with hitting:*

- We can work *preventatively*, so that the child experiences less of what is causing those feelings, and also so they get to release those feelings in safe and healing ways through laughter, crying and raging with our loving support.
- And we can respond in the moment, either with *attachment play* or *Loving Limits*. Instead of harshness or ignoring, we can meet our child with loving compassion, supporting them to release the feelings that are causing the hitting in safe and healing ways, so that they can return to their natural, gentle and loving selves.

## Exploring what shows up for us when our child shows aggression

*Self-Reflection Moment*

*Has your child ever hit, bit, thrown, or forcefully taken things out of other children's hands?*

*If so, how have you felt?*

*What have your thoughts been?*

*How have you responded?*

*I'm sending so much love and compassion to you and all the feelings and all the ways that you have responded in those challenging times.*

Let's look at the three different possible reasons for your responses, if you have found it hard to respond in calm and compassionate ways.

- What you *think*.
- What you *need*.
- What you *feel*.

## What you *think*

If we are telling ourselves harsh things about the reason for that behaviour, it is going to be very difficult to feel compassionate towards them. I want to remind you how normal and natural that is, given that you have grown up in a culture and live in a culture where core beliefs about the causes of aggression are not compassionate.

> *Self-Reflection Moment*
>
> *I invite you to reflect back on a time when your child was doing those things.*
>
> *What were you telling yourself?*
>
> *Can you see how these thoughts would have contributed to your feelings and your response?*

I'd love to offer some suggestions of ways of thinking that can really help us as parents. Do any of these resonate with you?

*"They're doing this because they feel scared or powerless or frustrated."*

*"They might look powerful, but they don't feel powerful."*

*"They don't look like they're calling for help, but this is a cry for help."*

*"They really need my help."*

> *Self-Reflection Moment*
>
> *I invite you to choose one (or more) that is a fit for you, or find a phrase that really helps you stay connected with your compassion for your child.*
>
> *Once you have it, I invite you to write it down where you will see it regularly, so you can be reminded of how you want to choose to think, especially if this behaviour happens a lot.*
>
> *That might be on your phone, on a note on the fridge, or on a Post-it note.*
>
> *Where would you like to keep note of this phrase?*
>
> *Can you imagine yourself thinking those thoughts during a time that your child is showing one of these behaviours?*
>
> *I invite you to imagine yourself in that situation, thinking those thoughts, practicing in your mind.*
>
> *What else might you need?*

## What you *need*

If your needs are not being met in the present, particularly in relation to agency, autonomy and choice – but any needs – you might easily flip into feeling frustrated, powerless, angry or outraged if your child takes something from another child, pushes their sibling, or is harsh with the dog. Those unexpressed feelings from your own unmet needs are likely to bubble up and out when you see your child doing that.

I'd also love to acknowledge how normal our fight or flight response is in those moments. If your child is about to hit you, or has just hit you, the impulse to fight back can arise. So, again, I invite you to be deeply compassionate with yourself if you have ever responded in those ways.

> *Self-Compassion Moment*
>
> *As always, I invite you to drop any sticks of self-judgment, guilt or*

*self-harshness if you have responded in harsh ways. I want to remind you again that those sticks are internalised from this culture, and just as punishing your child if they are aggressive will not help but will actually add to them having more pent-up painful feelings, so you punishing yourself if you react to their aggression will mean that you have more painful feelings and less ability to respond calmly and compassionately. Instead, you might choose to connect with and express any sadness you feel when you remember your past actions to a loving listener, so you can mourn what you did.*

*Self-Reflection Moment*

*Are you getting your needs for agency, autonomy and choice met?*

*How about your other needs, such as for sleep, emotional support, self-connection and practical support?*

*Are you willing for your needs to be met more?*

*What one tangible thing could you do to meet them more? (This might include a request to someone else.)*

I want to remind you that any time you make a choice to do something you love, that will be meeting your needs for agency and choice. The more you connect with how powerful you are in that way, the less you will feel powerless in those moments, and the less likely you will be to react in harsh ways to your child.

## What you *feel*

It is very common for our own feelings from the past to bubble up at times like this. Please only reflect on these next points if you have enough emotional spaciousness and a sense of support. When our child hits their sibling or is harsh in other ways, it is a part of our own healing process that old unexpressed feelings can bubble up from similar experiences we had as a child.

So, if you were:

- *tickled* by a sibling;
- physically *hurt* by a parent;
- *overpowered* by a parent, sibling or teacher;
- saw an adult physically *hurting* another child;
- treated *harshly* by other children or teachers at school; or
- experienced power-over in other ways such as *medical procedures* or traumatic dentist visits,

those feelings might show up when your child shows aggression.

This is where I want to remind you that this is part of your own natural healing process. You might be feeling that combination of feeling safe enough in the present (because you are now the adult and your child will not leave you) while connecting with the memories or feelings from the past.

That is your natural process of healing from stress and trauma in operation.

However, of course it is not our children's job to help us heal from our stress and trauma, nor do they have the capacity to help. In addition, our own reactions that are actually aimed towards that original person are not meant to be received by our child and may actually be stressful or traumatic for them to experience.

This is why it is *essential* for us to receive regular opportunities to express our feelings to another adult who is able to listen lovingly to us and who trusts our own innate wisdom to heal.

> *Self-Reflection Moment*
> 
> *Do you sense that some of your feelings are bubbling up from the past?*
> 
> *Are you willing to take those to another adult for listening?*
> 
> *What action are you willing to take over the upcoming days and weeks to support that process?*

## Four things to reduce or prevent the likelihood of aggression in the first place

One of the underlying causes of aggression is powerlessness.

How can you help a child to feel less powerless in the first place?

1. Offer more *choices*.
2. *Refrain* from *power-over, coercion, force, punishments, shaming and blaming*.
3. Regularly offer *attachment play*, particularly power-reversal games, to support them to release powerlessness.
4. Listen to plenty of *crying* and *raging* to help them release powerlessness, fear and rage.

### 1. Offer more choices

If we want a child to feel more powerful and less powerless, one key way is to meet their needs for choice, agency and autonomy.

Here are a few ways you can do that:

(for young children, just offering two choices can be most helpful!)

- *"Would you like this toothbrush or that one?"*
- *"Would you like to wear these trousers or those?"*
- *"Would you like to sit next to me or Daddy for the movie?"*

- *"Which book would you like me to read you tonight?"*
- *"What pyjamas do you want to wear?"*
- *"Do you want to hang out with us or your friends this afternoon?"*
- *"Would you like to come food shopping with me and choose what you want?"*
- *"What would you like for dinner? The options I'm willing to make are pasta and vegetables, that rice dish, or curry."*

In addition, meeting their needs for *autonomy* and *agency* can also include refraining from telling them what to do if they are working things out for themselves, and offering to help them do new things rather than just stepping in and helping without asking.

## 2. Refrain from power-over, coercion, force, punishments, shaming and blaming

Whenever we tell a child that they *should* do something, they *have* to do something, or we make subtle or not so subtle *threats*, a child is likely to feel powerless, frustrated or outraged. The more we *coerce* them, *force* them or use our greater physical, emotional, intellectual and economic *power* over them, the more feelings they will have and the more likely those feelings will show up as aggression.

If we *do* ever use power-over them, or force or coerce them to do things, then listening to their feelings and giving them empathy, and repairing where possible, will mean that those feelings will be released and will be less likely to accumulate to the point of aggression.

Since Aware Parenting includes non-punitive discipline, we are aiming to *refrain* from punishing children or shaming or blaming them. However, we may find at times that we do things to our children that were done to us. The more that happens, the more painful feelings and stress will accumulate in their bodies, possibly leading to aggression.

However, despite all our effort and care, the majority of children *will* frequently feel powerless, especially the younger and smaller they are. Simply not being able to do the things that they see us do can lead to powerlessness. In addition, growing up in this culture means many experiences of power-over for most children.

There will inevitably be times where they feel powerless, such as:

- when they have a new sibling;
- being put in a car seat, stroller or high chair;
- other children taking things from them, pushing them or hurting them;
- being told what to do by adults and older siblings;
- being told what to do at school;
- being exposed to parents fighting;
- parental separation; or
- moving house.

### 3. Regularly offer *attachment play* to help them release powerlessness

*Attachment play* can be used to prevent aggression from happening in the first place! The more they get to release feelings of powerlessness, fear and frustration, the less likely they are to ever get to the point of aggression.

**The magic wand game:** this is a contingency play game where you do what they tell you to do each time they wave a magic wand. You can adapt it to the remote control game, where they point a remote control at you and choose what you do.

Power-reversal games are *particularly* helpful to prevent aggression. Here are a few ideas:

**The swing game:** your child is on the swing, facing you, and each time they come forward, you pretend to go flying in the air or fall over. Again, mock surprise, fear or anger are more likely to bring the healing laughter.

**The scary puppet game:** this is a game where you pretend your child scares you with a crocodile puppet or a plastic spider. Pretend to be scared by jumping up in the air. Let them chase you with it.

**The "there's no time" game:** let them set a timer and you need to do something quickly. This can help if you often have time pressure and are asking them to be quick. It can also help with feelings they have in relation to you asking them to get off devices. This time they are choosing the finishing time and the more mock-stressed you can be, the funnier it can be for them!

> *Self-Reflection Moment*
>
> *Can you imagine yourself playing these games with your child?*
>
> *Are there other contingency or power-reversal games that you like playing with your child?*
>
> *Are you willing to play these more often?*
>
> *What might you need so that you are more willing?*

Chelsie Spence, who you met earlier in the book, shares about the power of *attachment play* as a preventative to aggression. She starts off by explaining the background scenario again:

*"My three-year-old son, Maximus had progressively become aggressive since the birth of his baby brother Finn, now one. He was aggressive towards Finn and me and generally carried a lot of tension in his body, often roaring at us with a tense stance. We started working with Rafa Guadalupe, an Aware Parenting instructor, to address his aggressive behaviour. She told us that the main reason for his aggression was a lack of expressing his uncomfortable feelings and stress after the arrival of Finn.*

*To address his aggression we started with ten-minutes of* attachment play *every day, including power reversal games. When Max would roar at me, I invited him to play tigers with me for ten minutes (which was the amount of time I was willing to play for without resentment or boredom). After putting on the timer, we began. He chased me around the house roaring loudly while I screamed in mock-terror. I would let him catch me and he would pretend to eat and scratch me, in response to which I screamed loudly, pretending about how much it was hurting. All the while I was screaming, he was roaring and laughing, and even though he was pretending to hurt me, he was being so gentle.*

*With daily* attachment play *and regular* Loving Limits *to help him release his uncomfortable feelings, Max did a complete 180 in his reactions to his brother. He stopped reacting when Finn came over to touch what he was playing with and stopped snatching toys out of Finn's hands, and instead would go and get toys Finn could play with. It was the most beautiful thing to finally see loving exchanges between my boys."*

> ### Self-Compassion Moment
> How do you feel after reading this chapter so far? I'm sending love to any feelings you might feel. We can experience a lot of emotional pain seeing our children use aggression towards others, particularly towards their siblings or ourselves.

### 4. Listen to plenty of raging and crying to help them release powerlessness

The larger a percentage of their feelings they get to express, the less feelings there are to accumulate to the point of aggression.

## Immediate interventions – *attachment play* in response to aggression

### Power-reversal games

Power-reversal games are an incredible way to intervene when children are acting aggressively. They help children:

- *feel* more powerful and safe;
- *release* feelings of powerlessness; and
- *heal* from past experiences of powerlessness.

### How do power-reversal games work?

They work because in the game, the child becomes the more powerful one. This *counteracts* feelings of powerlessness, while the laughter helps them *release* past powerlessness and fear. The child literally gets to complete the resolution of the fight or flight response but this time, they get to fight and be the victor, all in a fun, safe and connected way. Remember the *balance of attention*? Here, the child experiences being safe in the present, while attending to the past experience of powerlessness, and getting to feel powerful in the here and now.

Here are a couple of specific examples:

**The pillow fight:** your child knocks you with the pillow and you fall down dramatically, with either mock surprise, *"How did you do that?"* or pretend fear, *"Eek!"* or mock anger, *"Whatever you do, don't do that again!"* and let it happen again and again.

**The "you keep catching me" game:** Your child chases you, and you pretend to be clumsy, to fall over, to keep on being caught, and keep on being surprised.

In these power-reversal games, your child gets to be the more powerful one, and you pretend that they are knocking you over each time they swing or hit you with the pillow or chase you around the house. The more you can be goofy and exaggeratedly wonder about how they can possibly be that powerful, and the more they laugh, the more that laughter and experience of being more powerful than you helps them release and heal from old experiences of powerlessness.

> Self-Reflection Moment
>
> How do you imagine you would feel playing these in response to your child's aggression?
>
> Can you imagine which one/s your child might respond to?
>
> Can you think of any other games that might be helpful?

Suze shared an *attachment play* game she found helpful in response to her son's aggression:

*"One thing I have been doing recently is 'air fighting' with my five year old son. He can really lash out at times – hitting and kicking – and when he does, I flip it round and say, 'Oh you want to box or fight?' and then we pretend to punch and kick each other but don't connect, i.e. I stay far enough back that he almost makes contact but doesn't and then when he does it I move the body part he 'hit' as if he'd connected really powerfully, and I'd say, 'Awww' or, Pow' or, 'Aw, you got me'. I find it releases his need to lash out without anyone getting hurt or in trouble and gives him a good laugh."*

Alishya shared about how she responded to her son's aggression with a playful limit using nonsense play[36]:

*"I carefully put the baby down and turned my son's aggression into a game. Pressing buttons on his body and grabbing his hands saying, 'Is this button the off switch?' 'Is this button the sleep switch?' 'Is this button the lay-down switch?' 'Do I turn this first to turn this boy into lay-down mode?' etc. Well, it quickly turned his aggression into laughter and play, and eventually I found the right button. His little sister even joined in on*

---

36  You can find out more about playful limits in Aletha's *Attachment Play* book

*the game. She fell asleep after a few minutes of playing and he fell asleep much quicker than usual (by about half the time actually!)"*

In the following example, I also used nonsense play when my son was hitting and kicking me.

*When my son was nine, I created the "Shall We Dance?" game. He had been on screens a lot while he had been ill and I was wanting to support him to get off. After conversations and agreements, I then asked him if he was willing to get off the screen and he started to hit and kick. I did some other attachment play but nothing seemed to be bringing a shift – and then the new game came to me.*

*The "Shall We Dance?" game is sung to the tune of the song in The King and I. Every time he tried to push, hit or kick me, I would protect myself from getting hurt, pretend that he was inviting me to dance, and say in a silly voice, "Oh I'd LOVE to dance with you! Oh! A waltz!" (when he tried to hit my hand) and, "Oh, a new kind of rap dance" (when he tried to hit my chest), and "Oh, yes, I LOVE flamenco," when he started kicking his feet on my legs. And I'd pretend to do those dances with him, engaging and meeting him with whatever he was doing! And he smiled a lot. We did it for quite a while, and after that he happily and calmly played with his sister and was willing to connect all day, and showed no interest in screens.*

*What I loved about singing the song while playing the game was that it really helped me to stay calm and loving, even when he was trying to kick or hit me. I played the game a few times after that with him, and every time, I found it really helpful for both of us.*

> ### Self-Reflection Moment
> Can you imagine playing either of these games or something like them if your child is trying to hit, bite or kick?
>
> Can you think of games using your own songs that might help you stay connected with compassion and fun?

### What if your child keeps on hitting and *attachment play* doesn't seem to work?

In this case you may need offer a *Loving Limit*, and to see if your child can release the feelings that are causing the aggression through raging and tears.

## Immediate interventions – *Loving Limits* and *holding* in response to aggression

There are many times where *attachment play* doesn't work to stop the aggression and help the feelings be released, or we simply need to move in promptly to stop someone getting hurt.

This is where *Loving Limits* come in. I want to remind you of a few things about *Loving Limits* that I talked about earlier in the book.

- We are saying *no* to the *behaviour* and *yes* to the *feelings* that are causing the behaviour. That means, that once we've stopped the behaviour, *we don't expect our child to be relaxed. We expect them to express the feelings underneath the behaviour.*
- We need to be relatively *calm* and loving for *Loving Limits* to 'work'. If we move towards our child from a powerless or angry place, we are not likely to be providing the emotional safety for healing raging or crying to happen.
- We are aiming to do the most *minimal* action *required* to stop the behaviour. If we can simply hold our child's wrist to stop the hitting, then that is all that is necessary.

I also want to remind you of the phrase I enjoy. It is only one of many phrases you might use.

I like to say something like;

*"I'm not willing for you to hit, because I'm here to keep everyone safe, and I'm right here and I'm listening."*

We may often need to repeat this phrase after we stop them hitting (or whatever the aggression is), because they might try to start hitting again. I invite you to connect in with what you want to be thinking here, because at this point it's really easy to go into conditioned thoughts, rather than those that you choose. Then, if your child starts crying or raging, you might keep on doing the minimum physical action necessary to keep them and others safe, while offering empathy and the verbal limit if required.

I want to remind you about the healing that happens when a child completes the release that occurs after the fight or flight response. Often this includes vigorous lashing out with their arms and legs. However, it is our role to make sure that no-one gets hurt and that the child is actually releasing rather than still in the aggression of the fight response. For this, *they need to know they are safe.*

The most important thing here is your emotional state. If you are feeling frustrated, powerless, or scared, it is probably going to be hard for you to offer an embodied *Loving Limit* that helps them feel safe.

This is why it's so important to be working with:

- your *thoughts* at these times;
- increasing the amount your *need*s are met (particularly agency, autonomy and choice); and
- *healing* from your childhood experiences of powerlessness.

The more you are:

- choosing to *think* compassionate and clear thoughts;
- experiencing true *power* in your day-to-day life; and
- responding from your *adult* self rather than past powerlessness of your inner children,

the more likely you are going to be able to offer a true, embodied *Loving Limit*.

This is where your child feels:

- a sense of *emotional safety* and loving *presence*;
- a sense of physical *safety* in being prevented from hurting others or damaging things;
- a connection with the *painful feelings* that are causing the behaviour in the first place; and
- the *balance of attention* between the safety in the present while revisiting the painful feelings from the past.

If a child is being really destructive, we might need to come in with *holding* to prevent them from hurting others or damaging things. And again, this means doing the minimum *holding* required while still providing the physical safety of our arms. I talked more about *holding* in the chapter on *Loving Limits*, which I invite you to revisit for all the details.

## Please always listen to yourself here. If you feel uncomfortable doing something, please stop!

Ideally, during *Loving Limits* or *holding*, a child will express the big feelings that were causing the behaviour, will complete the healing process and will come out the other side feeling deeply calm and relaxed and you will be able to feel that in their muscles.

However, you might not feel able or willing to stay with the feelings until the whole chunk of them is released. In this case, you might see the remaining feelings showing up again later.

The more you listen to raging and tears at other times too, the less likely it is that those feelings will accumulate to the point of aggression.

> *Self-Reflection Moment*
> What do you need to be able to offer powerful and loving embodied Loving Limits?

> Are you wanting to focus more on attending to:
>
> Your thoughts in the moment?
>
> Your needs in general, including agency, autonomy and choice, so that you feel more truly powerful?
>
> Your feelings of powerlessness, fear and rage from your childhood?

Sometimes we will have a sense that the most helpful thing to respond with is by offering a *Loving Limit*. In other situations we can combine *Loving Limits* with *attachment play*.

If neither attachment play nor Loving Limits seem to be making a difference at the time of the aggression, then I recommend doing more preventative work – with connection and non-directive child-centred play, contingency play, power-reversal games and listening to feelings that come up spontaneously.

***From a child:*** *I don't know why, but one minute I feel calm, and the next minute I want to lash out. I know that Robert only bumped into me by accident, but I just had to hit him. I don't know what happens to me, Dad. All I know that it's like this red hot fire bursts out of me from a million kilometres below the ground. Whenever someone knocks into me, or says no, or does any little thing, this rage erupts. I kind of feel scared about it myself, because it's like it comes from nowhere. I know that people get shocked. Oh, Dad, he's done it again. He called me "stupid" and there it is, I want to hit him again. Please help me, Dad. Oh you do help! You are there! You get in between us and you use those weird words that I joke about you sounding like a parenting robot. But Dad, please keep doing that. Your big hand is bigger than mine and you stop me from hitting Robert again. The red hot fire comes up again and now I want to push you. Robert's going outside. Your hand is there, and I'm pushing you. I feel the heat of the fire all through my body. I want to roar. Perhaps I do. Then you smile.*

*I see your smile, Dad, and I wonder what you'll do next. Oh, you're pretending to do boxing, but you don't touch me, and you go "POW!" and "BIFF!" and "ZAP!" And kind of pretend that I'm knocking you over. It's so corny, Dad, but I find myself wanting to join in! "POW!" back to you, Dad! We do fake boxing moves around the kitchen and you keep on dancing about like a boxer. At first, I'm all fiery and I still want to hit you for real, but then we keep doing the corny words and I start to join in with your laughter. The fire bubbles out into the air whenever I laugh. How does that happen? We're boxing and biffing and saying weird stuff and I start to feel lighter. The fire's gone out and I feel kind of calm. Ahhhh... I'm back. I'm here. I can breathe again. I can see clearly. Thanks, Dad! Let's go and play some soccer with Robert!*

## Chapter summary

**It's normal and natural for us to have big feelings showing up when our child is showing aggression.** Getting support for our own feelings can help us be able to respond in helpful ways.

We talked about the things we can **do in the moment to respond to aggression, and things we can do to reduce the likelihood of aggression happening in the first place.**

*Attachment play* **is a helpful** way to both respond to and prevent aggression, particularly power-reversal games with laughter.

*Loving Limits* **and** *holding* are important and powerful ways to respond to aggression – with all the usual caveats.

I so celebrate you every time you can
stay calm and compassionate in the face
of your child/ren's aggression.

CHAPTER FIFTEEN

# Our own power-over and aggression and how we can repair

> *Self-Reflection Moment*
> *Have you ever become reactive or aggressive with your child, or used coercion or power over them?*

> *Self-Compassion Moment*
> *If you have, I invite you to drop any guilt or self-judgment sticks if you're reaching for them at this moment. I want to remind you about what I said at the beginning of the book about punishing ourselves. It really won't help. Self-compassion will be way more helpful for your and your child/ren. You might feel sad when you reflect back on those moments. I invite you to be compassionate with yourself and to hear the sadness, or express it to your Listening Partner or Aware Parenting instructor.*

If you have reacted to your child in this way, you're not alone. In working as an Aware Parenting instructor and mentor since 2005, I have heard from so many parents about those painful moments where they acted in ways that they really didn't want to. When I was in a lot of pain after separating from the father of my children, there were many times that I responded in reactive ways to my children.

I want to remind you of the thing I say so much – it is completely natural and understandable for us to act in this way, given:

- the culture we grew up in, where most of us received punishments, rewards and power-over – and didn't have our feelings heard so we could heal from those experiences, and
- the culture we live in, where parents have little of the wider community and support that is vital to healthy family life, and often feel stressed, stretched and overwhelmed.

However, there are things we can do to help ourselves be less likely to react in these ways to our children.

Remember earlier on in the book where I explained that what we learn in this culture is how to judge ourselves when we do things that don't fit with our values, rather than knowing how to discover the source of our behaviour and make changes there?

When we understand the origin of our behaviour, we can bring about true change. When we know why we are being reactive, shouting, or using threats or power-over, we can then attend to the source of that in compassionate ways, which means we're less likely to do that again.

Sometimes, we might catch ourselves as we're about to go into harshness. *Attachment play* can be an amazing go-to here, as a way of releasing our frustration so we feel relieved and are less likely to get harsh.

Here's a game I used to play with my son when he was younger, if I was feeling frustrated and about to do something I'd regret. I called it the 'Over the Top Game' and I learnt it from Aletha's book *Attachment Play*. Here's me sharing about it, nearly a decade ago:

*"One game I play with my son (who's eight) when I'm starting to feel frustrated, is I start to talk in over the top ways, something like this, 'If I get frustrated, then you will get frustrated, and you will hit me, and my head will fall off, and the dog will bark and the neighbours will cry and the house will fall down!' Each time I make up some ridiculous story about the calamities that will happen, and he laughs. He really loves it! I see him healing with the laughter."*

This game can also help our children and ourselves heal from past experiences where we've got frustrated and have been harsh or used power-over.

The other wonderful thing about Aware Parenting is that we can repair.

## We can help our child heal from the stress or trauma that we inflicted upon them in those painful moments.

In this chapter, we're going to go into the repair process in depth, including acknowledging, taking responsibility for our behaviour and feelings, listening to their feelings and helping them feel powerful again. This is very different from what most of us were taught to do – which is to judge ourselves, feel guilty, or say sorry a million times but not really be available to listen to their feelings and help them heal because we're so busy beating ourselves up with guilt and shame sticks.

**You really can change your behaviour at its source, and you absolutely can help your child heal from the times you behaved in ways that you wish you hadn't.**

## Exploring when our own aggression shows up

> *Self-Compassion Moment*
> 
> *Once again, I am going to invite you to be deeply compassionate with yourself here, and to drop any sticks that you feel tempted to pick up! Acting harshly is already painful enough for us, and adding a whole lot of guilt or shame to the mix does not help anyone in any way. I'm going to invite you to be really gentle with yourself. Perhaps you'd like to put your arms around yourself when you're reading this, or put one hand on your forehead and one on your belly? Perhaps you'd like to snuggle in bed when you're reading it?*

I also want to remind you that it is natural for us to move into aggression at times, given that most of us would have grown up with punishments, power-over and coercion, and very little opportunity to heal from those experiences. This means that most of us will have lots of pent-up feelings of powerlessness, frustration, anger and outrage. And just like with children, if we are not feeling safe to express those in healing ways, it's highly likely that they will accumulate and come out in aggression, particularly if we're feeling stressed in general, or if our child isn't willing to cooperate with us, or keeps doing things we ask them not to do.

For parents, I'm including in the aggression category things like:

- shouting;
- punishments;
- judging;
- shaming;
- power-over;
- threats; and
- hitting.

### Self-Reflection Moment

Have you ever done any of these or any other forms of aggression to your child?

Rather than judge yourself, I invite yourself to mourn what happened.

Do you feel sad when you remember doing this?

Are you willing to feel some of that sadness?

Do you experience enough support to express the sadness you feel when you remember doing that?

If you'd like to imagine me there with you, please do.

Would you like to connect with your Listening Partner and share your feelings with them?

I want to remind you that this is like Aware Parenting with yourself – feeling your feelings, rather than punishing yourself.

If you were your own best friend, what might you say to yourself while feeling that sadness?

### Self-Compassion Moment

I'm sending you so much love, and so much compassion to all the feelings you're feeling.

I invite you to notice if self-judgment, guilt or shame sticks come in, and see if you're willing and able to put those down and return to compassion for the sadness, or whatever other feelings you might be feeling, as part of mourning what happened.

***Just as punishments don't work, neither does self-judgment. We can judge ourselves for years and years, but because that does not address the source of our behaviour, it doesn't mean that we will be less likely to behave like that again. In fact, because it adds more pain, in the form of those emotional bruises of guilt and shame, it actually means we are more likely to repeat those behaviours again.***

## The source of our aggression

Growing up in this culture, we learnt to punish ourselves rather than:

- *feel* sadness and mourn that we did what we did;
- compassionately *understand* the source of our behaviour; and
- *support* ourselves at the causal level to be less likely to do that thing again.

In the last section, I invited you to mourn when you remember doing what you did. Next, I would love to invite you to compassionately understand the source of your behaviour.

Again, if you would like to imagine me with you as you do that, please do. Alternatively, would you like to take these questions to your *Listening Partner* or other emotional support person? And if you're already feeling overwhelmed or guilty, I invite you to skip these for now. You can always come back to them later, if you want to.

So, let's explore why you did what you did.

> *Self-Reflection Moment*
>
> *I invite you to remember a time when you did something you might call aggressive, harsh or reactive to your child, and then reflect back on that time. I imagine you might find the process is easier if you remember something fairly recent that you can remember clearly.*
>
> **Would you like to reflect on:**
>
> What were you thinking?
>
> What were you telling yourself about your child or what they were doing?
>
> What were you thinking about yourself?
>
> What were you telling yourself about that situation?
>
> When you think those thoughts now, how do you feel?
>
> How much were your needs met at the time?

*Were you experiencing much agency, autonomy and choice?*

*Were you needing cooperation or consideration or appreciation?*

*Were you wanting care or understanding or respect?*

*Were you feeling stressed? Tired? Hungry? Sick? Exhausted? Lonely?*

*Did the situation remind you of something from your childhood?*

*Were you feeling big feelings as a result?*

*Did you feel younger or smaller?*

*Did you feel powerless, frustrated or outraged?*

*Did you feel overwhelmed?*

*Did you feel scared or terrified?*

*When you reflect back on these questions and this situation, what could you do differently so that you are less likely to react again?*

I know it's tempting to skip over self-reflections, but I want to remind you that the more you understand the source of your behaviour and the more you attend to those sources, the less likely it is that you will do things that you don't want to do.

*Self-Reflection Moment*

*What might you like to replace those* **thoughts** *with, or what information might you need to help you at these times?*

*I invite you to write out 'Aware Parenting thoughts' that would be helpful to think if this happens again.*

*Is there some information you need about Aware Parenting or other things? What are you willing to do to access that information?*

*What* **needs** *are you willing to have met more?*

*What practical things could you do now so that those needs get met more?*

*Is there any action you are willing to take to reduce the amount of stress in your life?*

> *Is there anything you can do to help yourself feel less stressed?*
>
> *Are you willing to attend to your **feelings** and have them lovingly heard by either inner or outer loving presences?*
>
> *Are you willing to set that up now, eg. reaching out to set up a Listening Partnership, reaching out to one of your existing Listening Partners, or to an Aware Parenting instructor?*

I'm sending so much love to all your feelings and all your needs, and all the younger parts of you who experienced painful things and learnt to think in harsh ways!

## Offering ourselves compassion and not punishing ourselves

I know that I've said this a lot; I keep repeating it because I know what a huge difference it makes in practicing Aware Parenting!

***I want to remind you that all the ways you punish yourself in your parenting are ways that you learnt, through being punished, seeing other children be punished and shamed and judged, and through witnessing adults shaming and judging themselves.***

> I want to remind you that just as punishing children doesn't work because it doesn't address the source of their behaviour, neither does punishing ourselves. It doesn't attend to the source of our behaviour, it doesn't mean we are less likely to do it again, it doesn't help our child, and it's likely to add more emotional pain which means we are MORE likely to behave in ways we don't want to, rather than less!

So, any time you punish yourself in relation to how you've been or what you've done in your parenting, I invite you to see if you're willing to drop that stick.

Becoming conscious of the ways in which we judge ourselves can be very painful.

However, having awareness is an essential start in the process of change, which step by step can look a bit like this:

- punishing ourselves without being conscious of it and just feeling guilt, shame or other uncomfortable feelings;
- punishing ourselves and being aware of the thoughts – but still believing they are true;
- becoming really aware of exactly how we are punishing ourselves with harsh thoughts;
- being aware that the thoughts aren't true and didn't come from us;
- being willing to stop punishing ourselves some of the time;
- starting to be compassionate with ourselves some of the time;
- not being willing to ever punish ourselves ever; and finally,
- being compassionate with ourselves always.

*Self-Reflection Moment*

*So, again, please check in with yourself to see if you're willing to become more aware of the harsh thoughts you've been believing about yourself. If you have a no, please skip this. If you have a yes, perhaps you'd like to imagine me next to you, offering you unconditional love. I am here to ask you:*

*What are those harsh thoughts?*

*How do you feel in terms of sensations in your body when you think those things about yourself?*

*Are you open to the possibility that they aren't true?*

*Does it resonate with you that doing this to yourself actually doesn't help?*

*What happens in your body if you are open to these possibilities?*

*I invite you to share these answers with one of your loving listeners.*

## Offering repair to our child

Offering repair to our child after we have acted in aggressive or harsh ways is going to be so much easier if we're not bashing ourselves with guilt sticks.

However, if you are still feeling guilty (because it does take time to free ourselves from this cultural conditioning) you can still repair.

Here are some of the elements that I think are helpful in the repair process (they don't need to be in this order and if our child is already crying or clearly upset, we would listen to their feelings first):

1. to *acknowledge* what we've done (ideally, without the guilt sticks, self-judgment and shame);
2. to take *responsibility* for our behaviour and to make it clear that it's not their responsibility;
3. to *listen* to their feelings; and
4. to *help* them feel powerful.

Please note again that the language elements of this are from me and are not classical Aware Parenting.

### 1. To acknowledge what we've done and the regret we feel (ideally, without the guilt sticks, self-judgment and shame)

This continues on from what we were just talking about.

**Much of traditional apology is a form of self-punishment.**

For example, self-punishment in the form of:

- "I *shouldn't* have done that."
- "I was a *bad* mummy for doing that."
- "That *wasn't okay*, what I just did."
- "That was *naughty* of me to do that."

As I shared earlier, language is important to me because it affects both how we feel and how the recipient of the words feels.

So, I have an invitation for reflection:

> *Self-Reflection Moment*
> *If you think those thoughts, how do you feel in your body?*

In addition, our self-punishing apologies teach our children to also punish themselves if they act in harsh ways. It doesn't help them to compassionately understand why they did what they did.

If you're hitting yourself with those guilt or shame sticks, you'll feel shame or guilt, so you'll also be less present to listen to your child's feelings. Shame and guilt don't help us to change. Compassionately understanding the three reasons for our behaviour and making change there is what helps us less likely to be harsh.

**Skilled, compassionate and playful repair can build even stronger connection with our child while modelling to them how to repair with compassionate self-responsibility rather than guilt and shame.**

I'd love to offer something that you could say to acknowledge what you did and express the regret or sadness that you feel having done it, without judging yourself. I invite you to connect in with yourself to see if it resonates with you.

*"I really regret that I did that to you, because I want to take responsibility for my feelings so that you feel safe with me."*

I invite you to reflect on what you would like to say.

What words are a fit for you?

One way of connecting in with words that might be helpful is to reflect back on a time when you were a child and a parent or other adult did something harsh to you.

> *Self-Reflection Moment*
> *What would you have loved to have heard from them in terms of a repair?*
> *Would you like to say those things when you are repairing with your child/ren?*

### 2. To take responsibility for our behaviour and to make it clear that it's not their responsibility

This is vital and is one of the key differences from what most of us experienced as children. If our parents responded in harsh ways, it is likely that they didn't take responsibility for that. Because of a child's cognitive understanding, it is likely that we then believed that we were responsible for that reaction in our parents, especially if they said things like, "You made me feel…" or, "You made me do that".

This can have huge effects on us. Many of us learnt to take responsibility for our parents' feelings, needs or behaviours, learnt to believe harsh things about ourselves, and moulded ourselves in particular ways to be less likely to 'cause' those things to happen again. This can then transfer in adulthood to us taking responsibility for other adults' feelings, needs and behaviours.

***When we very clearly take responsibility for our own behaviour as parents, and the feelings and needs that caused that, something entirely different happens.***

Yes, our child might have still felt scared when we were reactive – or had other painful feelings – which still need to be heard. However, it is unlikely that they will take responsibility for what happened, blame themselves, try to change themselves, and believe all kinds of painful things as a result. These are huge differences from what most of us experienced!

> I invite you to remind yourself of this, whenever you act in ways that you wish that you hadn't. You can repair. You can take responsibility. You can give them clear information that they are not responsible for your needs, feelings or behaviours. You can help them heal. This is (probably) so different from what you experienced. Remembering this might also help you have more compassion for yourself and be less likely to judge yourself.

What kinds of things might you say?

I'd love to offer some suggestions, and I invite you to listen in to whether any of them resonate for you. You might want to mix and match them, like a repair smorgasbord!

Again, I want to remind you that choosing language that resonates with *you* is important, so that the repair process is something that you're really embodying.

What you say will probably also depend on the age of your child.

Here are some examples:

- "I take complete responsibility for reacting like that."
- "You're not responsible for my behaviour or my feelings."
- "That was nothing to do with you."

- "You didn't cause that."
- "I had a lot of big feelings that caused me to do that."
- "That was my big feelings that caused that."
- "I haven't been taking care of my own feelings and needs enough."
- "I'm taking responsibility to get some listening from another adult to help me."

> *Self-Reflection Moment*
>
> *What would you like to say at times like these?*
>
> *What would you have liked to have heard from a parent or other adult when you were a child?*
>
> *I invite you to write your ideas down and feel into which one/s you most resonate with.*
>
> *What can you do so you will be able to easily remember this phrase next time?*

### 3. To listen to their feelings

You might make some empathy guesses (thank you, Nonviolent Communication for this term) about how they feel:

- "Do you feel upset?"
- "Did you feel scared?"
- "Do you feel angry?

If you're not sure what they might be feeling, keeping it to a word that is all-encompassing can help, such as "upset."

You might ask them how they feel.

"How did you feel when I did that?"

They might already be crying or raging, in which case, you might want to say things like:

- "I'm here and I'm listening."
- "I'm here to listen to all of your feelings."
- "I'm right here with you."
- "I so understand that you're upset."
- "I'm listening."

> *Self-Reflection Moment*
> *How would you like to respond?*
> *What can you do to help you remember that phrase?*

### 4. To help them feel powerful

Remember that part of the process of helping children heal from stress and trauma, including that which they experience as a result of our actions, is through helping them feel powerful again – because they didn't at the time. *Attachment play* can be a helpful way to support this to happen.

Here are a few ways you can do that:

# Bring in a feature of what you did that you regret, and add *attachment play* to *it*.

So, if you spoke loudly, they could make loud noises and you could jump up in the air each time (this is contingency play), or fall over each time they make the noise. Mock-surprise can add to the healing factor.

If you used physical power-over or force, you could invite them to knock you over again and again, either with them on a swing, or in a pillow fight, or through pushing you on to the bed or sofa. This is a power-reversal game and can bring lots of healing laughter!

If you ran after them, they could chase you, but you keep on falling over, or being surprised that they keep on catching you (a power-reversal game).

If you shamed or judged them with words, you could suggest that they say those words to you and you could change them into different versions that are silly and goofy (nonsense play).

> There's also the do-over game. In this game, you go back to the original scenario, but this time the child chooses how the situation goes. This can also bring much repair and a sense of power for them.

Again, I'm sending you so much love and invite you to be deeply compassionate with yourself. This is big work!

Kaya shared about the power of *attachment play* to repair with her child:

*"Just wanted to share a repair success I had with my son today... so grateful for this* Attachment Play Course *for turning a rough situation into an opportunity to play! This afternoon my four year old decided to put ALL the toilet paper into our toilet, and we are renters with a not-so nice landlord and very old pipes, so when I discovered the overflowing toilet I lost my temper and yelled, "Goddamn it!" (yikes, I know!) Anyhow, after losing it and lecturing my boy about waste, backing up pipes, landlords, renting, etc, and showing him the flood in the basement that he had caused, I caught myself and took a moment to calm down (so thankful for diaphragmatic breathing!!).*

*When I came back (I had my son in the bath, as he had helped me fish out the toilet paper and clean up the mess), I apologised for losing my temper and talked to him a little about what happened inside my brain when I lost my temper and showed him on my hand-model brain. (We had done this before so he had a reference point.)*

*I then prompted him to talk about what happened inside his brain and how he felt when I lost my temper, and we had a nice talk about it. After a few moments my son led me to the basement to "Show me what I did!" in a classic power reversal, and together we shouted, "GODDAMNIT" again and again while laughing uproariously! After we got it out of our systems and both released a lot of tension, I had us 'put that harsh word away in a box since it isn't a very enjoyable thing to say,' and we pretended to lock it up inside a lunchbox I found. Of course the word tried to sneak out but we kept grabbing it and putting it back in! There was a lot of laughter and it felt so great to catch myself in a moment of low-brain parenting and be able to use laughter and play to come back to connection. I feel like play is becoming my default mode of late, and while I OBVIOUSLY still have my moments where I do things I regret, it feels so good that even those can result in healing and laughter."*

If you do ever blame your child for causing your reactions, you might want to help healing happen by adding in a parenting mantra – both to remind you what's really going on in the moment, and to offer them reparative phrases that they can internalise instead of any blaming ones.

These can stem from your inner mantra, which might be:

"They're not doing this deliberately, they're feeling upset, they need my help."

The outer phrase might be something like:

## "I know you're not doing this deliberately, I see that you're upset, I see that you need my help."

Saying this out loud can help us stay connected with loving and compassionate thoughts, and can also help them have compassionate rather than judgmental thoughts about themselves and their behaviour.

***From a child:*** *I can feel it in my tummy when you're feeling grumpy. I see how you move differently and your face looks all funny too. That's when you sometimes say things that are scary for me. I don't like it when you speak in that loud voice to me. I kind of know that you don't want to be like that with me, but it really helps me when you say that you regret that you did. Sometimes I get scared that it was because of something I did. When you tell me it wasn't my fault, I feel a big sigh all through my body. When you tell me that your behaviour is because of you, I feel this lovely feeling, kind of like cuddly clouds and feeling safe and home. I can relax again. Oh and I love it when we play that rewind game, and I get to choose what happens this time. I really like that. Can we play it again, now?*

## Chapter summary

Remember we talked way back earlier in the book how our culture only teaches us to judge ourselves, rather than understand the source of our behaviour and change it at that level? This chapter was all about **creating change at the source level**, starting with our own reactive moments.

From then, we can discover the source of our aggression, and **offer ourselves compassion rather than punishing ourselves as we were taught to**.

From here, we can **offer repair to our child**, including reparative statements so that they don't learn to judge themselves for their behaviour nor blame themselves for ours.

> You have so much power to help your child/ren heal from times you were harsh towards them.

## CHAPTER SIXTEEN

# Eating, food and feelings

**Important note:** please always listen to your intuition in relation to your child and food. If you suspect that there is something going on with their gut microbiome, or think that they might have allergies or intolerances, or other issues with their digestive system that require attending to, please trust yourself and reach out to your trusted health practitioner for information and support.

### Children's innate body wisdom

In Aware Parenting, we recognise that children's bodies are innately wise and know exactly when to eat, what to eat, and how much to eat.

We also understand that children are meant to learn to fit into the family, culture and place they are born into. Growing up in the *Disconnected Domination Culture*, where children's innate wisdom is not trusted, children will often learn to disconnect from the intrinsic knowing their bodies have in relation to food.

Living in the *DDC*, there are many things that can get in the way of them being connected with their intrinsic body wisdom, which we will explore in depth in this chapter.

In addition, most of us do not get taught how to differentiate between hunger (which is a needs-feeling) and healing-feelings, which means that many of us may regularly feed our babies or children when they actually have feelings to express to us. This can often lead to them thinking they are hungry when they're actually upset. This is one of the reasons why so many of us as adults tend to eat when we have painful feelings bubbling.

When we understand a child's innate body wisdom in relation to food, and also what can get in the way of it, there are plenty of things we can do to support children to be more connected with their intrinsic knowledge. This chapter explains how.

Whatever our own journey with food and feelings and trusting our innate biological wisdom, and whatever we have done so far in relation to our children's feelings and food, it is never too late to support them to return to being deeply connected with their innate wisdom and for us to do the same, too.

Haley shared, *"I've started having conversations with my daughter about changing some ways around food in our home and I'm already witnessing how our relationship is changing and her mood is relaxing."*

## The self-connected approach to eating[37]

One of the core tenets of Aware Parenting is a deep trust in babies and children and their innate wisdom in all areas of their lives, including in relation to food and eating. One of the most important things we can do as parents is to help our children stay connected to that intrinsic wisdom, or reconnect to it again if they have disconnected from it. That often invites us on our own parallel journey to reclaiming trust in our own bodies in relation to food. As parents, this is often a big journey for us to learn to deeply trust that their bodies know exactly when to eat, what to eat and how much to eat, and to understand how we can support them with that.

---

37  Also called the self-demand approach to eating and self-regulated eating in Aware Parenting.

## Innate body wisdom and its interplay with culture and conditioning

Central to Aware Parenting philosophy is that children come into the world with innate biological and psychological wisdom, including knowing what nourishment their body needs and when they need it.

They're also meant to learn about the family and culture they live in. If we reflect on our hunter gatherer origins, that would mean learning about what foods were poisonous, and how to gather, hunt, and prepare foods. So, children are constantly learning from us and others around them about food.

Unfortunately, this means that we can get in the way of their beautiful wisdom through our own cultural conditioning and *control patterns* in relation to food. The wider culture of course has a huge effect here too.

Aware Parenting supports parents to regain a deep trust in their child's body intelligence, while also honouring their wisdom in acquiring *control patterns* from us, because learning from adults about the family and culture they live in is essential to a child's development. This also means that they learn all kinds of other information that is helpful for them to fit into the *DDC*, but is not so helpful in terms of their optimal health and wellbeing (because the *DDC* doesn't have an accurate understanding of the true nature of human beings).

> I want to acknowledge and offer empathy for how difficult this can be, wanting to help our children stay connected with themselves and their innate body wisdom, while also living in a culture which makes it challenging to support children's emotional and physical health.

So, there is this ongoing and powerful interplay between their innate wisdom in relation to food and nourishment, and needing to fit into the family and culture they are born into.

In a healthy culture, they would be supported to stay deeply connected with their innate wisdom while also learning about the traditions and diet of their culture, as well as what foods were nutritious or poisonous and which places those would be found.

Their innate wisdom requires that they are present in their body, so that they can feel the sensations, including thirst and hunger, a drawing towards a food, disgust, displeasure, pleasure, satiation and discomfort from too much food. These sensations are there to communicate information, in the following ways:

- Thirst and hunger: that their body requires fluid or food.
- An interest in a food: that the food might be what their body needs.
- Disgust and displeasure: that the food isn't helpful for them.
- Pleasure: that the food is likely to be helpful for them.
- Satiation: that they have had enough.
- Discomfort from fullness: that they have had too much.
- Other discomfort: that they've eaten something that doesn't help their body.

However, as I shared earlier, in the *DDC*, there are many things that help children disconnect from their innate wisdom in relation to food.

*Self-Compassion Moment*

*When you read what follows, you might be tempted to pick up a guilt stick. I invite you to remember that it's so natural and understandable that we do these things that disconnect children from their bodily knowing, particularly because of the culture and time we are living in. Most of us experienced these things as children, too. Reconnecting with our own intrinsic wisdom takes time, as does freeing ourselves from unhelpful cultural conditioning, especially while we are still living in that culture. I invite you to be unwilling to pick up those sticks and to be deeply compassionate with yourself. Perhaps you*

> might choose to think, "I'm not willing to judge myself. I'm willing to be compassionate with myself instead. I'm willing to take in information that resonates with me and that will be helpful for me and my child/ren, and to learn to implement it."

## What gets in the way of children being connected with their innate body wisdom in relation to food

If our aim is for them to make the most optimal food choices based on their bodily sensations as well as information from us and from their own prior experience about whether they enjoyed the food and how they felt afterwards, then knowing what can get in the way of that can be helpful.

However, it's really important that we are also really compassionate with ourselves and hold in mind how hard it can be at times to lessen those influences because we live in a culture that is set against us being deeply connected with our bodies.

What can get in the way, or make it harder, for children to stay connected with their body wisdom in relation to food?

### Us not responding to their hunger cues accurately

Because they are learning from us about food and hunger, when we don't read or respond to their hunger cues accurately or in an attuned way, that will affect their relationship with their internal sensations.

See how important it is to be compassionate with ourselves here!

If we frequently give our child food when they actually have healing-feelings to express, they will learn to interpret the sensations of upset feelings as hunger, and may then search out for or ask for food whenever they feel upset. This is incredibly common in our culture. Many of us experienced this. It's generally passed down in families.

If our child uses food to dissociate from feelings, some of their desire to eat foods at particular times won't be because they're hungry, it will be to suppress feelings. And if they're dissociating *while* eating, it will also be harder for them to feel connected enough with the sensations and cues from their body to be able to discern that a flavour or texture isn't enjoyable, or that they are uncomfortable or full.

In addition, if breast or bottle-feeding is a *control pattern* for a toddler, they might rarely feel hungry and might show very little interest in food.

Aiming to prevent eating *control patterns* in the first place is really helpful if we want to help our child know what their body is telling them about food. One thing we can do is aim to differentiate more between when they are hungry and when they have healing-feelings to express, and then support them in having the opportunity to experience being fed after feeling sensations of hunger and to express healing-feelings when they need to.

If a child already has an eating *control pattern*, remember that presence is the antidote to suppression and dissociation. In other words, offering loving, warm connection while they are eating to dissociate, can help them be more able to connect with the sensations in their body. In addition, the more we are able to bring in a quality of joy, ease and pleasure to food preparation and family meals, the more that will support the dissolving of *control patterns* through the power of presence. These can be replaced with the child increasingly feeling and expressing emotions and eating from their body's needs and wisdom.

***Even if we have given our children an eating control pattern, it's still possible to help them reconnect with their innate body wisdom again and accurately read their own internal cues, so that they can differentiate hunger from upset feelings.***

> *Self-Compassion Moment*
> 
> *If you're feeling concerned as you read this, I'm sending you so much love and compassion. I want to remind you to drop the sticks, and to remember that whatever you've done up until now, it's possible to change how you've been with your child/ren and food.*

*To contribute to any needs for reassurance you might have that it really is possible to help change happen, I'd love to share about my experience with this with my daughter. I gave her a breastfeeding control pattern when she was baby but helped her get free from it from it by the time she was about three years old by continuing to practice all the aspects of Aware Parenting. I will talk more about that process later in the book.*

This muddling up of their sensations and internal food barometer can also happen if we don't give a baby or child food when they are actually hungry. This used to be very common in the 1950s, 60s and 70s, when parents were told to feed their babies 'on schedule'. It can also happen if a child is hungry and is told that eating now will 'spoil their dinner'. If they think that they might not be given food when they are hungry, it makes sense that they would eat as much as they can when food *is* available, overriding sensations of fullness in favour of building up reserves. All responses from babies and children in relation to food are deeply wise, and make sense when we enquire into what's going on and what they've experienced in the past, whether that's from their innate wisdom, or them responding to their environment.

## Us restricting what they eat but eating those foods in front of them

*I saw this when I was a young adult, before becoming a mother. I had friends with a young daughter and they didn't let her have any sugar, but they ate it in front of her. I remember as if it was yesterday one evening when we all went out for dinner and everyone else ate dessert but her parents weren't willing for her to have any. I remember thinking at the time how powerless I imagined she was feeling. A few days later, I was with another one of our friends, who was babysitting this little girl. We went into the kitchen, only to discover that she had gone through all of my friend's cupboards, had found sugar cubes, and was sitting on the kitchen floor, eating as many as she could. I saw really clearly that the forbidden foods had become incredibly desirable. This little girl was disconnecting from her physical sensations because the craving for the forbidden food had become the biggest drive. I imagine that if she had been connected with her body at that moment, the sensations of eating that much sugar would have been uncomfortable. But the desire to have what everyone else was having, and have as much as she could while her parents weren't around, overrode that.*

Later in this chapter, I'll talk more about what we can do as parents so that we still can choose what we are not willing for our children to eat when they are younger, without setting off this restricting and binging process. This includes not having food that we don't want them to eat in the house, not eating items that we don't want them to eat in front of them, and giving them free access to the food that *is* in our home.

Remembering what I'd seen happen for that little girl was one of the reasons why the self-connected[38] approach to food resonated so much with me when I first learnt about it in Aware Parenting when my daughter was a baby. When I first read that children will commonly crave certain foods because they are restricted or forbidden, rather than because their body is communicating that those foods are actually wanted, those two scenes with that little girl jumped out at me.

In practicing the self-connected approach with food with my children, I saw something very different to what I observed with that little girl.

---

38   More commonly called the self-demand approach or self-regulated eating in Aware Parenting.

*For years, my children had the door in the fridge filled with all the chocolates they'd received from family members at previous Christmases as well as Easter and Halloween. They had no urgency to eat it. At Easter, they would often just eat a small amount of chocolate and then saved the rest for days (or years). There was no urgency, so they were free to listen in to what their bodies were telling them. Many times, the chocolates my son has been given by family members go out of date because he just doesn't want them.*

## There's a big difference between restricting our children from eating certain foods but eating those foods in front of them, and not being willing for certain types of foods to come into our home. It's so important that we listen in to our values and the information we have about health, and to make choices based on that, particularly when our children are young.

*In my family, I wasn't willing for anyone to have artificial flavours and colours (after an experience I'd had eating them when I was younger), so none of those came into our home in the early years. If my children ever received these items, such as from relatives, I would offer to swap them from other sweets or chocolates that didn't include artificial colours and flavours.*

*Within our home, our children were welcome to eat whatever food was there, whenever they wanted, and however much they wanted.*

### Us using rewards, punishments, shaming, guilting or coercing with food

These can all get in the way of a child's innate body wisdom in relation to food, because the feelings that get overlaid as a result will make it harder for them to be guided by their internal barometer. This can include giving sweets to a child who has done their homework, or telling them they can only eat their pudding when they've eaten their main course. Coercing a child to eat when they don't want to, or when they are full up, shaming a child for not eating or wanting certain foods, forcing them to sit at the table when everyone else is or until everyone has finished can also lead to painful feelings which will make it harder for them to listen in to what their bodies are telling them.

All of these get in the way of a child's deep connection with their body and their innate wisdom.

If we give sweet food as a reward for savoury, research indicates that child will lose innate motivation to eat the savoury food and will prefer the sweet. If children are punished or shamed for wanting sweet foods, the overlay of guilt or shame can get in the way of them being able to feel what their body is telling them about those foods.

We might aim to be really compassionate with ourselves when we are tempted to judge, shame or use power-over our child when they want sweet foods, especially if we feel scared or powerless. We might also find ways to then reflect back to our child that we hear and understand how much they love that sweet food, which is likely to meet their needs for acceptance and being understood.

*Self-Compassion Moment*
*If you've given foods as a reward, or have tried to shame your child's food choices, I'm sending you so much love and compassion. Again, I want to remind you how understandable this is, given how common it is in the wider culture. And if this information resonates with you, it really is possible to change this and support them to feel more connected with their innate wisdom again!*

## Our reactions to them eating

I have my own powerful story to share with you about this!

*When my son was 2-3 years old, he loved eating spirulina tablets! They would leave a big green mark all around his mouth. Afterwards, he would often love to run towards the couch and land on it, and many times he would leave a big green spirulina stain behind. I don't know why I chose to have a cream couch cover at the time, with two children and two dogs, but I did! One time, feeling frustrated about the spirulina on the couch again, I had a big reaction to him doing this. After that, he was never again willing to eat spirulina tablets. I feel so sad when I remember this. I wish I'd found other ways to get my needs met so he would be willing to continue eating them for as long as his body enjoyed them (such as having a dark cover on the couch).*

## Our own relationship with food

Because children are designed to learn from us about what foods are healthy and which are poisonous, they are often affected by our own relationship to food. If we get really excited when we're talking about or eating a certain food, they're likely to also perceive that food as exciting. If we show disgust, they are likely to think that food will be disgusting. Again, this is part of them needing to learn about what foods are safe and helpful in their environment. If we talk about foods being 'treats' or 'naughty' or that we are 'bad' when we eat a certain food, that will also affect their relationship with that food, as will if we restrict ourselves and say that we 'shouldn't' or 'can't', or if we go on particular diets.

If certain foods are *control patterns* for us, our children might be affected by that too. If we go to eat chocolate any time we are upset, it's possible that our children will learn to do that too.

The wonderful thing about this is that the more we do our own inner work, and become relaxed in relation to food, trusting ourselves and enjoying food that our body loves, that will also affect them.

> *Self-Compassion Moment*
>
> *As always, I invite you to drop the sticks. This can be an invitation for us to develop a more self-connected relationship with food too. I'm sending you lots of love as you read this. I want to remind you that most of us experienced all of these things, and so it's so natural that we pass down some or all of them, or that we revert to them when we are stressed. I'm sending you a big hug right now.*

I'd love to also briefly name some of the other myriad sources of ways that our children's innate wisdom in relation to food can be affected in this era we're in, and I will suggest some ways that we can ameliorate those effects.

### Wider cultural influences

If children are not seeing where their food comes from, this can mean they're less connected with their food than children in families who grow their own food, or who have a farm, or who are hunters and gatherers. This can mean less intimacy with food and less understanding about it.

What can we do to help our children feel more connected with food? We can support them to learn about where food comes from, including from visiting farmers markets, having some herbs in plant pots, or even a vegetable garden if you have the room and resources.

Using cutlery means they don't receive so much sensory information about their food.

To increase sensory information for them, we might encourage them to eat with their hands with certain foods or at times that will also meet our needs, such as watermelon here in Australia in the summertime. The baby-led weaning approach is often very popular with many Aware Parenting families as it supports children's needs for connection with their bodies and food, and plenty of agency and autonomy.

### Influences from outside the home

Advertising can have powerful effects – by making foods look more palatable or interesting and through fusing food with other needs, such as fun or inclusion or connection. Children might want to have the food because they're being influenced by other people, and because they want those needs to be met. This is particularly significant when they're not able to fully understand that this is an advert and people are being paid to say these things.

How can we help? After receiving our own listening from others, giving children information can be helpful, although the needs they are wanting to meet might still override that.

Brightly wrapped sweets and coloured sweets tap into children's innate wisdom to choose the ripest fruit.

What might we do here? I'm remembering the glass containers I had in the fridge that also had brightly coloured lids. I filled these with cut up fruits, vegetables, cheese and so on. Giving older children information about how they might be being affected by the bright wrappings can also be helpful here. And remember, you might choose not to bring brightly packaged things into your home when your children are younger.

Let's be really compassionate with ourselves as parents. It's so understandable that we have lots of needs for ease, and buying things that are most readily available in shops and what is quickest to prepare may meet many of our needs. Again, finding ways to meet both our needs and our children's needs can be helpful to hold in mind here.

The effects of what is cheapest in shops affects our choices too.

Then there are the effects and influence of other children, daycare, school, etc. – children have needs for inclusion, acceptance, and community, and these needs can influence their food choices when they see what other children eat. It's natural for children to want to try things that they see their friends eating.

In response, we might give our children empathy and an opportunity to try out those foods, or to find things that are similar to what their friends are eating that we are willing for them to have.

### Influences from inside the home

Ease also comes into play in terms of what is quickest to get out of the cupboard or fridge and which food items need least preparing, particularly when children are hungry and are just wanting to get something for themselves.

What can we do? Having fruits and vegetables and other food items cut up into bite sized pieces in containers in the fridge can help meet those needs for ease as well as listening in to their bodies.

There's the effects of our stress or family tension around meals. It can be hard for a child to feel relaxed while eating and thus to feel the sensory feedback their body is telling them about food, hunger and satiation if they're feeling tense.

To reduce the tension happening at mealtimes, we might be called to receive some empathy for our feelings, and to bring in playfulness to help relieve and release the stress.

If we believe that children 'should' always eat a wide variety of food, that can lead to us feeling stressed or scared, and we might try to coerce our child to eat more variety. This might backfire, with them wanting more agency and not being willing to eat what we give them.

Understanding that it was common in many Indigenous cultures to eat a small variety of foods can give us reassurance that our child is likely to be receiving enough nourishment, helping us feel more relaxed to trust our child more with food.

Internalised should's or have-to's about certain foods might also get in the way of what their body is telling them.

So, avoiding telling them that they should or have to eat certain foods can help, again with lots of compassion for ourselves when we feel powerless or scared and are tempted to try to coerce them in these ways.

### Effects of feelings, stress and trauma

In addition to eating *control patterns* we talked about above, children who are feeling powerless may restrict their eating, what they eat or when they eat as a way to have control over something in their life. This means their food choices will be meeting their needs for agency more than reflecting their internal cues and sensations in relation to what their body needs with food.

*When I lived with my dad and didn't see my mum for 18 months as a 9-10 year old, I generally ate the same dinner every day – mashed potato, fish fingers and peas. I imagine that as well as helping me have some sense of agency and power, it also met other needs for me, such as consistency and reliability. Similarly, I noticed that my son's food choices drastically reduced after his dad and I separated, which matched the powerlessness I observed in him, which also showed up in him hitting.*

If your child clearly restricts what they're willing to eat after a stressful event, indicating powerlessness and a need for agency and choice, then offering plenty of choice in other places can be helpful. So can playing power-reversal games. In particular, listening to plenty of raging and crying can help release the feelings of powerlessness and increase the sense of power, so that they have less need to meet the needs for agency through their food choices.

With quite a few parents I've supported, I've discovered that intergenerational trauma can play a role in food issues. If there was famine or starvation in the family line, a parent may feel a desperate fear that their child isn't getting enough food and may frequently feed them when they aren't hungry.

I've found that supporting them in acknowledging what happened to their ancestors and bringing healing to the family system can then free them up to feel confident that their child is safe and is clearly having enough food.

Some children might have experienced trauma such as tube feeding, or being intubated as a baby or child, and any unexpressed feelings from these experiences can show up in a reluctance to eat, or expressing big feelings in relation to food.[39]

In this case, we can support them to heal from these traumatic events through *attachment play* and listening to crying and raging. *Attachment play* can also be incredibly helpful for children who have food restrictions because of food allergies or sensitivities.

### Physiological influences

Then there are many physiological influences on food choices, such as parasites and gut microbiome issues which can affect appetite and what is desired.

Being aware of all these possible effects and gathering clear information about food that resonates with us can help us be more compassionate with ourselves. It can also help us make choices about what foods we're willing to have inside our home and for our children to have free access to when they are young.

> *Self-Compassion Moment*
>
> *There is so much here, isn't there? Food and eating can be associated with so many aspects of our lives. It's so natural for children to be affected in these ways. I invite you to be deeply compassionate if you see your child reflected here.*

---

39  Thank you to Maru Rojas, an Aware Parenting instructor in the UK, for her suggestion to include this.

## General ways to help children be more connected with their innate body wisdom in relation to food

In general, if we're wanting to help our children be more connected with their innate body wisdom in relation to food, we might want to:

- Take in resonant *information* about food, and trust what resonates with us;
- Have *listening* time so we can get clear about what choices we're going to make about food for our family;
- Receive *empathy* for the feelings which bubble up for us in relation to our children and food;
- Give our children age appropriate *information*;
- Have *conversations* with them about food from a place of calmness;
- Support them to release stress and trauma with *attachment play* and crying and raging;
- Invite them to *notice* what their bodies are telling them before, during and after eating;
- Be *present* with them when they're eating.
- Convey confidence that their bodies are wise.

Many cultures have blessings before food. With your child/ren, you might enjoy looking at the different food items when they're in the shops, and where possible, touching it when choosing it, preparing it and eating it. You might encourage them to really smell and taste food.

> Most of all, offering our own presence makes a big difference. This helps support them to be more present during these processes as well as during and after eating food, to listen in to what their bodies are telling them.

As parents, we might become more present with food and eating by slowing down. When we're rushing, we're going to be less connected with our senses of smell, taste and satiation.

***And of course, presence is the essence of Aware Parenting.***

The wonderful thing is, that the more we can practice the three aspects of Aware Parenting, the more naturally children will be present and connected with their bodies and so more able to be present while eating.

*I remember the evening when my children and their dad were invited to dinner with a family we didn't know. I want to add, before sharing more, that I'm not judging this family (you already know that I'm not willing to judge people). They didn't know about Aware Parenting and I'm telling the story because the effects of Aware Parenting were so clear. There were several families at the dinner, and the parents and children were seated at different tables. At that time, my children were still in their super calm and present stage, before their dad and I separated. They would have been about three and seven. They sat at the table and calmly and slowly ate their food, with their usual quality of presence. It was evening time, and most of the other children had lots of big feelings bubbling up, (their innate wisdom trying to release these feelings before sleep), and after a short time all the other children were getting up and down, running around, playing, and were trying to cry. After about ten minutes, our son and daughter were the only two children left at the table, still calmly eating their food and observing the children around them, which they continued to do until they'd finished eating.*

I love children's innate body wisdom. Those children were indicating that they had feelings that they were trying to release. And because my children didn't have many healing-feelings at the surface at that time, they were able to eat with presence and peacefulness, facilitating their bodies to digest the food.

*This can often happen with food and eating. Have you ever tried to eat when you were really upset? When we're feeling painful feelings, or in fight, flight or freeze, our body is trying to focus on survival and healing, not eating and digestion. This can be the cause of many food battles – if a child is agitated and trying to release feelings after a busy day or before bed, it will be really hard for them to calm down enough to eat and digest their food. The most helpful thing here would be to support them to release the feelings first, before then giving them food, when their body is actually ready to digest it.*

Just as it makes sense that having enough needs met and enough healing-feelings expressed means that they can sleep restfully and restoratively – since sleep is such a vital need – so it's also understandable that when we're able to meet enough of their needs and listen to enough of their healing-feelings, children will be able to know what their bodies are telling them food-wise and will digest their food most optimally.

> Our bodies are so innately wise. The more we can understand this, get free from our conditioning and heal from our childhood unexpressed feelings, the more we can help our children be connected with what their bodies are telling them with regard to food and eating. While also having so much compassion for ourselves about how hard this can be, living in the *DDC*.

India Farr, an Aware Parenting instructor in the UK, who looks after young children in a childcare setting, shows that it's possible to support multiple children with this approach. She says:

*"We have snack times at 10am and 2:30pm from the snack cupboard which is locked but children can point at it if non verbal to show they're hungry. There is fresh fruit available which the children can reach at all times. And older children know that their lunch boxes from home are available any time for them to eat something from.*

*When we think a child is using food to suppress feelings – for example asking for more food immediately after eating a big lunch, we ask the child to let their food go down for 15 mins or have a drink of water and see how they feel. They usually don't come back to ask again and feelings will come up and we will listen to those feelings. If they do ask again, they have fruit available for them."*

I also want to remind you that because children's intrinsic biological wisdom is innate and powerful, we can always help them return to it, using the principles of Aware Parenting.

## Helping children stay connected to their innate body wisdom (or reconnect with it) with the three aspects of Aware Parenting

The self-connected approach to eating involves trusting children's innate wisdom, and giving them time to develop a healthy relationship with food (whether they have an eating *control pattern* or not). But this approach only works if we fully implement all other aspects of Aware Parenting and give them enough time to reconnect with their own bodies.

### Attachment-style parenting

Connection and attunement are so central here. The more we can connect with our children, the more we can support them to stay connected with their bodies or reconnect with when they are hungry, what they want, how much, and when they're full. Responding in a present and attuned way helps them to connect with and be attuned to their own body signals and cues.

**Parents often focus on the crying aspect of Aware Parenting, but that is third on the list. Connection, presence and attunement always come first.**

This might include having conversations about food. Asking them how they feel in their bodies when they ask for certain foods, during eating, and afterwards, will help them connect with the sensations and understand them. When they are babies, aiming to differentiate between hunger and healing-feelings – and listening to the healing-feelings – is pivotal in helping them interpret their sensations accurately. And I want to remind you that if you often fed your baby when they had healing-feelings to express, as I did with my daughter, it is still absolutely possible to help them return to reading their own body cues in relation to food.

### Non-punitive discipline

This means refraining from rewarding with food, not calling certain foods 'treats', or saving sweet food for after savoury, not judging, shaming, blaming or coercing. Not rewarding or praising children when they eat foods that we want them to eat eg. with, 'Good girl/boy,' or 'Good job,' or 'Well done'.

However, this can be hard for us at times, especially because most of us didn't receive this, so we might feel tempted at times to use coercion or threats to get our child to sit at the table or eat a certain food. One of the core elements of the *Disconnected Domination Culture* is to use power-over children to get them to eat what we want them to eat, when we want them to eat and how much we want them to eat. Undoing this conditioning in ourselves can be a huge process.

> *Self-Compassion Moment*
> *I'm sending you so much love and compassion right now. If you have issues and challenges in relation to food choices, eating and feelings for yourself and/or your child/ren, you are not alone. I think it's one of the most common experiences in our culture! As always, I invite you to drop any sticks you're tempted to pick up!*

### Healing through *attachment play* and crying and raging

If we have found it hard to trust our child in relation to food, and we've used power-over to try to get them to eat or stop them from eating, I want to remind you that *attachment play* can be really helpful for children to heal from those experiences.

Paula shares an experience of this:

*"My elder son is constantly running away from the table with food in/ on his hands. He refuses to eat a lot of things, and my sense has been that it is about his needs for autonomy and other feelings that come up with the close attention at the table. Hubby is really unnerved by it, especially about him not sitting still. I decided that I was going to start playing some* attachment play *with my son. He shared some pretend toy cakes with me and I pretended to eat them, and hubby came to ask us to go to the table, and we started running away from him and then pretended to eat on the couch as allies. Hubby played his part, complaining and insisting that we move to the table, then taking our 'cakes' away. We would obediently sit down at the table but then jump up and run to the couch again. It was hilarious. My son laughed heartily and I enjoyed it too. There was great healing laughter and togetherness. It was also a powerful autonomy (rebellion) experience for both of us too! Hubby got a bit tired in the end. It is really important for him that we eat in an orderly way. I also noticed for some seconds how very uncomfortable it is to experience this kind of lecturing from him! Oh my goodness, my son hears this stuff from both of us, on different topics, all day long! So I also gained some insight as to why he is saying no so often."*

In Aware Parenting, we aim to respond to food *control patterns* in similar ways to thumb sucking – and just as we don't recommend taking a child's thumb out of their mouth, it's important that we're very cautious about *Loving Limits* in relation to food. The use of *Loving Limits* with food is helpful primarily in the case of breastfeeding, because it is the mother's body, or if the child is overweight or has health challenges, particularly in relation to food.[40]

In *Cooperative and Connected* (p.171), Aletha Solter says: *"If your child overeats to numb painful emotions, the most effective approach, in the long run, is to address his underlying feelings instead of trying to control what he eats."*

We can also do plenty to increase emotional safety, so that they are freer to cry and rage in general. We can notice where we distract them from their feelings or try to fix things when they have *broken cookie* moments, and offer *Loving Limits* elsewhere. We might also use *attachment play* to help children feel more relaxed and present around food, especially if we have been restrictive or stressed.

However, we might still use *attachment play* with eating and mealtimes, such as pretending to be a cookie and our child is chasing us around the house to eat the cookie, and we're pretending to be scared and keep on getting caught! Responding with *attachment play* can be helpful when they are clearly upset and are wanting to eat to suppress feelings, as long as we're not distracting them from crying or raging.

## What can make it hard for us to help our children eat in a self-connected way?

Let's focus on the specific ways that all of these factors we talked about earlier can make it hard for us to practice these three aspects of Aware Parenting with our child in relation to food. We might find it challenging for us to trust our children's innate wisdom because:

- Our innate wisdom wasn't trusted;
- Our own *control patterns* or eating issues are a lens through which we see our child;

---

40  Remember though, that we are still choosing what foods we buy in the first place!

- The presence of intergenerational trauma, such as famine or starvation in the family lineage;
- Our cultural conditioning in our beliefs about children and food;
- Judging ourselves and our parenting in terms of what they eat or don't eat;
- The effects of the culture, such as advertising making certain foods enticing;
- The effects of the culture in terms of food that is most readily available and easiest to prepare;
- Influences of other children, parents, daycare, school, etc.

> *Self-Compassion Moment*
>
> *This is such a big topic here! If you're feeling overwhelmed, I'm sending you lots of love. However you're feeling, I'm offering you plenty of compassion. Supporting our children to be connected with their innate wisdom while living in this culture and at this time is a really big thing, isn't it? You're so not alone.*

Having compassionate understanding of the practical effects of this society as well as the emotional and cognitive effects on us is important in this process. Claiming our power in this culture, as well as doing our own healing, are both core here, including exploring our own *control patterns* and our own history in relation to food. The most important thing is for us to be doing our own inner work so that we can support our children to stay connected with their innate wisdom in relation to food, or to return to it.

I love working with parents in relation to these things. All Aware Parenting instructors can help with this. Having a *Listening Partner* to share feelings with can be vital as part of us being compassionate with ourselves in this culture and getting freer from our own conditioning.

## How might we experience these challenges?

### We might feel worry and fear,
### because of our value for health

If you ever worry that your child is not eating enough, or is eating too much, or not enough of the food that meets your need for health, you are so not alone. Of course you deeply value your child/ren's health! There is so much information out there about food, isn't there? Gathering clear information about what resonates with us and doesn't can help us make those clear decisions about what food we're bringing into the house in those early years (and of course, as they get older, they will have more agency to bring other things home, and that's where the conversations come in).

I invite you to receive lots of listening from your *Listening Partner* about this. The more we can have our feelings heard, the more likely it is that we will get clear, and this will help us also be more likely to respond in calm and compassionate ways with our child/ren.

I'd love to offer a Marion Method practice here. When we feel scared because we're thinking something about the future that we don't want to happen – which in this case is that our child might end up being unhealthy, we can first receive empathy for our fear until we feel relieved, secondly, turn around what we fear happening in order to connect to what we do want, ie. health, and thirdly, connect with our willingness for health as well as their needs, such as for agency, autonomy and choice. Then we can connect in with our embodied willingness any time we're having conversations about food, and perhaps even connect with, "I'm so willing for us both to get our needs met here." I found that process really helped me be much less likely to feel powerless and tempted to use power-over.

### We might feel hurt when they don't eat food we've carefully made, because we need appreciation

We might feel disappointed, powerless or rageful if they don't eat what we make, especially if we've put a lot of thought, care and time into cooking. These might come from our needs for acknowledgment, appreciation, support, ease, or community, or they might be our own feelings from our childhood. Lovingly exploring our own thoughts, needs and feelings that come up if they don't enjoy what we offer them can help us be less likely to have big reactions that might affect their relationship with food.

### We might shift into judgment, from our own cultural conditioning

Refraining from judging our child, even in our mind, can really help, and having a curiosity about what they love and wanting to contribute to them enjoying food as well as being connected to their body, can make the whole experience so much more enjoyable for us and for them.

### Our own self-enquiry is vital

When we're:

- reactive;
- judging ourselves or them;
- scared; or
- tempted to use coercion or power-over,

these are signs that we need some Listening Time for us. Enquiring into whether we were judged and shamed, punished and rewarded, guilted, fed to suppress feelings, made to wait when we were hungry, or whether our parents ate food in front of us that they didn't let us eat, can all really help us to express any feelings, while being lovingly heard! It's so natural that we might have a lot of big feelings about these things. It's really common and understandable.

> *Self-Compassion Moment*
> *If you have feelings bubbling up here, I'm sending you a big warm hug. It's so understandable that you would, and you are so not alone! I invite you to be deeply compassionate with yourself.*

## Tangible actions we can take to help them stay connected with their innate body wisdom

### Connecting with ourselves and making clear choices about what foods we have in our home

This is part of us listening to ourselves, and taking into account information about food that resonates with us, and creating the food environment for our children. We will each make unique choices about what to include or not. Some parents might only buy organic food, others might not bring meat or particular types of oils into the home. I had a no to anything with artificial flavours or colours. In different eras, there will be different information available about foods that we will be affected by. One of the most important things is to deeply listen in to ourselves about what we have a no for in our house, so we are really clear about that. As our children get older, this process will morph and become more of a conversation with them, taking into account their preferences, needs and knowledge.

### Connection with them – at home, giving them free choice about food

If this resonates with you, this means that they choose what they eat, when they eat it and how much of it they eat. We can offer a wide variety of food or food groups. With younger children, you might find it helpful to show them a selection of foods, including any sweet foods at the same time, so they can choose. That might mean going with them to the fridge or cupboard when they communicate that they're hungry, and supporting them to listen to their body when they are choosing when, what and how much to eat.

Making all the foods similarly easy and available to access – eg. in ready to eat, bite-sized pieces – can really help with this. Needs for ease can be quite important in relation to food, too. When our children are hungry, it's natural that they want to be able to easily and quickly access it and eat it. Having all kinds of food easily available to eat means that food in a packet won't be the easiest thing and thus the thing they always reach for when they're hungry.

When my children were younger, I'm grateful to say that I bought 90% of our food from a health food shop. They would always come with me (as we were homeschooling) and chose what they wanted. For a few years they each had a shelf in the fridge and they would choose the food at the shop that they wanted for their shelf.

Of course there might be restrictions for financial reasons too. That replicates the wild food model, when there would always be natural restrictions eg. due to climate or season. The important thing is that they get to choose from what is available in the home, just as in the wild.

> In episode 157 of *The Aware Parenting Podcast*, I talked with Clare Louise Brumley PhD, who said that in the wild food model, there's "...heaps of free choice, but lots of natural limits." That's really important information, isn't it? And I think what we're doing here is replicating that in some way. Especially with young children who are not going out to shops themselves. We're having those natural limits in the house of choosing what foods to bring in, especially in their earlier years, but within what is available at home, they have lots of free choice.

I love imagining this as three concentric circles. The biggest circle is all the food available to us, wherever we live in the world. The second biggest circle is what we choose as parents, with the information and resources we have, to bring into the home and give our children access to in other places. And our children start off as a smaller circle within those two bigger circles, having free choice within the circle that we create. As they get older and have access to more information and more agency, their circle becomes bigger and bigger, as they have more and more choice about what they eat within the biggest circle.

Ellie Gut-Silverman, an Aware Parenting instructor in Australia, shares about this process of trusting her daughter with food choices. She says:

*"When my daughter was 17 months old, we were cooking dahl together and she was playing with the different spices. After some time she picked up a jar of spirulina from the drawer and began saying, "Mum... Mum". I asked if she wanted to shake it as she had been doing with the other spices and she said, "No". I then asked if she wanted to eat some, and she excitedly said, "Yes!". I mentioned that it might be a little dry on its own, and asked if she would like it with some yoghurt to which she excitedly said, "Yes!" I then gave her the choice between sheep's milk yoghurt and coconut yoghurt and she requested, "Sheep's". She was delighted to eat her bowl of yoghurt with spirulina mixed through it, and I was so blown away by the way she knew exactly what her body needed, and how clearly she communicated it to me. This is one of many examples I could give where she has selected a very specific and very nutritious food. Last week she did the same with nutritional yeast flakes, which for two days she ate by the fistful! The week before she requested seaweed! I love witnessing her delightful relationship with food and I am so grateful for the deep trust that I feel in her awareness of what she needs."*

If you as parents have separated, your child/ren will probably have different foods available in each house, and they might need you to hear their feelings about that. It's very understandable that *you* might also have a lot of feelings about that, and taking them to your *Listening Partner* or Aware Parenting instructor will help you be more able to listen to their emotions.

I also recommend deciding what you're going to do in relation to food at seasonal holiday times. *For example, at Halloween, I would ask my children to replace the sweets that contained artificial flavourings and colourings with sweets or chocolates without them. As they got older, we would occasionally go to the sweet shop or sometimes have things that we didn't generally have in the house. By the time they were going to shops without me where they could buy their own food, they might at times buy things that we didn't have at home, but they weren't binging on them, nor eating lots of them, nor desperately wanting lots of things that we didn't have at home.*

As children get older and have more agency outside the home, there is more opportunity for discussions about the food choices they make and the things they buy. Doing our own inner work of putting down future-thinking sticks and getting clear about our needs and values, and listening to the younger parts of us, makes all the difference. That means we'll be more able to respond with compassion and connection, being interested in what they like and why they like it, and supporting them to keep on listening in to their body, even to keep tracking the sensations hours after they've eaten the food. We might choose to have fun eating a certain food together, and then see this as an experiment as we each check in with how we feel in our bodies and how those sensations change afterwards.

We might ask them questions, such as:

- what led you to want to reach for that food in particular?
- what thoughts and feelings were you having before?
- what were your feelings and sensations while eating it?
- when did you want to stop eating it?
- how do you feel in your body afterwards?
- is there any aftertaste?
- what were your emotions afterwards?

- how did you feel that night?
- what about the next morning?

In this way, they're actually getting this really nuanced experience of, "Here's me engaging with the world, and what do I experience as a result? What's the feedback loop? What information am I receiving about how my body responds to this food, and what do I want to do about that?"

***Eating different foods together can be a beautiful process that deepens connection and presence and the enjoyment of being a parent and supporting our children in this process of self-connection and experimenting to gather self-knowledge.***

I have a couple of examples of this in my own parenting.

*When I was a child, I used to say, "I'm so excited to be a grown up so that I can eat as much ice cream as I want." When I became a parent, I'd take my children out to our local seaside towns with gelato shops, and my son would often want three scoops of ice-cream. I supported him and said an enthusiastic yes! every time he asked. However, after lots of times of having three scoops, he found that they would often melt all over his hands, and he didn't like the sensations that went with that. He also discovered that he sometimes felt uncomfortable after eating three scoops, especially if he chose particular flavours. After this process, he would then generally just ask for one or two scoops of ice cream and knew exactly what flavours he enjoyed. I love that he learnt this from his own experimenting as a child. He didn't need to wait decades to wait to experiment, like I did as an adult, to discover that he didn't actually want three scoops!*

What I love about food and Aware Parenting is that it's an invitation to find out more about the uniqueness of each person. Even now, with my son and daughter as young adults, I love learning from them what foods they're loving at any one time, and buying or preparing those foods for them. To me, that's a way of communicating that I care about what they love and that their preferences matter.

*At 17, my son will say, "I'm sorry that I didn't eat it all," if he doesn't eat everything I've given him. I love saying to him, every single time, "I'm so glad that you listen to your body."*

So, we can see this as a process of discovery to find out what each person loves. Each child is unique. Some may not like particular flavours, textures, or mixtures. Having what they love in the house can also meet their needs for care, mattering, and being understood.

## Trusting them and supporting them to be connected with their bodily cues and sensations

This comes down to trusting that their bodies are innately wise and the more we can support them to listen in to their bodily experience in relation to food, and the more we can lessen all the effects we talked about earlier on, the more they will be able to feel how their body responds to different foods. Then they will naturally want to eat things that help them feel enjoyable sensations and not want to eat what leads to discomfort. They'll know when they've had enough and will naturally want to stop eating when they've had enough. Regularly conveying our confidence in their innate body wisdom can really help with this, too.

So it really is this interplay of trusting their innate wisdom, understanding the effects of the culture we live in, our own cultural conditioning and our past experiences with food, so that we do as much as we can to get freer from those and help them stay more connected with what their bodies know.

We might hold in mind that the amount of time that it takes a child to be able to discern that a food isn't helpful for them is affected by many different factors, such as:

- Whether eating – or eating particular kinds of food – is a *control pattern* for them;
- Whether those foods have been *restricted* before;
- Whether those foods have been used as a *reward* before:
- How *present* in their body they are;
- Whether the food has a number of different foods *combined* or not;
- How much *presence* and compassionate *support* they receive from us before, during and after eating it.

Understanding these things can also help us make choices about what foods we're willing for them to have unlimited access to at home, and which foods we're not willing to bring into our home.

## Being relaxed and playful around food and aiming to make mealtimes enjoyable

> This can often be a huge process for many of us, particularly if we experienced coercion, punishment or harshness at mealtimes when we were growing up. Becoming relaxed, playful and joyful in relation to food can take a long while and require a lot of inner work for some of us!

One of the main things I've noticed over many years of working with parents is that in families where there's a lot of relaxed pleasure around food, and where children are encouraged to join in with growing, buying, preparing and cooking food, often the children enjoy eating, and often eat a wider variety of food (and, remember it can also be really natural for children to only enjoy a small variety of foods, or to want to eat the same food repeatedly over a period of time).

Let's bring in the wider cultural context again here. In many Indigenous cultures, children would have been an integral and natural part of food gathering, growing and preparing. This is how they learnt how to become a part of the culture. So again, the more we can support our children to relate to food as our hunter-gatherer ancestors did, the more likely they will have a relaxed and enjoyable relationship with meals and eating.

## Aware Parenting is about helping children stay deeply connected with their innate wisdom and pleasure in relation to food.

I'd love to share another story about how my children's father and I got free from some of our own conditioning and how that helped us have fun as a family.

*For a couple of years when our children were young, we went to a particular cafe that sold the most delicious chocolate mousse cake that we all loved. I don't remember how it started, but it became a common occurrence that we would eat the chocolate mousse cake first and then the savoury part of the meal. It led to lots of interesting conversations with whoever the waiter or waitress was each time, and we became well-known for doing that. It was such a fun way to play with our old cultural conditioning and all four of us loved it!*

> ### Self-Reflection Moment
> How do you feel when you're preparing and eating food?
>
> Would you like to imagine me offering you lots of empathy and unconditional love to whatever your response is?
>
> Perhaps you'd like to share about this with your Listening Partner, counsellor, therapist or Aware Parenting instructor?
>
> Are you wanting and willing to bring in more harmony, ease and pleasure in relation to food?

> Are there any changes that you'd like to make to how you prepare and eat meals (that you also believe are possible) to bring more connection, joy, pleasure or enjoyment?
>
> Are there ways that you see or remember your child/ren experiencing more connection and fun when eating (eg. at a picnic)?
>
> Are you willing to bring more of those kinds of experiences into your family?
>
> Do you have any childhood memories of really loving food in a way that wasn't you suppressing feelings but was about being deeply connected with your body and perhaps also with others?
>
> Does that give you any ideas about what you could bring into your family for even more connection, pleasure and harmony?

## Modelling a healthy relationship with food and connection with our cues and sensations

Children are meant to learn from us about food and what is healthy, what is available, and what is culturally important, so as parents we have an opportunity to explore our own relationship with food. I often find that we might be willing to keep doing something painful forever, but when we see that our children are learning this from us, it is a powerful invitation for us to be willing to bring about change.

> *Self-Reflection Moment*
>
> Do you know the sensations of hunger in your body?
>
> What about the sensations of satiation?
>
> Do you stop when your body tells you to?
>
> Do you eat more than your body tells you to and feel uncomfortable afterwards?
>
> Do you pick up sticks after eating particular foods or certain amounts of food?

*Would you like to receive listening and support to connect more with your body's wisdom?*

*Are you willing to drop any sticks you're picking up around this?*

*What actions are you willing to take from deep self-compassion?*

## Having deep compassion for ourselves in relation to food, cooking and eating

As you know by now I will always suggest bringing deep compassion for ourselves – it is *so* vital. For example, for a few years after separating from the father of my children, I only made meals that had just a few ingredients and that were simple and easy to make. At the beginning, I definitely hit myself with self-judgment sticks, but I learnt to drop those sticks, and to be much more compassionate with myself and what I was going through at that time.

In summary, with Aware Parenting, our aim can be to support children to make food choices based on their bodily sensations and information from us and from their own experience, so that we lessen the possibility of effects from:

- craving because something has been restricted;
- shoulds or have-tos;
- desire to suppress feelings with food;
- inability to feel bodily sensations because they're eating to dissociate.

## My journey with eating, food and feelings

*I used to have a really distorted relationship with food and eating when I was in my twenties. I judged how my body looked. I also couldn't differentiate between when I was hungry, when I was tired and when I was upset. I used to hit myself with guilt and shame sticks whenever I ate foods that I would judge as 'bad', or if I ate a whole packet of something, and particularly if I dissociated while eating. So there was this repeated theme of eating to suppress feelings and then feeling guilt and shame, which were then of course more uncomfortable feelings that I'd need to dissociate from.*

*Through lots of psychotherapy and inner work from when I was 24, that gradually changed. I stopped shaming myself about what I ate and how my body looked. I learnt to differentiate between the sensations that indicate hunger, those that indicate tiredness and those that told me I was upset.*

*However, when I started practicing Aware Parenting, I still had so much to learn about trusting my own body sensations and therefore also in differentiating between when my daughter was hungry and when she was upset. I often fed her when she had healing-feelings to tell me. As a result, she learnt to suppress her feelings with breastfeeding and found it hard to express her feelings with me. However, as I kept learning about Aware Parenting, I got so much clearer about differentiating hunger from upset feelings, both in her and in myself.*

*I remember when she was three, and we used to play games where we would both listen in to the sensations in our stomachs before we ate food, during the eating, and afterwards. I was amazed to see how clearly she could tell when she was hungry and when her body had had enough. Despite my learning journey as a parent and often feeding her when she was upset when she was was a baby, she reconnected with her body's innate wisdom. I focused on deeply trusting her and her body, and supporting her to stay deeply connected to her intrinsic intelligence in relation to food. As an adult now, she has an incredibly healthy relationship with food and her body, which is so different from me at that age.*

*I loved supported my children in listening to their bodies in relation to food. As I shared earlier on, for a couple of years, each person had one shelf of the fridge. When we went to the shops, they would choose what they wanted and it would go on their shelf. I prepared food so that it was ready for them to eat, for example, chopping up carrots and celery and putting them in glass containers. They also could access water right from their toddler years, so they could always get a drink when they were thirsty. As I've also shared earlier on, for many years the whole fridge door became their chocolate door – and they had years of old Easter eggs and chocolate that had been given to them at Christmas – a clear sign that they had no urgency or fear of lack in relation to chocolate; something that took me many, many years to get to!*

*Trusting my children's innate wisdom in relation to food has helped me return to trusting my own. For many years now, I have generally eaten based on a deep attunement to my body. I mostly eat when I'm hungry and I eat what my body tells me to eat and I stop eating when my body tells me I've had enough. I don't ever judge or shame myself after eating. I never eat to a point of uncomfortable fullness. I wouldn't have thought it was possible to make so much of a change in relationship to food. It really is possible, and practicing Aware Parenting has definitely been a powerful part of that process. As we learn to deeply trust our children in relation to food, we can regain our trust in ourselves in relation to food too.*

I love how clearly Aware Parenting helps us understand how much food, feelings and love get confused in this culture, and how much the *DDC* can make self-connected eating more challenging. In our parenting journey, we can learn to support our children to stay deeply connected with their innate wisdom in relation to food so that they know the difference in their bodies between feeling upset, feeling hungry and feeling tired, at the same time as going on our own journey of reclaiming our body's innate knowledge about what we really need.

*I believe that this is one of the most important gifts we can give to our children; helping them be deeply connected with, and trusting of, their body's wisdom.*

## The process of practicing the self-connected approach to eating

In her book, *Cooperative and Connected* (pages 171-172), Aletha Solter suggests that if parents are wanting to support their children to return to a healthy relationship with food based on what their bodies need, they can experiment with the following things:

1. First try the self-demand approach to eating combined with all other aspects of Aware Parenting (including *Loving Limits* for non-food issues). Trust that children will eventually be able to self-regulate in a healthy way.
2. Playful approaches for encouraging or discouraging children from eating specific foods.
3. If a child has an eating *control pattern* and binges on sweets (for example), provide connection and attention and suggest a short waiting time. You could invite your child to hold the sweets while inviting a cuddle and connection, so that they can have reassurance that you're not trying to restrict what they eat.
4. As a last resort, use *Loving Limits* (restricting specific foods), especially for an overweight child.

## Why hunger and feelings can often become intertwined

This can often be one of the most challenging things for parents to take in with Aware Parenting, generally because in so many cultures, the cultural beliefs are to feed babies and children whenever they are upset. The terms 'comfort food' and 'comfort eating' describe this so clearly.

> *Self-Reflection Moment*
>
> *I wonder if you ever find it difficult to differentiate between when you are hungry and when you are upset?*
>
> *If so, it is likely that your hunger and feelings might not have been differentiated between as a child, which we are going to talk about later.*
>
> *I also want to remind you about the whole 'perfection' thing. The idea of being perfect at something, or that we 'should' be perfect at something, comes from the DDC. So, as you go through this chapter, I'm not suggesting that you 'should' (because I never use that word!) always differentiate between your child's hunger and other feelings, or that you 'should' always differentiate between the two for yourself.*
>
> *This is more of a loving invitation, to see if you would like to differentiate more between the two of these.*

Given those preambles, I'd love to say more.

Why might many of us have lost trust in our body's innate wisdom related to what, when and how much to eat?

Why might it be that so many of us reach for food when we're upset?

Why might we find it really difficult to know if our baby or child is hungry or upset?

Probably because of cultural practices such as:

- making children eat all the food on their plate;
- not giving children choices about what, when or how much they eat;
- making children wait until a designated meal time; and
- making babies wait for arbitrary lengths of time before feeding them.

In addition, we can also add the following reasons:

- culturally, eating is seen as an important way to express love (this can be even more so in particular cultures);
- historically, so many of us have a lineage where there has been starvation, famine or lack, and that trauma gets passed down;
- most parents naturally want to always make sure their baby or child isn't hungry, so will always veer on the side of feeding rather than thinking that other things might be going on;
- most of us didn't experience our feelings being heard and many of us were fed when we weren't hungry, to suppress our feelings; and
- many of us would have experienced being fed on schedule as a baby, or being told to wait for dinner as a child, and thus we don't want our child to ever feel hungry in the ways we did, and so we overcompensate for that.

> *Self-Compassion Moment*
>
> *You know what I'm going to say, don't you? By now you know that I will always be saying these two things. Please put the sticks down. Please be compassionate with yourself.*
>
> *The majority of us growing up in these cultures have all kinds of complex relationships with food, and between food and feelings. This isn't another reason to pick up the self-judgment sticks. This is an invitation for curiosity, compassion and awareness, and then seeing whether you want to make any changes.*
>
> *Also, if you've had particularly big experiences related to food and eating, such as what are called 'eating disorders' (rather than 'disorder,' your relationship with food is a totally understandable solution to the family, time and culture you grew up in), please go extra gently with this material. You might decide to skip it altogether. You might pause, or jump over parts. You might make sure that you have plenty of empathy and support with anything that you do read about and explore here.*

So, here are a few thoughts:

If we are consistently fed when we are upset as a baby or child, we will learn to interpret those sensations as hunger.

We will literally interpret the sensation that is actually an emotion such as sadness or frustration or overwhelm or outrage as "I am hungry."

So, when we feel those sensations, we ask for food.

The cycle is compounded because often our parents continue to respond as if we are hungry.

## Differentiating hunger from a need to express feelings

No wonder we then find it hard to tell whether we are upset or hungry when we are adults. We might have had tens of thousands, or even hundreds of thousands of experiences of being fed or eating when we were upset, not hungry.

> *Self-Compassion Moment*
> *Do you feel more compassion towards yourself now?*
>
> *So, doesn't it make sense then, that when our baby is upset, or our child wakes from a nap, or comes home from school, that we might often interpret that they are feeling hungry when they actually have some healing-feelings to express to us?*

This is how the pattern gets passed down.

Our parents thought we were hungry when we were upset, and fed us. → We think we are hungry when we're upset, and feed ourselves. → We interpret our baby or child's feelings as hunger, and feed them. → And so on, and so on!

Disentangling this whole thing is a big process, especially if we haven't examined it in ourselves before becoming a parent.

As I shared earlier, I used to not be able to tell the difference between tiredness and hunger. And this makes so much sense, doesn't it? If we were frequently fed when we were tired as babies and small children, to get us to go to sleep, then it's obvious that we might then feel confused between sensations of tiredness and sensations of hunger, isn't it?

In the next section, I'm going to gently invite you to explore your relationship with food.

## Noticing eating *control patterns* in yourself and your child

*Self-Reflection Moment*

*Do you ever find that you:*

- *Don't know whether you are hungry or not;*
- *Eat because it's a particular time of day, rather than because your body tells you that you are hungry;*
- *Don't know what to eat;*
- *Eat things that you know lead to you feeling uncomfortable;*
- *Eat more than your body needs, and then feel uncomfortable;*
- *Snack throughout the day and never really feel hungry?*

*I invite you to lovingly reflect on these over the next few days.*

*Let's narrow this down to control patterns – i.e. using food to suppress feelings.*

*And let's include drinks with this, too!*

*Are there particular foods or drinks that you know that you eat or drink almost always as a way to suppress uncomfortable feelings?*

*That might be chocolate or cake or coffee or chips or cookies or fizzy drinks or alcohol.*

*Do you eat or drink in general when you first wake up or when you are tired, to suppress feelings?*

> *That might be the sense that, "I NEED my toast first thing in the morning," or, "I HAVE to drink hot chocolate before I go to bed."*

Of course I want to remind you that food and drink might be meeting many other needs rather than hunger – they might meet needs for:

- warmth (hot drinks);
- refreshment (ice cream);
- community (going out for a meal)
- celebration (celebrating birthdays with cake); or
- entertainment (eg. when we're bored).

> *Self-Reflection Moment*
> *Do you recognise any of these needs for you?*
> *Do you notice when you feel called to eat to suppress feelings?*
> *For example, do you gravitate towards the fridge to see what's there, even though you know you're not hungry, or do you find yourself thinking over and over again about the next chocolate/cookie/chips?*

I also want to acknowledge that this is a very complex topic. Chocolate, coffee, alcohol and many other food and drink items might be addictive in themselves, aside from us eating or drinking them to suppress feelings.

This is why I am inviting you to be really curious here.

Our desire for food and drink might be from:

- our need for *sustenance* and *fuel*;
- a need for *community* and *connection*;
- the *addictive* nature of the food itself;
- the *chemicals* in the food deliberately placed there so that it's enticing;

- an attempt to meet *physiological* needs that aren't being met by other types of food;
- a way to *suppress* feelings;
- effects of issues with the *gut microbiome*, *allergies* or *intolerances*,

and so much more!

The more you can:

- think about these things in compassionate ways;
- receive empathy about these; and
- stay lovingly present with yourself when you're about to eat to suppress your feelings,

the easier it will be to feel and express your feelings rather than suppress them with food – and reconnect with and relearn how to trust the wisdom of your body in relation to what and when you eat.

I'm also going to invite you to reflect on, and observe, whether your child suppresses their feelings through eating or drinking.

We might ascertain that they are suppressing their feelings, when they:

- ask for the same foods or drinks that we use to suppress our feelings;
- want them immediately on waking, or always when they're tired;
- ask for them or get them when they are clearly upset, eg. if they fall over and ask for a cookie;
- ask really urgently for them even though they've just had a lot to eat or drink;
- want them repeatedly (but this could be their innate body wisdom needing that food); or
- seem dissociated when they're eating or drinking (eg. their eyes are glazed).

(Again, please bear in mind and hold the possibility that there are other reasons for these things too.)

*Self-Reflection Moment*

*Do you notice any of these in your child?*

*Do you think that there are foods or drinks that they particularly use to suppress feelings?*

*Self-Compassion Moment*

*I invite you to put down the sticks here!*

## Bringing in *attachment play* and *Loving Limits* with food and eating

The more compassion and connection there is, the more *attachment play* and *Loving Limits* will be effective, so I really deeply acknowledge all that you've already attended to here.

Remember, it's important to implement the self-connected approach first for all children, before introducing *attachment play*.

*For the self-connected approach to work, it's helpful to act as if we don't have big feelings about what children eat, and to avoid commenting on what they eat or pressuring them (even playfully).*

Important note about play and food:

With *attachment play*, we are not trying to trick children into eating specific foods.

The airplane trick is a common way to get children to eat something, by pretending the spoon is an airplane flying into the child's mouth.

Another common trick is combining some food that the child doesn't enjoy on the same spoonful as the food they do like.

> The ultimate goal is to help children be in touch with their bodies and their own innate wisdom about food. It's important that children have a choice about eating or not eating something.

> *Self-Compassion Moment*
> *If you have played the airplane trick, I invite you to refrain from picking up sticks. It's never too late to stop doing things like this and to help children reconnect with their own innate wisdom in relation to food and to trust them and support them to trust themselves, while still bringing in play and fun to mealtimes.*

You may find that simply bringing in playfulness around food and meals can make a huge difference, since many of us grew up with admonishments to "not play with your food," and may be unwittingly bringing a quality of seriousness to food and eating that gets in the way of deep connection.

Playing *attachment play* games can be very helpful with supporting our children to heal, especially if we have been stressed around food, or have been coercive or punitive towards them in relation to food.

Emma Mason, an Aware Parenting instructor in Australia, shares a game she played with her children about sugar. This is a game you might find healing if you have had issues in your home in relation to sugar, for example if your child has a *control pattern* of sweets/lollies/candy:

*"We had this game where I would run after my children, begging to catch them, and pretending that they were sugar, saying exaggeratedly, "I need some sugar!" and then chasing them, trying to catch, hug and kiss them, saying, 'Sugar, sugar, sugar, sugar!' as if they were the*

sugar. They could tell me, 'No!' I couldn't have them/sugar and I'd run around and beg to have them/sugar and eventually they'd let me kiss or hug them. Both kids loved it and there was lots of joy and laughter."

Here's some playfulness I enjoyed with my daughter:

*I had a playful response with my daughter when she was two to three years old, as she was regaining her connection with her innate body wisdom in relation to food after me giving her a breastfeeding* control pattern. *When she asked for food in ways that indicated to me that there might be healing-feelings underneath the request rather than needs-feelings, I would say to her, with a playful tone, "Are you hungry for food, or are you hungry for a hug?" and I would move in close with a warm and joyful expression. If she said food, I would support her with that, even if I thought there were feelings there. Remember that warm connection is the antidote to freeze (dissociation), so even the offering of our warmth at those times can support our children to connect more with themselves.*

Here are some more play ideas that can be really helpful if you've been stressed around food and want to help everyone to heal from that stress so there's more ease and relaxation in relation to food for everyone. I wonder if any of them resonate with you?

I've acquired so many *attachment play* games from Chiara Rossetti, an Aware Parenting instructor you've heard from before in this book. Chiara shares some games:

**Maria with the disgusting restaurant:** I would pretend to be this funny waitress, and they would order pretend disgusting foods like toenails on toast, and then they wouldn't pay the bill and I'd chase them around.

**The switch witch:** If they came home from Halloween or parties, I would be the switch witch, trading sweets for organic things. They would run around trying to get the new chocolate or sweets, and I would try to steal the Halloween/party sweets, and would touch them and melt to the ground like the wicked witch of the west, saying, "Oh these sweets are terrible!"

***Silly names for sweets:*** We'd make up funny names, like the stinky bum popping candy, or this poopy poopy fart sweets. This is something we'd do all the time: a way of expressing that that food is gross for you, but in a silly way.

***Rory:*** I had an alter ego called Rory, and I would pretend to suggest going to the shops and getting a chemical fizzy drink and pouring it everywhere, which was really silly and fun.

Here are some other games that participants of my *Attachment Play Course* have shared:

- **The dropping food game:** Pretend to keep dropping food every time you get it near your mouth!
- **The funny wall food game:** Announce that you are going to get some food, and get up and walk into the wall, and say, "Oops," and, "This way".
- **The hungry caterpillar game:** Pretend you are a hungry caterpillar and want to eat all the different foods on the table.
- **The "I'm the food" game:** Pretend to be the food talking and dancing on the plate and calling out begging to be eaten. Or the opposite and pretend to be the food trying to escape from the plate and your child's teeth and tummy.
- **The baby giraffe game:** Pretend your child is the baby giraffe and you are the mama or papa giraffe. Reach up to the lettuce tree and pull down vegetation and feed it to your child.
- **The birthday cake game:** Open your mouth and close your eyes, making a big deal out of them giving you some birthday cake, and then they give you vegetables instead and you make a big yucky sound of disappointment.

- **The "don't you know vegetables are poisonous for kids" game:** When preparing the vegetables, say in a big mock voice that vegetables are dangerous for kids, and whatever they do, they'd better not eat any of them while you aren't looking. And then, while you aren't looking, they will invariably take one of them, and you say, "NOOOOOO, didn't you know that vegetables are poisonous for kids!" (I wouldn't recommend this with very young children who might not understand that this is not true information).
- **The cement mixer food game:** The cement mixer arrives with the food, then it is the digger and the tractor, the jumping kangaroo, etc.
- **The cafe game:** Pretend you are a waitperson with a funny accent, give them menus and make up funny names for the food. Give them the bill afterwards. The more you mock or ham it up, the more fun it is likely to be.
- **The green moonbeams from space game:** Look deeply surprised and fascinated by each item of food, as if it were from space and you had never seen it before! Point at parts of the food and say things like, "I can see that was harvested on Mars because of the scorch marks!"
- **The "don't even think of putting that broccoli in your mouth" game:** "No, please don't! Not the carrot too! Nobody listens to me in this house! I'm so glad that you're not going to eat greens, because I fall over whenever that happens!"
- **The "I'm glad you won't eat vegetables" game:** "I'm glad that you won't eat vegetables, because I have this problem with people eating green things around me today!" and then each time they do eat some, do a ridiculous dance.

Joss Goulden, a Level 2 instructor who you've already met, shares a game she used to play with her children:

*"They would put a blindfold on me and then feed me small quantities of food and I had to guess what it was. I usually would really over-exaggerate how disgusting it was and complain about how unfair it was that they were doing this to me and how hard it was to guess. There was lots of laughter and power-reversal which was so healing for us all."*

Please remember that these games are not designed to try to trick children into eating certain foods. They're designed to help families release tension through play and laughter, so that children can be even more deeply connected with their bodies and the innate wisdom they hold about food.

> *Self-Reflection Moment*
>
> I wonder if you would like to play with any of these?
>
> Perhaps you'd like to print them out and keep them nearby so you can remember to play them?
>
> You might find that it helps loosen things up around food for you too, and brings more ease and joy to mealtimes.

## *Loving Limits*

*Loving Limits* are useful only as a last resort after fully implementing the self-connected approach to see if the child eventually reconnects with their body's innate wisdom in relation to food. In Aware Parenting, we recommend using *Loving Limits* with food in two situations:

1. In the case of a breast-feeding *control pattern* (the mother's body is involved, so she has a right to offer limits),
2. In the case of a child whose eating habits are beginning to cause weight or other health issues (as parents, we have a responsibility to keep our child healthy).

An eating *control pattern* is similar to a thumb-sucking *control pattern*, because it's something that children do to their own body. In Aware Parenting, we think of *Loving Limits* with eating *control patterns* in the same way (except as a last resort).

If you do offer *Loving Limits* with food in these rare situations, I invite the following order of things:

- Attending to your own inner work, having your feelings lovingly heard;
- Offering more loving compassion and connection to your child when they're suppressing feelings with food;
- Bringing in *attachment play*;
- Offering the *Loving Limit*.

As always with *Loving Limits*, I invite you to offer them when you are:

- thinking compassionate thoughts;
- feeling connected to your child;
- able to listen to the feelings underlying the suppression.

You probably remember the language that I enjoy, such as,

*"I hear that you want more chocolate, and I'm not willing for you to*

have any more, sweetheart, because I don't think it's helpful for your body right now, and I'm here and I'm listening."

Please also bear in mind that this is within the context of trusting a child's innate wisdom around food that has usually been affected by what we and the culture have done, so we are supporting them to regain connection with, and trust in, their natural wisdom.

As always with a *Loving Limit*, we expect them to express the feelings underlying the *control pattern*, so we expect crying or raging.

> Self-Reflection Moment
>
> Does your child fall in the category of having eating habits that are beginning to cause weight or other health issues?
>
> Have you already attended to supporting them with self-connected eating first, and then attachment play if that doesn't seem to be working?
>
> Do you have a sense that Loving Limits are necessary now in relation to food?
>
> Is this a particular kind of food, or at a particular time of the day, or in a particular situation?
>
> Do you feel called to offer a Loving Limit and listen to the feelings?
>
> What do you need so that you can do that?

As always, I invite you to share this with a *Listening Partner*. With this issue in particular, I would highly recommend having a consultation with an Aware Parenting instructor or Aletha Solter herself.

And also, please be gentle with yourself after this chapter. It's a big one!

**From a child:** *I know you want me to eat healthy, Mum, but wow, you do go on about it sometimes! Jo gets to eat whatever he wants and sometimes it's just not fair that he gets to have all this stuff that you won't let me have. Since I've been friends with Jo, sometimes I sneak* snacks in that he's given me. I don't want to tell you about it because I know that you'll get all serious again. I just want to have a bit of fun. Oh Mum, you're coming into my room and you have a smile on your face. What's going on here? You've got a cape on, that one that I used to have for dressing up when I was a little kid. What are you doing? Hahaha! You're pretending to be a superhero! WHAT! You're taking some of those forbidden snacks out from behind your back! How did you know that I've been eating those exact ones with Jo behind your back! You're being all silly, pretending they are snack weapons. You give two to me and clearly want me to join in. Mum, this is crazy! I roll my eyes a bit, but inside I feel quite relieved. You clearly know that I've been eating those snacks and you're not doing that sad serious face. So that means something! We're pretending to fight with the snacks and you keep making like you're falling over. Oh Mum, you're pretty crazy, but I love this. I can't help it, a smile comes out from inside of me, and then a chuckle. You're laughing too, looks like you're having fun. Phew! I laugh some more, and dive in to whack your snack with mine. Got it! Haha! We are both laughing out loud now. It's kind of hysterical. I don't know why I'm finding this so funny, but you clearly are, too, cos now neither of us can stop. We're laughing and fighting and the snacks are flying everywhere now. Looks like you've got more than four of them! This game seems to go on forever and I don't know what you're doing to me, but I feel all happy now. I don't feel all angry about the snacks. We run to the sofa together and fall on it, kind of tired after all that laughing. "I didn't know you knew about the snacks, Mum."

"I didn't, until recently, sweetheart, and I realised that I was being all tense around them. I know you and Jo are having fun, and I feel sad that you didn't feel comfortable to tell me about the snacks. It's up to me to help you feel safe to share whatever is going on for you. I take responsibility for you not feeling safe to do that."

"It's okay, Mum," I respond. "But can I have them sometimes now?"

"Sure, lovely boy, let's just keep talking about it, shall we? You're getting older now and of course you want to try the things your friends are eating. We can be like scientists, exploring different snacks."

"Thanks, Mum," I reply, "Do you wanna watch that movie we said we were gonna watch?"

"I'd love to," said Mum. "Let's make dinner together and watch it afterwards."

"Cool," I reply. Who knew the evening was going to turn out like this? I'm so pumped that it did.

## Chapter summary

Aware Parenting is based on a **deep trust in children's innate wisdom**, and the self-connected approach to eating is a central part of this. However, there are aspects of our culture and cultural conditioning that can make this harder.

This often invites us to **get freer from our own cultural conditioning and to heal the ways we stopped trusting our own innate wisdom** in relation to food, so we can trust our child's (and our own) and communicate that trust to them, too.

In our culture, it's so normal for hunger and feelings to get connected, so **learning to differentiate hunger from a need to express feelings is often a huge journey**, both for ourselves as adults but also in differentiating the two in our children.

In this chapter I invited you to **notice eating *control patterns* in yourself and your child and to have lots of compassion for yourself in the process**.

With Aware Parenting, we can **increasingly bring in harmony, ease and pleasure related to food. Conveying trust in our child's innate body wisdom can also really support them to trust themselves.**

If the self-connected approach does not seem to be working, we may choose to bring in *attachment play* in relation to food, but not to trick children into eating things that they don't want.

In Aware Parenting, we don't recommend offering a child *Loving Limits* in relation to food, except in two scenarios: a breastfeeding *control pattern*, or a child whose eating habits are beginning to cause weight or other health issues.

If you want more information about this topic, I recommend reading *Cooperative and Connected* by Aletha Solter, and listening to the *Food, Feelings and Trust* series on *The Aware Parenting Podcast*.

Your body is so wise.

## CHAPTER SEVENTEEN

# Screens

## The interplay between self-connection and culture

Just like in the previous chapter on food, where we talked about the interaction between self-connection *and* children's innate need to learn about the culture they live in, this combination is deeply relevant to children and screens. However, unlike with food, which obviously we've been eating forever, supporting children to stay connected with their innate wisdom in relation to screen use is a much more recent experiment. Television has been around for only a hundred years. Video streaming platforms started in 2005. Social media began taking off at a similar time.

There's a way, of course, that food and screens are different. Food is essential for our survival *and* can also be a *control pattern*. In contrast, screens, clearly, are not essential for us to live – even though our culture has become very used to using them for many everyday tasks and we have found many ways for them to meet a variety of needs for us – yet they are a very common *control pattern*. Food and screens are probably two of the most common *control patterns* used to suppress or dissociate from feelings. There are other ways we can compare screens with food, in terms of understanding what makes it harder for children to be deeply connected with themselves in relation to screens, just like with food. We can also take a similar approach with Aware Parenting and screens as we do with food.

Remember when we talked about cooperation earlier in the book, I shared about us giving information to a child about what we want to happen and then offer them choices within that?

As with food, we can make the bigger choices about what we are willing and not willing for them to watch or play on screens, and then give them choice *within* that. To do this requires us to get really clear about our own yeses and no's – such as whether they have access to a screen at all, and what we are willing and unwilling for them to watch or play.

Within that, we can then give children choices and support them with ongoing connection with us and with their body, needs and feelings, particularly in their earlier years. As with food, we might then give them increasingly more choice as they get older, while continuing to stay connected with them through conversations and experiments together about their screen use.

Holding in mind the three aspects of Aware Parenting is helpful here, so that that they have fewer unmet needs and less accumulated feelings, both of which have a powerful influence on screen use.

## How we can apply the Aware Parenting maps to screen use

### The three aspects of Aware Parenting

Holding the three aspects of Aware Parenting in mind is really helpful when we think about screens and parenting:

- attachment-style parenting (connection and attunement to our child in relation to screens);
- non-punitive discipline (refraining from rewarding with screens or punishing screen use and instead really understanding why children want to be on screens);

- protecting children from stress and trauma (this is deeply relevant to screens, especially for young children, in terms of what we are unwilling for them to watch and play); and
- helping them heal from stress and trauma with *attachment play* and crying and raging (these can all play a large role in our parenting around screens).

## Attachment-style parenting

The more we can stay connected with our children in relation to screens and the more attuned we are, the more likely we are to help them stay connected with their bodily sensations, needs and feelings when relating with screens. This will mean they are more likely to know what shows, movies or games they prefer and those that they don't enjoy and when they've had enough. We can support them to understand when they feel excited, joyful, scared, overwhelmed, agitated or numb during or after screens. This will generally require us to attend to our thoughts, needs and feelings so we can stay connected and respond with interest and compassion. Being attuned to them includes being curious about what they're interested in watching or playing, which can meet needs of theirs for love, acceptance and mattering.

Focusing on connection in the actual process of using screens can make a huge difference. Offering non-directive child-centred play and saying yes when they want to choose screens, and 'Screen Present Time' and *attachment play* are some of the ways we can stay connected with our child in their screen use. The more we stay connected, the more likely we are to feel compassionate and to respond in warm ways, and the more willing they will be to listen to us and cooperate with our requests.

## Non-punitive discipline

This includes refraining from using screens as rewards and not punishing children by taking away screen time, as well as avoiding judging, guilting or shaming children when they want to go on a screen or stay on a screen. This often asks a huge amount of us in our own inner work and within our *Listening Partnerships*, since most of us probably experienced many of these things growing up, and probably continue to judge ourselves or feel guilty when we're on a screen or when our child is. This aspect of Aware Parenting also invites us to give our child information about screens and to explore the needs that screens can meet for our child.

> *Self-Compassion Moment*
> 
> *I invite you to be really compassionate with yourself here. Our child/ren's screen use can help us connect to huge amounts of powerlessness, fear and rage, and it's so understandable that most of us might have used power-over our child/ren many times when we felt those big feelings. We'll be exploring this all more later in the chapter.*

Most of us grew up with either being told what we could watch and when we could use screens, or having no parental input in relation to screens. With Aware Parenting, our role is to stay connected with ourselves and our needs as well as our child's needs and experiences. Through conversations, agreements and experiments, we can explore together to find ways for our children to use screens while staying connected with their innate body wisdom and unique interests.

### Protecting children from stress and trauma where possible

# My personal perspective is that many of the movies and shows marketed to children are actually stressful or even traumatic for them.

When my own children were between the ages of two and five, I was only willing for them to watch a very small number of shows that I chose. That then widened as they got older, when they began to make their own choices about what they would watch.

I was not willing for them to watch shows that I thought would be harmful for them. But within what I was willing for them to watch, I was more flexible about how much time they had to watch those things, and for them to choose which of those they wanted to watch.

If I could go back again, I would hold more limits over what I was not willing for them to watch for *more years*, while also giving them choices within that. However, I did find that in those early years, they were deeply connected with themselves and would say if they felt scared or overwhelmed and would ask to turn it off.

I believe that the cinema is an even more stimulating, immersive and realistic environment than watching a small screen, and thus has an even more powerful effect. I didn't take my children to the cinema until they were much older than most children are.

## I recommend waiting as long as possible before showing children screens.

But similarly with food, if we're eating sugar in front of them, their innate desire to learn and fit in will mean that they want it. If we're using screens, they are likely to want to use them too. So most of all, it's an invitation to check in with our values around screens and consider reducing our own screen use, especially when we have young children and when we're with them, while also being deeply compassionate with ourselves when we use screens to meet our needs, including for ease, connection, community and entertainment, or as *control patterns*. For most of us, screens are such an everyday part of our lives, and often we use them to meet so many needs, and so using them less can be a really big thing for us. As always, I invite you to listen in to yourself, be deeply self-compassionate, and make choices that are most a fit for your own unique family situation.

## Supporting them to heal from stress and trauma

It's common for many children to have feelings after watching something or playing something on a screen, and to need to heal from those experiences through crying and raging or laughter and play. You might find that your child has a *broken cookie* moment after screens, or will ask for lots of different things in ways that invite you to offer a *Loving Limit*. Alternatively, you might find that they spontaneously want to play games that are similar to the show they've watched or the game you've played, and invite you to join in. Their innate wisdom for healing is trying to work! Understanding when and how to offer *Loving Limits* in relation to screens makes all the difference; knowing how to listen lovingly to how a child feels when we ask them to get off a screen is important. We'll go into that in more detail later in this chapter, including when we don't recommend using *Loving Limits* with screens in Aware Parenting.

Having this list of the three aspects of Aware Parenting in our consciousness can be really helpful whenever we're wanting clarity about something to do with screens and our children. We might literally go through the list in our mind:

- How can I respond in a connected and attuned way here?
- How can I find a way for everyone to get their needs met?
- How can I protect them from stress or trauma?
- How can I support them to release any feelings that they might have here?

We can also hold in mind another Aware Parenting map that I shared at the beginning of this book: the three causes of behaviour.

## The three causes of behaviour

If our child wants to go on a screen or we want them to get off a screen, we can consider:

**Information:** What information do we want to give them about screens, or about screen time that day? What are they thinking about screens? This can be particularly important for younger children, who often don't understand the difference between reality and what they see on a screen.

**Needs:** We will be exploring later in the chapter about what needs screens can meet. When we understand what needs screens *are* meeting, we might then find it easier to either be compassionate, calm and accepting of their screen choices, or to offer alternatives to meet the same needs.

When we don't live in communities like we're meant to, our child/ren being on screens can very often meet *our* needs for support or concentration. Sometimes we might want them to go on a screen to meet *our* own needs, when there could be several ways other than screens for *them* to meet their needs. At times like this, it's again so important for us to be compassionate with ourselves about how hard parenting can be in the *DDC*.

If we're wanting and willing for them to get their needs met in ways other than screens, we can address the needs.

For example, if they're needing stimulation or entertainment, might we tell them a fun story or would they like to listen to an audio book?

If they're needing connection with their friends, would we like to suggest that they get together in person?

If they're wanting information, would we like to suggest a trip to the library?

Finding ways to stay connected with our children, especially as they get older, can be a really important part of this. That might be offering to play board games with them, showing interest in what they're interested in, and going out places together.

**Feelings:** What feelings they might have bubbling before, during and after screen time? Are they using screens to suppress feelings in that moment, or are they feeling joy, curiosity and excitement when they're watching or playing on the screen? Later in the chapter, we'll be diving into this more.

## Helping children be connected with what their bodies are telling them about screen use

What helps children know in their bodies when what they are watching or what they are playing on a screen is not helpful for them? The more we can be compassionately connected with them, offering what we notice in them and asking them about what their bodily cues are telling them, the more that they will have clear information about their connection with screens.

The things that make it harder for children to be connected with what their bodies are are telling them with screens are:

- When screens meet *needs* that aren't getting met in other ways;
- When screens have been used as a *reward*;
- When screen time has been removed as a *punishment*;
- When they have been *shamed* or *judged* in relation to screens;
- When they are using screens to *suppress* or dissociate from feelings;
- When they need to dissociate while watching or playing because the content is *stressful* or traumatic for them;
- The *immersive* nature of screens; and
- The *dopamine* hits designed to be a part of many games and apps.

> *Self-Compassion Moment*
>
> As a parent, we can be so tempted to pick up sticks over screens, especially because of the amount of shaming of parents and children about screens in this culture. I invite you to put down the sticks. It is so natural and understandable that screen use can be highly charged.

What can we do to help children, given all of those factors? What help do they need from us? We can return to the three aspects of Aware Parenting for the first several points above. Connection and presence are first on the list, and our presence and connection with them have the most significant effects on our relationship with them and their relationship with screens.

As they get older, we can give them more information, such as about how gaming companies make things attractive and how creators of programmes (this word is so similar to 'programming'!) make the end of the episode enticing so we find it hard to stop, because we want to watch the next one.

What do we need so that we can support them in these ways? Alongside research, most of us will need a lot of listening from our *Listening Partner* or Aware Parenting instructor, so that we're communicating this information in helpful ways rather than from fear and powerlessness or with judgment, shaming or coercion!

It's so understandable that we might feel all of those feelings and more, given how immersive and enticing screens are, and how we live in a culture where many of the natural ways for needs to be met – eg. through living in communities where children would be playing with other children all day in nature – are now being met through screens.

## Judgments and screens

I remember being really scared that other parents would judge me and my parenting if my children were on screens. Do you ever fear the judgment of others when your child/ren are on screens?

There are so many complex questions for parents to address about screens:

- What content is suitable for children at what ages?
- How much is 'too much'?
- How much can we trust that they are truly listening to what their body is telling them?
- How much are they being affected by what big tech corporations, movie makers and game developers are wanting them to do?
- What about blue light and EMFs?
- How can we help children get off screens?
- Why might they have big feelings in relation to screens?

> Again, I want to bring in the wider culture here. Because we live in a fractured society where larger family clans no longer exist, screens can be helpful for parents when we need time to work, to concentrate and to get other things done. The immersive nature of screens can mean that they are really helpful in this way. However, the immersive nature also means that some children may find it really hard to get off screens and come back into the non-screen world when we want them to. I believe that this issue is going to become even bigger as virtual reality and AI become the norm.

### Dropping the self-judgment

Because of how much harder all of this becomes when parents are experiencing judgment in the *DDC*, one of the most helpful things I have found is to drop the self-judgment with screens.

> This whole issue is challenging enough without us judging ourselves. The self-judgment, judging of our child, and our fearful thoughts about the future, are generally what lead to us feeling powerless and responding to our children in ways that we regret. We're likely to also be less able to connect with them compassionately to find out what's actually going on for them when we are hitting ourselves with those emotional sticks.

### Dropping the comparison sticks

Secondly, I've found it vital to invite parents to stop comparing themselves to other families and to instead look at their own family situation. Each family is different and each child is unique. Each family will have ways to be with screens that work for them.

### Differentiating between screens to meet needs and screens to suppress feelings

Understanding how to differentiate between screens to meet needs and screens to suppress feelings is a vital part of dropping the sticks. When we have compassionate understanding about the needs that screens are meeting for ourselves or our child, we can more easily drop the judgment.

## Taking stock of your screen use and your child's screen use and being unwilling to judge yourself

*Self-Compassion Moment*

*Please refrain from judging yourself here! I think this is particularly important for this topic, because there is so much judgment in the world in relation to screens, and particularly screen use for children.*

*So, if you do judge yourself when you are using a screen, or you judge your child when they're using a screen, please understand that of course you do! You've learnt to do that, seeing all the judgment around. And as always, I want to remind you that the more you are judging them or yourself, the less likely you will be able to clearly observe what is happening and be able to respond in the most helpful ways.*

*If you can drop the sticks, I invite you to do exactly that. If you want to, you might like to write down the judgments, because being aware of them can sometimes help us notice when we're believing them.*

*Self-Reflection Moment*

*How do you judge yourself when you are using a screen? What kinds of thoughts do you think?*

*How do you feel when you think those thoughts?*

*What kinds of behaviours are likely to result from those thoughts and feelings?*

*What kind of judgments about yourself do you think when your child is using a screen?*

*How do you feel when you think those thoughts?*

*What do you tend to do when you think those thoughts and feel those feelings?*

*What judgments do you entertain about your child when they are using a screen?*

> How do you feel when you think those thoughts?
>
> What are you more likely to do when you think those thoughts and feel those feelings?

I'm going to invite you to have some more friendly ways of thinking about yourself and your child. The aim is to support you to respond in more compassionate and effective ways that help you connect with yourself and your child so you can address what is really going on and can support them in listening to their body and feelings with their screen use. Later on, I'll be inviting you to write down what you want to choose to think in these situations instead.

## Connection, needs, agreements and trust

The less we are judging ourselves and our child in relation to screens, the more we are going to be able to connect calmly and compassionately with them about their screen use, and from that, to trust them and convey confidence that they have the ability to self-regulate[41] with screens.

If we're feeling lovingly connected with our child, it's going to be much easier for us to have a calm conversation before they go on screens, and to have regular ongoing conversations about screens.

The more we understand what our needs are and what their needs are, the more we can keep in mind our willingness for both of us to get our needs met in relation to their screen use.

*Many times when I was having conversations with my son about screens, I found it really helpful to express the phrase, "I'm willing for us both to get our needs met here." I found that saying that*

---

[41] Please note that in Aware Parenting, we only use the term 'regulation' in the context of food and screens, and not to refer to emotions or feelings.

*would prevent me going into powerlessness or power-over, and I loved that it also communicated to him my willingness for his needs to get met.*

Here are some suggestions for harmonious screen use:

- **Staying connected:** There are many different ways of doing this. One of the ways I really enjoyed was when we had a low circular table that we would all sit around together when we had our screen time, which meant we could see each other and could easily engage with each other while on screens.
- **Negotiating agreements:** For example, we might suggest to our child that they watch one episode per day, and then give them an opportunity to monitor that themselves. Ongoing discussions are vital to this approach, as is us lovingly conveying our confidence that they can stay deeply connected with their body's wisdom. It's vital that we are interested in their experience, that we ask them how it is for them to be watching one episode, that we listen to their feelings, and we keep being willing for both them and us to get our needs met. What a child is doing on a screen will affect this 'negotiating agreements' approach. For example, watching an episode is very different from playing a game with levels. For the former, it can be easy to agree on a certain amount of time, eg. one episode might be 20 minutes, whereas with a game, the agreement might be to play two levels, which wouldn't have a fixed amount of time. Conveying trust that they will honour the agreement is also important.
- **Experiments, followed by sharing observations and feelings with each other:** I found this really helpful with my children. As a homeschooling family, I also joined in with the experiments and went on my computer at the same times as them. We played with all kinds of different options, such as:
  - *All of us having a set amount of time at the same time each day, eg. 90 minutes at 4pm.*

- *None of us using screens until a certain time, eg. 4pm;*
- *Having a set time that we would all be off screens by, and then having two timers, 15 minutes and 5 minutes before the time we agreed, that went off automatically each day;*
- *Having certain days where no-one went on screens;*
- *Unlimited screen use days.*

We would then have conversations about how we felt, whether that met our needs, and how much we were inspired to do non-screen things. For example, we really enjoyed the joint agreement that no-one would go on screens until a certain time because there was no temptation to get on earlier, and we would go about our day without thinking of screens until then. In our family, we found that the first two options of the experiments were those that we most enjoyed, and we used them for years.

## Each family is so different, and each individual is so unique, including in what they're using screens for. Experiments followed by conversations can really help us understand each person's experiences, preferences and choices.

*Self-Reflection Moment*

*Have you ever done experiments like this?*

*Do you feel called to experiment like this?*

*If so, what would you like to experiment with?*

*How would you like to build in conversations with your child/ren about this?*

## Differentiating between screens to meet needs and screens to suppress feelings

I find this process incredibly helpful and I'm so willing for you to, too!

> *Self-Reflection Moment*
>
> I invite you to reflect on the following:
>
> - the different ways you use screens;
> - the needs that they meet; and
> - how you feel when those needs are met.

For example:

- reading a book on a reading app: relaxation and entertainment; relaxed and happy;
- watching a particular video platform; learning and entertainment; inspired and interested;
- doing an online course: learning and stimulation; curious and engaged;
- voice app: connection and community; warm and touched;
- social media: inspiration and connection: inspired and happy;
- watching a film or documentary: learning and entertainment; intrigued and relaxed.

What about when you use a screen to suppress feelings? How can you tell that you're using it that way? For example, you might pick up your phone and scroll social media without even thinking, and then notice after some time has passed that you weren't choosing to keep going and you weren't really even concentrating on it.

Or, you might have picked up your phone to look at the weather app, and ten minutes later realised that you started scrolling through social media and had forgotten to even look at the weather!

> *Self-Reflection Moment*
>
> *How do you feel, during and after this?*
>
> *For example, you might feel numb, agitated, spaced out, frozen, or dissociated.*
>
> *How do you respond to yourself afterwards?*
>
> *For example, you might judge yourself and then feel even more uncomfortable.*
>
> *Now, I invite you to reflect on your child/ren.*
>
> - *what kinds of things do they use screens for;*
> - *what needs might those meet for them;*
> - *how might they feel during and after?*

Depending on their age and willingness, you might want to ask them about this, or even involve them in a conversation or do a project about this. This can be a very helpful way of bringing more clarity and compassion for everyone.

For example:

- gaming app: agency and competence; flowing and energised.
- movies: entertainment and learning; happy and interested.
- language app: learning languages; engaged and focused.
- social media: connection and community; warm and happy.
- watching sports: community and entertainment; excited and interested.

This can be a really helpful process, and as part of the information/thinking part of Aware Parenting, can help you think more compassionate thoughts about your child's screen use.

> **Self-Compassion Moment**
> *Have you already noticed a change here? Perhaps earlier on you had judgments of their screen use? Perhaps you are feeling more warm and positive towards (at least some elements of) their screen use?*
>
> *Now, what are you thinking and feeling? I am offering you so much compassion as you receive this information.*

In addition, when we understand what needs the screen use is meeting, we might also suggest non-screen activities to meet those same needs.

Next, how can you tell when they are using a screen to suppress feelings?

You might discern this when they want to go on a screen:

- as soon as they wake up;
- when they are clearly tired;
- when they are clearly upset.

You might also notice other things about their bodies or their behaviour that tell you that they are using screens to suppress feelings, eg.

- they look dissociated;
- they're avoiding eye contact;
- they're really agitated before and after going on a screen;
- they ignore their body's needs eg. thirst, hunger, needing to go to the toilet, tiredness.

## The more we can differentiate between when a screen is meeting needs and when it's being used to suppress feelings, the more we can respond in apt ways.

We can support our children when they are meeting a need with screens and we can offer *attachment play* and *Loving Limits* when they are using it to suppress feelings (while holding in mind not to just use *Loving Limits* without conversations and agreements).

I'd also love to offer a few words about one of the reasons why screens can be so effective at suppressing feelings. Have you ever been so immersed in a movie that it was almost as if you really were there, with those people, doing those things, and when the lights come up at the end, it takes you a few moments to reacclimatise to being in your here and now life?

Screens can transport us into other worlds and other times. This is what, on the one hand, makes them so powerfully entertaining and enticing (and is why they can be so helpful to us when we are wanting our child to concentrate on something for a while while we get something done).

However, their enticing nature can make it hard for a child to want to, be willing to, and be able to, move off the screen back into this world and reality.

I invite you to recall a time where you've been deeply immersed in something on a screen.

Imagine you were:

- Right in the middle of a movie and someone turned it off. How would you feel?
- Involved in learning something new, and just about to really understand it, and someone told you to get off. What would your response be?
- Doing a project and were just finalising something you'd been working on for ages. How would you feel if someone came along and told you it was time to finish?

This is why it's so important for us to really listen in to what our child is experiencing. Just as we might feel incredibly frustrated, outraged or powerless in these occasions, so can our child, particularly if we're not aiming to really understand their experience.

***Our children have the same needs as us – including respect, consideration, and completion. For them, playing an online game can be like a creative project is for us.***

Honouring and valuing their needs and having conversations which consider their needs as well as ours can all be part of building more emotional safety in the family.

---

*Self-Compassion Moment*

I'm sending you so much love to any and every time you feel frustrated, powerless or outraged when your child wants to be on a screen or isn't willing to get off. At these times, when we have big feelings, it can be so hard to listen in to what they might be experiencing. If you're reacted harshly to them, my heart goes out to you. The complexities of screens and parenting can help us feel really big feelings. I remember experiencing that too. You're absolutely not alone!

---

*Self-Reflection Moment*

Do you remember ever watching a screen as a child or a teen and your parents turning it off, or telling you that you shouldn't be watching it?

If so, how did you feel?

How would you have wanted to be responded to instead?

What would you like to remember from this experience when you're attending to your child when they want to be on a screen and you don't want them to be?

## Staying connected before, during and after screen use

Staying connected around screens makes all the difference, which is one of the reasons why I want to support you in having ways of thinking that are more likely to mean that you feel compassionate towards your child/ren in relation to screens. It can also help children make the transition between being on a screen and off one easier.

Imagine you are chatting to a friend about your favourite movie/series/book, and they started judging you, or telling you that you shouldn't be doing that. How would you feel? In contrast, if they listened avidly, showing interest and asking pertinent questions, how would you feel then? Holding this in mind when we're about to judge our child about them wanting to watch their favourite show or play another game can help us come back to compassionate connection.

When we clearly show them that we're interested in what they like, for example by listening to them sharing about what just happened in the most recent episode or level, remembering the names of characters and the story line, or understanding how the game works (or asking questions if we don't). This can meet lots of needs for them, particularly for being cared for, mattering, and being loved.

*Before* screen time, you could ask your child what they:

- are going to do on screens;
- enjoy about it;
- are looking forward to about it.

*During* screen time, you could:

- sit close and watch with them;
- ask to see what they are doing;
- offer to play a game with them;
- ask them what they enjoy or don't enjoy;

- ask about things you don't understand;
- be willing to enjoy it as much as they do;
- have your screen time too and sit together;
- discuss a time to get off, eg. at the end of the episode or the end of the next level (if you haven't already made an agreement before they get on); or
- play silly and goofy games at the end of the agreed time to support them in getting off the screen.

*After* screen time, you could:

- play a game that's similar in some way to what they have been watching or playing;
- ask them about the show or the game;
- act out the show or game; or
- do some activities with body contact to help them reconnect with their body, especially if they tend to dissociate when they're on a screen.

## *Attachment play* and screens

*Attachment play* can be very helpful with screen use.

It can help:

- us stay connected with our child, and help our child stay connected with us;
- them release feelings related to choice, agency, or autonomy;
- us release feelings related to our judgments and reactions to them being on a screen;
- them release any feelings that were caused by them actually being on the screen;
- them express feelings that they were trying to suppress with screens.

Joss Goulden, a Level 2 Aware Parenting instructor in Australia whom you've already met, shares about *attachment play* games she used to play with her children when they were younger:

*When my children were reluctant to come off screens I used to say sometimes, "Okay, but you can only watch another 246 episodes and then you really have to come off! Do you promise?" and this would often start some loving and silly connection around me becoming more and more ridiculous about what I was suggesting for them, like, "Okay, well if you have 23 hours screen time a day, would that be enough? Would it be fair if we switch off after playing another 974 levels?" This would support my children to feel connected and to laugh (so there was less need to suppress feelings with screens) and would support me to feel more connected and loose about it all (so I could then embody a* Loving Limit *more clearly without going into telling myself lots of unenjoyable things about my children, their behaviour and what their screen time said about them and about me)."*

I love these games from Joss! A game I found really helpful with my own children was what I called *Screen Present Time*. This is when our child chooses what to watch or play and we watch or play with them. I used to offer this to them regularly.

*I'll never forget one time when me and my son and daughter all played a video game together for about three hours. They were both offering me empathy and doing whatever they could to help me through the game, including their characters going back to the beginning over and over again to help my character. They were displaying such incredible compassion, encouragement, celebration and support that I was completely in awe. It actually gave me a really clear indication of what they'd internalised through experiencing Aware Parenting. Not something I had previously thought I would gain through gaming!*

Some children might choose screen-based activities during their non-directive child-centred play. This can meet many needs for them, including wanting to watch or play something that is normally restricted and having support with that, wanting acknowledgment for their gaming skills, or wanting us to understand why they enjoy that show or game. It's common for parents to need listening time to be able to freely say yes to these choices.

### Power-reversal games

Power-reversal games can often naturally come about if our child can do things on screens that we aren't able to do (which is very common). This reverses the usual direction of power, and can give them and us a true sense of them being more powerful. If we exaggerate what we're not able to do and pretend to be frustrated, this can make it a power-reversal game. We might not even need to pretend to be less powerful here! It's common in gaming in particular that children become more competent at it than us. Giving them experiences of feeling powerful can be profoundly healing for children.

*I remember so often playing online games with my children and being so incompetent, that it supported them to experience being more competent and powerful. Sometimes, it would also help me connect in with my own painful feelings. I remember one time playing an online game with them and not being able to do it, which helped me connect with younger parts of me and feeling so powerless and eventually depressed, as I reconnected with a sense of "I can't do this" and then gave up.*

So if you ever feel big feelings at times like this, I so understand and send you so much love! This is why our own listening time is so vital.

### *Attachment play* for releasing feelings related to our judgments and reactions to being on a screen

It is so understandable, given all the cultural judgments in relation to screens, that you might at times have judged your child when they were on a screen. If so, there are *attachment play* games that you can use to help them with that.

**The "whatever you do, you're not going to go on a screen when I go to cook dinner, are you?" game:** This is when you say this phrase in a mock surprised tone, making it clear that that is exactly what you are inviting. Then, you could come back into the room every now and again, and say, in a mock surprised way, "NOOOOOOOO! You said you weren't going to go on a screen! Now I will need to give you a huge HUG!" Then go over and hug them, and then repeat. This can also be healing for us, where we get to say what we'd really like to say, but in a silly way.

**The "please stop me from picking up my phone" game:** You pick up the phone and they point it out, and you jump in the air, surprised at how that happened. If there's laughter, keep repeating it. This can help them feel powerful and help you both heal from times when you were trying to get them off a screen.

## Release any feelings that were caused by them actually being on the screen

This is another game that a parent shared in my *Attachment Play Course*.

**The wolf game:** The wolf game was inspired by the dogs/wolves in the game of Minecraft – if you're not familiar, when you feed the wolves beef, they turn into tamed dogs with love hearts around their heads and they follow you around, and if you hit them they turn into angry wolves and try to eat you. When your child pretends to hit you, you turn into a ferocious wolf, get mock angry, growl and pretend to eat them.

## *Attachment play* can also help them when they are trying to suppress feelings with screens

**The "new phone tripod" game:** Earlier in the book, I briefly shared about this game. Here's me telling the story at the time I invented it nearly a decade ago:

*Today I came up with another game that I really enjoyed! My daughter and I were clothes shopping (lots of fun with a 13 year old), and my son (nine) was on my phone (not what I had wanted at all, but I do understand that shopping isn't much fun for him!!). When we got home, he was still on it! He was on the couch and his dad was there too, on the couch next to him. So I started talking to his dad, saying that did he know that they have a new phone tripod nowadays, that looks like a really realistic boy. You can even move the tripod's arms and legs. (And I moved his arms and legs!) The only thing is that it is stuck to the phone (and I pretended to try to get his hands away from the phone). My son was laughing and laughing, and I continued in this way, with his dad joining in, asking things like, 'Does it also crack open macadamia nuts?' and I demonstrated how. It was really funny, we all reconnected, and he happily got off the phone and stayed connected with us.*

> ### Self-Reflection Moment
>
> How do you feel, reading about these attachment play games?
>
> I want to remind you to refrain from picking up your judgment sticks if you feel powerless, fed up, frustrated or angry even thinking about it. I think that powerlessness is a really common feeling for parents to feel in relation to screens. This can be from unmet needs in the present, but also because we're connecting with powerlessness from our own childhoods when the adults around us wouldn't do what we asked. I'm sending so much love to ALL of your feelings! And you know what I'm going to suggest, don't you? Yes, to share your feelings with a loving listener.
>
> Are you willing to do that?

I want to remind you that the more you have your feelings heard, the more likely you are going to be able and willing to:

- think *compassionate* thoughts about your child;
- feel *connected* with them;
- be *interested* in them and their experiences and needs in relation to screens;

- *play attachment play* before, during or after screens; and
- *listen* lovingly to their feelings.

## *Loving Limits* with screens and listening to feelings

By putting into practice some or all of what talked about here, it's likely that your child will feel less painful feelings around screens (and you too), because they:

- feel more connected with you;
- experience being understood and that interests and needs matter to you and they are valued;
- feel more powerful, with more agency and autonomy needs met;
- experience being trusted.

As with food, in Aware Parenting, we see *Loving Limits* as a last option with screens, not something to do as an initial go-to.

An arbitrary *Loving Limit* without any warning or preparation could be experienced as authoritarian control to a child. Before using *Loving Limits* with screens, we can discuss screen use with them ahead of time, share our concerns, and strive for a mutual agreement about how many shows they will watch (or game levels they complete). This requires a willingness to negotiate. We can even have an ongoing written contract for older children and then trust them to honour the agreement.

If they don't honour the agreement, we can discuss the issue again and let them know that we will monitor their screen use and help them stop, if necessary. When their screen time is up, we can lovingly implement the agreement but also give them a choice, "Do you want to turn it off yourself, or do you want me to turn it off?" We can also offer suggestions for an alternative activity (with or without us), "Would you like to play a game of cards with me?" And, of course, it's important to welcome any feelings they might have.

Given that information, there are times when we may want to offer a *Loving Limit* in relation to screens.

I want to remind you again that a *Loving Limit* means not only saying no to the behaviour, but also saying yes to the feelings underlying the behaviour.

If we have:

- discussed ways for us both to get our needs met;
- given them agency and autonomy; and
- been playful,

and they are still not willing to get off, it could either be that:

- screen use is still meeting needs for them, or
- the screen use is helping them suppress or dissociate from feelings.

If we offer a *limit*[42], because we have our own reasons for wanting them to get off, they will feel feelings related to their needs now not being met.

If we offer a *Loving Limit*, they will connect with the feelings that were being suppressed or dissociated from by the screens.

Those can be a LOT of feelings!

I want to invite you, that if you are going to offer a *limit* or a *Loving Limit* in relation to screens, to pause for a moment and remember your thoughts, needs and feelings:

1. Choose to think some helpful thoughts, eg. "I'm here to help them get off the screen and I love them."
2. Connect with your needs and your body, eg. put your arms around yourself and connect with your breathing and your need

---

42  If you're wanting a reminder about the difference between *limits* and *Loving Limits*, and why they are still both loving, see the chapter on *Loving Limits*.

for connection and whatever other needs you will be meeting by them getting off the screen.

3. Give empathy to feelings and younger parts and choose to act from your adult self, eg. "I'm sending love to my frustration, and I am going to respond from my compassionate loving parent self."

> *Self-Reflection Moment*
> *I invite you to note some ideas for yourself here.*
> *What thoughts might be helpful for you?*
> *How can you support your body and needs?*
> *How can you care for your feelings and your younger parts?*

Then, we can move in with the *Loving Limit*:

For example, *"I see that you want to watch another show, and I'm not willing for you to watch any more, because I want us to keep to the agreement we made earlier about stopping after this episode, and I'm here and I'm listening."*

Or, *"I hear that you want to get to the next level, sweetheart, and I'm not willing for you to play any more, because I want to keep to the agreement we made earlier about stopping after this level. I'm here and listening, and I love you."*

Please hold in mind how you might feel if you were involved in something that was meeting your needs on your phone, or if you were scrolling Facebook to avoid feeling uncomfortable feelings, and your friend or partner stopped you from doing those. You might feel really big feelings, mightn't you?

# It's really normal and natural for your child to feel really big feelings – which might be from unmet needs including agency, autonomy and choice, or

might be feelings that screens were suppressing, or might even be feelings that the screen use created. Or a combination of them!

So, please be prepared for this.

They might start pleading to stay on. You might want to keep offering the empathy and the *Loving Limit*:

*"I really hear that you want to watch more/play more sweetheart, and I'm not willing for you to watch more/play more now. I'm here and I'm listening. I really hear how upset you are."*

They might scream or shout at you things like, *"It's not fair,"* or, *"I hate you!"* or, *"I never get to do what I want."*

I invite you to offer them empathy with responses like, *"I hear that you think it's not fair,"* or, *"I hear that you hate me,"* or *"I hear that you think you never get to do what you want. I'm listening."*

They might start crying or raging.

I invite you to listen.

*"I see you're upset. I understand. I'm here and listening."*

They might start moving into aggression.

In this case, I invite you to do all you know from the chapter on aggression – doing the minimum required to keep yourself and them safe, aiming for the *balance of attention* with a *Loving Limit*, and keeping on offering empathy.

*"I'm not willing for you to throw the books, sweetheart, because I'm here to keep everyone safe and I want to care for the books, and I'm right here and listening. I understand how you feel. I'm here with you."*

Ideally, see if you can keep listening for as long as the feelings are there and being expressed. This may require a lot of you. Repeating your parenting mantra, connecting in with your breathing and a loving inner presence might help you to stay calmer for longer.

Afterwards, you might want to reach out and send a message to your *Listening Partner*. This can be a challenging situation and it's so natural if you feel lots of feelings afterwards.

> *Self-Reflection Moment*
> How do you feel when you read this?
> Are there any parts of this that you imagine you'll find hard?
> What might you need so that you find it easier?
> Are there any parts of this that you want to do differently?

## Why exploring our own powerlessness as parents is so important here

I've found that screens have been one of the most common places in parenting that my own powerlessness has shown up. I wonder if you've found that too? It's generally when we're feeling powerless, such as if our child keeps going on a screen when we've asked them not to, or if they won't get off when we want them to, that we can flip into power-over and other forms of harshness. This is because powerlessness is so painful, that we'll do anything we can to avoid it.

I find it helpful to look at the three sources of powerlessness, and tend to them, so we're less likely to feel powerless and act in these ways.

## Thoughts

If we're telling ourselves harsh things or powerless things about ourselves or our child when they're on a screen, we're likely to feel powerless. For example:

*"I can't ever get my needs met."*

*"They never listen to me."*

*"Why doesn't he ever do what I ask him to do?"*

*"I don't know what to do."*

*"She's never going to stop."*

Noticing these thoughts, being compassionate with ourselves, and replacing them with more powerful thoughts, can really help, eg:

*"I'm telling myself that I have no power when he doesn't get off the screen. But I do have power here. I'm willing to feel my power here."*

*"I'm telling myself that I can't ever get my needs met. But that's not true. I do get my needs met. I'm willing for us both to get our needs met here."*

*"I'm been thinking that he doesn't ever do what I ask. My need here is cooperation. He does often cooperate!"*

*"I'm telling myself that I don't know what to do, but that's not true. I can return to information, needs and feelings."*

*"I'm thinking that she's never going to stop, and I really want her to. I'm sending myself love. I'm so willing to help her get off."*

## Needs

When our day to day needs aren't being met, particularly our needs for agency, autonomy and choice, we are likely to easily flip into powerlessness if our child goes on a screen when we don't want them to, or won't get off when we ask them to.

This is because those feelings of powerlessness are sitting below the surface and the screen use is helping us feel that. Our child is just helping us feel what's already there.

It's so important for us to be really compassionate with ourselves here. The *Disconnected Domination Culture* does everything it can to lead us to feel powerless and for it to be hard to get our needs met, particularly as parents. It's not your fault!

And, understanding this can help us be more willing to get our needs for agency, autonomy and choice met, when we see the huge effect that not having them met can have.

> *Self-Reflection Moment*
>
> *Are you willing to listen in to what you're needing, and to explore your willingness to have your needs met?*
>
> *Are you willing for your needs for agency, autonomy and choice to be met more?*
>
> *Are you willing to feel more true power in your life?*

In the moment of the screen conversation, we can also connect in with our willingness for both ourselves and our child to get our needs for agency, autonomy and choice met. Even if we have no idea how that might happen.

## Feelings

Most of us have many, many unexpressed feelings of powerlessness in our bodies, from growing up in the *DDC*. The majority of us will have been overpowered, told what to do, and not given choice, agency or autonomy hundreds of thousands of times, including at home and at school.

Of course we have a whole lot of unexpressed feelings of powerlessness! And of course they're going to show up when our child won't get off a screen when we really want them to. The magnetic nature of screens makes this it even more likely to help us connect with past unexpressed feelings. Them not doing what we ask has the potential to help us connect with thousands of times when we asked our parents or teachers to do what we wanted, and they didn't.

I invite you to take any feelings of powerlessness and express them in your journal, to your Inner Loving Mother[43], your *Listening Partner* or Aware Parenting instructor. The more you get to express those feelings to a loving listener, the less they will come out when your child gets on a screen when you've asked them not to. I want to remind you that those feelings are probably coming up because your wise body is trying to heal from the past times when you asked your parents, sibling, peers or teacher to stop doing something, and they kept on doing it anyway. Or you asked them for help, and they didn't.

> Tending to our feelings of powerlessness can make a huge difference. The more we feel our true power when we're talking with our child about screens, the more likely it is that we can stay calm and compassionate, be willing to find a way for everyone to get their needs met, and be able to listen to their feelings if expressing them is their most vital need in the moment.

**From a child:** *Sometimes I see your face go all funny when I say I want to watch something, and I just know that you don't like it. I wonder why you don't want me to do something that I love so much. I'm so excited about the new episode – I've been waiting for ages for this new one, to see what happens to my favourite character. I wish I didn't need to hide from you how much I love it. Sometimes I wish you'd just sit with me and watch it and I could tell you afterwards about all the things that I noticed. I remember that one time you did that and I loved it so much. But also, I do need your help sometimes.*

---

43  From The Marion Method work.

*The other day I got into watching that old show I used to watch, and I kept on needing to watch another episode. I wasn't even really enjoying it. It was like I couldn't stop. I really liked it when you came over and helped break the spell, and then how we played that fun game afterwards, pretending to be the bear. I felt so relieved. Oh, Dad, you're coming over to watch the new episode with me! I'm so excited to tell you all about it! You must care about me, after all! Isn't it so fun! I love the way that the main character has that magic power. I'd love to have magic powers. I sometimes wish I had more power, and watching this show helps me feel powerful in my body. I love knowing more about all the characters than you, so I can tell you about them all. Oh, you're listening, Dad, and you look interested! Wow! This is like a dream come true! I remember how you used to say that this show was stupid and I felt so sad back then, like you didn't love me. But you're here now, and you're watching it, and we're together. Oh, the episode is over. Wasn't that amazing, when he jumped over that huge building and saved his friend! I felt SO excited then! I just love how I feel when I watch him do things like that. I'd love to be like him. Dad, after I tell you more about his origin story, could we go and play in the garden, where I'm him, and you're his friend, and I jump over the wall and save you? Oh, you said YES! This is my best day ever! Thanks, Dad!*

## Chapter summary

Holding in mind **the three aspects of Aware Parenting and the three causes of behaviour** can be really helpful when anything challenging happens around screens. These can prevent challenges from occurring in the first place, too.

One of the key things that can make the most difference to us is **being unwilling to judge ourselves in relation to screens**. The less we judge ourselves, the more likely we are to be able to respond compassionately to our child in relation to screens.

With screens, we can aim for harmony and trust. **Staying connected with our children, negotiating agreements and then giving children an opportunity to monitor that themselves, along with ongoing discussion and experiments, followed by sharing observations and feelings with each other,** can all be part of this process.

When we can **differentiate between when screens are being used to meet needs and when screens are being used to suppress feelings,** we are going to be able to respond in a more attuned and compassionate way to our child.

We can use *attachment play* **in relation to screens once we have already worked with negotiating agreements, doing experiments and having discussions.** *Attachment play* can help us and our children stay connected and can help it be easier for them to get off screens.

*Loving Limits* **with screens and listening to our child's feelings are a last resort with screens**, remembering how we might feel if a loving adult offered us a *Loving Limit* in relation to our screen use.

Looking at our **own power and powerlessness**, especially from our own childhood, can be vitally important if we're going to be able to respond with more compassion and true power to our children when they're on a screen.

## I'm sending you so much love any time you feel powerless!

# CHAPTER EIGHTEEN

# Sleep

## The innate wisdom of children's bodies to sleep peacefully

As you've seen in many other chapters of this book, one of the premises of Aware Parenting is that we can trust the innate wisdom of children and their striving for emotional and physical wellbeing. Because the culture most of us grew up in doesn't trust or understand that, most of us have a whole lot of cultural conditioning and unhealed stress and trauma that gets in the way of us being able to see, trust and cooperate with their intrinsic wisdom.

This also applies to sleep. If you're new to Aware Parenting, you might be surprised to hear that children want to sleep peacefully as much as we want them to. You might also be interested to hear that children are using their innate body wisdom to do that, but we are often working against it because of our cultural conditioning and our own hurts.

In this chapter, I'll explain the three things that children (as well as babies and adults) need for truly restorative sleep. I'll also talk about how we can help ourselves get free enough from our own conditioning and heal from enough of our own childhood experiences with sleep, so that we can cooperate with their natural wisdom.

## What gets in the way of children sleeping restfully

From an early age, my children slept long and restful sleeps while co-sleeping, breastfeeding and being securely attached. I'm here to offer an alternative to the myth that you need to choose between secure attachment and sleep for the first few years of parenting.

The most common reason for children taking ages to go to sleep and waking up lots during the night isn't because children just aren't biologically able to sleep peacefully for the first few years. Rather, it's generally because unexpressed feelings and stored up tension from unhealed stress and trauma prevent them from feeling truly relaxed enough to go to sleep and sleep peacefully for as long as they need.

This can be challenging to hear if we believe that most children don't experience painful feelings, stress or trauma. However, if we take as a central point that *all* children experience painful feelings pretty much every day, it's much easier to also be open to the possibility that in our culture we are taught to suppress their feelings and it is that suppression and dissociation which is getting in the way of them feeling the kind of true and deep relaxation that sound sleep requires.

> It's those suppressed feelings that lead to them feeling uncomfortable and agitated in their bodies.

It's that agitation that we see when they're clearly tired but they:

- keep on wriggling in bed;
- are constantly kicking off the covers;
- are asking for the fifth book while yawning;
- are saying they want more drinks, more snacks, or more playing;
- fall asleep sucking their thumb or a dummy;
- move around a lot in their sleep;

- wake up frequently at night;
- wake up 'grumpy'; or
- wake up crying.

I wonder if you recognise any of these?

Aware Parenting turns the common understanding of sleep on its head.

***Babies and children want to sleep when they're tired as much as we want them to. They're not fighting sleep. Often the things we are doing to try to make them relaxed enough to sleep are actually preventing them from feeling truly relaxed enough to sleep. That's why I often say, 'Children don't fight sleep. It's generally us that is fighting their natural relaxation and healing response.'***

They're not 'overtired'[44]. When we really understand what's happening in a child's body, and how to cooperate with the natural relaxation processes they are born with, everything changes, because we:

- know how to cooperate with those natural processes;
- stop working against those processes;
- support a child's natural homeostasis process;
- facilitate them to express their feelings in healing ways;
- support them to heal from stress and trauma;
- help them feel unconditionally loved; and
- support them to sleep more restfully and restoratively.

## The three things needed for sound sleep

Aware Parenting has a very different perspective on sleep to many other parenting paradigms. However, when I talk about it, I want to remind you about the three aspects of Aware Parenting, because they all are relevant to sleep, in ways that I will explain later.

---

[44] The term 'overtired' isn't used in Aware Parenting

- attachment-style parenting;
- non-punitive discipline;
- the prevention of, and healing from, stress and trauma.

You know I love lists of three! Now I'm going to share a list that I made, based on Aware Parenting: the three things that babies and children need for sound sleep.

But before I do, I'd love to invite you to reflect on what you grew up believing about sleep and what you learnt about sleep in your family and culture.

> *Self-Reflection Moment*
>
> *What did you grow up believing about children and sleep?*
>
> *What have you believed about children and sleep until you came across Aware Parenting?*
>
> *What do you believe now about children and sleep?*
>
> *Are any of these phrases are familiar to you?*
>
> *"My child fights sleep."*
>
> *"My child is a bad sleeper."*
>
> *"My child hates sleeping."*
>
> *"All children wake up really early for the first several years. It's just what we need to put up with as parents."*
>
> *When you reflect on these thoughts and beliefs, do you see any ways that they have affected how you feel when your child takes a long time to go to sleep or wakes in the night?*
>
> *How have they affected how you have responded to your child's sleep?*
>
> *Now I'm going to offer you that list of three I talked about.*
>
> *As you read it, I invite you to listen in with yourself. Does it resonate with you?*

Babies and children need three things to have relaxed and restful sleep:

1. to feel tired *(sleepy)*;
2. To feel connected *(closeness creating a sense of safety)*; and
3. To feel relaxed *(by releasing any healing-feelings present)*.

Let's look at each one of these in turn.

## 1. To feel tired (sleepy)

This one might seem obvious, but Aware Parenting has a different perspective on this to many other parenting paradigms. Yes, yawning, rubbing eyes, clinging and lying down are signs of sleepiness. They are the body communicating tiredness and a need to sleep. However, crying, agitation, playfulness, and 'silliness' are not directly caused by tiredness.

Instead, when children are tired, they are less able to suppress feelings. That means that feelings that have been suppressed bubble up to the surface when they are tired.

And we are the same, aren't we? Do you find that you get much more reactive when you are tired? What that also means is that you're less able to suppress your feelings at those times.

As always, because Aware Parenting is all about honouring the wisdom of the body, we can see that there is a beautiful reason for this. We'll talk more about it in point three.

Basically, this is part of the natural relaxation and healing process. Their bodies are trying to release stress hormones, stored feelings and tension from the fight or flight response, so that they can sleep more restfully and peacefully, which is helpful for their physical and emotional health.

***Why is this important and what difference does it make?***

Let's look at this more closely.

If you think that crying, agitation, playfulness and silliness are all signs of tiredness, you're probably going to want to help your child go to sleep as soon as possible once you see any of these signs. You might even feel concerned, frustrated or powerless if they're doing these things but then don't go to sleep straight away. You might feel confused seeing their tiredness and wondering why they aren't going to sleep.

Maybe you might even tell yourself that they are fighting sleep. If you're thinking those things, and they're still kicking off covers, jumping in and out of bed or crying in response to the way you handed them their cup, you're likely to get even more frustrated. Perhaps you might think that they are doing it deliberately to 'annoy you', or that they just 'can't sleep' and you may feel more and more agitated, frustrated or powerless.

> *Self-Compassion Moment*
> *If you've experienced this, and have felt confused, overwhelmed, agitated, frustrated or outraged at these times, I'm sending you so much love and compassion. I so deeply acknowledge how painful that is. If you've responded in harsh ways to your child as a result of those thoughts and feelings, my heart goes out to you. And I want to let you know that it really can be different, with Aware Parenting.*

If you perceive the kicking off covers or crying over the way you handed them their cup as indications that your child is trying to use their amazing natural relaxation and release process to do exactly what it's designed to do, you're much more likely to feel compassionate towards them, and will want to cooperate with those processes.

This overturns some beliefs and phrases used in other parenting paradigms.

There's the whole 'overtired' concept, which isn't a term we use in Aware Parenting. In many parenting paradigms, the belief in overtiredness says that if a child hasn't got to sleep when they are first tired, they get 'overtired' and then aren't able to sleep.

In Aware Parenting, we see it in a very different way, which we will talk more about in point three.

Another common belief in other parenting paradigms is that tiredness is painful. If a child is clearly tired and is crying, and we believe that the tiredness itself is painful, we are of course going to do whatever we can to try to get them to sleep as soon as possible, by hurrying them up, distracting them from the crying, admonishing them for playing or being silly, and trying to get them to 'calm down'. You might then feel all kinds of painful feelings, such as frustration, powerlessness or rage if they are taking a long time to go to sleep. These behaviours, thoughts and feelings are likely to work against their natural relaxation processes.

*Self-Reflection Moment*
*What thoughts do you think when you read this?*
*How do you feel when you read this?*

## 2. To feel connected

The second thing that children need to sleep restfully is to feel connected.

This again points to the innate wisdom of a child's body.

Until a short time ago in human history, children slept with their families. It's only a relatively recent phenomenon to put children in their own rooms. If a child was alone, they might be threatened by predators or other dangers. They wouldn't be safe. In addition, warmth is a primary need of young mammals, so closeness would also have been a way to protect against exposure to cold weather.

Until they were old enough to escape from danger themselves through fast running or strong fighting, closeness would have been important for survival, so that parents or other adults in the community could pick them up and carry them while running away from danger.

If a young child doesn't have closeness, it is natural for them to be on alert, ready to sense danger and to call out if necessary. This isn't conducive to falling asleep or sleeping restfully.

A lack of closeness or connection can not only cause a child to take a long time to go to sleep. It can also cause them to wake up in the night. Their body might go into light sleep during sleep cycles, and will feel the lack of closeness, and that need for safety will wake them up. They might call out for their parent, or they might suppress those feelings from that unmet need with a *control pattern*.

Once a child gets older, they are then able to go to sleep and sleep restfully without being close, because they are stronger and more competent to be able to fight if necessary or flee to their parent/s' room, and also because they have internalised the closeness they have experienced.

How does a young child go to sleep if they *are* alone? From an Aware Parenting perspective, they will need to suppress, or dissociate from, the feelings of alertness, agitation or fear in their bodies. To do that, they will need to use a *control pattern*. That might be one that we've given them, like a dummy. Or it might be something that they find themselves. You may have seen a young child going to sleep sucking their thumb, clutching on to a soft toy or blanket, or needing to always be in a particular position when they go to sleep.

These actions are often suppressing feelings related to being alone. They might also be suppressing feelings from stressful or traumatic experiences that are bubbling up at the end of the day, ready to be expressed and released.

> **Self-Compassion Moment**
>
> *If you have helped your child go to sleep with a dummy, or they've sucked their thumb to go to sleep, I invite you to put any sticks down that you might be tempted to pick up. I want to remind you – for all the reasons I've shared before throughout the book – that feeling guilty will not help them or you, and being compassionate with yourself will! Healing is always possible. It's also incredibly common for children to suppress or dissociate from their feelings before they go to sleep. If your child does that, they are not unusual. And it is also possible to support them with Aware Parenting so that they need to do that less of the time.*

In comparison, lying next to a younger child while they go to sleep or connecting with an older child before sleep is supporting those innate needs for closeness before sleep. This is likely to help the child feel a sense of safety in their body, and signal that it is safe for them to go to sleep, since the adult is looking after them and protecting them.

What is going on if a child is clearly tired (eg. they're rubbing their eyes), and they do have closeness, but are still wriggling around, kicking off covers, talking a million miles an hour, wanting ten different things, asking you to read them a thousand more stories, running away, jumping on the bed, and generally looking as if they don't want to go to sleep and that they really are 'fighting sleep'?

This is where the third part of the map comes into play.

## They are not feeling relaxed.

If we have done lots of things to try to 'make' them feel relaxed, such as sing songs, read books, give them a bath, put soft lighting on, and so on, and they still aren't relaxed, we can understand why we might feel frustrated and might tell ourselves that our child 'doesn't like sleep' or is 'fighting sleep'.

> *Self-Compassion Moment*
> *Have you ever spent ages doing things to try to help your child/ren feel relaxed, and they're still not relaxed? And have you felt frustrated, powerless, overwhelmed, tired, exhausted or simply fed up? If so, I'm sending love to all of those feelings. I so deeply acknowledge how painful those times were.*

If we understand that there is a deeper reason for them not feeling relaxed, that can change everything. We have information and thoughts that will lead to us feeling different emotions and taking different actions to support them to sleep restfully.

We're going to talk about that in the next section. So, let's turn to point three, the understanding of which can make a huge difference to parents.

### 3. To feel relaxed

We might do loads of things to 'make' a child feel relaxed, and some of those things might be really lovely and effective. However, if we do them and a child is still agitated, not only does it tell us that they didn't work, it's possible that they were working against the natural relaxation processes of the body.

We might have:

- "shhhed" them when they started to cry.
- told them to "calm down" when they tried to do rambunctious play.
- read them stories when they started to get agitated.
- sung to them when they tried to cry.

# Isn't this a paradox, then, that we often say that a child is fighting sleep, when so often what is going on is that we are fighting their natural relaxation processes?

> *Self-Compassion Moment*
> I invite you to drop any sticks here, and be deeply compassionate with yourself. I imagine that you didn't ever hear this information growing up. I imagine that until you came across Aware Parenting, you might not have known these things. It is so natural that we believe what our culture tells us, until we question things or they simply don't resonate any more.

***So, you know what those natural relaxation processes are, don't you? You guessed it – they're the same as the natural innate processes for healing from stress and trauma:*** **attachment play** ***and crying and raging.***

With Aware Parenting we can:

- see a child's inability to go to sleep when they are clearly tired not as a sign of 'overtiredness,' but a sign of unexpressed feelings;
- observe the ways our child is trying to use their innate relaxation and healing processes rather than think they are fighting sleep; and
- support ourselves so that we can cooperate with those natural processes.

When we work against those processes, they keep attempting to do what they are designed to do.

If we sang to our child to get them to be calm enough to go to sleep when they actually have healing-feelings to express to us, or shushed them, or patted them, then when they come into lighter sleep, they may wake up, ready to cry.

***As they have more and more accumulated feelings in their body, the natural process will happen more and more often, as those feelings attempt to be expressed. This is why babies and toddlers often start waking up more and more frequently as they get older and as their feelings accumulate.***

There is nothing flawed about what they are doing. They are attempting to do something biologically healthy – to release the tension, stress and feelings that are preventing them from sleeping restfully. See how powerful our cultural conditioning is to work against their innate biological wisdom!

This is why children find it hard to go to sleep, stay asleep and sleep for as long as they need if they have had a stressful day, and they haven't had the opportunity to express those feelings at the end of the day by playing, crying or raging with loving support.

*The younger a child is, the more likely it is that they will need to cry with us before sleep in order to feel relaxed enough to sleep. If they don't get to do that, they will need to use a* **control pattern** *to mildly dissociate and feel 'calm' enough to sleep.*

However, *control patterns* only provide a temporary relaxation, which then wears off, usually when a child moves into lighter sleep. This is why, if we do things to children to make them feel calm rather than supporting their innate wisdom of what they need to feel truly and deeply relaxed, they will often wake more and more often.

The kind of relaxation that happens through *attachment play* and laughter, and supported crying and raging, offers a deep and true sense of relaxation, which thus continues for longer than the temporary calm that happens when we suppress a child's feelings. This effect also depends on how many accumulated feelings a child has. The larger percentage of their feelings we're able to listen to, the more relaxed they feel.

The wonderful thing is, supporting their natural relaxation processes doesn't only help our child feel deep relaxation, rather than the superficial relaxation that distracting them from their feelings achieves. It also helps them know:

- how to differentiate between the sensations of tiredness and upset feelings; and

- how to sleep restfully and restoratively as they get older.

In the next section, we'll look at how we can cooperate with these natural relaxation processes.

# IMPORTANT NOTE
Lots of *physical* things lead to children not feeling relaxed in their bodies. With Aware Parenting, I invite you to always check out physiological needs before assuming that feelings are creating the agitation.

Physical things that might lead to children not feeling relaxed enough to sleep may include: sickness, teething, food intolerances or allergies, worms, gut microbiome or digestive issues, the effects of wifi, polyester bedding or nightwear, chemicals in washing powder, and so on.

## Creating connection before sleep

I want to remind you about something we talked about earlier in the book in regards to presence. If we're not present, or not connected with ourselves, it's going to be very hard, or almost impossible, to be connected with our child. This is one of the reasons evenings can be so hard.

I wonder if you ever experience getting to the end of the day and just longing for your child/ren to go to sleep quickly so that you can have time to yourself, go to sleep, tidy the kitchen, get some work done, or connect with your partner (if you have one)?

> *Self-Compassion Moment*
> *If you do, I want to remind you that of course you do! Living in nuclear families, away from our extended community, is not how we were meant to live. You are doing the work of many people. I*

> *invite you to drop any sticks you might be tempted to pick up, and be deeply compassionate with yourself instead.*

If we're feeling desperate for self-connection, and we're trying to rush the process of them going to sleep, they will likely feel that, and won't feel connected, thus are going to find it harder to go to sleep. One of the things that can make a big difference is if we are willing to find a way to feel more connected with ourselves at the end of the day.

I'm going to offer a few suggestions. Because each of our lives are so different, only you can know what might work for you in your family system.

> *Self-Reflection Moment*
>
> *I invite you to connect in with whether you would like to:*
>
> *Make things easier for yourself in the evenings? Is there anything you can drop? Can you make double dinners and heat them up the following day? Are you making complex meals when you could be making something more simple?*
>
> *Could you leave tidying the house for a bit? or a lot?*
>
> *If you have a partner, could you take turns each having 10 or 15 minutes to go off in the early evening and do something that will help you feel connected with yourselves?*
>
> *Are there things that you're telling yourself that you 'should' do that you really could say no to?*

If you need loving support to change any of these things, I hereby offer that to you now.

You really don't have to do anything that anyone else does.

You can create your own family evenings, rituals, routines, or lack of them. You are the parent now.

I invite you to choose.

I so support you in deeply
listening to yourself.

> *Self-Reflection Moment*
> *If you could change evenings any way that you dream of, what would you do?*

Another possibility is to continue to do the things you usually do, while keeping really connected with yourself and inviting connection with your child/ren.

These can be really small actions.

- Connecting in with your breathing when you're making the dinner.
- Touching your child's back with presence in your hand as you put their food in front of them.
- Choosing to make eye contact with them while eating.
- Speaking with warm endearments to them if they're having a bath or shower.
- Having a bath with them, or sitting on the edge of the bath, listening to them tell you about their day.
- Cuddling them up with the towel and staying in the cuddle.
- Doing stretches together.

I'm sending love if you're thinking, "But I don't have time to do all this!" or "That's so many extra things to do!" However, you may find that in prioritising connection in this way, you actually feel more warm and loving towards your child/ren and actually enjoy evenings so much more. You might even sleep more restfully too!

> *Self-Reflection Moment*
>
> *I invite you to brainstorm some ideas.*
>
> *Are there any that you're willing to do tonight (or tomorrow night, if it's already late at night)?*

## *Attachment play* before sleep

I want to remind you that Aware Parenting is all about trusting your child's innate capacity to heal from stress and trauma and release the feelings of the day before sleep, so a lot of this process will be about following their lead.

***If they're clearly tired, connected and relaxed, and are drifting off to sleep, you obviously wouldn't add in* attachment play.**

I invite you to observe them for invitations for play throughout the evening.

They might be being silly and goofy at the dinner table. If so, I invite you to remember that they are trying to get relaxed through the silliness. Perhaps you could pretend to be a waitperson at dinner and use a different accent to announce the food, even making up funny foods!

If they're jumping up and down in the bathroom, could you join in and pretend to be jumpy kangaroos, ready to jump in the billabong-bath.

Rather than trying to 'wind them down', how about experimenting with going the other way! Being playful during bath time, putting on pyjamas and teeth brushing.

This can all create lots of connection and provide lots of release.

I want to remind you that you get to play with this and you get to choose. You could experiment with something for just one night, or just one week, and see how it goes. You can always change it back again.

> **Self-Reflection Moment**
>
> When you reflect on the past few nights, do you see any invitations for play from your child/ren?
>
> If they were to do that again, how could you respond even more playfully?
>
> What thoughts, needs met and feelings heard might help you do that?
>
> Are you willing to tend to those thoughts, needs and feelings in the upcoming days?

However, not only can we *respond* to our child's invitations for play, we can also *offer* our own *attachment play* ideas to them. I'm here to remind you that not all games will resonate with all children, and that some might be welcome on some days and not on others. You might find that you offer a game to your child/ren, and they change it. As you get more more familiar with *attachment play* (if you're not already), you may find that you and your child/ren make up more and more of your own games.

Here are a list of some ideas. I wonder if any of them call to you? I received lots of these from other parents over the years, mostly in my *Attachment Play Course* and also from Chiara Rossetti, the Aware Parenting instructor you've already met. I thank them for these ideas. Aletha's *Attachment Play* book also has lots of amazing play ideas and I really recommend reading it and re-reading it if you haven't already.

## Bathtime games

**The "footies" game:** In the bath, your "footies" poke out from the water and you talk to them in a ridiculous voice about ridiculous things.

## Toothbrushing games

**The silly toothbrush game:** In this game, you can pretend that you don't know where their teeth are. You might say something like, "Oh

I know where your teeth are!" and try to brush your child's arm. They will probably keep trying to show you where their teeth are, and you can keep on pretending to be confused about where their teeth are, brushing all different parts of their body, saying things like, "Oh, your teeth are very furry today," while pretending to brush their hair with the toothbrush.

**The missing the mouth game:** Pretend to keep missing their mouth with the toothbrush. Swoop the brush over them and wiggle it about and 'miss' their mouth and then say, "Oh I missed again! Funny toothbrush! Why do I keep missing! Where are those teeth anyway? Oh I'll try one more time... oh I missed AGAIN!" and then finally find them.

## Putting on pyjamas games

**The "this is your hat" game:** Pretend to put their pyjama bottoms on their head and admire what a beautiful hat they have. Do this with all different items of clothes, putting them on in inaccurate places.

**The "these fit me perfectly" game:** Get their pyjamas and put them on you, and pretend that they are your clothes and that they fit perfectly.

## Playful reading games

**The funny reading game:** If you are reading to them, make the words in to funny words, like "the dog went to the moon" instead of the dog went for a walk. Each time they tell you how it is meant to be in the book, you insist in a funny way that you are reading the book, or say that you perhaps need special glasses to read the book. You could put funny glasses on and pretend that it makes you read words differently, and change the words. Or you announce that it is the end, when you have only just started!

**The biting books game:** You're reading them a book and keep on pretending that the book bit you, and it jumps up in the air each time.

## Bedtime

**The "it's morning" game:** Pretend that instead of going to bed, that it is morning, and act all surprised that they are in bed. Be goofy about all the morning things you are doing; tell them that breakfast is ready and what you have planned for the day, and so on. Act surprised when they insist that it is night time and they are going to sleep.

**The "I-hope-you-aren't-on-the-bed" game:** Announce in a loud voice, "I hope you aren't on the bed!" and when you go there, act all surprised that they are on the bed. "What are you doing in bed!?" in a mock-angry voice. This can help bring about healing if you have felt frustrated or angry in the past about them not going to bed.

**The tired-eyes game:** You say things like, "Let's make sure our eyes don't close!" and if they close them, say in a mock surprised voice, "You've got your eyes closed!" And you can also make big eyes and funny eyes and crossed eyes, all the while talking about not going to sleep. Pull on their arms to pretend to wake them up.

**The "let's get up again" game:** You can say things like, "We'll just try to stay awake and get up again! Let's leave our eyes open." After some time: "Hey, your eyes are closed again!"

**The "don't lie down on the pillow whatever you do!" game:** You get the idea!

**The grilled cheese sandwich game:** Your child lies on top of you on the bed and you have a cuddle called the grilled cheese sandwich. Your child literally melts onto you. This can be a way of feeling close and connected.

## If you've been agitated, grumpy or harsh

**The "can we find mummy/daddy's grumpy feelings?" game:** In this one, you go hunting for mummy or daddy's feelings under the covers and when you find them, you squish them.

Joss Goulden, a Level 2 Aware Parenting instructor in Australia who you've met already, shares about her experiences of *attachment play* with her children before sleep:

*"One way I used to ensure that everyone's needs were met at bedtime was to offer nonsense play about books and reading. That might be starting a book with "once upon a time" and then flicking to the end straight away, "and they all lived happily ever after. Goodnight!" and the children would laugh and complain and tell me how silly I was. Or reading the book upside down and getting confused about why I couldn't read it anymore. Or bringing in lots of rude words or silliness into the story, or lots of poo and wee jokes into the middle of the story when the children weren't expecting it. My children would then cry with laughter and their laughter is always so contagious so I would laugh too and the feelings of exhaustion, overwhelm or resentment would be released for me, leaving us with beautiful, calm, balanced connection for us all."*

> **Self-Reflection Moment**
> Would you like to choose one of these and experiment with it tonight? Or tomorrow, if you're reading this in the evening and they're already asleep.

All of these games can also be used to help reduce night waking. It is generally feelings coming up that wake children up at night. Instead of the thoughts about 'settling' a child at night, or trying to suppress feelings in the evening, aiming for connection and release (through laughter and tears if necessary), will help them feel more and more relaxed, so that they can sleep more and more peacefully and restfully.

## *Loving Limits* and listening to feelings before sleep

*Remember that old adage, "It will all end in tears!" With Aware Parenting, we're trusting that tears are part of a child's natural release and relaxation process, and we welcome and invite those tears, if they are needed.*

Elizabeth shared about what a difference listening to her two year old's feelings made to his sleep, and to their connection:

*"When my first son was a baby I was wondering why he wasn't laughing so much or making much eye contact. I thought something was wrong with me. When he was two years old, he woke up many times at night to feed. I felt frustrated and tired and wanted to stop breastfeeding him and looked for a gentle way to stop. I came across Aware Parenting, and after reading watching Marion's videos I was clear that he had accumulated feelings to express. The next day I told him that from that day, I would not feed him to sleep, but that I would hold him and listen to his feelings.*

*The first days I listened to hours of crying. He cried mostly for two hours and then fell asleep. I saw drastic change in his sleep and in his body. He suddenly started to sleep longer stretches at night and for the first time he deeply looked me in the eyes and smiled at me. His eyes were smiling and he was so present. I felt so connected to him, like I finally got my son (back). His eyes were shining and his energy was so clear and relaxed. For the first time in two years I felt really connected on a soul level. I've practiced Aware Parenting with my second son from the beginning and he is such a sunny baby, he smiles a lot, is very present, makes eye contact and is very aware of his surroundings. Such a difference between my first and second baby. I'm grateful for Aware Parenting and the connection it brings to me and my children."*

## What happens if they are clearly tired, and they keep on playing and playing?

We can assume that the *attachment play* isn't enough to bring the needed relaxation and that they probably need to cry or rage. We can support that to happen by offering a *Loving Limit*.

*Does your child want to play with you for hours before bed?*

You may find yourself saying things like, "Sweetheart, could we please stop now?" – and feeling powerless;

or, carrying on playing, not saying anything and feeling exhausted and resentful;

or, your frustration building into, "That's enough now! No more! Bed time!"

I invite you to hold in mind the three things needed for sound sleep and secure attachment (to feel tired, connected and relaxed).

Remember that if your child is tired and connected, but still not going to sleep, it probably means they have painful feelings sitting at the surface, preventing them from feeling relaxed enough to go to sleep.

I invite you to experiment with offering them a *Loving Limit*.

Offering them a *Loving Limit* means saying no to the behaviour and yes to the feelings that are underlying the agitation and desire to keep playing and inability to sleep. You might try saying, *"I see how much you're enjoying playing, sweetheart, and I'm going to set the timer on my phone for three more minutes. When the timer goes off, I'm not willing to play any more and I want you to go to bed, because I think you're tired."*

Remember that *Loving Limits* aren't about your child just saying, "Okay!" when the timer goes off. If they had uncomfortable feelings sitting underneath, the *Loving Limit* is designed to help those feelings come out. Remember that we are expecting tears, because those unexpressed feelings are probably what is keeping them from being able to go to sleep.

When the timer goes off, you might say *"I hear that you want to play more, lovely, and I'm not willing to play any more now, because I don't think it's the most helpful thing for you. I hear how upset you feel. I'm here with you. I'm listening."*

If they had painful feelings sitting at the surface, this can be the opportunity for the feelings to come out in some big tears or some loud raging.

You might keep repeating something like, *"I really hear that you'd like me to play more, sweetheart, and I'm not willing to play any more."* Then we can expect the crying and the raging and the expressing of the feelings that were getting in the way of them feeling relaxed enough to sleep. Our role is to stay lovingly present with them, listening to those feelings that are preventing them from sleep. Once they've expressed a chunk of those, it's likely that their body will then feel relaxed enough to sleep.

## What happens if they keep asking for lots of things before bed?

When your child is tired, and you're moving towards them going to bed, do they often start asking for lots of things?

- One more story?
- Going to get one more toy?
- A bit more playing?
- Yet another drink?
- Another visit to the toilet?
- Another snack?

Do you ever feel frustrated, when you keep on responding to these requests but each time you do, it's followed by yet another thing that they want? Do they seem agitated and antsy, and not fulfilled or satisfied even when you *do* give them each thing that they appear to want? Do you think it's possible that something else is going on here? That they're not actually wanting these things to meet needs of theirs, but that they're trying to suppress the feelings that naturally come up when they're tired and less able to suppress them?

If this was the case, what might happen if, after a couple of these requests (and of course making sure that they aren't physically uncomfortable and all their needs are met), you offered a *Loving Limit* instead?

*"I really hear that you want another story, sweetheart. I see how much you love stories. And after this one, I'm not willing to read any more, because I don't think it's the most helpful thing for you."*

And at the end of that story, when they ask for more, *"You really want another one, lovely, and I'm not willing to read any more. And I'm here with you and listening."*

The aim of the *Loving Limit* is to help them express the feelings underlying their attempts at suppression, which have left them still feeling agitated and unable to sleep. So, we expect our child to start crying or raging, perhaps begging for another book, or another game, or to go to another room.

We lovingly keep hearing them and offering them empathy: *"I really hear that you want me to read another book,"* and the limit, *"and I'm not willing to read any more, sweetheart, and I'm right here with you. I'm listening."*

The aim is for them to express all the feelings that the requests for a million things have been trying to suppress, so that afterwards they actually feel relaxed enough to be able to sleep. Our role is to stay lovingly present, keep offering the limit if necessary, and continue to listen to all of their feelings.

### What happens if they start pinching or hitting in the play?

Again, we can trust that all the *attachment play* we've done has helped them feel connected and has helped deeper feelings bubble up, which we can help them express through offering a *Loving Limit*. This is why it's so important to be aware of what we're telling ourselves. If you're thinking, "I've done all this *attachment play* with them, and now they're hitting me!" we're likely to get frustrated or angry, and it's almost impossible to offer a *Loving Limit* from there.

However, if you're thinking, "Wow, that *attachment play* really helped. They're feeling connected and the deeper feelings have been loosened up so that they can tell me what's really going on for them," you're likely to feel calm and compassionate, and to be able to respond with a beautiful and powerful *Loving Limit*. Remember the invitation to do the minimum possible to prevent the hitting or whatever it is, such as holding their hand. *"I'm not willing for you to hit, sweetheart, because I'm here to keep us both safe, and I'm right here and listening."* Again, we expect tears and raging to come.

### What happens if they suddenly start crying over something small, or something else happens that brings tears?

Again, here is where you can trust that the *attachment play* has created connection and emotional safety and has supported the lighter feelings to bubble up, so that the deeper feelings can now be expressed. You can simply be there with them, and listen lovingly, offering them empathy. *"I'm right here with you. I'm listening. You're letting it all out, sweetheart."*

### What happens if they wake up soon after they went to sleep?

This usually tells us that they had feelings to tell us (or more feelings to tell us), that we didn't get to listen to. If we can get close, ready to listen, they might be able to move into crying with us. On a long term basis, we can focus on supporting more release of feelings before bed so they are less likely to need to wake up at night to express them then.

### What happens if they wake up with increasingly short intervals as the night wears on?

This is generally a sign of accumulated feelings. Again, what we are telling ourselves here can make a big difference. If we think they are doing it deliberately, or choosing to do it, we're likely to feel frustrated. However, if we remember a time when we were agitated and antsy and kept on waking up even though we really wanted to sleep, it can help us feel more compassionate.

***They need our help to utilise those natural relaxation processes, and we are usually the ones who have got in the way of those processes.***

(Here's why it's also important to not pick up those guilt sticks, because that's not going to help anyone either.)

## They want to sleep as much as we want them to!

> *Self-Reflection Moment*
>
> *Would you like to create a sleep mantra, to remind you of these things? For example,*
>
> *"They want to sleep as much as I want them to. They're not waking deliberately. They need my help to let out their feelings so that they can feel more deeply relaxed."*

It's up to you what actions you take and when. Do you want to listen in the night, or would you like to focus on supporting more *attachment play* and crying *before* sleep? The larger the percentage of feelings they get to express before they go to sleep, the less feelings will be held in their body to wake them up at night.

## What if they wake really early in the morning?

This *can* be another sign of accumulated feelings, but isn't necessarily one, because there is evidence for the heritability of circadian rhythms and sleep traits, so it can be a genetic disposition. This implies that some children have a natural tendency to wake up early even when there are no accumulated feelings. For other children, early waking *can* be a sign of accumulated feelings.

As always, with Aware Parenting, we will be able to tell the difference by observing our child. If they wake up early but are relaxed in their body, happy, and willing to make relaxed eye contact, that's more likely that they simply are an early bird. However, if they wake up and are tense or agitated, are avoiding eye contact, are trying to cry or are crying, or are wanting a *control pattern*, it's likely that accumulated feelings are waking them up.

If accumulated feelings are causing your child to wake up early in the morning, you could focus on offering *attachment play* and listening to their feelings in the evening. The more you do that, the more you are likely to see them sleep for longer in the morning. You might also choose to listen to their feelings first thing in the morning, if you are willing to. There is no 'right' or 'wrong', it's simply a matter of finding what you can do and when you can do it, playing with that, and seeing what happens.

Nic Wilson, an Aware Parenting instructor and Marion Method Mentor, shares her moving story of how Aware Parenting changed not only her and her daughter's sleep, but her life (content warning: her story includes feelings of desperation and despair):

*"As a baby, my daughter just wouldn't sleep and I had no idea why. She wouldn't sleep during the day. She slept two 20 minute catnaps up until about eight months and then never slept in the day again. And those catnaps were facilitated by me walking around my garden, which is about 10 square metres, in a circle with her in the pram, just*

*like a crazy person, or putting her in the car and just driving around the streets. It got to the point when she was about 16 months and I would just often find myself falling asleep in places so randomly because I was that tired. She was awake every 45 minutes at night. I just could not function. I was like, 'What is going on here?'*

*And I myself was a baby that apparently didn't sleep till I was five, so the support system that I had around me was like, oh, well, babies don't sleep and, you didn't sleep till you were five, so this is karma and I just remember thinking, 'It's not supposed to be this hard'. So we'd tried every sleep nurse under the sun, and there's a facility here where you go where your baby doesn't sleep. And they kicked us out after three nights and said, 'We can't help you. Buy a hammock. You'll be fine. Just pop her in the hammock and bounce her to sleep.' That wasn't working.*

*And when she was just about to turn four, that Christmas of that year, my sister in law at the time gave me Marion's* Love Being a Woman Course *and it was my first introduction to Marion's work and I did the first three modules and it was all about self care and filling your cup and I'm like, 'What? People actually do this! This is insane! How do they have time to do all this with a baby that doesn't sleep or eat or anything?'*

*And the further I got into that course, I think it was even just Marion's voice. I just remember feeling like this person had come in to just give me a big warm hug just with her voice and so I started researching and I found her site with Aware Parenting and I was like. 'Oh, what's that?' And I just dove in head first to absolutely everything.*

*My daughter was just about four when I'd really started implementing a lot of the listening to her crying, holding space for crying and listening to tears and emotions. And within three months of us doing a lot of catch up crying there was a lot of tears in that time and a lot of holding space. And also me because I started asking for a little bit more help which gave me a fuller cup to be able to listen to her feelings, and within three months I remember there was one night where she slept a five hour block and I just remember checking her 13 times. And I didn't sleep, but she actually slept for five hours. And I just remember waking up with her and she was just so alert and awake and happy and smiling and it just was this light for me in the darkest of dark times.*

*I remember how many times when every day I would tell myself, 'I can't do this anymore, I just want it to end. I can't do this any more.' And so yeah, so Aware Parenting, when I say it saved us, it absolutely saved my life. It was the light that I needed at that time."*

### Self-Compassion Moment

How do you feel, after reading this? If you've also had a really hard time with your child/ren's sleep, I'm sending you so much love and compassion. And if the challenges are continuing, I want to let you know that it really is possible for that to change, as Nic shows. If you're feeling desperate, please reach out for support from a health professional and Aware Parenting instructor as soon as possible.

**From a child:** *Mummy, I know that I'm five now, but I still like cuddling with you and chatting as I go to sleep. You got so grumpy tonight when I was all wriggly and I kept on kicking off the covers. I really did want to go to sleep, Mummy, but I just couldn't. I closed my eyes and they kept on popping open again like popcorn. I wanted my legs to be calm but they were like a kangaroo. Oh but then, Mummy, I loved it when I told you that and you jumped up and asked me if I wanted to pretend to BE a kangaroo! That was SO fun, when we bounced around the room and kept on pretending to bump into each other and fall over. We laughed and laughed so much. I don't think I've ever seen you laugh that much before, Mummy. And then when we bumped that last time, I fell over and suddenly it was like shaking a milkshake and I just started to cry and cry. I didn't even really know why I was crying, although I did miss* *you today when I was at school. I loved it when you held me in your arms and just kept telling me that you loved me and you were listening. I was like the little kangaroo in your pouch. It was such a funny thing, Mummy, because after that jumping and crying, I felt all relaxed. My legs weren't jumpy kangaroo legs any more, and my eyes just fluttered closed like a little butterfly. I love going to sleep cuddled up next to you. Nighty night, Mummy, sleep tight!*

## Chapter summary

There are **three things needed for sound sleep: to feel tired, to feel connected, and to feel relaxed**. Children have natural relaxation processes that we are often taught to work against in this culture.

**Creating connection before sleep is important**, because otherwise, a child's body communicates that it's not safe enough to go to sleep.

*Attachment play* **before sleep is powerful** because it creates connection and aids relaxation, through releasing lighter feelings.

However, **sometimes this isn't enough to help a child feel truly relaxed, which is where** *Loving Limits* **and listening to feelings before sleep comes in. Sometimes, feelings bubble up spontaneously without us needing to do anything, and we can just listen lovingly to those tears and tantrums.**

If you want to learn more about sleep from an Aware Parenting perspective, I recommend the following:

The sleep series of *The Aware Parenting Podcast* (episodes 125-141).

My next book, *Sound Sleep and Secure Attachment with Aware Parenting*.

My course, *The Sound Sleep and Secure Attachment with Aware Parenting Course*.

CHAPTER NINETEEN

# Supporting friendships and sibling relationships

## My children's relationship with each other, and my joy and grief

When I think about sibling relationships, I remember the two very contrasting experiences I have had with my own children.

*For the first five years after my son was born (my daughter is four and a half years older than him), they were completely in love with each other, for 99% of the time. They wanted to wear similar clothes, loved hugging and playing together and were gentle and loving with each other. They were together the majority of the time, and were so happy together. I absolutely loved seeing them together. It was one of the biggest joys of my life.*

*That delight turned to one of the most painful things I've experienced, when their dad and I separated. My son, deeply affected by the separation and loss, went from being one of the most present and relaxed beings I've ever seen to often hitting and head butting his sister and me.*

*You'll know from reading earlier chapters that his behaviour was caused by the trauma of the separation and the powerlessness and grief my son felt. It was really hard for me because I was also in so much emotional pain myself, and so didn't have my usual parenting capacity. So although I did aim to respond with compassion, listen to his feelings, do attachment play and offer* Loving Limits, *many times I also responded from my own emotional pain, being reactive in response to the hitting, or not getting in between them in time to prevent my daughter from being hit. This meant that she then had the added trauma of being repeatedly hit by him. After about six months of experiencing this quite a lot of times, her previous deep compassion towards him turned to harsh words. I felt even more devastation, seeing this process happening. This was exacerbated by the rupture in my relationship with my daughter, when she experienced me not protecting her from being hurt by her brother many times.*

*This led to lots of years of healing for all of us. I'm so grateful that eventually I did help my son come back out of that aggression and return to his natural gentle self. They did return to a loving relationship again, and I gradually rebuilt my relationship with my daughter, but it was a long and hard journey and there are still emotional scars there.*

One of the biggest regrets I have of that time is not getting even more emotional support than I did.
If I had been willing to do that, I believe that I could have done much more to listen to my son's feelings and to get in earlier with *Loving Limits* to prevent any hitting. So, if you're in the midst of something painful in your parenting, I really deeply invite you to reach out for more emotional support, eg. more *Listening Partners*, or working with an Aware Parenting instructor or Aletha Solter herself.

There was one gift from the experience, and that was a profound and deep compassion I gained towards all parents, however they respond. I knew first-hand how very hard it is to practice Aware Parenting when we are going through a deeply painful time in our own lives. That compassion is with me still.

That personal experience also helped me understand a lot about how sibling relationships can be, and what might be going on when there's harshness and fighting.

In a way, I did my own experiment.

I saw what happens when we know about Aware Parenting and are in the position to meet a lot of our children's needs, not use punishments and rewards, protect children as much as possible from stress and trauma and listen to as many tears and tantrums as we can (I listened to a *lot* of feelings). That resulted in all the loving harmony, connection and fun they had together for those first five years. And I also saw what happens when children experience stress or trauma and when they have lots of accumulated painful feelings.

> *Self-Compassion Moment*
> *I am sending you the biggest, widest hug right now if you have children who are fighting with each other. I'm giving unconditional love to all the feelings you're feeling. I want you to know that I deeply understand, and that you're not alone. My heart goes out to you. I'm so willing for things to change for you all towards more harmony, ease and connection.*

Some paradigms say that siblings fighting all the time is just how things are and there's nothing we can do about it.

Aware Parenting offers a very different perspective.

## Siblings actually want to love each other and have harmony and fun together.

However, it's also very normal and natural for all siblings to have lots of feelings in relation to each other – most often, jealousy, and feelings related to sharing parental attention and love, but also feelings from family stresses and stress outside the home, such as from school.

When those feelings don't get to be expressed in healing ways, through *attachment play*, laughter and crying and raging – or, if we do support those expressions but at not quite a high enough percentage level to make that difference, the pent-up feelings lead to unenjoyable behaviours – hitting, harsh words, taking each other's things, and so on.

In addition, all the other feelings that are unexpressed and sitting in children's bodies also tend to come out in their interactions with their siblings, even if those things have nothing to do with them (just like we can be antsy with our partner if we've had a hard day at work). It's similar with children's friendships.

> Any accumulated and unexpressed feelings that children have will tend to show up in their relationships with other children, including their siblings.

There are two things we can do here. One is preventative, and the other is in the moment.

But before we attend to the siblings (or friends), the most important thing here is empathy for ourselves. Seeing our beloved children hurting each other or being hurt by each other can be incredibly painful. The more we receive empathy for our own feelings, the more we are going to be able to support our children in the most helpful ways. It's so natural that if we are in a lot of emotional pain we are going to find it really hard to respond calmly and compassionately, and to be able to offer them empathy, support, *attachment play* and *Loving Limits*.

---

*Self-Reflection Moment*

*If you're seeing your children fighting, or your child in conflict with another child, do you feel really big feelings of overwhelm, fear, powerlessness or rage?*

*If so, it's likely that this is helping you reconnect with unexpressed feelings from your own past.*

> *If you feel enough emotional presence, I invite you to reflect on what this fighting reminds you of.*
>
> *That might be memories of fighting with your sibling or peers, or seeing your parents fight.*
>
> *I invite you to share the feelings that show up with your Listening Partner.*
>
> *If you're familiar with the Inner Loving Presence Process from The Marion Method, you might like to do that, and afterwards to have your Inner Loving Mother, Father, Sibling or Friend be with you when your child starts fighting, so you have that extra emotional support and are more likely to be able to stay calm and help your child.*

The key to prevention of conflict is to listen to as high a proportion of our child's crying and raging as we can. All children have big feelings that need to come out in these ways, and the higher proportion they express, the less feelings are pent-up in their bodies. The less pent-up feelings, the less behaviours caused by accumulated feelings will occur, such as fighting, taking, pushing, hitting and harsh words.

In the moment, we can get in between our children and either offer *attachment play* or *Loving Limits*. The *attachment play* helps them release the feelings that are showing up in harshness, through laughter and play. The *Loving Limits* help them express the bigger feelings that are creating those harsh behaviours, through crying and raging.

> Children want harmony and connection, fun and love. We can help them have more of that in their sibling relationships and friendships by meeting more of their needs and listening to more of their feelings.

## Preparing for harmony

If we're wanting harmony within a sibling relationship or friendship, one of the biggest things we can do to prepare for that is to listen to as many feelings as we can. This is as relevant for preparing for a new sibling as it is for going out on a playdate. A child who already has a lot of accumulated feelings, who then has a new sibling, is going to find it a lot harder when all the new feelings of jealousy and hurt get added on top. This is when things like hitting, pinching and being rough tend to happen (or alternatively, lots of dissociation).

*Remember, a child wants to be loving to their new sibling. It's their painful feelings that are getting in the way of that. So, one of the most powerful ways you can support a child to be a gentle older sibling is listening to as many of their feelings as you can before the new baby comes along.*

A child who already has a lot of accumulated feelings who goes to meet a friend is likely to find it hard to be gentle, to share, to be aware of the other child's body and needs, and is likely to need help with the connection. So again, if you can listen to some feelings before going out for the playdate, that is likely to help your child be more able to enjoy the interaction.

## Another core element that will help prepare for harmony is connection with us.

Again, this is relevant whether you are preparing a child for a new sibling, whether you have three children, or whether you're taking your child to play with another child. Even short periods of 1:1 connection, ideally in the form of non-directive child-centred play, can make a huge difference to how a child feels.

India Farr, an Aware Parenting instructor who cares for children with Aware Parenting, shares how she helped two children who were soon to have new siblings:

*"I was caring for two boys, both aged three, whose mums were both pregnant and due a month apart from each other. Both boys were Highly Sensitive, had more of a tendency to be hyperactive and struggled with transitions and demands. One now has a diagnosis of autism with extreme demand avoidance.*

*They were both showing some very aggressive behaviours. Bouncing around the room, pushing people and laughing, ignoring any requests to keep people safe and listen to people's no's, throwing things, tipping toys from boxes, taking toys. Their behaviours were quite extreme. So I sat down on the floor close by and I started saying, 'Hey boys, your Mummies both have a baby in their tummy, don't they?' I picked up a baby doll and I said, 'Just like this one. One day it's going to pop right out of her tummy, isn't it? Just like this!'*

*And then I put the baby doll up my jumper and got its head and popped it out the bottom, in a quick puppet-like way. And I said in a funny squeaky voice, 'Who's that out here making all that noise and pushing everyone?' They squealed with delight and started pushing and hitting the baby in my jumper. I made big noises about being hurt and then said in my squeaky baby voice, 'Right! that's it! I'm going back in my mummy's tummy!'*

*They then hit and pushed the baby in my jumper and I quickly popped its head out and in its voice said, 'Who's that hitting and pushing me? Right, that's it, I'm going back in my mummy's tummy!' And that repeated on and on until they were all laughed out.*

*After that, they were content, engaged and cooperative for the rest of the week and there was no extreme behaviour again. Later on, they would ask for the game when they needed it. They are both now very doting older brothers and they never pushed or hit their mums' tummies with the real baby inside. And they didn't ever hit the babies, either."*

# If you have a new baby, even five or ten minutes of non-directive child-centred play every day can be an emotional life saver for your older child.

If you're going to hang out with friends, spending the first ten minutes with each parent giving non-directive child-centred play to their own child, or as much as possible to their multiple children, can help children go into the play feeling connected.

As parents in the *DDC*, it can be so natural that we desperately want to connect with our friends, but if we start off first connecting with our child, then playing with the children, then engaging with the adults, this can support the children to be far more likely to play harmoniously, and far less likely to act harshly from unmet needs.

So, preparing for harmony involves:

Giving 1:1 connection, ideally non-directive child-centred play and other forms of *attachment play*, to meet their needs for connection;

Listening to their feelings, ideally via their crying or raging, so that accumulated feelings are less likely to show up in hitting or hurting.

> *Self-Reflection Moment*
> 
> *I wonder how you feel when you read this?*
> 
> *What would you like to do to increase your child/ren's experience of connection with you?*
> 
> *Would you like to take any opportunities to increase the amount of attachment play and listening to their feelings that you do?*

## Being with the crying of two siblings at the same time

It's really normal for two siblings to both want to cry together. I would recommend experimenting with how you can give them both closeness while they're crying. That might be sitting on the bed or floor, with one tucked under each arm, or with one on your chest and the other next to you. If they're both crying and you're there and present, you can trust that they are feeling enough emotional safety for the crying to be healing.

## How to support harmony

One of the biggest things that can help us be a powerful supporter of harmony in friendships and sibling relationships is our own inner work, because so often what gets in the way for us is our own conditioning and childhood experiences.

Things that can show up that get in the way are:

- us thinking harsh thoughts, eg. "They are so mean to their brother," or, "They will never have any friends," or
- our own painful memories and unexpressed feelings from the past, eg. when our child hits their sibling or a friend, we are reminded of being hurt by our sibling or 'friend' and feel the outrage we would have felt back then.

We can support harmony to be more likely through:

1. choosing to think about our child in compassionate ways;
2. having healing experiences in relation to our own childhood;
3. setting up the environment to support harmony;
4. giving empathy to both children;
5. staying with them during challenges, mediating and communicating our support; and
6. asking the child who has an object if they are ready to give it to the child who wants it.

## 1. Choosing to think about our child in compassionate ways

> *Self-Reflection Moment*
>
> *Do you notice yourself thinking harsh thoughts about your child/ren in relation to their siblings or their friends?*
>
> *If so, I invite you to write down all the harsh thoughts (as part of turning them around):*
>
> *Would you like to create an easy to remember alternative when you get tempted to believe those harsh thoughts?*

For example, phrases like:

- *"They love their sibling. They want to be gentle and caring. They need my help here."*
- *"They love their friends. They want to be gentle and caring. They need my help here."*

## 2. Having healing experiences in relation to our childhood

> *Self-Reflection Moment*
>
> *Do you ever feel really big feelings when your child is harsh towards their sibling or friend? If the feelings are really big, by definition, this generally tells us that the feelings are likely to be from the past.*
>
> *Do you sense that these big feelings are from past painful experiences with your sibling or friend that you are being reminded of?*
>
> *If so, are you willing to receive some loving listening or do some journaling?*
>
> *What experience are you remembering?*
>
> *What happened?*
>
> *How did you feel?*
>
> *How would you have liked to have been supported by your parents or teachers? How would you have liked them to have stepped in?*

*Would you have liked them to offer a Loving Limit?*

*How do you feel after getting to express this?*

*If these big feelings show up when your child does something, what can you do to support these younger parts of you so that you don't act from them?*

*Could you remind your inner children that you are an adult now?*

**Speaking phrases like, "I'm here to keep everyone safe," can help both our younger parts[45] and our children feel safe, and can help remind us that we are an adult now.**

*Can you think of another phrase that you would like to remember to support both your child/ren and your inner children?*

### 3. Setting up the environment to support harmony

This can make a huge difference! With siblings, this includes giving the older child their own space where they can set up their toys where younger children cannot reach them.

With multiple siblings, they might each have a special area where they get to keep things of theirs that they don't want anyone else to play with, which we support with *limits* or *Loving Limits* if another child wants to come and get those things.

When other children come to play, you might ask your child/ren which toys they don't want other children to play with, and either put those toys away or cover them with a cloth, and then communicate this to the child and parent, and support that with a *limit* or *Loving Limit* if necessary.

---

45  Remember that 'younger parts' is from The Marion Method, not Aware Parenting.

### 4. Giving empathy to both children

If something happens between two children, giving empathy to both of them makes a huge difference. For example, "You both really want to go on the swing, don't you? Zen, I see how you're wanting to go on it, and Peta, you've got hold of it."

This includes if one has hit, pushed or hurt the other. They still need empathy. Often, just giving empathy to both of them can restore connection and harmony, or it may indicate where one or both need lots more listening. Clarity will often come about through the process of deeply hearing both (or all) children, as we all work out what happened and who is feeling and needing what.

### 5. Staying with them, mediating, and communicating our support

Supporting children through challenges helps them feel safe, know they're supported, and learn to find ways for everyone to get their needs met.

On page 147 of *Cooperative and Connected*, Aletha Solter says, *"You can help them find a solution through mediation. First give each child a chance to explain what happened, what she needs, and how she feels. After listening to each child, reflect back what you heard, or ask the other child to do so. After you have listened carefully to each child, summarize the conflict..."*

After that, you can ask the children if they can think of a solution that meets everyone's needs. We might say to them, *"Can you think of a way for you both to get your needs met here?"*

We might also offer our support, with phrases such as, *"I'm here to help,"* or, *"I trust we can find a way to meet everyone's needs,"* which can be a way to help children experience that we are there with them and are supporting them. I've so often found that staying with children in this way, they often come up with amazing ideas for everyone to get their needs met that I would never have thought about.

Staying close with them and remaining clear on what we are willing for in the interactions has a powerful magnetic effect. *"I'm here to support everyone getting their needs met,"* or, *"I'm here to help everyone have fun in this game."*

They may not come up with anything, in which case we might then offer some ideas that we think might be helpful, to see if they like those.

Aletha continues on p.148 of *Cooperative and Connected*: *"Mediation with young children requires time and effort, but it helps them learn to identify their own feelings and needs, and think about those of the other person. These are important conflict-resolution skills."*

Children clearly learn from us how to mediate. Nic Wilson, an Aware Parenting instructor and Marion Method Mentor shares this story about how her daughter did some mediating between two of her friends:

*"My daughter was playing with two younger girls who are sisters and the two sisters started arguing over a toy. Bella got down and she sat in the middle of them. She held both of their hands and said to them, "I'm really willing for us to all find a way to get our needs met here," and then she said, "So, Chizu, you want the Barbie, right?" and Chizu said, "Yes, I want the Barbie and I want those shoes," and Bella says, "Okay, you want the Barbie and the shoes," and then she turned to the other sister, and she said, "Nami, would you be willing to play with this Barbie for a little bit of time and then Chizu can play with this Barbie and then I can even set a timer and we can swap after five minutes. Chizu, would that be okay with you?" And Chizu said, "Yes," and then Nami said, "Oh no I just really want that Barbie, and Bella said, "Oh I really hear that you want the Barbie. Chizu had the Barbie first, and Chizu is not willing to share it at the moment but I'm really willing for you to love this Barbie because it has this dress and this and this and this and this." And then she asked her again, "So are you willing to wait five minutes and then play with it, it's only five minutes and then Nami said, "Yeah, okay Bella," and then they just played so happily and I just watched this whole thing play out and I'm just mind blown. This is incredible!"*

Ellie Gut-Silverman, an Aware Parenting instructor, shared about how she supports her daughter in social situations:

*"As a result of practicing Aware Parenting from when she was three months old, my 17 month old daughter is accustomed to making her own choices and to being treated with respect by those around her. When we spend time with other toddlers in our local community, they frequently attempt to grab things out of her hands, and when this happens I see the look of bewilderment in her eyes as this is not something she is used to experiencing. I feel she is too young for mediation to be appropriate in these situations, and so when they occur and the other child's parent or caregiver doesn't prevent the item being taken without consent, I feel it is my role to advocate for my daughter. I do the minimum possible to stop the child from taking whatever it is, and I say something like, "Zeva is having her turn with that right now and I'm not willing for you to take it from her." I will then ask Zeva if she feels willing to give it to the other child, and sometimes she will gladly choose to give it to them, and other times she will clearly say no. In that case, I tell the other child, "Zeva isn't willing to give it to you right now." I might support the other child to find something else to play with if needed. It has taken inner work for me to have the confidence to speak up for my daughter especially in settings with parents who don't share my values. I now feel grounded and steady in my choice to honour my daughter's feelings and to meet her needs while also being respectful of the other child's needs and feelings. I love that my daughter expects to be asked for her consent, to be treated with respect and for her no to be acknowledged. I am so willing for these powerful imprints to continue to be her sense of the normal way to be treated and to treat others."*

## 6. Ask the child who has an object if they are ready to give it to the child who wants it

This is very different to approaches that tell children, "You have to share." We can support children to find ways for everyone get their needs met, while also stepping in to prevent children forcefully taking a toy from another child wherever possible. We might say, *"Susie wants to play with the red car, are you willing for her to play with it?"* Meanwhile, we can stay lovingly present with the child who wants the thing and prevent them from taking it with a *Loving Limit*, listening to their feelings if any bubble up.

**Often, the feelings that show up in relation to sharing things are deeper feelings that have accumulated, and may be to do with sharing our attention, particularly with siblings.**

So, we might say to Susie, *"Oh sweetheart, you really want to play with the red car, and Amy isn't willing to finish with it yet. I see how upset you feel. I'm here with you. I'm listening."* Often these can be wonderful opportunities for them to express feelings that haven't had the chance to be expressed.

Some parents enjoy the rule that the child who has the toy gets to play with it until they've finished. In *Cooperative and Connected* (page 147), Aletha Solter says: *"This approach can work, but you may be missing an opportunity to help your children think about each other's needs and learn conflict-resolution skills... Furthermore, it's not always clear who had the toy first."*

I invite you to read Aletha's book *Cooperative and Connected* to learn more.

---

*Self-Reflection Moment*
*Are there any changes that you'd like to make, having read this?*

## *Attachment play* in friendships and sibling relationships

*Attachment play* can make ALL the difference in friendships and sibling relationships!

Joss Goulden, a Level two Aware Parenting instructor in Australia whom you've already met shares about an *attachment play* game she played with her children when they were younger:

*"Missy Kissy was a wonderful game that I played with my children which brought in so many elements of attachment play – closeness, connection, laughter and power-reversal, where they were in control and winning almost all the time. It included physical touch and affection, collaboration and relationship building between the children, and contingency play, where they could predict what would happen when they shouted and controlled my movements. And, as was so often the case, my children invented the game themselves. Children are true geniuses at play and know exactly what to choose to support themselves to heal and to make sense of and process their experiences.*

*In the Missy Kissy game, I would chase my children and try to catch them. If I succeeded, I would take them back to my castle to give them kisses and make them promise not to run away while I fell asleep. They would then run away, or rescue each other as I 'slept' and I would act so confused and upset when I woke up that they had got away again. They also had a secret metal marble which they could hold and use to freeze me when I was chasing them by shouting 'Invizolate'. Once I was frozen, they could run away to their safe spot and unfreeze me by shouting 'Un-invizolate.'"*

As for the power of play in friendships, Joss shares some more games:

*"At our homeschooling group, I used to invite all the kids to chase me to help them connect with each other – they always caught me and I would escape and then they would catch me again. And we used*

to play soccer, parents versus kids together and we always lost and always had the most ridiculous names for our team!"

## 1. If games are getting a bit rough

If games are getting a bit rough, we might join in and say, *"Hey, pick on someone your own size!"* and then do some power-reversal play, where we keep falling over and the children climb on us.

## 2. If children are needing extra reassurance that they are loved

**The "s/he's mine!" game:** The "s/he's mine!" game is helpful when children have feelings related to sharing attention with a sibling or friend. In this game, two adults fight over a child: "S/he's mine!" says one parent, then, "No, s/he's mine!" and back again to the first, "No! I want her/him!" If your child giggles and laughs as you gently pull them towards you each time, it's likely they are releasing feelings related to sharing you, and are feeling filled up with a sense of being deeply loved and wanted, which so often loosens challenges in friendships and sibling relationships. (Thank you to Lawrence J. Cohen, PhD, for this game, the previous one, and any others I might not have credited him for. I highly recommend his book, *Playful Parenting*.)

## 3. If siblings or friends are feeling tight over things

Here's a wonderful game shared by Fiona in my *Attachment Play Course*: **The "this nail in the floorboard is all mine" game:** *"One of my attachment play celebrations was in relation to the kids getting upset when they thought that the other one's game was getting too close to the elaborate play scene they had set up. It usually resulted in them getting really upset and saying, "This area from the couch is all mine," etc. So I started pretending to desperately try to protect something silly like, "This nail in the floorboard here is all mine and whatever you do never, ever touch it". So of course they both would run over to touch it and I would pretend to be shocked and then I* *would say something else silly which reconnected them and all of us."*

Another game can be to jump in and be goofy about each child sharing parts of us: *"You can play with my arms, and you can have my legs. No! You can have my head, and you can have my feet to play with!"*

## 4. When children have been away playing with other children

What about when our child has been away playing with friends. What can we do to help, when they return home with feelings?

Doing some non-directive child-centred play with them when they first come home can be helpful, and will likely help us see if anything happened where they felt powerless or were not included, as they are likely to bring it into the play. If we sense that they felt powerless with another child, or we know that they've been playing with a child who tends to use power-over, we might specifically bring in some power-reversal games so that they can release those feelings of powerlessness with us and feel powerful again. If they've been playing with a large group and we know that sometimes they don't experience being included, we might play games such as the, 'We're glued together and we can't be separated' game. Understanding the themes that they are experiencing in their friendships, we can bring in particular forms of play to support healing and empowerment.

> *Self-Reflection Moment*
>
> *Does your child/do your children tend to feel powerless or disconnected in friendships?*
>
> *Do they tend to be the one who uses power-over?*
>
> *What kinds of games would you like to play with them after they've been playing with other children to support them to heal and feel connected and powerful again?*

## 5. When there are ongoing challenges

What about ongoing challenges in a friendship or sibling relationship?

You could offer a special space for the relationship or friendship. You could set it up first: *"I see that you've been having some challenges in your friendship, and it's really important to me to help you have a lovely relationship, so I'd love to put aside some ongoing time to support you both."* You might then give them all your focus. Depending on their age, you might support them by:

- asking them to each describe what they are finding challenging;
- asking them both to share their feelings about what's going on, and listening lovingly;
- ask them if there are things that they want help with;
- offer particular kinds of *attachment play* that you think might help;
- keep offering confidence that their relationship will return to harmony; and
- letting them know that you are always there to help.

Feyza Celik shares two games that she enjoys playing with her children to support their connection:

*"One is the usual game I go to when they don't want to share a toy with each other. I usually use a funny voice and say, 'I'm 'teddy bear' (or whichever toy). I really want to play with both of you pleaseeeee!!! Please don't fight for me, I love you both so much WAHHH!!' And they usually start laughing after that, and usually one of them allows the other to play with it at that point.*

*Another game we played recently is when they were both telling each other that their hair looks ugly. 'Your hair is ugly!' and the other said, 'No, your hair is ugly!'" What I did in that moment was I messed up all my hair on my head and started using a funny sound to say, 'No! MY hair is ugly! Wahhhh!' They laughed and with their hands they messed up my hair even more. After that they stopped telling each other harsh things about their hair and moved on to play games together. I'll add that the comments they were making about hair being ugly started happening after one of them got a haircut and many people started commenting about how nice the haircut looks on her. Big feelings probably started bubbling up as a result of that."*

## 6. Addressing the specific themes that come up

Tailoring the play to each child can be really powerful. First of all, we need to observe the children to see what each child's themes are. Does one talk about how unfair it is? Does another keep on wanting to be in charge? We can ascertain from this to what is going on for them. One needs fairness. One needs to feel powerful. Or one needs to know that they are loved, and another needs to know that they are included. Then we can play specific games that attend to those issues:

- For fairness, we can play a nonsense play game where we say all kinds of things are unfair, like not being able to get to the moon and back before dinner.
- For power, power-reversal games such as pretending that they knock you off the sofa and falling in a big exaggerated way, coming back to say, *"You're not going to do that, again, are you?"* with a big smile to show that that's exactly what we are inviting them to do!
- For being loved, lots of kisses and cuddles and the "S/he's mine!" game.
- To be included, body contact games where they're right in the middle.

By attending to the specific theme that is showing up for each child, they are likely to feel calmer and more present, their needs met, and thus able to play in harmonious ways.

## 7. How can you practice non-directive child-centred play if you have more than one child?

First of all, it's really important to be compassionate with ourselves about how hard this can be, and to remind ourselves that we are not meant to parent in nuclear families. If you're finding it hard, it's not your fault.

If you have a partner, are there times where one of you can give non-directive child-centred play to one child, or if you only have two children, can each parent focus on one child? Even short periods like this can make a huge difference to how a child feels and how they behave.

If you are a single parent, I am sending so much compassion to you. Lots of planning will help you meet everyone's needs. Does one of your children take naps? Does one go to school? Finding even small chunks of time to give your child non-directive child-centred play can make a big difference to your child experiencing the power of your connection, the sense of mattering, being loved, and being cared about.

If you have multiple children, there are still lots of things you can do to fill up everyone's cups. Cuddles with everyone on the couch or in bed! Fun family games like sock fights, where everyone tries to take off each other's socks, or pillow fights, where everyone gets the adult!

Belynda Smith, Aware Parenting instructor and Copy Editor of this book says, *"I worked with one mum who scheduled one five minute session of special time each day with each of her seven children!!!"*

## 8. Supporting children to play *attachment play* with each other

*One of the many things that I loved about* attachment play *with two children was seeing my daughter do* attachment play *with my son, from when he was about 18 months old and she was six years old. I remember them running around the kitchen, her offering power-reversal games, eg. "Whatever you do, don't chase me!" and him laughing and laughing!*

The laughter in power-reversal games helps them release feelings of frustration and powerlessness which might otherwise accumulate and turn into hitting or throwing or biting. Younger siblings can often have feelings of powerlessness about not being able to do what their older sibling can do. Imagine getting to release those feelings – actually with the sibling in question!

Belynda Smith, who you've heard from just now, says,

*"This has been a lovely reflective point for me. My ten year old spends at least one day per week with his cousins, aged four and two. He is a master of power-reversal play! They LOVE playing with him. I was just yesterday watching how relaxed the siblings are together and feeling so happy that this is their experience. And I know that all the hours of* attachment play *their big cousin offers to them has had a profound impact on their relationship."*

The same can happen with sibling friendships. The more our children experience us playing *attachment play* with them, the more likely they are to bring therapeutic play into their games with their friends too!

Chiara Rossetti, an Aware Parenting instructor who specialises in play who you've met several times before, shares some games she used to play with her children:

*"Mainly I would go in with empathy and play rivalry games at times there wasn't conflict, like pretending my two hands were always squabbling, lip syncing when we were watching birds or any animal,*

*pretending they were arguing over silly things (also good with sound off on a tv), pretending to be the annoying sibling and fake arguing with each child.*

*For games in the heat of the moment, I'd rush in and pretend to be a lawyer and listen to both sides. Sometimes I'd ask each child to 'represent' the other side but that takes a lot of skill to do.*

*A few times I'd pretend there was a knock at the door and garden gnomes were there saying that they hear arguing and could they please have lessons in how to squabble.*

*Sometimes, when the kids were very young, I pretended I was a bulldozer and would sweep up one child and the other had to chase us.*

*Distraction helped a few times in the heat of the moment, such as me melting to the floor the more they argued, pretending I was a malfunctioning robot that needed help to reboot.*

*Some other ideas are: a fake freak out that your puppies in puppy school are fighting and that you need help!*

*Pretend you are watching the news on tv and mutter that you wanted the weather, not the arguing.*

*Set up a How To Squabble School and invite each kid on with the best tips on how to be really annoying.*

*Play Squabbling Charades with annoying scenarios written on paper that they have to demonstrate."*

### Self-Reflection Moment

How are you feeling?

Is there any particular attachment play game you'd like to play with your child/ren?

Dace Flynn, an Aware Parenting instructor in Australia, shares an experience of using *attachment play* to support her daughter and a friend have a harmonious time together:

*"My daughter had her friend over this morning and they just couldn't agree on anything. They wanted to play different games, they both wanted the same toy and on and on it went. I could feel the tension rise between them (as well as my own frustration)! So, I playfully said, "Come here my little puppies. Come sit on the couch. This is your little house and I'm going to look after you. I'll go get some food for you, but you have to stay in your little house and wait for me. Whatever you do, don't run away." As soon as I left, of course they both jumped off the couch and ran away. When I got back, I pretended to be surprised that I couldn't find them on the couch. I went looking for them and heard their laughter from another room where they were hiding under the table. The girls loved the game and asked to play it again. When we had finished, they happily went off playing together. There was no more bickering and fighting over toys. This game took me less than five minutes! It was easy, effortless and effective."*

## *Loving Limits* in friendships and sibling relationships

In working with many adults over years, one of the things I have heard so often is the pain that people felt as children that their parents or other adults did not step in to stop unenjoyable things that were done to them by siblings or peers.

In this culture, we are so often told to let children work things out themselves, but what children often go away with from those experiences is not a sense of power, but rather, a lack of safety and protection. Staying close by when children are playing is important, so that we can make sure that we are stepping in with *Loving Limits* where necessary.

This might be:

### 1. Loving Limits with our child's harsh words

*"I'm not willing for you to say those words to them, because I'm here to keep everyone safe, and I'm right here and I'm listening."*

*Loving Limits* with harsh words can be hard, because of course we are not going to put our hands over their mouth.

I have found that the following is one way we can work with this.

One way can be to say to the child who is saying the harsh things, *"I'm not willing for you to talk to Rachel like that, because I am concerned about how she would feel, but I am here to listen to what's going on for you. Let's go into the other room."* If the child is willing, we can then go into another room, so that they get to say all the things that they want to say, and we listen to those feelings, without the other child hearing. We might first hear the feelings of the other child, *"Did you feel upset being talked to like that? I'm here. I'm listening."* If there are two adults present, one can listen to each child. Alternatively, we can see if the other child is willing to put on some noise-cancelling headphones. If this happens regularly, the headphones could even be given a funny name! *"Here's the happy headphones!"*

### 2. Loving Limits with our child's harsh actions

It's important that as much as possible, we step in and prevent harm from happening. Ideally, before it happens, with a statement such as, *"I'm not willing for you to hit because I'm here to keep everyone safe, and I'm right here and I'm listening."*

I want to remind you that the child who is hitting really needs help, so whenever we don't step in with a *Loving Limit*, we are doing them a disservice, because they are likely to feel uncomfortable that they've done that, and may even start to judge themselves or believe harsh things about themselves.

This is why, if a child is frequently hitting or hurting other children, it's really important that we assume that it will happen, and stay close, so that we can prevent it from happening again. So often in our culture, children who are hurting others are not supported. But you really can make a huge difference to a child when you support them in this way.

What happens if you don't get there in time to stop the hurting?

Again, we might say, *"I regret that I didn't get here in time to stop this, because I really want everyone to be safe."*[46] What I love about this is it helps us as parents stand in our power to help children.

## It really is our role to help them and prevent these things from happening.

Remember that the third aspect of Aware Parenting includes preventing stress and trauma from happening in the first place.

This phrase can also be a powerful thing to say to help us be more likely to feel compassion towards our child, rather than going into believing harsh thoughts about them hitting or hurting. When we communicate that we are taking responsibility for keeping children safe, that can help them feel a deep sense of safety, of being cared about and protected, which is of course really powerful.

As with all *Loving Limits*, our intention is not only to stop the behaviour, but to help the child express the feelings that were causing the behaviour. And as we talked about in earlier chapters, if we offer the *Loving Limit* but the feelings don't come, they are still sitting there

---

46  Inspired by Patty Wipfler of Hand in Hand Parenting

just under the surface; it's important that we hold in mind that at any moment, more harsh behaviour, or the feelings causing it, can bubble to the surface, so staying close to the children is vital.

### 3. Supporting children to say no and in being assertive in general

As part of creating safety for children, we can also make sure we offer clear ways that children can communicate a 'no' during their play.

You might want to make an agreement between children as to what a no is – for example, if they are both jumping on a trampoline, what the clear signal will be to stop – that might be a specific word. Then, if a child makes that signal, we support that and give information about why we want the child to stop jumping. *"Helen said she wants to stop. It's not safe for you to keep jumping while she is getting off,"* or, *"It's hard for her to get off when you are jumping,"* or, *"She wants you to stop jumping while she gets off."* Otherwise, she may not understand why we want her to stop jumping.

This is all part of creating safety in friendships and sibling relationships.

For children who tend to let harsh things happen to them without speaking up, practicing with us to say no can be really powerful. For example, we might set up a situation where we walk towards them, and they say "NO!" and we stop whenever they do. Or we might invite them to say what they really want to say to others who take a toy or push them, for example. Having conversations with them, giving them information and empathy, and sharing ideas about what they can do, can also help – as well as giving them space to act out different scenarios, with our loving support. We might also repair and acknowledge that we have put them in situations where we weren't there to protect them. There are many different options, and each child will have different specific needs.

> Self-Reflection Moment
>
> How are you feeling?
>
> How do you imagine you would have felt as a child if the adults around you took responsibility for making sure that the children were physically and emotionally safe?
>
> Is there anything that you'd like to do differently, having read this?

***From a child:*** *Mummy, when my brother was born, my world changed forever. I was at the centre, it was you and me, and suddenly, where had you gone? I missed you. I love little Ben, but once he came along, things were different. Your eyes were different with me. Your voice changed that time when I was singing and he was asleep and he woke up. I want to love him, but sometimes I'm just so mad that you love him so much and where is the space for me? My tummy gets all funny with all the love and my angries and sads and I don't really know what to do. Sometimes it all just explodes out of me like a rocket ship and I don't know what's happened, like today when he took the car you got me for my birthday and I just wanted to push him to the moon so you could be all mine again. Please help me, Mummy. I want to love him, but all these feelings swirl around inside me and I keep doing things I don't want to do. Oh, you're coming over to me. You tell me that Ben is with my other Mum, and you're going to just be with me for a while. Oh wow, Mummy, I already feel so happy hearing that. You're always holding him and I never get to just be with you on your own. You tell me that you'll play whatever I want to play for the next half an hour, and you put a timer on your phone. Oh WOW! My heart is jumping up and down a bit. I feel so happy! I've been wanting to play this game with my giraffes for ages. So, Mummy, you be the middle sized giraffe and I will be the big giraffe. Let's put the tiny weeny giraffe way over there. Let's be giraffes together and eat some lovely leaves. I'm so big and tall, I can see the whole sky. I love that you're doing everything that I say. I even feel just like I think a giraffe would feel. I seem to* *be getting taller. Then I jump on your back and tell you where to go and that's so much fun! I love feeling you close and warm. I love the way your hair smells. Then we play the magic wand game and I get you to jump in the air a lot of times. That is so fun. Oh, now the timer is going off. Nooooooo! That can't be half an hour already. We've only just started! I want to play with you more! But you tell me no. Suddenly, I'm a river of tears. My heart is broken. Don't you want to play with me? I cry and I cry and I cry. I miss you so much, Mummy. You and Mum are always with Ben now. I feel so lonely. I'm as sad as the moon. I cry and cry. I climb into your lap and cry some more. You listen to me with those lovely love eyes and the sadness is going. Now I can just feel the warmth of your arms and your lap. I'm cuddling in with you, and it's funny, but now I can feel that you do love me. I know that you do love me. Oh Mummy, you DO love me! Yayyyyyy! We cuddle some more, and then I want to go and play with Ben and Mum in the garden. Let's go now, Mummy!*

## Chapter summary

Preparing for harmony, whether it's between siblings or friends, can include the following:

**Receiving lots of emotional support** for ourselves, particularly if there is conflict between siblings or friends. It's natural for this to be very painful for us, not only in the present, but also in terms of helping us connect with painful similar experiences from the past, such as if we were overpowered by a sibling or friend, or saw our parents fighting.

Giving 1:1 connection, ideally **non-directive child-centred play, to meet their needs for connection and listening to their feeling**s, ideally crying or raging, so that accumulated feelings don't show up in hitting or hurting.

Then there's **supporting harmony**, which includes:
- us choosing to think in compassionate ways;
- having healing experiences for our own painful memories;
- setting up the environment to support harmony;
- staying with them and communicating our support;
- giving empathy to both children; and
- mediating between the children.

*Attachment play* **can make a huge difference in friendships and sibling relationships**, and I offered some suggestions for usual challenges.

Finally, we can also **offer *Loving Limits*** in friendships and sibling relationships, with the core premise that we're saying no to the behaviour and yes to the feelings that are underlying the behaviour.

# I so appreciate all that you do to support your child/ren.

CHAPTER TWENTY

# Partners, exes and other family members

## Compassion for us all

One of the things I hear most from parents I work with is how hard it is to practice Aware Parenting if one's partner or extended family are not on board. If you're experiencing that, I'm sending you so much love. This is all part of parenting in the *Disconnected Domination Culture*. If we lived in a healthy culture that trusted humans, honoured attachment and community needs, and welcomed all feelings, our parenting journey would be entirely different.

So, if your partner, ex, parents or family-in-law don't understand what you're doing, are telling you to do it differently, are judging what you're doing, or are reacting harshly in other ways, the first step is oceans of compassion for you.

> *Self-Compassion Moment*
> *Are you feeling any painful feelings at the moment in relation to how others are responding to your parenting? If so, I'm sending you so much love and empathy. I welcome all of your feelings here. Do you feel called to reach out to your* Listening Partner *or Aware Parenting instructor to share some of your feelings?*

The second step, once you're feeling relief from having your own feelings empathically heard, is to step into their shoes (if you are ready and willing to). For an older generation, the idea of meeting needs, listening to feelings and avoiding punishments can be scary and foreign. They may experience their own parenting being judged when we share information with them, because they grew up learning to judge themselves or others instead of feel their feelings and needs. Their own feelings may well be buried very deep, and even the idea of feeling their own pain might be terrifying for them.

To take in this information means also being willing to feel the pain of realising how much we have unwittingly hurt our own children, despite our most loving of intentions. Facing and feeling those feelings requires a lot, particularly if their feelings were not heard and if they learnt to judge themselves and pick up guilt sticks. This can all be overwhelming and intense.

If your partner or ex is a man, you may have observed that men can often find it much harder to welcome feelings, particularly sadness, and not to use punishment or power-over, because growing up in this culture, they were often shamed even more for crying and punished even more than girls were.

But I invite you not to stop at the point where you can understand why the information can be hard for them to hear. We can also find all kinds of ways of doing our own inner work, such as getting to say all the things we wanted to say to our parents, but saying them to someone who really can hear those feelings without judging themselves or us, and then getting to receive compassionate and reparative responses. This is what I offer in The Marion Method work.

The more inner work we've done, and the calmer and more compassionate we're feeling, the more we are going to be able to respond in helpful and powerful ways in these relationships; that are more likely to help them be able to move towards Aware Parenting if they are able to.

## Compassionate listening to your feelings and thoughts

*In a quest to be compassionate towards others, parents can so often judge or overlook their own feelings and thoughts. Instead, I am going to invite you to compassionately listen to all the feelings and thoughts that you have in relation to your partner, ex-partner, co-parent and other family members.*

What I have experienced many times with parents is that there is a natural process that happens. The more we welcome our feelings and needs with deep loving compassion, the more we come naturally to a sense of compassion towards the other. However, if we bypass our own feelings, for example, because we understand *why* our parents did what they did and dismiss the emotions we experienced growing up, we miss out a vital part of the healing process.

If we meet our own feelings with deeply loving listening, we can then have absolute unconditional love for all of our emotions, for all of the younger parts of us, and all they experienced, while *also* having compassion for our parents (or whoever else it was) and understanding for exactly why they did what they did, growing up in the family, culture and time that they did. That compassion is more than just cognitively understanding them, because our heart feels more open as a result of having our feelings heard. It's true and natural compassion that arises as a result of our own healing.

This process can also happen with partners, co-parents and other family members.

# Natural compassion for others arises from deep compassion for ourselves first.

As always, I invite you to connect with a loving presence in your life, and to share about your feelings in relation to others.

> *Self-Reflection Moment*
>
> *Do you have any feelings bubbling in relation to your parents, your partner (if you have one), your ex or co-parent (if you have one) or other family members?*
>
> *Are you willing to express those feelings?*
>
> *Would you like to make a time with your* Listening Partner *or an Aware Parenting instructor to do that?*

## Healing on the inside

So often, people believe that if they have feelings towards their parents or partner or ex, then they need to express those feelings to that person in real life.

Sometimes, in some cases, with some people, that can be a helpful thing to do.

However, many times it won't, and I'd love to share which times those are likely to be.

They are if the other person:

- doesn't have the capacity to listen to our feelings with empathy and reflect them back to us;
- will receive our feelings as judgments and will judge themselves;
- will receive our feelings as judgments and will judge or punish us in retaliation; or
- will respond to us in the same way that has hurt us in the past.

***There is often a developmental process we get to, when we are no longer willing to put the younger parts[47] of us in a position where yet again, we are not heard, our feelings are not welcomed, where the other goes into their painful feelings, or where we are judged or shamed.***

In this important part of the journey, we may get to the point where we say, *"I'm not willing for the little parts of me to experience being hurt in that way again, and now I am going to go to people and places where my feelings are welcomed and lovingly heard."*

> Self-Reflection Moment
>
> I wonder if you've experienced this?
>
> Have you felt the relief of rather than yet again having a parent or ex simply not knowing how to respond empathically, you have instead shared your feelings with a Listening Partner or Aware Parenting instructor, and heard a beautiful and empathic response?

# Most people didn't grow up receiving empathy and have no idea how to listen empathically. You can choose to take your feelings to places where they *will* be lovingly heard.

This is one of the many things that I have loved about being a part of the Aware Parenting Community. Parents who are aiming to listen to their children's feelings also aim to listen to their friends' feelings. Right from early on, I experienced the profound emotional safety of sharing my feelings with other parents who were practicing Aware Parenting.

---

47   Younger parts is a term from The Marion Method, not Aware Parenting.

> **Self-Reflection Moment**
>
> *Have you experienced that yet?*
>
> *If you don't yet have a Listening Partner, would you like one? I recommend having lots!*

The other wonderful paradox I have found in working with parents is that the more we are willing to have our feelings heard by other people, the more that mysterious and delightful changes can happen in our families and partnerships. When we consistently have our feelings heard by a *Listening Partner* or Aware Parenting instructor, changes open up in our family systems.

> **Self-Reflection Moment**
>
> *Have you experienced that yet?*

Over and over again I've seen relationships shift, partners becoming more able to offer empathy and learn about Aware Parenting, grandparents become more open to listening to their children's and grandchildren's feelings, and interesting dynamics changing, all when there is more compassion and empathy available in the system.

> Your willingness to have your feelings heard has a powerful effect on your family system, not only going down the intergenerational line, but also going back up it!

## Seeing what they are doing and understanding their feelings, needs and values

Another thing that can be very hard for parents is when the other parent or co-parent, or grandparent or family member, treats their child in a way that doesn't fit with their values or Aware Parenting.

> *Self-Reflection Moment*
> *Do you ever experience this?*
> *If so, I'm sending you so much love and compassion.*

If this happens for you, my suggestion would always be to see if you're willing to receive listening around the situation first.

First, empathy for ourselves. Then, we can listen in to what might be going on for the other.

What might they be thinking?

What might their needs and values be?

What feelings from the past might be showing up?

For example, if your parents are saying to your child, "Be a good girl, and I'll give you some chocolate," you may not agree with the practice, but what might their needs or values be? Often we can discover that our values and their values are the same, for example, for our children to grow up to be helpful and happy members of society – it's just that we have different ideas of how to help that happen.[48]

Connecting with our shared needs or shared values can help us be more likely to be able to stay connected with these family members.

What about if your child is crying and your partner, ex or parent does everything they can to stop the crying. What might be going on there?

---
48  I'm so grateful to Marshall Rosenberg, whom I learnt this from back in 2003.

One very common experience is that their painful feelings are bubbling up for them from all the times that their feelings weren't heard, and they find the pain unbearable (because no-one was present with their pain), so they try to distract our child, to protect themselves from their own feelings.

If we see things in this way, we're going to find it much easier to be compassionate with them and to make choices about what we do from that place of compassion, while also including compassion for our child and ourselves.

> *Self-Reflection Moment*
> *Is there something that your parents, partner or ex does to your child that you find painful?*
> *Does it remind you of something you experienced as a child?*
> *How do you feel and what do you need?*
> *What might be going on for them in terms of their thoughts, needs and values or unexpressed painful feelings?*
> *What do you want to do now that you have this information?*

## What conversations do you feel called to have?

Sometimes, we really are called to have conversations about these things, but it's usually preferable to do that *after* receiving compassionate listening for ourselves, so we're more likely to be able to respond from a calm and centred, adult place, rather from the younger parts of us or from painful unexpressed feelings in us.

In Aware Parenting, we recommend having these conversations away from the child and at times when the issue is not happening (unless it is harmful behaviour – in which case it's important that we step in to stop the harm immediately). There may be certain occasions where the person is hurting our child and where we intervene immediately to stop that from happening and to protect our child, in which case, there would be no time for us to receive compassionate listening for ourselves first.

> *Self-Reflection Moment*
>
> *Do you feel called to have a conversation with a family member about how they are with your child/ren?*
>
> *What is the behaviour that you want to talk about?*
>
> *What are your concerns about the effect of this on your child?*
>
> *Do you feel able to listen to the other person's thoughts, needs, values and feelings in relation to this?*
>
> *Do you have any requests?*
>
> *Are you willing to believe that there's going to be a way for everyone to get their needs met here?*
>
> *Would you like to journal about this?*
>
> *How would you most like to communicate? Would you prefer to write a message or to talk in person or over the phone or other format?*
>
> *I'm sending you love and am so willing for you to have the outcome you are wanting here!*

## Using *attachment play* to help our children heal from judgments from family members

If our children have been the recipients of judgments from other family members as a result of our different parenting choices, we can of course listen with empathy to whatever they may feel after that. In addition, *attachment play* can be a powerful way to bring about healing.

Joss Goulden, a Level 2 Aware Parenting instructor in Australia, whom you've already met, shares about how this happened in her family.

*"We often used to use* attachment play *when we were experiencing harshness or judgement or criticism by family in relation to Aware Parenting or our homeschooling journey. I always found it so helpful to bring laughter and empowerment for my children. One of our favourite games was when we used to imitate the person who we felt had been harsh or critical about us.*

*So for example, I remember a time when my father had questioned our homeschooling and was suggesting that my children would be behind in maths. So later on that day, when my parents weren't there, my son pulled his trousers up quite high like my dad likes to wear his pants and walked in a way that was imitating my dad and put on his voice and started making jokes about all the things that their cousins were able to do that they weren't – "By the time James was their age, he could do his 67,000 times tables!" They made lots of silly jokes, which became more and more outlandish about all the things that their cousins could do that they couldn't. It brought so much laughter and fun and connection and it became something we did in relation to lots of things that were painful or uncomfortable.*

*It was something that my children did spontaneously and, bringing laughter, silliness and connection to what were often painful situations, took the charge out so that I was then less likely to be activated and more likely to just feel deeply trusting and connected with my children. And I noticed that it also supported my children to have no lasting feelings at having been criticised or judged and instead to just know that they were unconditionally loved and supported."*

***To your inner children:***

*I'm sending so much love to the pain you feel when you see your parent/s do to your child what was done to you.*

*I so deeply acknowledge that your parent/s did what they did to you back then.*

*I'm here to listen to all the feelings that you felt back then. All the hurt and all the pain.*

*I'm here with you and I'm listening.*

*I so hear how painful it is to see this happening again, this time to your own child.*

*I want to remind you that adult you can now be the protector and advocate for your child, in ways that you didn't experience growing up.*

*Adult you is a powerful and wise being and knows how to help your child.*

*Adult you is also taking care of you now, so you don't need to keep on experiencing this.*

*What would you like to tell adult you about how you felt back then?*

*What do you need now to heal from that experience back then?*

*What do you want adult you to do to support your outer children now?*

*What words would you like adult you to say?*

*I'm here with you. I'm supporting you. I'm sending you so much love.*

## Chapter summary

**Compassionate listening to our feelings and thoughts is vital** if we want more healthy and healing relationships.

**Often, people think that they need to have the conversations with the actual person**, but so much healing actually happens through sharing thoughts and feelings with other people who are able to deeply listen to our experience, including when they stand in for the original person (as in The Marion Method).

I invite you to search to **understand your family member's feelings,**

**needs and values and then to notice what conversations you feel called to have.**

You have the **power** to bring about change for your child/ren and in your family system.

## IMPORTANT NOTE

I invite you to listen to your no. If a family member is consistently treating you or your child/ren in harsh ways, I so support you to do what you need to do to say no to that, which might include not being in contact with that person. Having listening support to get clear about what you will do to safely stand in your no is vital here. If you're in this position, I'm sending you so much love.
Your child/ren's and your physical and emotional safety really matter. You are powerful.

I believe in you.

CONCLUSIONS

# Trusting our child

## Trusting children is one of the core foundations of Aware Parenting

Aware Parenting is so different to the culture that most of us grew up in and live in because it recognises the innate wisdom of human nature, and so it deeply trusts children. As I imagine you've seen so clearly through reading this book, in Aware Parenting, we trust that children are innately loving and compassionate and don't need punishments and rewards to behave in loving ways. This approach deeply trusts the human body, and the intuitive knowing that each child has about how to heal from stress and trauma and how to feel naturally relaxed enough to sleep. It trusts that their bodies know what, when and how much to eat. It trusts that they know what and how to learn. It trusts that each child knows how to be securely attached and seeks their own journey and timing of individuation.

Clearly, trusting our innate wisdom is one of the core tenets of Aware Parenting. Aletha Solter says in *The Aware Baby*: "*The first assumption is that babies are born knowing basically what they need, not only for survival, but also for optimal physical, emotional and intellectual development ... babies know and indicate what they need, and we can therefore trust them to be in charge of their own lives as much as they are physically able. Babies will communicate their needs... and it is the caretaker's role to interpret their signals correctly.*" (pp.4-5)

# However, Aware Parenting also recognises all the challenges in parenting that are caused by growing up and living within a culture that fundamentally does not trust that human nature is wise.

As we've seen, the *Disconnected Domination Culture* has waged war with the innate wisdom of children – and has demonised attachment needs, crying, tantrums and play. It has denied body wisdom including in relation to food, sleep, and each individual's individuation process.

So, it is so common for us as parents to not have our own natural wisdom trusted about what we needed to flourish physically, emotionally and intellectually when we were growing up. Those around us didn't know how to cooperate with our innate wisdom, including how to heal from stress and trauma through laughter, crying and raging with loving support. Most of us weren't trusted in relation to food, sleep, learning or individuation. And what we experience, we internalise, which means that we are likely to find it hard to trust ourselves in particular areas.

**The most difficult parts of parenting are generally where our child is inviting us to trust their innate wisdom in places ours wasn't trusted. It is at these places that our own conditioning and hurts get in the way of us being able to recognise and cooperate with the intrinsic knowing of our child's body and feelings.**

Aware Parenting helps us see those places where we weren't trusted, where we find it hard to trust our child, and even where we unwittingly work against their natural wisdom. Our desire to trust them and support them to stay deeply connected with themselves will invite us to revisit these places in ourselves, so we can tend to our own healing, unlearning and relearning so we can reconnect with ourselves and trust our biological and psychological wisdom.

Aware Parenting thus invites and supports us to reclaim our intrinsic wisdom so we can trust our own bodies, feelings and intuitive knowing as well as our child/ren's.

## Exploring how we were trusted and not trusted

*Self-Compassion Moment*
*I invite you to be deeply compassionate with yourself as you go through this list. You might like to do it with the loving presence of a Listening Partner. If you read things here that you've done to your children and you get tempted to pick up guilt sticks, I invite you to put them down. It's so natural and understandable if you have, because these responses are central to the Disconnected Domination Culture. I'm sending you so much love as you do this.*

*Self-Reflection Moment*
*So, I'm going to invite you to connect in with:*

*How were you trusted and not trusted in each of these areas growing up?*

*As always, please reflect on these with a sense of loving support, and please skip this if you feel overwhelmed.*

*If you don't know the answers, please also skip each one; the later questions will probably also help bring you clarity.*

*Were your needs, particularly your attachment needs, trusted and met growing up?*

*How can you know the answer to this?*

*Do you remember plenty of closeness, cuddles, warm affection, being able to sleep in your parents' bed if you felt scared?*

*Or do you remember being left alone, being lonely, or calling out from your bed and no-one coming?*

*Did you get to co-sleep when you were a baby and then choose when you were ready to be in your own bed in your own room?*

*Or were you in a cot in your own room from an early age?*

*Was your body wisdom in relation to food trusted?*

*Do you remember getting to choose what to eat, when to eat and how much to eat?*

*Or do you remember being told things like, "You have to wait until dinner time," that, "You can't choose, because everyone is having the same," or that, "You can't leave the table until you've eaten all your food," or, "You can't have pudding until you eat all your main course."*

*Did you get to learn things at your own pace, learning about things that you were interested in, and being able to immerse yourself in what you wanted to learn for as long as you wanted?*

*Or were you told that you should learn certain things at certain times, and were you stopped from learning things you were interested in?*

*Was your own separation and individuation process trusted? In other words, did you get to do things separate from your family at your own pace, when you were ready?*

*Did you get to choose the timing of milestones like your first sleepover, even if it was a lot earlier or later than other children?*

*Were you forced to separate earlier than you wanted, or prevented from individuating in the times and ways that you wanted?*

*Did you get to play with things that you wanted to play with and were interested in? Did your parents join in with your play? Did they show interest in what you were interested in?*

*Do you remember not getting to choose what you played, or playing alone a lot?*

The *DDC* believes that children need to be taught to sleep, to be gentle, and to learn, and need to be told what to eat and when to eat, and so on. As you've seen, Aware Parenting is completely the opposite.

## Trust in relation to attachment, food, sleep, healing, learning and play

We really can trust children in all of these areas! We can trust that children will indicate their needs, including their attachment needs, when we are available and attuned to listen.

We can trust that children know what they need to eat and when, with our loving support to help them stay connected with their body's cues.

We can trust that they know how to sleep and are trying to use their natural relaxation processes to feel deeply relaxed.

We can trust that they know how to heal and are trying to do so through play, laughter, crying and raging.

We can trust that they know what they need to learn and when.

We can trust their own individuation process and pace.

*However, we can also recognise that they are deeply affected by the family and culture they are born into. So, they may learn to eat, sleep and learn based on experiences and information that aren't in tune with their natural wisdom (including from us). Understanding these cultural and familial influences and how they can get in the way is profoundly important if we are to be able to help our children stay connected with their innate wisdom.*

# Where do you find it easy and hard to trust your child?

*Self-Reflection Moment*

*Which of these core categories in Aware Parenting do you find it easy and hard to trust in your child?*

*And does that correlate with where you do and don't trust yourself?*

Their:

- needs, including their attachment needs;
- food choices;
- sleep;
- healing;
- learning;
- play;
- relationship with screens.

Do you notice a correlation between this and where you don't trust yourself, or where you find it hard to connect in with your innate wisdom in relation to each of these?

## Increasingly learning to trust your child

*Self-Reflection Moment*

*Where would you like to focus on learning to trust both yourself and your child/ren more?*

*What help might you need in order to do that?*

*What information do you need to help with that process?*

*Are you willing to explore this more?*

**To your inner children:**

*Hello, lovely you!*

*I so deeply acknowledge all the ways that your innate wisdom wasn't seen, acknowledged or trusted.*

*I see you. I see your intrinsic wisdom and worth.*

*I love you exactly as you are.*

*I know that you know exactly what you need in your relationships and life.*

*I see that you know precisely what your body needs and when.*

*I recognise that you understand how to sleep restfully and restoratively.*

*I trust that you know how to heal from all the stressful and traumatic events that you've experienced.*

*You are deeply wise. I see that wisdom.*

*I deeply acknowledge all the ways the adults around you didn't trust your inner knowing.*

*That wasn't your fault, sweetheart.*

*That was simply because they had also lost their own way when they grew up.*

*We trust you.*

*We see you.*

*We understand you.*

*Your wisdom is always within, waiting to be welcomed.*

*We welcome it.*

*We welcome you.*

I trust your own unique journey here. As you've experienced already in this book, parenting invites us to enquire deeply into our core beliefs about human beings – and to the effects of our own past and the culture we grew up in and live in – on what we think, feel and need.

When each of us practices Aware Parenting in our own subtly unique ways, holding in mind the core concepts of trust, connection, understanding and healing, this supports change in our culture. What you do every day with your child/ren is so important and significant. Your increasing trust in your child's innate wisdom, and your capacity to cooperate with that knowing, will support them to grow up being deeply connected with themselves, being able to listen in to themselves and to trust what they find.

***This is one of the clearest outcomes I have seen, not only in my own daughter and son, but also in the other young adults I know who were brought up with Aware Parenting.***

## They are deeply connected with themselves.

I believe that larger and larger numbers of young people growing up deeply connected with themselves, willing to speak up and live in alignment with that deep self-connection, as well as with connection and compassion for others, can bring about great change in the world.

I so appreciate you reading this book, and your willingness to see children, and human beings, through a different lens. Your parenting is important. I acknowledge you and all that you do in caring for your child/ren and I am so willing for your journey together to be more enjoyable, connected and fulfilling as a result of knowing about and practicing Aware Parenting. I deeply trust that what you are doing is making a difference not only to your child/ren and their children, but also to the wider world.

I invite you to keep on being willing to drop the guilt sticks, until you're not ever willing to feel guilty any more.

I support you to keep reaching out for the most loving and empathic listening, and to increasingly experience your inner dialogue as deeply self-compassionate too.

I celebrate all that you're doing to help your child/ren be more connected with themselves and their innate wisdom.

And I acknowledge all the ways you're returning to more deeply connect with yourself and your own intrinsic and wonderful wisdom.

Thank you for hanging out here with me here in this book. I deeply appreciate your attention, awareness and presence.

See you in the next one!

Big love,

Marion

January 2024

## Chapter summary

**Aware Parenting is all about trust.** Exploring how we were trusted and not trusted can help us understand our own process of learning to trust ourselves.

From an Aware Parenting perspective, we can **trust our children in relation to attachment, food, sleep, healing, learning and play**.

**However, understanding how cultural influences and conditioning makes that harder, and what our children need from us to stay connected with their innate wisdom, is vital.**

**Where do you find it easy and hard to trust your child** and how does that relate to how much you trust yourself and how much you were trusted?

I'm so here to support you in increasingly **trusting** your child and their development, and yourself and your innate **wisdom and worth**.

**Your parenting makes a difference to the future culture we're co-creating together.**

## I so appreciate you!

## ACKNOWLEDGEMENTS

I am deeply appreciative of Aletha Solter, PhD, the founder of Aware Parenting, for her profound work, her books, her clarity of thinking, and her wise guidance and support, including in the process of editing this book and making many editorial suggestions, helpful additions and contributions. If you haven't already read her books, I highly recommend reading all of them (several times). You might find that *Cooperative and Connected* is the most helpful one of them to read next after this book, but I trust whichever one you feel called to! You can find them on her website: **www.awareparenting.com**

Thank you again, beyond all thank you's, to my book publishing consultant, the wonderful Julie Postance, without whom this book wouldn't exist, and to the amazing Sophie White, for her beautiful typesetting and cover editing. You two really are the dream team!

I'm in love with this cover, just as I was with the last one. Thank you again, Jelena Mirkovic for creating so much beauty and bringing exactly what I saw in my mind's eye into form.

I'm so grateful to everyone who read and edited the book, with special thanks again to my lovely Editors Belynda Smith and Jenny Exall as well as friend and colleague extraordinaire Joss Goulden. I'm so grateful to everyone who was a beta reader, including Amanda Trim, Eirini Anagnostopoulou and Anna Haberfield.

Big thanks again to Michael, the father of my children, for the photo of our daughter and his daughter on the cover and for the picture of me on the back, subtitle conversations, being willing to trust and join with my initial calling to practice Aware Parenting all those years ago, and the parenting journey we've been on together ever since.

Yet again, I'm immensely thankful to all the people who offered ideas, information and suggestions, including many of my friends on

Facebook, and my Marion's books Support Team. A special thank you goes to Chiara Rossetti, the queen of *attachment play*, for all your play ideas. Finding the subtitle was quite a journey, and I so appreciate everyone who helped with it, with a special mention to India Farr, Lynda Silk, Clare Peace, Feyza Celik, Joy Borish, Thalia Tilly and Jenny Exall.

To all the parents I have mentored over the years, and who have joined my workshops, groups and online courses, thank you for giving me the honour of contributing to you and your family. I'm so grateful for all that I learnt through walking alongside you and all the ways you touched my heart. In particular, I so appreciate all the parents in my *Attachment Play Course* who contributed so many wonderful games – and big appreciation to your children too!

The biggest love and gratitude goes to my daughter Lana and son Sunny, who have always been my most wise teachers. Thank you for being you.

Although my dad is no longer here, I'm grateful to all that he did to support me in my callings and I always sense his continued support and celebration. Thanks, Dad, for inspiring me to step off the beaten path.

And to my inspirational and powerful Mum, thank you for trusting my unique journey and being willing to support me, however much my journey has looked different to the road less travelled. You living with us since the floods and doing all the washing up – and all the other things you do around the house – has made such a huge difference and given me extra time for writing and editing. Thank you for always being interested in me and what I'm doing, for always wanting to contribute to me, and for always being here.

# GLOSSARY

## Aware Parenting Terminology

*Attachment play*

Nine specific kinds of play between parents and children as described in Aletha Solter's book *Attachment Play*. This type of play creates connection, elicits cooperation, and supports children to both prepare for, and heal from, stressful or traumatic events.

*Balance of attention*

A state in which a child feels physically and emotionally safe while revisiting past stress or trauma. The *balance of attention* is necessary for emotional release and healing to occur (crying, play, laughter, etc.).

*Classical attachment parenting*

This term refers to the original attachment parenting paradigm, which was first described by William and Martha Sears. The Aware Parenting version of attachment parenting has several key differences from this original version. (This term was created by Marion Rose and has been adopted by Aletha Solter.)

*Control pattern*

Repetitive or compulsive behaviours which are usually acquired during infancy and childhood to suppress crying and strong emotions. A typical *control pattern* is thumb-sucking. *Control patterns* can put babies and children into states of mind dissociation. They are also called emotional suppression habits and self-soothing behaviours. They are sometimes called 'repression mechanisms'.

*Dissociation ("freeze or surrender")*

This is one of two primary physiological reactions to real or perceived threats or trauma. (The other is hyperarousal.) During dissociation, the parasympathetic nervous system is dominant, and children are quiet, passive, compliant, inattentive, unresponsive, and numb. They are often using a *control pattern*.

### *Emotional release*

Any behaviour which helps restore homeostasis by releasing tension from the nervous system that was acquired during stressful or traumatic experiences. Forms of emotional release in children include crying, raging, trembling, laughter, certain kinds of therapeutic play, and body movements. These are also called healing mechanisms and tension-release processes and are often shortened to the term, 'release'.

### *Hyperarousal ("fight or flight")*

This is one of two primary physiological responses to real or perceived threats or trauma. (The other is dissociation.) During hyperarousal, the sympathetic nervous system is dominant, and children are agitated, distractible, impulsive, hypervigilant, defiant, reactive, aggressive, or destructive.

### *Loving Limits*

These are the combination of a verbal or physical limit paired with empathy to create a pretext for a child to cry to release pent-up stress. *Loving Limits* say no to a behaviour or a child's request and yes to the underlying feelings causing the behaviour. (This term was developed by Marion Rose and adopted by Aletha Solter.) We may offer a *Loving Limit* in response to a child's behaviour, such as if they are hitting or biting. We might also offer a *Loving Limit* in response to a child's requests, such as if they are asking for the breast and we don't think that they are hungry. As Aletha Solter says, in this second situation, this is essentially a limit on our own behaviour.

### *Suppression*

This is when children are disconnecting from their feelings or using a *control pattern* so that they stop feeling their feelings, either when they move their attention to something else, or when we distract their attention away to something else.

## Marion's Terminology

### Crying dance

When we stay deeply connected with children who are crying to heal, and follow their lead in a nuanced way, as well as gently inviting them to stay connected with their bodies, especially if they are trying to move away to distract themselves from their feelings. The crying dance is one way that we help create the *balance of attention*.

### Disconnected Domination Culture

The culture that has been firmly in place since industrialisation and has spread around the world through colonisation, but has its roots thousands of years before. The core tenet of disconnection is disconnecting babies from families, and disconnecting us from our bodies, feelings, wisdom, nature, seasons and traditions. From that disconnection comes domination – force, coercion, guilt, should and have-to, power-over and authoritarianism. This is a Marion Method term.

### Emotional shepherd dog

When we are staying close to our child to help maintain the *balance of attention* so that they can continue to laugh or cry to release healing-feelings.

### Emotional sticks

These are ways we learn to judge or shame ourselves in the *Disconnected Domination Culture*. Examples of emotional sticks include guilt and shame and all other forms of self-judgement. This is a Marion Method term.

### Healing-feelings

Feelings that are caused by stress or trauma and when expressed through crying and raging with vigorous movement in loving arms or with loving support, help a child release that stress or trauma and move back into homeostasis.

### *Needs-feelings*

Feelings that are caused by immediate needs in the present moment and which go away when the need is met.

### *Research triangle of Aware Parenting*

A triangle between your cognitive understanding of Aware Parenting theory and practice, your own internal resonance, intuition, sense-making and conclusions, and your observation of your child.

## Terminology and concepts NOT used in Aware Parenting

### *'Overtired'*

In Aware Parenting, a child who is tired and connected but isn't going to sleep and who is crying, isn't 'overtired' but is utilising their innate healing and relaxation response to release stress and trauma from their body before sleep.

### *'Fighting sleep'*

In Aware Parenting, rather than fighting sleep, we see that parents are more often fighting a child's natural processes to feel relaxed enough to sleep, often through crying with loving support. Children need to feel tired, connected and relaxed to be able to sleep restfully.

# RECOMMENDED READING AND RESOURCES

## Books by Aletha Solter

*Attachment Play: How to Solve Children's Behavior Problems with Play, Laughter and Connection*

*Cooperative and Connected: Helping Children Flourish without Punishments or Rewards*

*Healing Your Traumatized Child: A Parent's Guide to Children's Natural Recovery Processes*

*Raising Drug-Free Kids: 100 Tips for Parents*

*Tears and Tantrums: What to Do when Babies and Children Cry*

*The Aware Baby*

For more information: **www.awareparenting.com/books.htm**

Aletha Solter's Aware Parenting Institute website:
**www.awareparenting.com**

## Books by Marion Rose

*I'm Here and I'm Listening: Empathic and empowering responses to needs, feelings, and behaviours with Aware Parenting*

*Raising Resilient and Compassionate Children: A parent's guide to understanding behaviour, feelings, and relationships* (Co-authored with Lael Stone)

*Sound Sleep and Secure Attachment with Aware Parenting*

*The Emotional Life of Babies: Find closeness, presence, and sleep for you and your baby with this compassionate approach to crying*

Marion Rose's website: **www.marionrose.net**

## Aware Parenting Courses by Marion Rose, PhD
https://marionrose.net/aware-parenting-courses/

## Podcasts by Marion Rose, PhD

*The Aware Parenting Podcast*
This was co-hosted with Lael Stone until episode 124.

**https://podcasts.apple.com/au/podcast/the-aware-parenting-podcast/id1455772681**

*The Aware Parenting and Natural Learning Podcast*
This is co-hosted with Joss Goulden.

**https://podcasts.apple.com/au/podcast/the-aware-parenting-and-natural-learning-podcast/id1643837590**

I also have a non-Aware Parenting Podcast, *The Psychospiritual Podcast.*

**https://podcasts.apple.com/au/podcast/the-psychospiritual-podcast/id1344385341**

## Aware Parenting Community

The Aware Parenting (based on the work of Aletha Solter, PhD) Facebook group: This is a free Facebook group facilitated by a team of Aware Parenting instructors.

## Further Reading

Lawrence Cohen, *Playful Parenting*

Jean Liedloff, *The Continuum Concept*

## YOUR NOTES AND OBSERVATIONS OF YOUR CHILD

*I invite you to use this space to make notes as you observe your child.*

Eye contact / presence in their eyes:

___

___

___

___

___

___


Facial expressions and tension around their eyes and mouth:

___

___

___

___

___

___

___

Speech (agitated or calm):

General agitation / calmness:

Muscle relaxation / tension:

_____
_____
_____
_____
_____
_____
_____
_____

How they went to sleep and number of night wakings:

_____
_____
_____
_____
_____
_____
_____
_____

Movement during sleep:

Other:

## WAYS YOU CAN WORK WITH ME

If you enjoyed this book, and would like to work with me, here are some of the ways you can do that.

### Articles on my website
https://marionrose.net/articles/

### Free Aware Parenting Courses
https://marionrose.net/aware-parenting-courses/#free-intro-courses

### Aware Parenting Courses
https://marionrose.net/aware-parenting-courses/#specific-topics

### Aware Parenting Instructor Mentoring Training
https://marionrose.net/aware-parenting-courses/#aware-parenting-instructor-mentoring-course

### 1:1 Mentoring
https://marionrose.net/mentoring/

## IF YOU ENJOYED THIS BOOK

If you enjoyed this book, I'm so glad! I would love for Aware Parenting to spread to even more parents and I wonder if you are willing to consider letting others know about this book as part of that. Here are some ways you can do so.

Please share your review on Amazon – it helps people see if this book might resonate with them.

Please leave a review on Goodreads.

Are you willing to tell your friends about it via your blog, podcast or YouTube channel, or on Facebook, Instagram, X (formerly known as Twitter), Pinterest or Linkedin? Are you willing to mention it to your friends and family members or colleagues?

I so appreciate your support!

MARION ROSE, PHD

## AUTHOR CONTACT PAGE

Email:
marion@marionrose.net

Website:
https://marionrose.net/

Instagram:
@_marion_rose_
@awareparenting
@theawareparentingpodcast

Facebook:
https://www.facebook.com/MarionRosePhD

www.ingramcontent.com/pod-product-compliance
Lightning Source LLC
Chambersburg PA
CBHW022023290426
44109CB00014B/728